**"A visit to the supermarket will soon be good for the soul as well as the body."**
*The New York Times*

"Trash the coupons. Ignore the sales. And, by all means, stop comparing prices. Thousands of people already have decided to make their grocery-store shopping reflect their consciences rather than their wallets. With the help of a new shopping guide, they can size up the ethical values of the corporations that make the TV dinners they eat, the headache pills they pop and the shampoo they use. Even long-time product favorites may lose their appeal when consumers discover firms' foibles, such as a poor record on minority advancement or community outreach."
*The Philadelphia Inquirer*

"No organization has been more important, more catalytic, more dynamic in helping corporations realize their responsibilities as citizens as CEP. This is a David that has grown up in its own right to be a Goliath."
Bill Moyers

"For 20 years CEP has been making a major contribution to the greening of America. It empowers consumers to buy from companies whose environmental policies they support, and it brings pressure on irresponsible firms to change harmful policies."
Denis Hayes
Chairman
Earth Day 1990

"'Corporate citizen' is often heard as a phrase, but the Council on Economic Priorities takes it to heart. By monitoring and encouraging corporations to be good citizens, CEP is changing the workplace, the marketplace, and the world."

Gloria Steinem

"Easy to use...Good news for those who want to turn their shopping carts into vehicles for social change."

*New Age Journal*

"SHOPPING FOR A BETTER WORLD has been very positive for us internally; it helps us look at what needs improvement, and it gives us an unbiased view. If we don't measure up to other companies, we're not doing what we need to do."

Celestial Seasonings

"This is consumerism at its finest. You vote with your dollars for companies you believe in or economically boycott those you don't agree with."

*Salt Lake City Tribune*

"An easy, practical way for all of us to support companies that recycle waste, make biodegradable products and are environmentally responsible."

Mike McCloskey
Chairman
Sierra Club

"Now you can let your conscience be your guide when you go to the supermarket."
*The Denver Post*

"Consumers with social consciences have a new tool to help support their causes by 'voting' with their money at the grocery store cash register. It's called SHOPPING FOR A BETTER WORLD."
*The Des Moines Register*

"While (the) Council on Economic Priorities has for years enlisted investors in its push for environmental enlightenment and other signs of corporate responsibility, these days it's found a new ally: the women who wander the supermarket aisles. (The) wildly successful checklist for the checkout, which weighs in on whether the companies behind the products are doing the right thing, has companies increasingly paying attention."
*Adweek*

# SHOPPING FOR A BETTER WORLD

A Quick and Easy Guide to
Socially Responsible
Supermarket Shopping

by
Alice Tepper Marlin,
Jonathan Schorsch,
Emily Swaab, and
Rosalyn Will

## COUNCIL ON ECONOMIC PRIORITIES

Council on Economic Priorities, Inc.

BALLANTINE BOOKS • NEW YORK

The Council on Economic Priorities wishes to thank especially the Cook Brothers Educational Fund and the Mary Reynolds Babcock Foundation for their vision and generosity in making this guide possible. Our deep appreciation also to the Right Livelihood Foundation; to Lyn Severance, Sarah Lee Terrat, Joette Spinelli and Michela Griffo for graphics; the intelligent and devoted interns who helped research the guide: Josiah Brown (Yale University), Peter Colavito (Yale University), Stephen Dyott (Cornell University), Jeffrey Lox (Stanford University), Kenneth Scott, Fumiyo Tanaka (Matsushita Institute of Government and Management, Japan); special thanks to Katy Androski, Bobby Ballard, Gene Chollick, Ben Corson (for years of commitment), Sheila Ratner, Robert Rubovits, Edie Stone Tshering and Marjory Vandenberg; to the enormous and successful efforts of CEP's international counterpart, New Consumer (U.K.) and to the Asahi Journal (Japan) for their research; and last but not least to all the CEP staff who pitched in.

Council on Economic Priorities, Inc.
30 Irving Place, New York, NY 10003
212-420-1133

Library of Congress Catalog Card Number: 91-92187

ISBN# 0-345-37083-X

This edition published by arrangement with the Council on Economic Priorities, Inc.

Manufactured in the United States of America

First Revised Edition: February 1992

# **TABLE OF CONTENTS**

# WHAT IS SHOPPING FOR A BETTER WORLD?

American consumers have had to learn all over again how to deal with tough times and shrinking paychecks. It hasn't been easy. Yet even with less money to spend, your regular trips to the supermarket or gas station can lead to changes in corporate policy. Companies wield tremendous power: your individual influence on corporate practice has leverage and can actually help change the world. It's the simple, positive activism of casting your economic vote conscientiously.

But how much do you really know about each company you support with your hard-earned dollars? Does it spew toxic materials into our rivers and atmosphere? Does it aggressively promote cigarettes even though an estimated 2.5 million people die every year as a consequence of smoking? Or does it donate large portions of its profits to charity, revitalize local communities, and value the expertise of women and minorities at the highest levels of management?

**SHOPPING FOR A BETTER WORLD** provides you with the information you need to select products made by companies whose policies and practices you support. You can not only find out what company makes your favorite products but also see that parent company's social record at a glance — all in a convenient pocket-size guide.

Of course, no one but you can decide which products to buy for yourself and your family. Quality, safety, nutrition, and price may be of paramount importance. If a certain brand is on sale, or is the only peanut butter your child will eat, chances are that's what you'll put in your shopping cart. But often, among all the competing detergents or canned peas, these differences are minimal. Product differentiations created by advertising can be artificial, trivial, or just plain misleading. **SHOPPING FOR A BETTER WORLD** was created to enable you to cut through advertising hype to reality.

**SHOPPING FOR A BETTER WORLD** empowers you by providing information that is hard to track down on your own. We've even made it easier to write or call companies and tell them why you're switching brands. The addresses, phone numbers, and names of chief executive officers for all the companies in this guide are listed on page 364. Ultimately, companies want your business. The sensible ones will listen if enough people let them know they monitor company performance. Managers know that for every customer who bothers to write and mail a letter, 200 to 500 more feel the same way and will vote silently with their pocketbooks. Apparently a lot of you are doing so. *Fortune* magazine, in its December 3, 1990 issue, reports "Today's tougher U.S. consumers ... are insisting on high quality goods that ... come from a manufacturer they think is socially responsible."

You may want to apply our rating system to your own place of work, whether you are a production line worker or the president. To rate your workplace, use the worksheet provided on page 316.

# HOW TO USE THIS GUIDE

The ratings in **SHOPPING FOR A BETTER WORLD** are divided into two main sections. The first section lists alphabetically, in four categories, all the companies that appear in the guide: large companies, small companies (between 16 and 100 employees, indicated with a #), supermarkets, and oil companies. Very small companies, with fewer than 15 employees, are marked with an asterisk (*) beside their names.

The second section is arranged by product category (e.g., Baby Food or Bread). Within each product category, brand names are arranged alphabetically. The company that makes each product is identified by an abbreviation, found next to the product name.

As you shop, look for the company or the brand name of the product you'd like to know more about. Each entry is followed by 12 columns. The first contains the abbreviation for the company that makes the product. (See abbreviation index on p. 396.) The information in the next 11 columns applies to that specific company. All the products made by that company or its subsidiaries will have the same rating. **SHOPPING FOR A BETTER WORLD** rates companies according to their performance in the following issue areas: Charitable Giving, Women's Advancement, Advancement of Minorities, Animal Testing, Disclosure of Information, Community Outreach, South Africa, Environment, Family Benefits, and Workplace Issues. Involvement with Military Contracts and Nuclear Power, previously under separate columns, are now flagged in the ALERT column.

Nine issues are rated using the three symbols ✔, ✔̸, or ✖. A ✔ indicates outstanding performance, ✔̸ indicates moderate or mixed performance, and ✖ indicates poor performance. Involvement in South Africa is rated "Yes" or "No." "Yes" indicates the company has some kind of business ties in South Africa and "No" indicates no involvement in South Africa. A "?" means that despite much searching, we could not find sufficient information to assign a rating.

Please see the RATING KEY on page 14 for detailed explanations of each rating.

The final column, labelled "ALERT," contains important information about the company that is not revealed by the ratings alone. The SHOPPING ALERT section on page 24 explains each phrase or symbol.

This year, we've added interesting new sections on the performance of Japanese and British companies whose brand name products are distributed in the U.S.A. In the Japanese company section, information and symbols denote where a company's social responsibility stands relative to other Japanese companies. These evaluations are excerpted from a special issue of the *Asahi Journal*, a leading Japanese newsweekly. Please see page 333, for this section. The ratings for British companies denote a company's social performance relative to other U.K. companies. These ratings are excerpted from CEP's British counterpart, New Consumer's **SHOPPING FOR A BETTER WORLD** (Kogan Page Ltd., 1991). Please see page 317.

# SMALL CAN BE BEAUTIFUL

Small businesses, whose number increased 12% from 1980 to 1988 (the latest year for which figures are available) are testimony to the fitness of America's entrepreneurial spirit. In 1988, there were nearly four million firms with fewer than 100 employees and a majority of these had fewer than 20 employees. By that year, women owned 20% of all small businesses.

You may wonder why CEP has included such companies along with corporate giants with international personnel figures running to six digits. Not only do small companies make up 98.9% of all U.S. companies (U.S. Small Business Administration), but they often also lead the way in innovative management, provision of organically-grown products and those made without the use of animal testing, and responsiveness to employees and consumers.

In 1991, none of the 39 small companies studied by CEP had military or nuclear power contracts, or ties to South Africa. Not only do they avoid animal testing, but they usually are also strong advocates for animal welfare. Most small companies we analyzed recycle raw materials, use recyclable packaging, and take steps to ensure no toxic chemicals are used or released in the manufacturing process.

Some small businesses, particularly those with a majority of female employees, often have considerable flexibility in work arrangements: employees may work at home, work part-time or on alternative schedules, or bring infants to work with them. Companies report that these arrangements cost little and have resulted in greater productivity, higher morale, and lower turnover.

A number of small businesses are set up as worker-owned cooperatives. These tend to be particularly conscientious on nutritional and environmental issues. CEP has noted the size and structure of a company when making its rating determinations.

Of the more than three million companies with fewer than 20 employees, an estimated 200,000 have sprung up just in the last four or five years. These ventures may have been launched by friends of long standing or by families. During the first crucial years, building up clientele and making the business profitable generally take precedence over consideration of community involvement, family benefits, minority advancement, and workplace issues. In a few cases, however, these issues are given top consideration from the very beginning.

If an enterprise employing fewer than 15 employees is based in a region with few minorities, it rarely has the capacity to seek them elsewhere to fill positions on its Board or in top management. A few very small companies rated ✓ or higher. CEP has given the others a ✓ø (neutral) rating in Minority Advancement.

# SHOPPING FOR A HEALTHIER LIFE

Honest informative labels on food packages can help you live a healthier life. Consumers have a strong new ally in Food and Drug Administration Commissioner David A. Kessler, who wasted no time in early 1991 chastising companies he felt were making false claims about freshness or cholesterol content. The agency also plans to work toward a ban on misleading fat percentage claims.

Reacting to scientific evidence that the way Americans eat is in itself a bad habit, the U.S. Department of Agriculture and experts in nutrition have called for revision of the basic four food groups, in place since 1956. The new plan would de-emphasize the importance of meat and dairy products. It would declare grains, fruits, and vegetables the major building blocks of a healthy diet.

As consumers become more educated about healthy eating, some manufacturers and processors are responding to demands for less fatty meats, for organically-grown fruits and vegetables, and for foods that are high in fiber and low in cholesterol. Look for these and avoid the fat-ridden, pesticide-laden products that still crowd your supermarket shelves.

Write letters to companies that continue to use misleading or obscure labels and/or objectionable ingredients. Tell them why you've stopped buying their products. (See COMPANY ADDRESSES on page 364.) Remember as you shop to:

**REDUCE** PURCHASE OF FOOD CONTAINING:

- Sodium – fresh foods contain enough salt.

- Fat and cholesterol – cut down on animal fat; avoid pork and beef, especially fatty cuts; avoid egg yolks and fried foods.

- Sugar and alcohol – they provide empty calories, no nutrition.

- Additives – especially avoid sulfites, nitrites, and artificial coloring.

**INCREASE** PURCHASE OF FOOD CONTAINING:

- Fiber – more fruit, vegetables, whole grains, bran, and nuts.

- Look for organically-grown foods; use fish and well-washed poultry; cook by steaming to retain optimum nutrients; pick olive or sunflower over other oils or butter.

Highly processed foods lose much of their nutritive value and require substantially more energy to produce. You *can* choose alternatives. Fresh foods rich in fiber, for example, not only help guard against digestive diseases like colon cancer – but also generate less waste and use less energy in the production process. For the best nutrition, eat vegetables and fruits that are grown locally or come from your own garden. Serve fresh vegetables raw or steamed. Avoid "fast food" restaurants that do not offer a healthy alternative.

You may have noticed that though CEP includes food products made by tobacco companies in the guide, it does not list cigarettes. If you are interested in living a healthier life, cigarettes (which are responsible for an estimated 1,000 deaths a day in the U.S. alone), have no place on your shopping list. Early in 1991, the Board of Johns Hopkins University joined several other institutions of higher learning in selling its investments in tobacco companies. A Board spokesman said, "the holding of tobacco stocks is incompatible with the university's mission to disseminate information on the treatment and prevention of disease and illness." The Council on Economic Priorities considers manufacturing and promoting cigarettes antithetical to social responsibility, because it is a direct and major threat to public health.

# WHAT IS THE COUNCIL ON ECONOMIC PRIORITIES?

In 1969, when the Council on Economic Priorities, Inc. (CEP) was founded, few corporations acknowledged their responsibility for the environment, charitable giving, or fair employment.

Today, that climate has changed. CEP and our members have helped change it.

CEP has painstakingly gathered and documented facts in more than 1,000 publications, major studies, and research reports on subjects as diverse as child care, air pollution, occupational safety, and the politics of defense contracting.

CEP's goal is to inform and educate the American public and provide incentives for corporations to be good citizens, responsive to the social concerns of all their stakeholders, employees, neighbors, investors, and consumers.

Our major recent publications include: *Rating America's Corporate Conscience* (Addison Wesley, 1987), which assesses the social records of 130 U.S. companies and identifies the products they make; *Building a Peace Economy* (Westview, 1991), which details the economic consequences of defense budget cuts; and *The Better World Investment Guide* (Prentice Hall, 1991), which traces the history of the ethical investing movement, profiles major ethical funds, and rates 100 publicly-held companies.

CEP also produces the annual America's Corporate Conscience Awards ceremony. The gala event honors corporations for outstanding citizenship in a particular area and also cites corporations that have disregarded the public good. The Chairman for 1992 is Martin Payson, Vice Chairman of Time Warner Inc. Bill Moyers, Jane Pauley, Coretta Scott King, Ed Begley, Jr., Gloria Steinem, George Plimpton, and Joanne Woodward are among the celebrities who have presented these coveted awards. See page 346.

- CEP is an independent, non-profit public interest research organization supported by a nationwide membership as well as by individual and foundation grants.

- All CEP members receive a free updated copy of **SHOPPING FOR A BETTER WORLD** every year, and a CEP *Research Report* every month. To join, simply send in the order form at the back of this book.

# SHOPPING FOR A BETTER WORLD – THE IMPACT

The Council on Economic Priorities first released **SHOP-PING FOR A BETTER WORLD: A Quick and Easy Guide to Socially Responsible Supermarket Shopping** in December 1988. Many of you let us know the guide was just what you were looking for. What happened next?

• Since then, more than 900,000 copies have been sold.

• In an early CEP poll of buyers of the guide, an impressive 78% of the 968 respondents said they had "switched brands" because of **SHOPPING FOR A BETTER WORLD** ratings; 98% told us that all issues CEP rates were important to them; 64% referred to the **SHOPPING FOR A BETTER WORLD** ratings whenever they shopped; and 97% considered the environment their top or near-top priority.

• A May 1989 *Business Week*/Harris Poll posed corporate social responsibility questions in a nationwide survey. More than 60% of Americans agreed that "Business has gained too much power over too many aspects of American life." When asked, "If you believed that business was doing something bad for society, what would you be willing to do to stop it?" — 76% said that they would boycott the company's products by refusing to buy them.

• In a July 1990 Roper Poll, 52% said they would pay 10% more for a brand made by a socially responsible company and 67% said they were concerned about a company's social ratings. Brands made by socially responsible companies, incidentally, are often competitively priced.

• A January 1991 *Fortune* article described today's consumers as "demanding, inquisitive and discriminating ... No longer content with planned obsolescence, no longer willing to tolerate products that break down, they are insisting on high quality goods that save time, energy, calories, preserve the environment, and come from a manufacturer that they think is socially responsible."

- Thousands of people continue to join our nationwide membership. Many of them are increasingly writing to companies, not only criticizing bottom ratings and praising top ones, but also questioning "?" ratings.

- And the companies are responding. For example: more companies try to cooperate with CEP to eliminate "?" ratings. Companies that never answered CEP's questionnaire before are now making the effort, including many privately-held companies which have never disclosed social information to private organizations before. In the process, some discover good programs they were not aware of, and poor policies that need review. Several have even thanked CEP for prodding them to self-examination! CEP's disclosure rate has steadily increased from 34% our first year to a 69% our fourth year.

- New Consumer, a British research organization modelled after and affiliated with CEP, published its first two books in 1991, *Changing Corporate Values* (Kogan Page Ltd., 1991) and **SHOPPING FOR A BETTER WORLD** (Kogan Page Ltd., 1991). *Changing Corporate Values* presents detailed profiles and charts for 128 U.K. companies. The group's **SHOPPING FOR A BETTER WORLD** rates the social responsibility of 125 U.K.-based and other European companies.

- In Japan, a special issue of the leading newsweekly *Asahi Journal* published results of a seventy-company survey on Japanese corporate social responsibility (*The Corporation and Society*, February, 1991). *Asahi Journal* Editor-in-Chief Mitsuko Shimomura consulted with CEP on research methods. *Asahi Journal* will conduct the survey annually, expanding research to include information from sources outside the companies and to cover more companies. Groups in Australia, Sweden, Germany and Holland are embarking on similar research.

Excerpts, including company ratings, from the New Consumer guide and *Asahi Journal*, are included in this edition of **SHOPPING FOR A BETTER WORLD**. See pages 317 and 333 respectively for research from abroad.

• Alice Tepper Marlin and CEP won the 1990 "Right Livelihood Award" for "the courage and vision to show the directions in which the Western economy must develop if it is to contribute to — instead of harm — global security and the well-being of humanity." The award is presented in the Swedish Parliament on the day preceeding the Nobel Prize presentations.

# RATING KEY

✔ Outstanding performance in an issue area as defined by the rating key;

✅ Moderate performance or a mixed record;

✖ Poor performance or little evidence of a good record.

For all categories, a rating of "?" means insufficient information, except where otherwise indicated.

Small companies whose entire staff numbers between fifteen and one hundred persons, are marked with a number sign (#) on the rating sheet. Very small companies, with fewer than 15 employees, are marked with a (*) on the rating sheet.

## $ GIVING TO CHARITY: LARGE COMPANIES

Total worldwide cash donations (including direct corporate giving, foundation giving, and matching gifts) for the most recent year is figured as a percentage of the average of three previous years' pre-tax worldwide earnings. For companies taking a loss for two or more of the last three years, no calculation was made and their rating is a "?".

In-kind (non-cash) giving may constitute a large part of a company's charitable giving. Due to inconsistencies in the measurement of the monetary values of these donations, however, CEP is not able to factor it into large-company total giving, except for those whose in-kind giving alone is so substantial that it assures them a top grade.

# GIVING TO CHARITY: SMALL COMPANIES

Small-company charitable giving is often strictly non-cash. We do include in-kind giving when estimating a small company's total donations. Total charitable giving is figured as a percent of the average of three previous years' pre-tax worldwide earnings.

✔ + - 2% or more of net pre-tax worldwide earnings given to charity.

✔ - Over 1.2%.

✓ - 0.7% to 1.2%.

✖ - 0.6% or less.

? - Insufficient information or company experienced losses in two or more of the last three years.

#  WOMEN'S ADVANCEMENT

CEP looks at representation of women on a company's Board of Directors and among the company's top officers (vice-presidential level or higher at corporate headquarters or President/Chief Executive Officer of a subsidiary or division). This is only one indication of a company's responsiveness to its female employees. See the Family Benefits and Workplace Issues categories for other information on how companies are responding to the changing workforce.

✔ - At least three women on the Board of Directors or among top officers.

✓ - At least two women on the Board or among top officers.

✖ - Only one or no women on the Board or among top officers.

? - Insufficient information.

Where information is available, these ratings are adjusted up or down according to Equal Employment Opportunity Commission reports on percentages of women among Officials and Managers, company size and industry, purchasing from women-owned firms, and representation of women among the top 25 salaried officers at the company.

#  ADVANCEMENT OF MINORITIES

CEP looks at representation of minorities on a company's Board of Directors as well as among the company's top officers (vice-presidential level or higher at corporate headquarters or President/Chief Executive Officer of a subsidiary or division). This is only one indication of a company's responsiveness to minority employees.

✔ - At least two minorities on the Board of Directors or among top officers.

✐ - One minority on the Board or among top officers.

✖ - No minorities on the Board or among top officers.

✐ø - Pertaining to very small companies (indicated with an (*) ), with too few employees to reflect the national demographics, and/or in geographic locations that do not reflect national demographics.

? - Insufficient information.

Where information is available, these ratings are adjusted up or down according to Equal Employment Opportunity Commission reports on percentages of minorities among Officials and Managers, company size and industry, purchasing from minority-owned firms, banking with minority-owned banks, and representation of minorities among the top 25 salaried officers at the company.

NOTE: Ratings in this category apply to U.S. operations only.

# ANIMAL TESTING

✔ - No animal testing.

✔* - Company tests on animals but has reduced the number used in testing by 40% or more over the last five years and/or has given $250,000 or more annually to alternative research through in-house or independent labs.

✔⊛ - Same as ✔* but the company manufactures surgical/medical supplies and/or prescription drugs.

✘ - Company tests on animals; less than a 40% reduction in the number of animals used in testing in the last five years and/or less than $250,000 annually given to alternative research; or no quantitative report of reductions or major contributions to research for alternatives.

✘○ - Same as Bottom but the company manufactures surgical/ medical supplies and/or prescription drugs.

? - Insufficient information or company does "nutritional testing," the effects of which, if any, CEP has been unable to determine.

Where information was available, ratings were adjusted upward if company: was close to threshold on either reductions or expenditures on alternative research; had significant reductions in animal use more than 5 years ago; is a leader in researching alternatives by convening seminars, establishing grant programs, or providing scientific expertise to industry committees.

# DISCLOSURE OF INFORMATION

✔ - Company provides current and substantive materials on their social programs and policies either by completing CEP's questionnaire or by providing comparable information in printed matter or phone interviews.

✓ - Company provides some specific information either by partially completing CEP's questionnaire or by providing comparable information in printed matter or phone interviews. Some key questions were left unanswered.

✖ - Company provides only the most basic information: an annual report, proxy statement and 10-K, or less; or, if additional information has been provided it is not detailed enough to give a real indication of the company's performance.

 ## COMMUNITY OUTREACH

✔ - Strong programs promoting education, housing and/or volunteerism; substantial investment in any programs related to these areas.

✓ - Moderate community programs or mixed record; some good initiatives.

✖ - Little or no evidence of programs designed to benefit community and/or record shows major lawsuits or citizen campaigns or other problems that adversely affect the community.

? - Insufficient information.

NOTE: Ratings in this category apply to U.S. operations only. Citizen campaigns related to environmental issues or other issues CEP rates will be considered in the relevant category.

 ## SOUTH AFRICA

No - No involvement in South Africa.

Yes - Licensing, distribution, and/or franchising agreements.

YesIN - Investment in South Africa: over 100 employees in South Africa.

YesIS - Investment in South Africa: strategic in terms of nature of product, e.g., selling fuel to the military or police.

? - Insufficient information.

 **ENVIRONMENT: Large companies**

✔ - Substantial positive programs, such as the use and encouragement of: recycling, alternative energy sources, waste reduction, green products and packaging, etc. A record relatively clear of major regulatory violations.

✓ - A mixed record: some positive programs such as use and encouragement of recycling, alternative energy sources, waste reduction, etc. Problems such as accidents, regulatory infractions, fines, complaints, etc.

✓ø - Nothing outstanding either positively or negatively. As far as CEP can ascertain, company is in compliance with minimum legal standards, but has no significant proactive programs.

✖ - Company has a poor public record of significant violations, major accidents, and/or history of lobbying against sound environmental policies.

? - Insufficient information.

NOTE: Environmental ratings for companies with worldwide operations are based on their global environmental impact, where data is available to CEP. The availability of such information, however, is limited.

**ENVIRONMENT: Small companies**

✔ - Positive programs such as the use of biodegradable and/or recyclable materials in packaging and products, the disposal of waste from manufacturing process in an environmentally sound way, and the use of only natural ingredients and growing techniques for food.

✓ - Moderate effort to achieve above.

✓ø - Nothing outstanding either positively or negatively. As far as CEP can ascertain, company is in compliance with minimum legal standards, but has no significant proactive programs.

✖ - Little or no effort to implement proactive programs and/or company has significant regulatory infractions.

? - Insufficient information.

# FAMILY BENEFITS

CEP rates companies according to how many family benefits are offered company-wide. CEP looks at three major areas of benefits coverage: 1) flexibility in workplace policies (parental leave, flextime, job-sharing, and flexible benefits); 2) child and/or dependent care assistance (reimbursement, referral, on-site or near-site day care, adoption subsidy, elder care, and disabled-dependent care); 3) education and information (onsite seminars, distribution of educational materials, and caregiver fairs).

CEP focuses on programs offered in the Flexibility and Dependent Care areas and uses the education programs as a "kicker" to boost a company's grade.

✔ - Company offers company-wide at least eleven of the benefits in areas 1) and 2), and offers educational support information.

✓ - Company offers all benefits in either area 1) or area 2), company-wide but fewer than three in the other area. Very strong educational support may boost a company to a top grade.

✖ - Indicates that a company offers fewer than three of the options in parts 1) or 2) to its employees.

? - Insufficient information.

If a benefit is in an experimental stage or in the process of being implemented, CEP counts it as a "yes." A benefit still in the research stage is counted as a "no." The size of the company and type of industry are also considered. A benefit granted through "departmental discretion" or on a "case-by-case basis" is counted as a "no" for large companies. CEP feels that for large companies only a company-wide written policy can eliminate the possibility of discrimination. For small companies, however, handling employee needs on a case-by-case basis is common. CEP credits case-by-case benefits for small companies only.

NOTE: Ratings in this category apply to U.S. operations only.

 **WORKPLACE ISSUES**

1 A) If the company is unionized: good relations exist with its union(s), with no major adversarial incidents (major disputes, strikes, lockouts, or unionbusting attempts);

1 B) If the company is not unionized: there is some form of employee representation or participation in decision-making or a grievance process allowing employees to be heard;

2) Company has no record of serious, willful or repeat OSHA violations in the past five years;

3) Salaried employees have a pension plan at least half-vested and/or fully portable after 5 years, and all full-time employees have medical coverage, of which at least half is paid by the company.

✓ - Company has two of the three components mentioned above.

✖ - Company has fewer than two components of a top rating. Company may offer strong benefits but has had a record of serious, willful, or repeat OSHA violations within the past five years. Any company appearing on the AFL-CIO Boycott List.

? - Insufficient information.

Ratings may be boosted upward for having at least three of the following benefits: 1) employee participation on an ESOP advisory board, pension plan management committee, or labor-management health and safety committee; 2) a company-wide policy limiting compensation/salary differentials; 3) outplacement and retraining for displaced workers; 4) a stated policy banning discrimination based on sexual orientation and toward employees diagnosed with AIDS or ARC (Aids-Related Complex).

NOTE: Ratings in this category apply to U.S. operations only.

## MILITARY CONTRACTS  (⚓ appears in the ALERT column)

Rating appears if company was a weapons maker or fuel supplier in 1990, and/or was among top prime contractors for research, development, test and evaluation work. CEP has counted only those companies with contracts totalling $500,000 or more. Contracts for food, clothing, etc. are not counted.

Nuclear weapons-related contract(s) - Company has nuclear weapons-related contracts of any amount. These may include nuclear weapons or their components; and/or systems aiding launch, guidance, delivery or deployment of nuclear weapons.

## NUCLEAR POWER  (✵ appears in the ALERT column):

Rating appears if company supplies one or more of the following to the nuclear power industry: construction, production equipment, fuel, or consulting.

## ALERT

Highlights important information that cannot be indicated by the ratings alone.  Please note that ratings for military contracts and nuclear power appear in the ALERT column throughout the guide.  See the chapter SHOPPING ALERTS for explanations of the ALERTs.

# SHOPPING ALERTS

**✈ - military contracts** - Company has conventional weapons-related and/or fuel contracts totalling $500,000 or more for fiscal year 1990.  Contracts for food, clothing, etc., are not counted.

**✳ - nuclear power** - Company supplies one or more of the following to the nuclear power industry: construction, production, equipment, fuel, or consulting.

**nuclear weapons-related contracts** - Company has nuclear weapons-related contract(s) of any amount.  For example, in 1990, General Electric received $2.7 billion in contracts from the Departments of Energy and Defense for nuclear weapons systems.  These may include nuclear weapons or their components; and/or systems aiding launch, guidance, delivery or deployment of nuclear weapons.

**⊕ - foreign-based company** - In an effort to obtain more accurate and usable information for our readers, CEP has revised its research methods for evaluating transnational corporations headquartered abroad.  Our questionnaire now asks the company to provide **worldwide** data for charitable giving, women's advancement, animal testing, and nuclear power involvement.  It requests **domestic (U.S. only)** information for minority advancement, community outreach, family benefits, and workplace issues.  Military contracting and South Africa are no longer included in the questionnaire, since CEP receives sufficient data from other sources to evaluate involvement in these areas.  In the environment category, a two-part questionnaire asks for separate information for domestic operations and those outside the U.S.

**1% For Peace** - 1% For Peace, Inc. is a non-profit, non-partisan, national organization whose purpose is to create, promote, and fund a positive peace agenda.  One of the campaign's goals is to pass a Federal law requiring that 1% of the $300 billion defense budget (i.e., $3 billion) be redirected to peace through understanding.

**1st to ban CFCs** - In 1975, the National Academy of Sciences found a link between fluorocarbons and depletion of the earth's protective ozone layer. Samuel C. Johnson, chairman of S.C. Johnson & Son, Inc., was concerned and announced that the company would no longer use fluorocarbons in its aerosol spray cans. Johnson urged other companies to follow suit, but it was not until 1978, when the EPA banned fluorocarbons and chlorofluorocarbons (CFCs) for use as propellants in most aerosol sprays, that other companies stopped using the chemicals. CFCs are still used as refrigerants, in plastic foams, in electronic components as cleaners, and in the two percent of aerosols deemed necessary in medical and pharmaceutical products. However, CFCs have recently been regulated by the Montreal Protocol, an international agreement signed by more than 60 countries. The Protocol calls for phasing out production and use of these chemicals by the turn of the century. Substitute chemicals are currently being developed and most major users of CFCs have announced they will phase out their use in manufacturing. The timetables for the phase-outs vary from company to company. Available chemical substitutes such as hydrofluorocarbons (HFCs), hydrochlorofluorocarbons (HCFCs), and halons may also pose environmental problems.

**100% organic ingredients** - The basic principles of organic farming were codified in 1981 by the West German-based International Federation of Organic Agricultural Movements: (1) to work as much as possible within a closed system (minimal waste), and to draw upon local resources; (2) to maintain the long-term fertility of soils; (3) to avoid all forms of pollution that may result from agricultural techniques; (4) to produce foodstuffs of high nutritional quality and sufficient quantity; (5) to reduce to a minimum the use of fossil energy in agriculture; (6) to provide farm animals living conditions appropriate to their physiological needs and to humanitarian principles; (7) to make it possible for agricultural producers to earn a living and develop their human potential.

Currently, labeled organic products are not required to be certified organic. Some companies seek third-party certification while others do self-certification. By 1993, the Organic Foods Production Act of 1990 requires the United States Department of Agriculture (USDA) to define the use of the word organic on a label, develop a list of non-toxic pesticides that are acceptable for organic farmers to use, and set manufacturers standards for organic production and approval of certification organizations, all with the advice of a National Organic Standards Board (composed of organic farmers, manufacturers, environmental specialists and consumer interest advocates).

**100% profit to charity** - Newman's Own, Inc., the all-natural food company founded by actor Paul Newman, has donated 100% of its profits (total $40 million plus since 1982) to charitable causes. Notable among the 400 organizations to which Newman's Own donates is the Hole-in-the-Wall Gang Camp for children with life-threatening diseases. Children who ordinarily spend much of their lives in the hospital are given the chance to enjoy the outdoors. The camp charges no fees.

**ACT NOW** - ACT NOW is a consortium of companies working together to create positive social and environmental change. The group hopes to mobilize consumers to take an active stance on matters of national importance via a series of campaigns. Participating companies deliver their common message to consumers via product labels and packaging, promotional inserts, and space in mail-order catalogues. Telephone numbers and postcards addressed to Congress are provided for consumers to express their support. ACT NOW's first campaign is to promote the passage of Federal legislation that would increase automobile fuel efficiency requirements from present levels of 27.5 miles per gallon to 40 miles per gallon by the year 2001, thereby lowering oil consumption and cutting harmful emissions.

**C.C.A.** - For information on CEP's Corporate Conscience Awards (C.C.A.) and Dishonorable Corporate Conscience Awards (D.C.C.A.), please see page 346.

**cigarettes** - These addictive products are aggressively marketed, especially to women and minorities, by the two cigarette manufacturers that CEP studied for this guide – Philip Morris and RJR Nabisco. Health officials, consumer activists, and other leaders have objected for years to the practice of concentrating tobacco billboard advertising in poorer urban neighborhoods where, they claim, people are dying in disproportionate numbers from diseases related to smoking. As anti-smoking forces continue working to ban all print and outdoor cigarette ads, the tobacco industry is considering a shift to direct marketing, such as mail offers, magazines, posters, and sponsorship of televised sporting events. They are also seeking to reap huge profits overseas, in countries where regulations are few and health warnings often are not required.

**clearcutting** - Of all the methods of logging, clearcutting is the cheapest, easiest, and most destructive, as all trees in a given section are cut down. Clearcutting often results in heavy soil erosion which may lead to serious damage of streams. Old-growth forests, with trees over 200 years old, cannot be replaced. Unfortunately, many timber companies use clearcutting as a way to quickly pay back burdensome debts incurred as a result of a corporate takeover or the fight to fend off a merger. In "maximizing return on assets," debt-ridden companies often cut and sell lumber as quickly as possible.

**co-op** - The cooperative companies in this book are all owned by groups of either dairy or agricultural farmers. There are certain differences in the accounting practices of cooperatives as compared to investor-owned firms. Charitable giving as a percentage of actual pretax earnings of the cooperative is difficult to ascertain because published "net proceeds" figures include earnings of the cooperative plus the "pass-through" market value of the product owned by farmer-members. Additional disclosure by cooperative companies has allowed us to more accurately rate this category. Land-O-Lakes and Tillamook Cheese, for instance, give more than 2% to charity, earning each of them a Top+ rating.

In the Women's and Minority Advancement categories, farmer member-owners of the co-op are nominated for the co-op's Board of Directors by their peers in each district. Directors are then elected by a vote of the entire cooperative membership. Directors, in turn, elect officers from among the Board members. According to officials at two of the cooperatives, 1) few women in farming communities choose to run for office, and 2) there are few or no minorities in the co-ops, largely because of geographic location. Some co-ops, such as Ocean Spray Cranberries, make an effort to recruit women and minorities for management positions in engineering and manufacturing, sales, and management information systems.

**D.C.C.A.** - For information on CEP's Corporate Conscience Awards (C.C.A.) and Dishonorable Corporate Conscience Awards (D.C.C.A.), please see page 346.

**disposable diapers** - Single-use diapers, introduced in 1962, have been marketed as a way to revolutionize child care. They can free parents from the chores of diaper washing, rinsing, hanging, and folding. But the manufacture and disposal of these plastic diapers have significant environmental and financial impacts. Disposable diapers have become a symbol of our penchant for using disposable products that are more expensive and more harmful to the environment than re-usable products. They now make up 2% of municipal solid waste in the U.S. Procter & Gamble and Kimberly-Clark control 80% of the disposable diaper market, a $3.3 billion-a-year industry. Procter & Gamble has built a prototype recycling facility for disposable diapers and has initiated programs to make its diapers safely compostable. These steps, both far in advance of the rest of the industry, have still come under criticism by environmentalists who argue that they are more geared to public relations than a currently-feasible solution.

**factory farming** - The small family farm has largely given way to huge, modern complexes engaged in intensive animal production. In the broiler industry, chickens routinely have less than one square foot of living space per bird. Birds are genetically selected for weight gain. As a result, they often have difficulty supporting their own weight and develop painfully crippled legs. Maintaining dense populations of animals in a confined, indoor space increases the likelihood of disease. The U.S. Department of Agriculture in 1989 estimated that roughly one third of all raw poultry in this country carries Salmonella or Campylobacter bacteria. The agency maintains that proper cooking and handling by consumers will prevent illness. However, the poultry industry only recently has begun providing labels with this information.

Veal calves are often kept in narrow stalls too small for the animals to turn around. To maintain a light flesh color, the calves are fed a liquid, iron-deficient diet which can cause anemia and lower resistance to disease. Sick veal calves may be injected with antibiotics and sent quickly to slaughter, causing drug residues to be found in some marketed veal. Most beef-cattle are fed high-calorie grain diets with little roughage, sometimes leading to liver disease. (See also "safe food controversy" and "safe chicken controversy" ALERTs.)

**Fair Share** - The National Association for the Advancement of Colored People (NAACP) is the oldest civil rights organization in the United States. In December 1981, the NAACP created the Fair Share Program. The program seeks to establish a relationship between the African-American community and corporate America to ensure that a fair share of dollars spent by African-American consumers are reinvested back into their communities in the form of jobs and business opportunities. The Fair Share Program promotes:

- Minority vendor programs for purchases of goods and services from African-American contractors, professionals, and financial and insurance institutions.

- Aggressive affirmative action programs and opportunities for the advancement of African-Americans into senior management positions.

- Representation of African-Americans on corporate boards.

- Philanthropic contributions to worthy African-American organizations and causes.

**forestry criticized** - The Scott Boycott Committee charges Scott with using highly destructive clearcutting and dangerous insecticides and herbicides in Nova Scotia. Scott's policy of replanting clear-cut areas with monoculture – softwood forests that are highly susceptible to insect outbreaks – has also come under criticism by the boycott committee. Scott denies the boycotters' charges, maintaining that its forestry practices are outstanding for the area and have been cited as model programs.

**heart valve suits** - Bjork-Shiley (a subsidiary of Pfizer Corp.) manufactured a prosthetic heart from 1979 to 1986, when the device was withdrawn due to a small percentage of reported strut fractures. Over 80,000 of these heart valves are in use around the world, as a means to extend the lives of patients whose own hearts had become diseased. According to the company, by 1990 at least 394 valves had broken and 252 patients had died. Pfizer has resolved a number of cases related to the heart valve through out-of-court settlements. A class-action suit brought by Public Citizen Health Research Group to require Pfizer to contact valve recipients was dismissed in May 1990. Soon after Public Citizen had filed a petition with the Food and Drug Administration asking that implantees be contacted directly, Pfizer announced it would establish a registry of valve recipients to facilitate the provision of information to doctors and, "if necessary," to patients. In January 1991, a new class-action suit was filed on behalf of 55,000 U.S. valve recipients.

**INFACT boycott** - INFACT is a grassroots action organization whose campaigns seek to hold corporations directly accountable for practices that endanger the health and survival of people around the world. On June 12, 1986 INFACT initiated a boycott of General Electric Corp. for its role in promoting and producing nuclear weapons, creating numerous Superfund sites, and causing serious health problems for workers and neighbors of its plants. The boycott, now estimated to have more than 3.5 million supporters, is having an effect. General Electric no longer makes triggers for nuclear weapons. The company has also realized losses of more than $30 million in its Medical Equipment division, which was the focus of much INFACT activity.

**infant formula** - There are currently two separate issues in the infant formula debate: 1) free supplies to the Third World, and 2) direct public advertising to mothers in the U.S.

1) FREE SUPPLIES TO THE THIRD WORLD: The morality of corporate donations of supplies of infant formula to Third World hospitals has been questioned for years. These free or subsidized samples are used as a marketing tool by the companies. The health implications can be severe. If breast feeding is interrupted in the early stages of post-natal care the production of breast milk ceases. Upon leaving the hospital the mother, now dependent on the costly formula, may mix it with contaminated water or dilute it to make it last longer. These practices often result in "Bottle Baby Disease," which can lead to death. In 1981, the World Health Organization (WHO) and UNICEF established an International Code to regulate the marketing of breast-milk substitutes.

Infant formula companies have stated a new goal to end free supplies of formula in developing countries by the end of 1992. Unfortunately, however, the companies are awaiting action on the part of Third World governments and refusing to end these Code violations voluntarily. In addition, all companies with this ALERT will continue to provide free supplies to developed nations. Nestle, Bristol-Myers Squibb, and American Home Products have refused to end free supplies unilaterally or to commit to a timeline. The previous Nestle boycott has been reinstated and continues.

2) DIRECT ADVERTISING TO MOTHERS IN THE U.S.: The WHO Code is intended to be applied universally. However, Bristol-Myers Squibb and Gerber in a joint effort, and now Nestle/Carnation, are spending tens of millions of dollars on TV and magazine ads that promote new formulas directly to mothers in the United States. These practices have been condemned by groups as diverse as the American Academy of Pediatrics and the National Council of Churches. A broad-based campaign to end direct advertising has begun. Note: Abbott Labs and American Home Products have pledged *not* to conduct direct infant formula ad campaigns in the U.S.

**makes pesticides** - Company makes or uses pesticides, which kill the natural enemies of certain crops. Although pesticides clearly reduce certain risks and losses in farming, they can cause a number of problems. Many are washed by rainwater from farmland into rivers and streams and can eventually make their way into our drinking water; they can be harmful and even fatal to farmworkers applying them without proper protection; their toxic residues may remain on and in fruits and vegetables; and they have in some cases made their intended targets immune so that more and stronger chemicals must be used. Of the 316 pesticides registered with the Environmental Protection Agency, current testing methods at the Food and Drug Administration can detect only 163. Alternative organic and biological methods of dealing with crops' natural enemies are increasingly being used with successful results.

**oil spill** - The Good Friday, 1989, grounding of the tanker Exxon Valdez on a reef in Alaska's Prince William Sound, resulted in the worst oil spill in U.S. history. Some 11 million gallons of oil spilled, washing up on over 400 miles of pristine Alaskan shoreline. The spill killed and injured thousands of otters, seals, fish, and birds, and riveted the nation's attention on the price that oil extraction and transportation exacts on our environment. Investigations into the tragedy revealed a trail of broken oil industry promises for improved accident prevention and quick emergency response.

**on-site day care** - A small but growing number of U.S. corporations offer child care at the workplace. Campbell Soup Co. subsidizes 50% of the tuition for 110 children of its Camden, NJ headquarters employees. It has also helped upgrade day care facilities overall in the Camden area. Other companies offering on-site/near-site daycare in at least one location include Ben & Jerry's, Hershey, Johnson & Johnson, and S. C. Johnson and Son, Inc.

**pesticide sterilization suit** - A suit brought by 500 Costa Rican farmworkers charges that Standard Fruit Co. (whose parent company, Dole Food Co. Inc. was formerly known as Castle & Cooke), for years used pesticides in Central America that were banned in the U.S. The company used dibromochloropropane (DBCP) on banana plantations in Costa Rica until 1979, when cases of alleged worker sterility influenced the Costa Rican government to outlaw further use of the pesticide. The company then sent leftover DBCP to Honduras, where health protection for workers was lax. There, many more workers allegedly became sterilized.

In March 1990, a Texas Supreme Court ruling allowed the personal damage suit against Standard Fruit (Dole), Dow

Chemical and Shell Oil Co. to be tried in the U.S. The latter two companies developed and produced DBCP. Dow allegedly continued to sell DBCP to Dole after it was banned in the U.S.

Dole says it has not used DBCP for more than five years, and that it is currently using Integrated Pest Management (IPM) techniques to reduce the amount of pesticides needed. The company states its policy is 1) "to not use anywhere any chemical that has been banned by the Environmental Protection Agency" and 2) "to comply with the laws of each country in which the company operates and sells its products."

Nevertheless, CEP considers this ALERT current and has included it for two reasons: 1) For seven years, the lawsuit has been blocked from trial in the U.S. by Dow and Shell. The new consolidated suit that also names Dole is being fought by that company as well. All are trying to have the case tried outside the country. 2) As of September 1991, the suit was still awaiting trial in Texas.

**removed tobacco** - In 1988, Von's Companies, Inc., the largest supermarket chain in Southern California, removed all cigars, pipes and chewing tobacco from its shelves because the companies that make the products failed to put consumer warning labels on them. "Clear and reasonable warnings" on all products that expose consumers to chemicals known to cause cancer or birth defects are required by California's Proposition 65 referendum, passed in 1986. The stores continue to sell cigarettes, which carry Federal health warnings.

**safe chicken controversy** - In 1991, new concerns were voiced about the safety of chicken, which Americans eat at an average rate of 75 pounds per person per year. The Government Accountability Project and other consumer groups have been focusing on this problem for some time. In June 1991, Sen. Howard Metzenbaum (Ohio) called for a study of sicknesses associated with poultry, expressing concern about the high rate of bacterial contamination found in virtually all brands of chicken sold in the supermarket. These chickens are stamped with the USDA Seal of Approval, but increased production line speed often means inadequate time for inspection. "A few giant corporations," Sen. Metzenbaum declared, "produce the same product with the same problems." ConAgra, Perdue, and Tyson (all listed in this guide) are among the top four chicken processors, which collectively produce 40% of U.S. poultry. Products from all are alleged to have high rates of microbial contamination.

The National Broiler Council (NBC) is concerned that news coverage has largely presented only the views of broiler industry critics. It announced that large-scale tests of new poultry-processing procedures would begin in August 1991. The president of NBC stated last summer that labels with poultry-handling instructions "are already being implemented by a substantial number of its members" and that all members are being urged to provide such labeling (*Feedstuffs* agribusiness newspaper, 6/24/91).

**safe meat controversy** - During the past year, this issue has been much in the news and has widened to include the broiler chicken industry. (See also "safe chicken controversy" ALERT.)

Since 1986, ConAgra's Monfort food plants (Greeley, CO and Grand Island, NE) have been two of five facilities using the "Streamlined Inspection System" (SIS), a U.S. Department of Agriculture (USDA) pilot program designed for greater inspection efficiency. Under SIS, a number of tasks usually performed by USDA inspectors are transferred to plant employees. According to the Government Accountability Project (GAP), an independent investigation found the microbial contamination rate had increased by at least eight times since SIS started. The Project reports: "Employees, often poorly-trained, perform primary inspection of beef on a speeded-up assembly line; workers, afraid for their jobs, are reluctant to slow or stop the line; Federal inspectors have only a few seconds to check each carcass for signs of disease or infection." Monfort's Vice President of Quality Control rejected these criticisms in a July 10, 1990 *Washington Post* article, saying GAP staff was "not trained in microbiology." He said SIS had helped improve "the process and the product" and pointed to Monfort records indicating a drop in the incidence of contaminants.

In September 1990, a report by the National Academy of Sciences stated that none of the inspection systems currently in use or being tested by USDA Food Safety Inspection Service (FSIS) are "designed to detect or eliminate microbial or chemical hazards presented by meat products." A representative of USDA/FSIS stated that the streamlined system was originally devised to avoid spending taxpayers' money for inspectors to be "foremen for industry."

**Salvadoran coffee** - Coffee beans grown in El Salvador generate an estimated $184 million in annual tax revenues for the right-wing ARENA government and military. The military in El Salvador has been accused by Amnesty International, members of Congress, and U.S. church groups of gross human rights abuses, including the murder of as many as 40,000 civilians. A boycott of coffee beans from El Salvador, led by the activist group Neighbor to Neighbor, is directed at Procter & Gamble, Nestle, and Philip Morris. The boycott is supported by five national religious bodies and five major U.S. unions, as well as several large trade unions in El Salvador.

Procter & Gamble asserts it has been unfairly singled out by boycott organizers, and that it is not the largest U.S. buyer of Salvadoran coffee. The company says it welcomes any new, verifiable information that would indicate a connection between its coffee purchases and wrongdoing in El Salvador. Critics of the boycott include the U.S. Ambassador to El Salvador, White House Chief of Staff John Sununu, and some Catholic bishops in both the U.S. and El Salvador. They argue that the boycott would cut off the only source of income for thousands of peasants, yet have no significant effect on the government.

**some organic ingredients** - These companies have some ingredients in their products which are organically grown. Please see ALERT entitled 100% organic ingredients (in the front of this chapter) for a more comprehensive discussion on organic farming.

**U.K.** - Company has been researched and rated by New Consumer, CEP's British overseas affiliate, as well as by CEP. For a discussion of New Consumer's research and their ratings, please refer to BUYING FROM BRITAIN, on page 317.

**Valdez Principles** - In 1989, in response to the Exxon Valdez oil spill, the Coalition for Environmentally Responsible Economies (CERES) established the Valdez Principles. The Principles are a set of ten commitments to a healthy and sustainable environment, which corporations are encouraged to sign: 1) protection of the biosphere; 2) sustainable use of natural resources; 3) reduction and disposal of wastes; 4) wise use of energy; 5) risk reduction; 6) marketing of safe products and services; 7) damage compensation; 8) disclosure; 9) employing environmental directors and managers; and 10) allowing an annual environmental audit. In signing, a company makes a pledge to uphold the Principles by using only environmentally-friendly policies and methods, and to submit an annual progress report to CERES and to the public. The Principles are designed to push investment dollars toward companies that are environmentally responsible. The Principles are broad and do not mandate specific actions. Consequently, a signatory is not necessarily complying with them. CERES states that it will publicize companies that aren't following the Principles and pressure those corporations to change their behavior. By mid-1991, 28 companies had signed, none of them in the Fortune 1000.

**Workplace Principles** - In 1988, the Citizens Commission on AIDS developed the Workplace Principles, a 10-point "bill of rights" on AIDS issues in the workplace. The Washington-based National Leadership Coalition on AIDS, was formed by business leaders to promote corporate action on AIDS. It has asked companies and organizations nationwide to adopt the Workplace Principles and abide by them. Signatories pledge not to discriminate against workers with AIDS, to educate all employees about how AIDS is spread (and how it isn't), to keep medical records confidential, and to not require HIV screening as part of hiring practice. As of early 1991, 404 companies and organizations have endorsed the Workplace Principles.

# SHOPPING FOR GENEROUS CHARITABLE GIVING

Corporate donations have come a long way since a major manufacturer supplied soap and candles to the town hospital. In recent years, many corporations have helped to alleviate problems caused by deep cuts in Federal funding for housing, education, and child care. They have contributed money and products to food banks such as Second Harvest, instituted job-training programs for disadvantaged youths, and set up partnerships with local governments to revitalize communities. Some have joined the flagship 2% and 5% Clubs, whose members pledge that portion of their pre-tax income to charitable causes. Newman's Own gives 100% of profits; Tom's of Maine and Ben and Jerry's Homemade give over 9%.

At one time, companies contributed their charitable dollars to a wide range of causes, giving many small grants to groups with diverse concerns. Now more companies are concentrating on one or two causes.

The cause currently attracting most attention is education. In the past, contributions for education went to research universities and colleges. The newest recipients of corporate gifts are public secondary and elementary schools. Corporations realize that a growing number of graduates are unprepared even for the most basic entry-level jobs. Thus, by helping schools financially they are combining self-interest with philanthropy.

Most corporate giving is done through company foundations and direct corporate donations. Many companies also have programs that match employee gifts. Others give grants to groups for whom their employees volunteer.

Of increasing interest to today's profit-minded CEOs is cause-related marketing, in which companies promise to donate a certain amount of the purchase price of their product to charity. The terms differ case-by-case and in some instances precipitate controversial commerical invasions into the classroom.

Still other companies make substantial in-kind (non-cash) gifts. Many small company donations are entirely in-kind. Some large companies, especially supermarkets, donate products to various social services such as food banks, or computers to schools. There is no standard measure of the value of these donations, so it is difficult for CEP to incorporate in-kind giving into our rating criteria.

Neither cause-related marketing proceeds nor in-kind donations are included in our charity ratings for large companies, which are calculated as a percentage of worldwide pre-tax earnings. If, however, a company's primary form of philanthropy is through product donations, as is the case with many supermarkets, then CEP does consider in-kind donations when making a rating. For small companies, we consistently included in-kind giving in our calculations.

Corporate charitable giving for foreign-based companies is often not as common as it is in the United States due to more extensive government support for public welfare. Likewise, multinational companies based in the United States may have few charitable giving programs in other countries where they operate abroad but give generously in the United States.

Giving as a percentage of pre-tax net income rose steadily for 16 years, until 1985, when it reached its peak of almost 2%. Since then, corporate generosity has fallen as low as 1.6% in

1988, the lowest level in seven years. In 1990, corporate giving in adjusted dollars was 1.9%. These national figures include in-kind donations and are figured as a percentage of domestic, rather than worldwide, pre-tax earnings. They thus tend to be higher than CEP figures.

In **SHOPPING FOR A BETTER WORLD**, CEP's rating criterion is: A company must give between 0.7% and 1.2% in order to earn a ✓, and over 1.2% to earn a ✔. Companies giving 2% or more earn a ✔+.

**You can help shape the future of charitable giving:**

• "Give Five." Contribute 5% of your income to charity. The current U.S. average for individuals is 2.4%.

• Support companies that are members of 2% or 5% clubs. Publicly-held companies can take tax deductions for up to 10% of their pre-tax income donated to charity. Privately-held companies can give any amount.

• Ask your employer to match your gifts generously, giving at least $2 for every $1 you donate.

• Ask your employer to donate money to the organizations where you volunteer.

• Help raise money for your favorite causes.

• Select products made by companies rated ✔+ or ✔.

# SHOPPING FOR EQUAL OPPORTUNITY

The U.S. Department of Labor estimates that three-fourths of all new entrants into the workforce in the 1990s will be minorities or women. A comparison of earnings patterns bodes ill for their prospects.

• 1991 Bureau of Labor Statistics (BLS) figures show:

• Black Americans earned $355 per week. Hispanic Americans earned $324 per week. White Americans earned $451 per week.

• Women working full-time earn only 73 cents for every $1 a man earns.

• Many Boards of Directors of major companies still do not have even one female participant; a greater number lack members of minority groups.

As CEP researched the composition of corporate Boards and upper management over the last six years, it has seen an almost universal pattern: slow but steady movement from a "token woman" to two or maybe three women at the top in many large corporations. Few, if any, minorities, especially are at the Board level.

A prime focus of the Labor Department's Office of Federal Contract Compliance Programs (OFCCP) this year has been investigating the so-called "glass ceiling" - an invisible barrier that limits the advancement of women and minorities beyond a certain level in the corporate hierarchy. OFCCP Director Cari Dominguez observes "tremendous imbalances" between the numbers of white men and those of women and minorities in upper level corporate management. Her office is examining how people are being groomed for the top jobs and will scrutinize attitudinal and other barriers that perpetuate this form of discrimination.

Some companies, such as Avon and General Mills, have effective systems in place right now to eliminate barriers to the advancement of qualified women and minorities. They use Upward Mobility Committees and mentoring programs. They advertise in women's and minorities' publications and/or regularly review their personnel managers' records in hiring women and minorities.

In 1990, women were directors at 817 Fortune 1000 companies, up from 719 in 1989 and roughly 30 in 1966. Still, 183 Fortune 1000 companies had no women on their Boards. Minorities had even less representation.

It is possible for corporations to support equal employment opportunity even if minorities make up only a small portion of the surrounding population or if the company is in an industry where the pool of qualified women applicants is limited. Some companies, even small ones, have appointed minorities from other geographic areas to their Boards.

Companies may choose to keep funds in banks owned by minorities or women, or in "greenlining" banks like Shorebank in Chicago, which has turned its entire neighborhood around by making local home mortgage and small business loans available to minorities. Quaker Oats' business with minority banks exceeded $160 million in 1990.

By seeking out suppliers among businesses owned by minorities or women, companies provide invaluable experience and revenues. PepsiCo, for example, has a $228 million minority purchasing program. The growth of minority purchasing and banking programs has been encouraging. In 1972, purchasing programs reported $86 million in business. The National Minority Suppliers Development Council (NY) states that by 1989 (the latest year for which figures are available), purchasing programs it monitors exceeded $13.5 billion. One-hundred seventy of the Fortune 500 companies participate as national members.

Now, greater opportunity is being extended to people with disabilities, thanks to a new Federal law passed in 1990. The Americans With Disabilities Act (ADA) ensures equal employment rights and access to public businesses for the 43 million citizens of the U.S. who are disabled. A recent Harris poll found that two thirds of disabled people of working age are not employed. More than 8 million of these would like to find jobs. Under the new law, companies with 25 or more workers have until July 1992 to comply; small companies with fewer than 25 employees have until July 1994.

In 1963, Martin Luther King, Jr. had a dream. To realize it, there is still a long way to go, and you can help:

- Encourage your place of work to eliminate "glass ceilings" and to seek out banks and suppliers owned or operated by women, minorities or people with disabilities.

- Let your elected representatives know you support enforcement of Equal Employment Opportunity laws.

- Practice equal opportunity and teach your children to do the same.

- Join organizations that speak out for equal employment opportunities.

- Select products made by companies rated ✔ in Women's Advancement and Minority Advancement.

# SHOPPING TO END ANIMAL TESTING

An increasingly aware public continues to oppose the needless suffering of animals. Concerted action is getting results. Several giant cosmetics and personal care companies such as Avon and Revlon, as well as others, no longer test on animals.

Most of these companies now use non-animal test alternatives and data banks of previously tested ingredients to ensure the safety of future consumer products. Other sectors of the corporate community have launched programs – from special in-house committees to industry-wide symposia – to promote non-animal alternatives. These new methods may well be faster, cheaper, and more reliable.

Recent efforts have substantially reduced use of the LD50 test (which determines the toxicity level of a substance required to kill 50% of animals in a test group), the Draize rabbit eye test (in which products being safety-tested are placed in the eyes of rabbits, frequently causing blindness or death), and other tests.

Some companies, such as Tom's of Maine and Aubrey Organics, were established on the principle of no animal testing. Among companies that still use animal testing, CEP has identified consumer product companies, such as Colgate Palmolive and S.C. Johnson and Son, Inc., that have substantially reduced the number of animals used and/or actively joined the search for alternative test methods.

The Animal and Plant Health Inspection Service of the U.S. Department of Agriculture (USDA/APHIS) is considered the best source for overall data on numbers of animals used at in-house corporate testing laboratories in the U.S. The agency does not track animal tests performed by outside labs for corporate clients. In 1983, the USDA estimated in-house use was 17 to 22 million animals. In 1989, Dr. Andrew Rowan of Tufts University estimated that between 29 and 39 million animals are used in lab research each year. The overwhelming majority are rodents. Testing by consumer products companies accounts for a tiny fraction of all research animals; the others are used by pharmaceutical companies and in government, academic, and medical research.

In the past, cures or relief for acute and chronic illnesses have been developed on the basis of research performed primarily on animals. Therefore, efforts to completely eliminate such research are likely to be life-threatening. Nonetheless, there is significant scope for reduction in the number of animals tested, even for medical research. The National Cancer Institute's (NCI) anti-tumor drug discovery program reduced its use of animals in tests from 6 million in 1986 to less than 300,000 in 1989. The organization chose to use "human tumor cell lines" instead, which it says may actually be more dependable and cost-effective.

Several organizations formed by disabled or incurably ill people favor animal research. Other such organizations oppose it. (Interested readers may obtain a list of either/both of these from CEP.)

To help you in making personal buying decisions, we have indicated with a ○ those companies that manufacture drugs and/or surgical equipment. The animal protection movement has effectively raised public awareness about the use of animals for safety testing, especially for cosmetics and household products. But, for every one animal suffering in this area, thousands of animals suffer from birth to slaughter through "factory farming." The movement is steadily expanding to include and address the enormous suffering incurred in the raising, transport, and slaughter of animals on factory farms.

The family farm we may remember from childhood or that we've viewed on "Little House on the Prairie" has become a rarity in America today. Such traditional farms have largely been replaced over the last two decades by efficient but cruel industrial operations that mass produce most of the nation's meat, milk, and eggs.

Factory farming denies animals the most elemental freedoms: to stand up, lie down, extend their limbs or spread their wings and turn around. The veal calf is taken from its mother hours after birth and chained in a crate often less than two feet wide, where it will spend the entire sixteen weeks of its life. In the broiler industry, birds are debeaked at birth and packed into buildings with less than one square foot of living space per bird. Breeding sows are often confined in "gestation crates" for three and a half months at a time, unable to turn around.

In this guide, ratings in the animal testing category do not take account of factory farming, because CEP has not been able to gather reliable, company-wide data on agribusiness practices. We have, however, identified three companies to receive a "factory farming" ALERT. Please see "factory farming" ALERT explanation on page 29. We encourage consumers to become informed about factory farming, to query companies, and to support an end to abuses in the animal agriculture business.

Here are some things you can do:

• Ask companies from which you buy cosmetics, household products, or pharmaceuticals to report what they've done to promote alternatives to animal testing. Company addresses appear on page 364.

- Ask legislators to provide you with reports on what regulatory agencies are doing to promote non-animal alternative testing.

- Ask companies from which you buy meat, eggs, and dairy products what they are doing to improve the quality of life for farm animals.

- Buy meat only from distributors that sell free-range or organically raised animals.

- Become an informed vegetarian; learn the basics of nutrition for a meatless diet.

- Shop for a better world by selecting products made by companies rated ✔ or ✔* or ✔⊛ .

# SHOPPING FOR OUR RIGHT TO KNOW

Consumers, investors, employees, and non-profit groups working in the public interest all need access to facts and figures in order to form knowledgeable opinions about corporations. A company's willingness to share information on its basic operations and its social endeavors is essential to this effort, and is an indication of good corporate citizenship.

Until recently, most corporations have resisted providing comparable data on social initiatives. Attempts to require companies to do so by law have been largely unsuccessful.

Though a majority of firms still do not publish information on social performance, many companies with a definite commitment to social responsibility have made it a priority. More and more companies are adding a small section to their annual report discussing their "commitment" or "public responsibility." Other companies publish more extensive reports. Many of these reports are full of feel-good pictures and words but provide little substantive information on the company's social programs. Others routinely inform the public of the social impact of their operations, in measureable terms and use a format comparable year to year and among companies. The best ones, such as Bristol-Myers Squibb Co.'s and Ben and Jerry's, document company efforts, demonstrate results or indicate shortcomings, and use comparable data.

Of the 166 companies rated in this book, 85 cooperated fully by providing extensive information, 31 provided more limited information, and 50 gave us little or no information.

ABOUT THE RESEARCH tells how we gathered information.

Let companies know that you want information about their social performance:

- Ask companies that did not cooperate to provide information for our next edition.  They received an ✖ for disclosure.  Company addresses appear on page 364.

- Urge members of Congress and the Securities and Exchange Commission to require annual disclosure of comparable data on corporate social performance.

- Encourage companies to publish meaningful social responsibility reports, often called social audits or stakeholder reports.

- Select products made by companies rated ✔.

# SHOPPING FOR A THRIVING COMMUNITY

Walk through any community in America and you catch its spirit right away. Do a little checking and you're likely to discover the town's persona is influenced by the major companies in the area.

The lack of affordable housing for low- and middle-income families and of quality public education has taken a sad toll in communities across the nation. In some cases, the corporate community has heard and begun to respond with innovative community outreach programs. In other cases, it has turned a deaf ear.

Companies can invest in low-cost housing in a variety of ways: the construction of new housing; the refurbishment of existing housing; or the revitalization of entire neighborhoods. S.C. Johnson and Son, Inc., for instance, supports the Racine Habitat for Humanity and is an active member in the Racine (WI) County Economic Development Corporation. Procter & Gamble organized an equity fund of $4.5 million from Cincinnati companies to provide housing for low-income people in the community.

Corporations can also contact experienced intermediaries to help evaluate local housing needs, manage housing programs, and distribute corporate funds to local community organizations. The Local Initiatives Support Corporation (LISC) in New York City, the Enterprise Foundation (EF) in

Columbia, MD, and the National Equity Fund (NEF) in Chicago, IL, are three such intermediaries. LISC has collaborated with over 600 community groups on the development of more than 21,000 housing units. NEF has worked with local groups in 27 cities and has created 9,500 housing units for the poor since 1981.

By staking these organizations with grants and investing in the consortia they put together, companies provide housing and can also aid their workforce. Affordable housing near company workplaces aids both in recruitment and in retention of employees.

Seeing that our education system is severely crippled, business is stepping into the classroom. Vast numbers of students are either graduating from schools without basic skills or not graduating at all. The Federal government has thus far been unwilling to substantially increase its financial commitment to education. Spending by the Department of Education, as a percentage of total federal outlays, has actually fallen from 2.5% in FY 1979 to 2.0% in FY 1990. Federal, state, and local expenditures per pupil go up slowly – the latest available figure is $4,639 for the 1988-89 school year. The corporate community cannot possibly function as the primary funder of public education, but may respond with imaginative programs: Adopt-A-School, literacy projects, vocational training, employment programs, and volunteer and tutoring projects. With these programs, companies hope to breathe new life into the school systems they depend on.

Adopt-A-School can be a fine example of a program that brings the corporate world and the community together. A business may help students prepare for the job market by supplying public schools with updated equipment, enhancing incentives for good academic performance, and placing employees in these institutions as instructors or counselors. However, schools should be wary of companies that use them primarily as marketing extensions – where the emphasis is on familiarizing young minds with brand names and not centrally on improving the quality of education, or when the corporate financial and staff commitment is minimal and lacks substance.

A company's greatest resource is its employees. Volunteerism is a positive way to help the community and a visible way to enhance the company's name. Through executive assistance, work release for other employees, grants to organizations for which employees volunteer, job banks, and involvement of retired employees, communities receive much help to address local problems.

Not all corporations, however, are community minded. Many companies abandon towns that have been dependent on them or lay off large numbers of employees without adequate notice or retraining programs. Some companies are engaged in unionbusting.

To make your community a better place, you can:

• Volunteer at a community center, public interest group or school.

• Encourage your employer to establish a strong volunteer program.

• Join a local organization that promotes housing and economic development or public education efforts.

• Ask companies in your community to involve themselves in upgrading education or local family recreation facilities.

• Consider a career in community work or teaching.

• Support companies rated ✔.

# SHOPPING TO END APARTHEID

Events in South Africa since CEP published the 1991 edition of **SHOPPING FOR A BETTER WORLD** show the country moving dramatically toward ending apartheid. One year after the freeing of African National Congress leader Nelson Mandela and the legalization of banned anti-apartheid groups, the South African government in February 1991 repealed three laws which have upheld the apartheid system for 44 years:

- The Population Registration Act (divided individuals by race);

- The Land Acts (86% of land reserved for whites);

- The Group Areas Act (zoned residential areas according to race).

Critics have noted, however, that these pillars of apartheid were not totally eradicated, and that other structures supporting apartheid are still in place. Despite the changes, Nelson Mandela and the rest of South Africa's black majority still cannot vote and are not represented in Parliament. They still receive health care vastly inferior to that provided the white minority. And low-paid black workers who fuel South Africa's economy still have a limited stake in it.

For decades, U.S. and other foreign corporations have played a key role in South Africa's industrial development. More than 200 companies have withdrawn from South Africa since

1986.  But according to the Investor Responsibility Research Center, 106 U.S. companies and a number of foreign corporations still had operations in South Africa at the end of 1990. Whether these companies make candy or computers, they all pay taxes to the South African government at a rate of 72%. These taxes still support South Africa's military and its imbalanced social programs.

Companies that have investments in South Africa defend their decisions, saying that the most effective way they can fight apartheid is to continue operating there.  They contend that they provide employment and important services and benefits to blacks, and that if they leave, the employers who replace them won't feel any obligation to maintain the social responsibility programs now in place.  Most companies with direct investment in South Africa endorse certain workplace guidelines as outlined in the Statement of Principles (for U.S. companies) or the European Community Code of Conduct (for foreign companies).

President George Bush has now lifted the U.S. Comprehensive Anti-Apartheid Act of 1986, which prohibited new U.S. investment in South Africa and banned companies from deducting taxes paid to South Africa from their U.S. tax bill. This legislation spurred exits from South Africa by several of the largest U.S. companies, including Mobil Oil, which had been the largest company until it left in 1989.  Companies that left commonly sold their assets to South African owners who retained the workforce.  Black workers were in a few cases given a stake in the new company through share ownership or representation on the Board of Directors.  Many U.S. companies also continue to fund social responsibility programs after divestment.  Coca-Cola did both: it gave employees a percentage of ownership in the company when it divested, and it donated $10 million to fund the Equal Opportunity Foundation.

Anti-apartheid activists both here and in South Africa are disappointed that sanctions were dropped before voting rights for blacks were achieved. They argue that public pressure and sanctions – which some estimate have cost South Africa more than $32 billion since 1985 and severely restricted its access to foreign markets and capital – provided the leverage necessary for change.

# SHOPPING FOR A GREENER WORLD

Since Earth Day 1990 we have seen an explosion of claims about how environmentally responsible companies are. At both the manufacturing and sales ends, companies continue to jump on the "green marketing" bandwagon. Some of these claims are sincere, others cynical. But at least one thing is certain: the greening of the marketplace is no passing fad.

There are many examples of corporations' "green" activities. Xerox is collecting copy cartridges from some machines for recycling. Two large California utilities were the first in the country to announce they would reduce total carbon dioxide emissions by 20% over the next twenty years. Furniture maker Herman Miller eliminated rainforest hardwoods from its line of office chairs. Procter & Gamble has increased the recycled content of many of its packages. Fort Howard introduced 100% recycled Green Forest toilet paper. Natural Brew Coffee filters are unbleached and contain no dioxins. Loblaw, Canada's largest supermarket, introduced a Green Line of environmentally-friendly products ranging from non-chlorine bleached coffee filters to organic food products. Wal-Mart asked its suppliers for products they claim are better for the environment, and the store highlights these with shelf displays and explanations.

How can you tell whether or not a product is really green? Many products advertised as environmentally sound do not prove to be so under careful scrutiny. Mobil Corporation was sued by seven states in 1990 for falsely advertising its Hefty trash bags as degradable. "Degradable" plastics will only break down when exposed to air and sunlight. What Mobil didn't mention is that most discarded bags end up in the dark, airless atmosphere of a landfill. The Federal Trade Commission and the state attorneys general have recommended that strict guidelines on plastics labeling be developed. Unfortunately, few standards currently exist for assessing a company's or a product's environmental impact, and there is little agreement about what "safe for the environment" really means.

While there are few absolute answers at this time, many groups and individuals are working to shed light on these questions and to develop solutions. Some states are developing standards for environmental terms like "recyclable" or "degradable." Several groups are organizing to certify rainforest woods logged in a sustainable manner. A national organic agriculture certification program, part of the 1990 Farm Bill, must be implemented by the U.S. Department of Agriculture by 1993. Model legislation has been drafted by the Northeast states to help reduce toxic chemicals in packaging. Researchers are also working to compare the environmental impacts of various types of packaging. Federal government procurement offices spending over $10,000 a year must now purchase, when available, "EPA-preferred" materials and supplies that are recycled or contain recycled material.

The U.S. will soon join the many countries which have eco-labeling programs, so that environmentally-friendly products may carry a validated seal of approval. Unlike other countries' programs, U.S. programs are privately operated as nonprofit organizations. Green mail-order businesses are thriving, and stores specializing in green products have sprouted in several major U.S. cities, including New York, San Francisco, and Buffalo.

While many changes still need to be made at the policy level, it is clear that companies and the Government are responding to consumer and citizen pressure about environmental issues. Below we've provided a long list of things you can do individually to help keep up the momentum. If you would like to receive additional suggestions in the form of a simple poster, please fill out and return the request form at the back of this book.

- Reuse containers and products as often as possible.

- Take a mesh, string, or canvas bag to the store for your shopping trips. For major shopping, fill it with your accumulated paper or plastic bags and reuse them.

- Recycle newspapers, corrugated cardboard, bottles, cans, and whatever other materials your community or municipality collects. The Environmental Protection Agency estimates that 70% of all incinerator ash is glass and metals, which we should be recovering.

- Buy fresh ingredients. They are usually more nutritious and less enveloped in packaging. Whenever possible, shop at farmers' markets and farm stands. Chances are, the farther food must be shipped, the more synthetic preservatives it will contain.

- Start a backyard compost pile to dispose of kitchen scraps. An estimated 20-30% of household trash disposed of in landfills could be converted into useful garden fertilizer through composting. Apartment dwellers can compost through the use of in-kitchen systems such as worm boxes.

- Choose personal care and paper products that have no artificial scent or color, as these are often toxic.

- Many shaving creams contain ammonia and ethanol. Look for natural alternatives. Or just use a little soap.

- Look for natural or non-toxic alternatives to household cleaners, paints, garden supplies, building materials, and so on. Contact CEP for a list of suppliers.

- Convince your local supermarket to begin a shelf labelling program that highlights products that are less harmful to the environment. Here are four areas to start with: reusable products, products made from or packaged in recycled material; products containing no toxic ingredients; and organically-grown food. Ask the store to set up an advisory board for the program and to invite the participation of community environmental activists.

- Eliminate the use of lawn chemicals. Almost 70 million pounds of potentially hazardous chemicals are applied to American lawns each year. A green, healthy lawn can be maintained with organic fertilizers, non-toxic pest control techniques, and a little elbow grease. Better yet, replace your lawn with a field of wildflowers and save on water and labor while eliminating the need for chemical treatments.

- Plant trees. Trees turn $CO_2$ into oxygen. Well-placed trees around a house can lower air-conditioning needs by 10 to 50%.

- Start or join a community garden. In urban areas, gardens bring communities together and bring a bit of nature into the city.

- Urge your school(s) to provide environmental education. We might yet restore a healthy harmony with nature if consideration for the environment becomes second nature.

- Conserve energy. Make sure household equipment and fixtures are maximally efficient in their use of electricity and water. Weatherize your home. See SHOPPING FOR CONSERVATION AND ENERGY OPTIONS on page 66.

- Reject disposable products when possible. Use cloth diapers. Buy a pen with a replaceable cartridge or one that is refillable. Use razors with replaceable blades instead of totally disposable ones.

- Avoid products that contain ozone-depleting CFCs, such as: cleaning sprays for sewing machines, VCRs, and electronic equipment; aerosol dust-removers for cameras; rigid insulation; and foam packaging. Unfortunately, many of these products have no workable substitute currently on the market.

- Leaky car air conditioners are a major source of CFC emissions. If your car has air-conditioning, make sure it's well sealed. An increasing number of shops will capture and recycle your car's CFCs.

- Don't buy products made from endangered or over-exploited species. Avoid furs, ivory, reptile skin, tortoise shell, and exotic hardwoods such as teak, koa, or zebrawood that aren't harvested sustainably.

- Write to company executives and tell them what you like (or don't like) about their policies.

- Choose brands in this guide made by companies rated ✔.

# SHOPPING FOR BETTER PACKAGING

Americans love packaging. And the products on supermarket and drugstore shelves reflect that love affair: nearly everything, it seems, is wrapped in something, sometimes a lot of things. Even produce – onions and corn-on-the-cob – sit neatly on a plastic foam tray, encased in clear plastic wrap. Some products have layer upon layer of packaging, for no apparent reason.

Some packaging is important – it prevents tampering and theft, ensures cleanliness, and can be imprinted with helpful information. But a great deal of it is unnecessary and wasteful.

You needn't walk far down any supermarket aisle to find a plastic bowl covered with a plastic lid, contained in a cardboard box, which is shrink-wrapped in yet more plastic. Ironically, some of these overpackaged goods are given awards by the packaging industry for their innovative designs. It is precisely these "innovations" that contribute to our clogged landfills. Of the roughly two tons of trash discarded by the average American each year, packaging accounts for an estimated 30%, or about 1,200 pounds a year for every man, woman, and child.

The problem isn't just the amount of packaging, it's also the type of materials used. A growing number of products are being wrapped in "composites"–packages containing several layers of materials and adhesives. Juice boxes, which contain layers of polyethylene, paperboard, and aluminum are one example. The components of these materials cannot be separated from each other before being thrown away and cannot currently be recycled. These packages will end up in landfills, where they may take centuries to break down.

Even when packaging consists of only one type of material, it is often an unrecyclable one. The vast majority of Americans have no means to recycle most types of plastic or polystyrene, or even the kind of coated paperboard used in many product packages. Many manufacturers, attempting to lure environmentally conscious consumers, are labeling their packages "recyclable." That may be technically true – given the right technology and enough financing, the package could be recycled. But for now, glass, aluminum, steel, and corrugated cardboard are the only packaging materials conveniently recyclable.

What about plastic? The good news is that two types of plastic are now viably recyclable: polyethylene terephthalate (PET) plastic, used in soda bottles; and high-density polyethylene (HDPE), used in milk jugs and some shampoo bottles. (These may also be identified by a plastics-industry coding system stamped on the bottom of the container. The codes contain a number inside the recycling triangle. The code for PET is #1, for HDPE #2.)

The latest recycling figures show that 15% of all PET plastic and 1.6% of all HDPE plastic, is being recycled. Yet many communities still do not have facilities which accept these plastics for recycling. Still, only about 1% of all other plastics are being recycled, and there is little market for the recycled materials. This situation will undoubtedly change in coming years. But for practical purposes, most plastic packaging remains unrecyclable.

What's the best type of packaging? The best packaging is made from the least amount of material possible, and contains materials you can readily recycle. An aluminum or steel can is one such type of packaging. Even a plastic soda bottle is acceptable if there is a recycling facility in your area that accepts it. Plain boxes made from recycled cardboard are also good. (You can identify recycled cardboard easily: the unprinted side of the cardboard is grayish-brown. If it is white, the cardboard is not recycled.)

Many companies, including the largest consumer product firms, are working to reduce or change the type of packaging they use. But for each reduced-packaging product, there seems to be at least one new "convenience" product brimming with packaging. Few, if any, industry or government restrictions are placed on such products, so it will be up to consumers to pressure manufacturers.

For more information, check *The Green Consumer Supermarket Guide* (Penguin Books, 1991) or subscribe to the monthly *Green Consumer Letter*. Write The Green Consumer, at 1526 Connecticut Ave., NW, Washington, DC 20036; 1-800-955-GREEN.

Meanwhile here are things to look for and others to avoid:

- Reject packaged produce. Most fruits and vegetables have their own natural "packaging."

- Avoid multi-material packages such as juice boxes and squeezable ketchup containers. They are almost impossible to recycle.

- Look for products packaged in recycled materials or materials that you can readily recycle in your community. For most Americans, that includes glass, aluminum, steel, and some kinds of cardboard and plastic. Take the empty packages to be recycled.

- Buy the largest-sized package you'll use, to minimize excess packaging.

- Look for concentrated products. They reduce packaging by putting more product in less packaging.

- Look for egg cartons made of paperboard instead of plastic foam.

- Avoid plastic milk cartons unless there is a recycling program in your area that accepts them.

- Avoid aerosols. The cans cannot be recycled, and most aerosol products contain propellants that contribute to photochemical smog.

- Let manufacturers and supermarket managers know that you are interested in products packaged in materials that can be recycled in your community. Press supermarkets to provide for recycling on-site.

- Urge your community to set up curbside recycling collection and central recycling collection and to actively seek markets for the recyclable materials.

- Bring your own containers and buy in bulk.

- Avoid multiple packages, one inside another.

# SHOPPING FOR CONSERVATION AND ENERGY OPTIONS

Safe, clean, and cheap. Nuclear power sounded promising at first. The performance has been quite the contrary.

In the early seventies, nuclear power was widely considered the ideal answer to our heightened energy needs. But since 1978, not a single new nuclear plant has been ordered in the U.S. because of safety and reliability questions and high cost. Accumulated nuclear waste poses another serious problem.

It is clear that of all the sources of energy that are now feasible (nuclear, fossil fuels, solar, geothermal, hydroelectric, biomass, wind), energy conservation and improvements in energy efficiency are by far the most sustainable, the cheapest and the least harmful to workers, neighboring communities, and the environment.

- By year-end 1989, nearly 190 publicly-held utilities in the U.S. were spending a total of $1 billion a year on conservation, according to the Investor Responsibility Research Center. Even the electric utility industry admits these expenditures will save 21,000 megawatts, equal to the output of 21 large nuclear plants whose construction would have cost *$10 billion* a year (assuming a 10-year building period).

- The Rocky Mountain Institute, a leader in the study of energy efficiency, reports that since 1979, the U.S. has gained seven times as much energy as a result of insulation and fuel efficiency gains as from **all** net increases in energy supply. As a result, our annual national energy bill has been lowered by $150 billion.

- The Worldwatch Institute, in its *State of the World Report* for 1990, projects that overall energy efficiency improvements worldwide between 1990 and 2010 could make a three billion ton difference in the amount of carbon released into the atmosphere each year.

- According to the Natural Resources Defense Council, recycling a ton of glass saves 9.8 gallons of oil.

We need a sensible national energy policy that encourages appropriate technologies where they can be most useful. Almost 9% of our energy already comes from renewable sources, such as burning organic material and hydropower, according to the Environmental Defense Fund. Federal policy must also encourage new approaches – through incentives, investment tax credits, or mandatory minimum standards. These include the installation of maximum efficiency equipment and fixtures in new building construction, the use of cogeneration (the steam from fuel burned for heating is captured to spin turbines to generate electricity) where appropriate in industrial plants, and a firm improvement in fuel efficiency standards for new cars.

There are many ways you can contribute to energy conservation:

- Homeowners should take efficiency into account when buying new equipment and fixtures like windows, boilers, furnaces, air conditioners, and insulation. The extra cost for maximum efficiency will be paid back through savings of fuel costs within a few years.

- Use public transportation, ride a bicycle, or walk whenever possible.

- If you must drive to work, join or form a car pool. If you own a car, keep it tuned-up to make it more fuel-efficient and avoid gas-wasting by unnecessary idling.

- Recycle. Not only is this good for the environment, it saves energy too. Each recycled aluminum can saves the emission of 0.8 pounds of carbon dioxide.

- Weatherize your home; don't overdo air-conditioning and heating.

- To begin taking advantage of the immense potential of renewable resources, you might consider ordering catalogs from renewable energy companies like Real Goods Trading Co. (1-800-762-7325) and Seventh Generation (1-800-456-1177).

- Use fluorescent light bulbs. An 18-watt compact fluorescent screw-in bulb is equivalent to a 75-watt incandescent, lasts 10 times as long, saves $40 to $60 over the bulb's lifetime, and prevents the emission of 1,020 pounds of carbon dioxide at the power plant. Although sometimes hard to find, there are many alternatives, including: Cromolux, full spectrum incandescent bulbs imported from Finland by Lumiram, 914-698-1205; Duro-Lite, made in the U.S. by Duro-Test, 800-526-7193; ECOWORKS, made in the U.S. and distributed by Nuclear Free America, 301-235-3575; Marvel, made in the U.S. by Marvel Lighting, 800-631-1614; Regency, imported from Taiwan, Korea and Poland by Regency Lighting, 800-669-5544; and Viva-Lite full spectrum fluorescent bulbs, made in the U.S. by Duro-Test, 800-526-7193. Ask your local hardware store to order these bulbs if they don't have them already.

# ENVIRONMENTAL ALTERNATIVES
# RESOURCE LIST

**Citizens Clearinghouse for Hazardous Waste**
P.O. Box 6806
Falls Church, VA 22040
703-237-2249

**Earth Island Institute**
300 Broadway, Suite 28
San Francisco, CA 94133
415-788-3666

**Environmental Action Foundation**
1525 New Hampshire Avenue, NW
Washington, DC 20036
202-745-4870

**Environmental Defense Fund**
257 Park Avenue South
New York, NY 10010
1-800-CALL-EDF
EDF sponsors a recycling information service. Call them and leave your address; they will send you their free recycling brochure and a phone number to call in your area.

**Friends of the Earth**
218 D Street SE
Washington, DC 20003
202-544-2600

**Greenpeace**
1436 U St., NW
Washington, DC 20009
202-462-1177

**Green Seal**
   1875 Connecticut Avenue, NW
   Washington, DC 20009
   202-986-0250

**Natural Resources Defense Council**
   40 W. 20th St.
   New York, NY 10011
   212-727-2700

**Sierra Club**
   730 Polk Street
   San Francisco, CA 94109
   415-776-2211

**United Nations Environment Program**
   2 U.N. Plaza
   New York, NY 10017
   212-963-8093

**Worldwatch Institute**
   1776 Massachusetts Ave NW
   Washington, DC 20036
   202-452-1999

# RENEWABLE ENERGY RESOURCE LIST

**American Solar Energy Society**
   2400 Central Avenue
   Unit B-1
   Boulder, CO 80301
   303-443-3130

**American Wind Energy Association**
   777 North Capital Street NE, Suite 805
   Washington, DC 20002
   202-408-8988

**Conservation & Renewable Energy Inquiry/Referral Service**
P.O. Box 8900
Silver Spring, MD 20907
1-800-523-2929

**National Appropriate Technology Assistance Service**
P.O. Box 2525
Butte, MT 59702-2525
1-800-428-2525

**Renew America**
1400 16th Street NW, Suite 710
Washington, DC 20036
202-232-2252

**Rocky Mountain Institute**
1739 Snowmass Creek Road
Snowmass, CO 81654-9194
303-927-3851

**Solar Energy Industries Association**
P.O. Box 10095
777 North Capital Street
Arlington, VA 22210
703-524-6100

# SHOPPING FOR FAMILY BENEFITS

By the turn of the century, an estimated 80% of American women aged 25 to 54 will be in the workforce. In practical terms, this means not only that most mothers will work outside the home, but also that they will be joined by many of the family members and friends that traditionally helped them with child and elder care. Right now, women are the sole support of more than 7 million families. Single fathers head up 2.9 million more. Child care has become one of the most needed family benefits. Modest help has come from the Child Care and Development Block Grant passed by the Federal government in October 1990. It provides $12 billion in tax credits to low- and moderate-income families, and grants to states to subsidize child care centers. But ensuring adequate, quality care for children in all parts of the country is a goal as yet unmet.

New initiatives in the crucial area of child care are the most visible evidence of corporate response to a range of family benefit needs, which include parental leave, flextime and job-sharing. In 1978, only 110 companies and institutions employing 100 or more workers offered any form of child care assistance. According to a 1987 Bureau of Labor Statistics survey (latest figures available), about 5,400 employers provide their employees with some kind of child care benefits. While this is dramatic growth from a very small base, it remains a tiny portion of the estimated 6 million corporations, hospitals, and government agencies. Almost 40% of companies with more than 10 employees still fail to provide family benefits of any kind.

The response of corporate leaders to the needs of the family has improved in the last decade. Still, a 1990 Bureau of Labor Statistics study found that only 37% of female workers in companies of 100 or more employees were covered even by unpaid leave for maternity. This is up slightly from 1989 when 33% were covered.

The United States still lags far behind other countries in terms of family benefits, largely due to lack of Federal commitment. At least 127 countries, including Japan and most of Europe, require maternal or parental leave. The Family and Medical Leave Act (FMLA), which would require employers with 50 or more workers to provide up to 12 weeks unpaid leave for childbirth, adoption, or family illness, with job guaranteed on return, was passed by both houses of Congress in 1990 – but was vetoed by President George Bush. The bill, essentially unchanged, has since gained broad support and is expected to be signed into law in 1991.

The National Federation of Independent Business, a critic of parental leave legislation, recently commissioned a Gallup survey of 950 small business executives. Nearly half said they would be less likely to hire women of child-bearing age and low-skilled workers if parental leave is federally mandated. But two other studies show FMLA is likely to impose minimal costs on business: a 1990 study commissioned by the Small Business Administration found that "the net cost to employers of placing workers on leave is always substantially smaller than the cost of terminating an employee." It estimated that FMLA would cost employers about $6.70 per covered employee per year. A second study, performed by the Families and Work Institute (NY) in 1991, analyzed the impact of existing family/medical leave legislation in four states. An overwhelming 91% of employers reported they had no problems implementing the new leave policies. Researchers found no significant increase in costs to businesses after the laws went into effect.

Flexible benefit plans, through which employees can choose to save tax-sheltered dollars for dependent care, extra medical care, and other options, are on the rise. Workers want them and they help corporations control costs, according to a Foster Higgins survey cited in the *Wall Street Journal*. Some 27% of 1,106 large firms offered these plans in 1990, and that number is expected to rise to 38% in 1991.

Some companies are beginning to recognize another area of increasing concern to employees: caring for elderly dependents. General Mills, one of the top-ranking companies in this guide, set up Altcare – a non-profit venture with the St. Paul-based Wilder Foundation – to develop innovative alternative care for elderly people with chronic ailments. Corporate assistance with eldercare should grow as employers find it improves employee attendance, productivity, and attention to the job.

You can work for a better quality of life for America's children and elder citizens:

- Find out what you or your employer can do to improve the life of a child through day care, scholarships, better family benefits like flextime, and child care assistance.

- Volunteer at a child care center or with an eldercare program.

- If no Federal bill has passed, promote family or medical leave legislation in your home state.

- Consider a career in teaching or in early childhood education.

- Choose products from companies with good family policies, indicated by a ✔.

# SHOPPING FOR A BETTER WORKPLACE

Not every employee aspires to become chief executive officer; not every employee seeks a job in management. Nor is everyone qualified. But all people who work expect to be treated fairly and with respect. At socially responsible companies, all are entitled to: a competitive salary, comprehensive health insurance for themselves and their families, pension plans that can move from job to job, the right to organize into a union without intimidation or harassment, opportunities to improve skills through in-house education programs or tuition reimbursement, job security or adequate notice (with opportunities for retraining or job placement), a grievance apparatus for handling complaints, a bonus program for ideas that make a difference, and rewards for work well done. Workers who participate in profit-sharing or employee stock ownership plans, called ESOPs, tend to feel a personal stake in their company's success. Critics argue, however, that ESOPs are sometimes offered as substitutes for good employee benefit plans and compensation.

Advances in computer technology and engineering have transformed the way our offices and factories function. But the benefits of technology can be offset by newly discovered threats to the environment or to workers' health. Computer screens emit low-level radiation and certain types of assembly line work or data-processing jobs may lead to repetitive motion injuries. Exposure to asbestos or other dangerous substances may cause fatal illnesses that are not detected until years later.

Cumulative-trauma disorder and repetitive-motion injuries account for an increasing number of workplace illnesses in today's automated society. The Bureau of Labor Statistics says that cumulative-trauma disorders accounted for 48% of the 240,900 workplace illnesses in 1988, compared to 18% of the 126,100 illnesses in 1981. Cases of repetitive-motion disorders are spreading from physical, blue-collar jobs to jobs that involve "white collar work with blue-collar rhythms and discipline." Data-entry workers are particularly susceptible. Supermarket checkers and cashiers have also experienced these disorders. The Occupational Safety and Health Administration plans to issue guidelines for preventing cumulative-trauma disorders. These may eventually become mandatory. Meanwhile, better workplace and equipment design and scheduling of breaks, could reduce the risks of these disorders.

Some companies also make a point of announcing policies of non-discrimination based on sexual orientation. Progressive workplaces support the right of all individuals to work regardless of race, religion, gender, ethnicity, sexual orientation, and other "identifiers." One of the most pressing issues of the 1990s has been the AIDS epidemic and the impact it has on the workplace. Socially responsible workplaces assure confidentiality to those who want it, and encourage affected workers to stay on the job as long as possible.

To reflect evolving workplace issues and adviser recommendations, CEP strengthened its rating criteria this year. Companies now must offer comprehensive medical and pension benefits, have in place some mechanism for handling employee grievances, and be free of significant OSHA violations and National Labor Relations Board cases, in order to earn a ✔ rating.

For a discussion of equity for disabled workers, please read SHOPPING FOR EQUAL OPPORTUNITY. For a discussion of family benefits in the workplace, including dependent care and flexibility, please read SHOPPING FOR FAMILY BENE-FITS.

You can show your support for a better workplace:

- Make sure your own workplace adheres to local and Federal rules and regulations.

- See that your office workplace provides regular breaks, ergonomic seating, and company-subsidized eye examinations for operators of video display terminals.

- Support or join groups that promote workplace safety and individual human rights.

- If your workplace already offers good programs, take advantage of them so you can improve your skills, do a better job, and advance.

- Avoid patronizing companies with documented records of poor safety, and write to the chief executive officer informing him or her of your action.

- Look for the union "bug" or other union identifiers on items you buy. If your company has unions, become a member.

- Make yourself heard where you work. If your company has a newsletter that solicits employee input, take the time to write in with suggestions to improve the workplace.

- Select brands made by companies rated ✔.

# CEP'S
# TOP-RATED
# CONSUMER PRODUCTS
# COMPANIES

# CEP'S TOP-RATED CONSUMER PRODUCTS COMPANIES

Of the 166 consumer products companies rated by CEP in **SHOPPING FOR A BETTER WORLD**, the 24 charted and profiled in this section either 1) have earned at least 7 top grades and are not involved in nuclear power, military contracting or South Africa, or 2) have earned at least 8 top grades and no more than one of the following: involvement in nuclear power, military contracting, or South Africa.

Of course, no company is perfect. In fact, only one small company, Eden Foods, earned top grades in all twelve categories. But these certainly are companies that deserve a lot of credit, companies whose products you may want on your shopping list, where you might want to work, and whose securities you might like to see in your investment portfolio.

There are, however, a few caveats. For this "Honor Roll" we have weighted all categories of social performance equally. Most of our readers tell CEP they consider them in this way. Quite a few consumers and activists, however, value one aspect of social performance so highly that a poor grade in a single category will significantly lower his or her opinion of the company. If you feel especially strong about one issue, you may want to look carefully at each specific grade rather than simply at the number of top grades.

In addition to recognizing companies with the strongest overall record on social responsibility, CEP honors those that have excelled in specific areas at our annual America's Corporate Conscience Awards. For a list of the recipients and details on the ceremony, see page 346.

The company profiles are often very interesting, and you may want to know more. You'll find the stories for many of these top-rated companies in *The Better World Investment Guide*

(Prentice Hall, 1991). Copies should be in your local bookstore, or you can order one from CEP.

In the following company profiles, a number sign (#) after a company name indicates it has under 100 employees, and an asterisk (*) indicates under 15 employees.

## Alexandra Avery *

| Abbreviation | $ | ♀ | 🐾 | 🐰 | 🏔 | 🌲 | 🌳 | 🏠 | 🏙 |
|---|---|---|---|---|---|---|---|---|---|
| ALEX | ✔+ | ✔ | ✔∅ | ✔ | ✔ | ✔ | No | ✔ | ✔ | ✔ |

Alexandra Avery gives 7% of its pre-tax earnings to charity and donates products to homeless shelters and a women's crisis center. All four employees are women, the company has never tested on animals, and all packaging is made from recycled material collected from other local businesses. The company educates employees and community members on health issues and aromatherapy, provides time off for volunteerism, and sponsors dance classes at a local elementary school.

**Products**: Alexandra Avery Purely Natural cosmetics, fragrances, soaps, hair care needs.

## Autumn-Harp, Inc. *

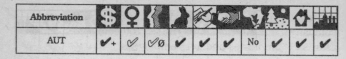

| Abbreviation | $ | ♀ | ⧘ | 🐰 | ✍ | 🐄 | 🌲 | 🏠 | ⊞ |
|---|---|---|---|---|---|---|---|---|---|
| AUT | ✔+ | ✔ | ✔∅ | ✔ | ✔ | ✔ | No | ✔ | ✔ | ✔ |

Autumn-Harp's generous charitable donations represent over
15% of its pre-tax income. One of the company's three directors and two of its highest paid officers are women. Autumn-
Harp conducts no animal testing, coordinates community
recycling efforts, and offers environmental education programs at nearby schools. Autumn-Harp uses recycled, non-
bleached office paper and soy-based inks. The company
provides computers to facilitate work-at-home arrangements.

**Products**: Autumn Harp hand & body creams, baby oils,
shampoo; Lip Sense; Ultra Care.

## Aveda Corporation #

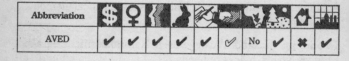

| Abbreviation | $ | ♀ | ⧘ | 🐰 | ✍ | 🐄 | 🌲 | 🏠 | ⊞ |
|---|---|---|---|---|---|---|---|---|---|
| AVED | ✔ | ✔ | ✔ | ✔ | ✔ | ✔ | No | ✔ | ✖ | ✔ |

Aveda was the first American company to sign the Valdez
Principles, ten corporate commitments to a healthy, sustainable environment. Aveda conducts no animal testing and offers subsidies to employees for carpooling and mass-transit
use. Aveda is a member of ACT NOW, and sponsored Catalyst, a nation-wide environmental conference of student activists. The company contributes 2% of its pretax income to
charity. Three women and two minorities are among the
company's top 11 officers.

**Products**: Aveda cosmetics, shampoo.

# Avon Products

| Abbreviation | $ | ♀ | 〰 | 🐰 | 〰 | 〰 | 🌲 | 🏠 | 🏭 |
|---|---|---|---|---|---|---|---|---|---|
| AVP | ✔+ | ✔ | ✔ | ✔ | ✔ | ✓ | No | ✓ | ✔ | ✔ |

Avon's generous in-kind giving, which represents 3% of its
worldwide pre-tax income, is outdone only by its dedication
to the advancement of women. Two-thirds of its officials and
managers are women and two serve on its Board of Directors. Avon's employee networks at company headquarters
provide support and a forum for discussion for minority staff.
In 1990, Avon announced an end to its animal testing. The
company spends $500,000 or more a year to research and de-
velop non-animal alternatives.

**Products:** Avon Color, Daily Revival cosmetics; Moisture
Therapy, Skin-So-Soft bath oil, Sun Seekers suncare.

# Ben & Jerry's Homemade, Inc.

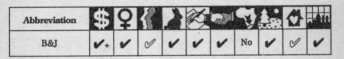

| Abbreviation | $ | ♀ | 〰 | 🐰 | 〰 | 〰 | 🌲 | 🏠 | 🏭 |
|---|---|---|---|---|---|---|---|---|---|
| B&J | ✔+ | ✔ | ✓ | ✔ | ✔ | ✔ | No | ✔ | ✓ | ✔ |

Ben & Jerry's (B&J) donates an impressive 7.5% of its worldwide pre-tax earnings to charity. The company purchases
nuts from indigenous groups in Brazil to produce its Rainforest Crunch ice cream (creating a viable economic alternative
to deforestation), donates proceeds from sales of its Peace
Pop to 1% For Peace, and promotes ACT NOW environmental
initiatives on product packaging. B&J's maintains a policy
that the highest paid employee earns no more than seven
times the salary of the lowest.

**Products**: Ben & Jerry's Homemade Ice Cream.

## Body Love Natural Cosmetics *

| Abbreviation | 💲 | ♀ | | 🐰 | | | | | |
|---|---|---|---|---|---|---|---|---|---|
| BLN | ✔ | ✔ | ✔ | ✔ | ✔ | ✔ | No | ✔ | ✔ | ✔ |

Two of Body Love's four directors are women and two minorities are in its upper management. Its cash and product donations amount to over 1.2% of its pre-tax income and have been directed to animal rights organizations and homes for abused teenagers. Body Love never tests on animals and uses organic ingredients in its Herbal Facial Steams and Love Mitts soaps. The company recycles all waste other than water and plans to use 100% recycled packaging by the end of this year.

**Products**: Amazing Grains soap, Aroma lotion, Herbal Facial Steams, Juniper massage oil, Love Mitts soap.

## Church & Dwight

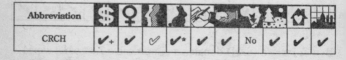

| Abbreviation | 💲 | ♀ | | 🐰 | | | | | |
|---|---|---|---|---|---|---|---|---|---|
| CRCH | ✔+ | ✔ | ✔ | ✔* | ✔ | ✔ | No | ✔ | ✔ | ✔ |

Church & Dwight (C&D) recently received the Packaging Award from Citizens for Recycling. Its Arm & Hammer Baking Soda serves as a non-toxic household cleaner and the company resisted the temptation to plasticize its container. C&D gave 5.2% of its pre-tax income to charity — one of the highest of the large companies included in this guide. C&D's employee housing assistance program helps workers bridge the financial gap to own a home in exchange for a five-year commitment to community volunteering.

**Products**: Arm & Hammer Baking Soda, toothpaste, air fresheners, laundry detergents.

## Clientele, Inc. #

| Abbreviation | $ | ♀ | 🐰 | 🐇 | ✍ | 🌲 | 🏠 | 🏙 |
|---|---|---|---|---|---|---|---|---|
| CTL | ✔+ | ✔ | ✔ | ✔ | ✔ | ✔ | No | ⊘ø | ⊘ | ✔ |

Clientele is a cruelty-free cosmetics company whose in-kind donations have ranged between 7 and 10% of its pre-tax income. Ninety percent of its employees are women, two of its four regional managers are Hispanic, and the company has an assembly factory staffed primarily by senior-aged women. Clientele offers paid time off for volunteers and conducts education programs at local schools. Clientele has hired persons with AIDS and rejected policies with insurance firms who refused to provide coverage for such individuals.

**Products**: Clientele cosmetics, shampoo.

## Colgate-Palmolive

| Abbreviation | $ | ♀ | 🐰 | 🐇 | ✍ | 🌲 | 🏠 | 🏙 |
|---|---|---|---|---|---|---|---|---|
| CL | ✔+ | ✔ | ✔ | ✔⊛ | ✔ | ✔ | YesIN | ✔ | ✔ | ✔ |

Colgate-Palmolive (CP) contributes 2% of its worldwide pre-tax earnings to charity, has two women on its 12-member Board, has 11 minorities among its 37 subsidiary heads, and has cut testing on animals by 78% since 1982. Just one example of CP's countless community outreach projects is a world-wide oral health care program that reaches 24 million children around the globe. CP has cut waste and emissions, often beyond legal requirements, and uses solar energy at selected plants.

**Products:** Colgate toothpaste, shaving cream, Palmolive dishwasher detergent, Ajax cleanser, Irish Spring soap.

## Earth's Best, Inc. #

| Abbreviation | $ | ♀ | { | 🐰 | ✍ | 🐄 | 🌲 | 🏠 | ▦ |
|---|---|---|---|---|---|---|---|---|---|
| EBI | ✔+ | ✖ | ✔ | ✔ | ✔ | ✔ | No | ✔ | ✔ | ✔ |

All of Earth's Best products are 3-year certified organically grown and processed. The company sponsors numerous events regarding sustainable agriculture and organic farming methods. In 1990, Earth's Best donated $85,000 worth of juice to international relief work in Romania, the Soviet Union, and Jordan. Earth's Best has paid parental leave for both mothers *and* fathers and provides free cases of organic baby food for newborns of employees.

**Products:** Earth's Best baby food.

## Earthrise Company *

| Abbreviation | $ | ♀ | { | 🐰 | ✍ | 🐄 | 🌲 | 🏠 | ▦ |
|---|---|---|---|---|---|---|---|---|---|
| RIS | ✔ | ✔ | ✔ | ✔ | ✔ | ✔ | No | ✔ | ? | ✔ |

Earthrise's aquacultural (water-based agriculture) growing methods not only produce a healthy, abundant nutrient source, but also have such environmental benefits as eliminating soil erosion, deforestation, pollution, and water contamination. Earthrise is helping rural villagers in West Africa, India, and Peru implement this technology. The company is also assisting efforts to determine if microalgae production may lead to insights on dealing with AIDS and radiation exposure.

**Products:** Earthrise natural vitamins, supplements.


## Eden Foods, Inc. #

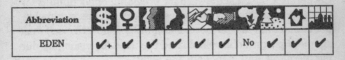

| Abbreviation | 💲 | ♀ | | | | | | 🌳 | | 🏠 | |
|---|---|---|---|---|---|---|---|---|---|---|---|
| EDEN | ✔+ | ✔ | ✔ | ✔ | ✔ | ✔ | No | ✔ | ✔ | ✔ | |

Eden Foods is a social responsibility success story. Eden is the only company rated to get top marks in all 12 categories. The company donates 10% of its pretax income to charitable causes, has three women among its eight top officers, and conducts no animal testing. Eden uses soy-based inks and recycled materials in packaging. The company assumed the cost of, and further expanded, a local recycling program that was slated to close.

**Products:** Eden flour, pasta, snacks, tea bags, vegetables, condiments; Edensoy soy milk.

## General Mills

| Abbreviation | $ | ♀ | ⟨ | 🐇 | ✍ | 🐾 | ☁🌲 | 🏠 | 🏭 |
|---|---|---|---|---|---|---|---|---|---|
| GIS | ✔+ | ✔ | ✔ | ✔ | ✔ | ✔ | No | ✓ | ✔ | ✔ |

General Mills has been widely recognized for meeting the needs of working mothers, supporting minority enterprise, and expanding the employment opportunities of Native Americans. General Mills also received the 1988 America's Corporate Conscience Award for providing opportunities for disabled individuals. The company gave 2% of its worldwide pre-tax income to charity. General Mills' innovative self-management program has eliminated the need for managers during the night shift at its Lodi, CA plant.

**Products:** Betty Crocker, Bisquick, Cheerios, Gold Medal flour, Nature Valley granola bars, Pop Secret, Wheaties.

## Giant Food Inc.

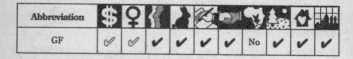

| Abbreviation | $ | ♀ | ⟨ | 🐇 | ✍ | 🐾 | ☁🌲 | 🏠 | 🏭 |
|---|---|---|---|---|---|---|---|---|---|
| GF | ✓ | ✓ | ✔ | ✔ | ✔ | ✔ | No | ✔ | ✔ | ✔ |

Giant Food's (G.F.) commitment to the African-American community earned the company the Dr. Martin Luther King, Jr. Corporate Community Service Award in 1989. G.F. donates over 3 million pounds of food annually to local food banks, and installed 7,000 free computer systems in the first year of the "Apples for the Students" program. G.F. stocks reusable mesh bags made by a company staffed by the visually-impaired, is using alternatives to CFC's in its refrigerators, and is testing natural gas in its company-owned vehicles.

**Products:** Giant Food supermarkets, private label goods.

## Hershey Foods Corporation

| Abbreviation | $ | ♀ | | | | | | | | |
|---|---|---|---|---|---|---|---|---|---|---|
| HSY | ✓ | ✓ | ✓ | ✓* | ✓ | ✓ | No | ✓ | ✓ | ✓ |

Hershey's record on social responsibility is as sweet as its chocolate. Perhaps most recognized is the Milton Hershey School, which provides free education, housing, medical care, and college aid to 1,200 disadvantaged youths. Hershey was among *Good Housekeeping's* top 69 companies for working mothers, is one of six companies in this guide with a Minority Enterprise Small Business Investment Company, and has a program to improve the social and economic conditions of cocoa growers in Belize.

**Products:** Hershey's, Cadbury & Reese's chocolates; Luden's cough drops; Ronzoni & San Giorgio pasta.

## Johnson & Johnson

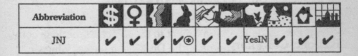

| Abbreviation | $ | ♀ | | | | | | | | |
|---|---|---|---|---|---|---|---|---|---|---|
| JNJ | ✓ | ✓ | ✓ | ✓⊛ | ✓ | ✓ | YesIN | ✓ | ✓ | ✓ |

Johnson & Johnson (J&J) is among a mere handful of companies that have three women on their Board of Directors. In 1989, the company dedicated over $4.5 million to research non-animal testing alternatives. J&J initiated New Brunswick Tomorrow, a program to revitalize the city where it makes its corporate headquarters, and provides thousands of grants to organizations at which its employees volunteer. J&J offers on-site day care and has signed the Workplace Principles for equitable treatment of workers with AIDS.

**Products:** Johnson & Johnson Baby Powder & Shampoo, Act mouth wash, Band Aids, Reach toothbrushes, Tylenol.

## S.C. Johnson and Son, Inc.

| Abbreviation | 💲 | ⚥ | | 🐰 | | | | | | |
|---|---|---|---|---|---|---|---|---|---|---|
| SCJ | ✔+ | ✔ | ✔ | ✔* | ✔ | ✔ | YesIN | ✔ | ✔ | ✔ |

S.C. Johnson (SCJ) gives between 3% and 5% of its pre-tax income to charity, received the Catalyst Award for its innovative women's leadership and development programs in 1991, was the first company to ban CFC's, and has reduced animal testing by 50% since 1985. The company provides substantial support to Habitat for Humanity and other housing partnerships. SCJ offers on-site day care and has a no lay-off policy that places displaced workers in another position for which they qualify, with no reduction in pay.

**Products:** Johnson's Wax, Agree shampoo, Edge Gel, Glade air freshener, Off!, Pledge furniture wax, Shout.

## Kellogg Company

| Abbreviation | 💲 | ⚥ | | 🐰 | | | | | | |
|---|---|---|---|---|---|---|---|---|---|---|
| K | ✔ | ✔ | ✔ | ✔* | ✔ | ✔ | YesIN | ✔ | ✔ | ✔ |

Kellogg received an America's Corporate Conscience Award in 1988 for improvement in social disclosure and has received a top rating in that category ever since. The company was listed in *Working Mother Magazine* and *Black Enterprise Magazine* as an outstanding employer for women and minorities, respectively. Kellogg's cereals have been packaged in recycled cardboard since the company was founded in 1906. Kellogg's "Feeling Gr-r-reat" wellness program encourages employees to adopt healthier and more productive lifestyles.

**Products:** Kellogg's cereals, Diner's Choice tea, Eggo waffles, Mrs. Smith's baked goods, Whitney's yogurt.

## Newman's Own *

| Abbreviation | $ | ♀ | | | | | | No | | | |
|---|---|---|---|---|---|---|---|---|---|---|---|
| NEWO | ✔+ | ✔ | ✓∅ | ✔ | ✔ | ✔ | No | ✔ | ✓ | ✔ |

Newman's Own contributes 100% of its profits to charitable and educational causes. Much of this is directed to the Newman-founded Hole In The Wall Gang Camp. Children with cancer and other serious diseases leave the camp "with a soaring spirit of freedom and independence, and a wider vision of their lives and of the future." Three of the company's four top officers are women. Newman's funded the distribution of a recycling leaflet to every household in its home town of Westport, CT.

**Products:** Newman's Own juices, salad dressings, pasta sauce, popcorn.

## Procter and Gamble

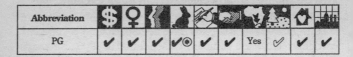

| Abbreviation |  |  |  |  |  |  |  |  |  |  |
|---|---|---|---|---|---|---|---|---|---|---|
| PG | ✔ | ✔ | ✔ | ✔⊛ | ✔ | ✔ | Yes | ✔ | ✔ | ✔ |

P&G hires women and minorities at more than twice their representation in college engineering programs. P&G won an America's Corporate Conscience Award in 1988 for reductions in, and promoting of alternatives to, animal testing. The company supports youth education programs and maintains volunteer placement services at all its North American offices. P&G's parental leave policy is among the most generous of those offered by companies in this guide. P&G employees own 25% of the company's stock.

**Products:** Bounce, Cascade, Citrus Hill, Comet, Crest, Downy, Duncan Hines, Jif, Sure, Tide, and many others.

## Quaker Oats

| Abbreviation |  |  |  |  |  |  |  |  |  |  |
|---|---|---|---|---|---|---|---|---|---|---|
| OAT | ✔+ | ✔ | ✔ | ✔ | ✔ | ✔ | No | ✔ | ✔ | ✔ |

Quaker gives 1.8% of its worldwide pre-tax income in cash contributions and supports Second Harvest Food Bank with substantial in-kind donations. Quaker has four women vice-presidents at its corporate headquarters. The company is one of three non-supermarket companies in this guide which have a Fair Share Agreement for minority advancement with the NAACP. Quaker uses cogeneration and solar energy at selected plants and has a bicycle rack and showers at its central office.

**Products:** Quaker Oats, Life cereal, Aunt Jemima, Gains, Ken-L Ration, Pounce pet food, Gatorade, Rice-A-Roni, Van Camp's.

## Supermarkets General Holdings Corp.

| Abbreviation | $ | ♀ | { | 🐀 | ✍ | 🐄 | 🌲 | 🏠 | 🏘 |
|---|---|---|---|---|---|---|---|---|---|
| SGH | ? | ✓̃ | ✔ | ✔ | ✔ | ✔ | No | ✔ | ✔ | ✔ |

Supermarkets General (SGH) has a Fair Share Agreement to support minority advancement and gave over $170,000 to charity in 1990 despite three years of losses. SGH's Pathmark subsidiary has an award-winning program for training and hiring mentally disabled individuals and opened a store in Newark's turbulent Central Ward as part of an effort to revitalize the area. The company will sell neither irradiated foods, nor dairy products derived from herds treated with the controversial bovine growth hormone.

**Products:** Pathmark supermarkets, Rickel Home Centers.

## Tom's of Maine #

| Abbreviation | $ | ♀ | { | 🐀 | ✍ | 🐄 | 🌲 | 🏠 | 🏘 |
|---|---|---|---|---|---|---|---|---|---|
| TOM | ✔+ | ✔ | ✘ | ✔ | ✔ | ✔ | No | ✔ | ✔ | ✔ |

Tom's of Maine gave 10% of its pre-tax earnings to charity in 1990, has five women on its Board, and encourages employees to devote 5% of their work time to community projects. The mood at Tom's was described as one of "environmental activism" by a Maine environmental regulation enforcer. The company sells cruelty-free products and gave $25,000 for a curbside recycling program. Tom's has a non-discrimination policy regarding sexual orientation and persons with AIDS.

**Product:** Tom's of Maine deodorants, shampoo, toothpaste.

## Upjohn Company

| Abbreviation | 💲 | ♀ | | 🐰 | | | | | | |
|---|---|---|---|---|---|---|---|---|---|---|
| UPJ | ✓ | ✓ | ✓ | ✓⊛ | ✓ | ✓ | YesIN | ✓ | ✓ | ✓ |

Upjohn donated over $4 million in pharmaceuticals to assist children affected by the Chernobyl nuclear disaster. The company has a decade-old Minority Vendor Program and supports the National Minority Supplier Development Council. Upjohn encourages community service among retirees through its Seniors Volunteer Program, is active in assisting local education initiatives, and contributed $80,000 in 1990 to attract child care providers as part of its Child Care Resource and Referral service.

**Product:** Cortaid, Kaopectate, Motrin IB, Nycitracin, Progaine shampoo, Unicap vitamins.

# CEP'S
# X-RATED
# CONSUMER PRODUCTS
# COMPANIES

# CEP'S X-RATED CONSUMER PRODUCTS COMPANIES

Of the 166 consumer companies rated by CEP in **SHOPPING FOR A BETTER WORLD**, the 13 profiled in this section are X-rated. An X-rated company has 1) 4 or more ✖ ratings or 2) at least 3 ✖ ratings and one or more of the following: involvement in nuclear power, military contracting or South Africa.

Of course, no company is entirely without merit. In fact, none were "X-RATED" in all twelve categories. But these are certainly companies whose social record will displease many consumers, whose products you may not want in your shopping cart, where you might be wary of working, and whose securities you might prefer not to see in your investment portfolio.

There are, however, a few caveats. For this "Dishonor Roll," we have weighted all categories of social performance equally. Most of our readers tell us they consider them in this way. Quite a few consumers, and activists, however, consider one aspect of social performance so important that a good grade in a single category will significantly raise his or her opinion of the company. So if you feel especially strong about one issue, you may want to look carefully at each specific grade rather than simply at the number of bottom grades.

In the Fall of 1991, CEP's Corporate Environmental Data Clearinghouse published detailed environmental reports on 100 major companies. All the companies in this section are among those analyzed. (See the free offer at back of this book.)

In addition to recognizing companies with the weakest overall social responsibility records, CEP annually accords "Dishonorable Mentions" to those that have exhibited particularly reprehensible behavior in specific areas. For a list of the "Dishonorable Mentions," see page 349.

The company profiles are often very interesting, and you may want to know more. You'll find the stories for many of these X-rated companies in *The Better World Investment Guide* (Prentice Hall, 1991). Copies should be in your local bookstore, or you can order one from CEP.

## American Cyanamid

| Abbreviation | $ | ♀ | | | | | | | |
|---|---|---|---|---|---|---|---|---|---|
| ACY | ✓ | ✖ | ? | ✖○ | ✖ | ? | YesIN | ✖ | ? | ? |

American Cyanamid (ACY) was the nation's third largest emitter of toxic waste in 1989. Prior to a 1990 Supreme Court ruling that prohibits such policies, some employees charged that ACY barred women of child bearing age from working in certain hazardous environments. ACY continued until at least 1989 to export mercury waste to a South African company with a known record of improper disposal. It has been alleged that a stream near the plant, used by residents of the KwaZulu homeland for drinking and bathing, had mercury levels 1,500 times the U.S. standard.

**Products**: Centrum vitamins, Heritage, Thrive, and New Image shampoo; Night Spice after shave, So Dry deodorant.

## Archer Daniels Midland

| Abbreviation | $ | ♀ | 🧥 | 🐰 | ✍ | 🐁 | 🌲 | 🏠 | 🏭 |
|---|---|---|---|---|---|---|---|---|---|
| ADM | ✖ | ✖ | ? | ? | ✖ | ? | No | ✖ | ? | ? |

Aside from marketing vegetable-based products, Archer Daniels Midland (ADM) shows little reverence for the environment: 1) The company's operations in Clinton, Iowa are a major cause of the area's severe sulphur dioxide pollution levels; 2) In Minnesota, ADM has had a "disturbing" record of non-compliance with air quality regulations, according to the Minnesota Pollution Control Agency. The company gave under 0.5% of its pre-tax earnings to charity.

**Products**: Various brands of flour, Lean 'N Crisp bacon, Russo & Gooch Foods pasta.

## Bayer AG

| Abbreviation | $ | ♀ | 🧥 | 🐰 | ✍ | 🐁 | 🌲 | 🏠 | 🏭 |
|---|---|---|---|---|---|---|---|---|---|
| BAG | ? | ? | ? | ✖○ | ✖ | ? | YesIN | ✖ | ? | ? |

Some of Bayer's operations are bad medicine for health and the environment. Bayer has been charged by the EPA with 110 pesticide export violations and accused by Greenpeace of exporting hazardous wastes to Canada. Bayer is conducting genetic research to develop herbicide-tolerant plants. If successful, this innovation would encourage even greater applications of herbicides and bring big profits for Bayer (higher costs for farmers), more environmental damage, and increased chemical residues on crops. Bayer's animal testing is entirely for medical products but the company gives no indication of reducing the numbers of animals used or funding of alternatives.

**Products:** Alka-Seltzer, Bactine, Cutter insect spray, Flinstones & One-A-Day vitamins, S.O.S. scouring pads.

## Chevron Corporation

| Abbreviation | $ | ♀ | 🖐 | 🐇 | ✋ | ☁ | 🌲 | 🏠 | 🏭 |
|---|---|---|---|---|---|---|---|---|---|
| CHV | ✓ | ✖ | ✓ | ✓* | ✓ | ✓ | YesIS ✖ | ✓ | ✖ |

Chevron appears to have undertaken strong efforts to reduce waste. But Chevron's past operations continue to threaten the environment and human health: 1) Chevron is a potentially responsible party at 170 Superfund sites; 2) In 1986, Chevron's El Segundo refinery in California was charged with 880 Clean Water Act violations and fined $1.5 million by the EPA. No women serve on Chevron's Board, nor are any among its top officers. In 1990, Chevron ranked 55th in prime military contracts, worth $303 million in fuels.

**Products:** Chevron gasoline, car supplies.

## ConAgra

| Abbreviation | $ | ♀ | 🖐 | 🐇 | ✋ | ☁ | 🌲 | 🏠 | 🏭 |
|---|---|---|---|---|---|---|---|---|---|
| CAG | ? | ✖ | ✓ | ? | ✖ | ✖ | No | ? | ? | ✖ |

ConAgra received a 1991 America's Corporate Conscience Dishonorable Mention for threatening worker safety and public health. ConAgra's Monfort subsidiary has had "numerous, pervasive, and outrageous" labor law violations according to the National Labor Relations Board. ConAgra is a prime supporter of legislation designed to increase the speed of food processing although proper food safety inspection may be jeopardized. No women serve on the company's 12-member Board of Directors.

**Products:** Armor bacon, Butterball chicken, Hunt's Catsup, Orville Redenbacher's popcorn, Wesson oil.

## General Electric Company

| Abbreviation | | | | | | | | | | |
|---|---|---|---|---|---|---|---|---|---|---|
| GE | ✖ | ✔ | ? | ✖○ | ✖ | ✓ | No | ✖ | ? | ✖ |

Its ads say G.E. "Brings Good Things to Life." G.E.'s role as a major contractor for the nuclear weapons and nuclear power industries, however, prompted the citizen's group INFACT to sponsor a broadly supported nationwide boycott of G.E. products. A *Multinational Monitor* study of the nation's 10 largest corporations found that G.E. had by far the most Federal worker safety citations (1,495) between 1982 and 1990. The company gave a scant 0.63% of its pre-tax income to charity in 1990.

**Products:** G.E. & Miser light bulbs, Magicube flash bulbs.

# Kimberly-Clark Corporation

| Abbreviation | 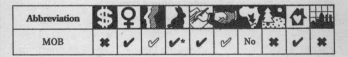 $ | ♀ | { | 🐇 | ✍ | 🐄 | 🌲 | 🏠 | 🏭 |
|---|---|---|---|---|---|---|---|---|---|
| KMB | ? | ✔ | ✔ | ✖ | ✖ | ? | YesIN | ✖ | ? | ? |

Kimberly-Clark has $8.3 million in assets in South Africa and has not signed the Statement of Principles for providing equal opportunity there. The company continues to test on animals with no indication of a serious effort to reduce or find alternatives. Kimberly-Clark is one of the largest makers of disposable diapers and recently lobbied successfully against a one-cent tax on such products, despite their significant contribution to our solid waste crisis.

**Products:** Clout paper towels, Huggies disposable diapers, Kleenex tissue, Kotex, Softique.


# Mobil Corporation

| Abbreviation | $ | ♀ | { | 🐇 | ✍ | 🐄 | 🌲 | 🏠 | 🏭 |
|---|---|---|---|---|---|---|---|---|---|
| MOB | ✖ | ✔ | ✔ | ✔* | ✔ | ✔ | No | ✖ | ✔ | ✖ |

Mobil's Torrance, CA refinery was fined in July 1989 and again in April 1990, a total of $191,000 for improper labelling and disposal of hazardous material, by the California Department of Health. A former Mobil Chemical employee was awarded $1.375 million in damages after he was fired for refusing to cover up pollution problems. Mobil's 0.5% pre-tax charitable giving is among the lowest in the oil industry. In 1990, Mobil had $237 million in military contracts, primarily fuel-related.

**Products**: Mobil gasoline, auto supplies, Baggies sandwich bags, Hefty trash bags.

## Perdue Farms Inc.

| Abbreviation | $ | ♀ | 🦷 | 🐰 | 🏭 | 👐 | 🌲 | 🌙 | 🏠 | 🏙 |
|---|---|---|---|---|---|---|---|---|---|---|
| PRDU | ? | ? | ? | ? | ✖ | ✖ | No | ✖ | ? | ✖ |

Perdue received an America's Corporate Conscience Dishonorable Mention in 1990 for maltreatment of its employees, animals, and the environment. National Public Radio reported that workers at Perdue's Lewiston, N.C. plant were routinely fired after developing debilitating workplace injuries. Animal Rights International states that Perdue chickens often have less than one square foot of space to move. The company was the first ever to be fined for water pollution by the state of Virginia.

**Products**: Perdue packaged poultry products.

## Pfizer Inc.

| Abbreviation | $ | ♀ | 🦷 | 🐰 | 🏭 | 👐 | 🌲 | 🌙 | 🏠 | 🏙 |
|---|---|---|---|---|---|---|---|---|---|---|
| PFE | ✓ | ✖ | ? | ? | ✖ | ✓ | YesIN | ✖ | ? | ? |

Pfizer asked not to be included in this guide, but its social responsibility record merits attention. Pfizer has no women among its top corporate officers. It has $9 million in net South African investments. Pfizer paid a total of $70,000 to 10 states as part of an agreement to terminate misleading advertising for its Plax mouth rinse. Pfizer is in litigation concerning the failure of hundreds of prosthetic heart valves manufactured by one of its subsidiaries, which the company estimates has resulted in 252 deaths.

**Products:** Barbasol shaving cream, Ben Gay, Musk for Men, Stetson cologne, Unisom sleeping aid, Visine eye drops.

## Texaco Inc.

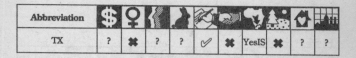

| Abbreviation | $ | ♀ | | 🐰 | | | | 🌲 | | ⌂ | |
|---|---|---|---|---|---|---|---|---|---|---|---|
| TX | ? | ✖ | ? | ? | ✓ | | ✖ | YesIS | ✖ | ? | ? |

In 1990, the EPA reported that Texaco's Port Neches, TX refinery posed a greater risk to local health than any other U.S. industrial facility. The Trans-Ecuadorian Pipeline, operated by Texaco until 1989, has spilled over 16 million gallons of crude oil into the Amazonian watershed during the past 20 years. There are no women among Texaco's directors or senior managers. Texaco had over 100 Federal worker safety citations from 1982 to 1990. Texaco has substantial military fuel contracts.

**Products:** Texaco gasoline, auto supplies.

## Tyson Foods, Inc.

| Abbreviation | $ | ♀ | | 🐰 | | | | 🌲 | | ⌂ | |
|---|---|---|---|---|---|---|---|---|---|---|---|
| TYSN | ? | ✖ | ? | ✔ | ✖ | | ✖ | No | ✓ | ? | ✖ |

Tyson subsidiary Holly Farms is the object of an ongoing AFL-CIO nationwide boycott initiated in November 1989. The company cut the wages of its drivers and yardmen and refused to recognize the Teamsters Union as the group's legal bargaining agent, then interrogated employees who protested. Tyson has just one woman among its directors and corporate vice-presidents. The Government Accountability Project claims that Tyson's high speed production line doesn't permit adequate food safety inspection.

**Products:** Tyson frozen dinners, Holly Farms chicken, Tasty Bird, Weaver lunch meats, frozen poultry dishes.

## USX Corporation

| Abbreviation | 💲 | ♀ | | 🐰 | | | | | | |
|---|---|---|---|---|---|---|---|---|---|---|
| X | ✖ | ✖ | ✖ | ? | ✖ | ✖ | Yes | ✖ | ? | ✖ |

USX, with charitable giving of 0.4% of its pre-tax earnings, is among the stingiest corporations analyzed by CEP. The company has neither a woman nor a minority among its Directors. In February 1991, USX agreed to pay $41.8 million to settle a 15-year old case alleging discrimination against thousands of black job-seekers. USX is a potentially responsible party at 47 Superfund sites. USX received an America's Corporate Conscience Dishonorable Mention in 1990 for worker safety violations and arbitrary plant closings.

**Products:** USX & Marathon gasoline, auto supplies.

# RATINGS FOR
# THE COMPANIES

| Company or Product | Abbr. | 💲 | ♀ | 🖐 | ⚒ | 🐕 | 🕊 | | | 🏠 | ALERT |
|---|---|---|---|---|---|---|---|---|---|---|---|
| **LARGE COMPANIES** | | | | | | | | | | | |
| Abbott Laboratories | ABT | ? | ✓ | ? | ? | ✓(*) | ✓ | ✓ | YesIN | ✓ | ✓ | infant formula |
| Alberto-Culver | ACV | ? | ✓ | ✓ | ? | ✗ | ✓ | ✓ | No | ? | ? | |
| Allied-Lyons PLC | ALP | ✗ | ✓ | ✓ | ✓ | ✓ | ✓ | ✓ | Yes | ✓ | ✓ | 🌐, U.K. |
| American Cyanamid | ACY | ✓ | ✗ | ✓ | ? | ✗○ | ✗ | ? | YesIN | ? | ✓ | makes pesticides; D.C.C.A.; nuclear weapons |
| American Home Products | AHP | ✗ | ✓ | ✓ | ✓ | ✓(*) | ✓ | ✓ | Yes | ✓ | ✓ | infant formula |
| Anheuser-Busch | BUD | ✓+ | ✓ | ✓ | ✓ | ✓ | ✓ | ✓ | No | ✓ | ✓ | |
| Archer Daniels Midland | ADM | ✗ | ✗ | ? | ? | ✓ | ? | ✓ | No | ✓ | ? | |
| Avon Products, Inc. | AVP | ✓+ | ✓ | ✓ | ✓ | ✓ | ✓ | ✓ | No | ✓ | ✓ | on-site day care; C.C.A. |
| Bayer AG | BAG | ? | ? | ? | ? | ✗○ | ✗ | ? | YesIN | ? | ✓ | makes pesticides |
| Ben & Jerry's | B&J | ✓+ | ✓ | ✓ | ✓ | ✓ | ✓ | ✓ | No | ✓ | ✓ | 1% For Peace; on-site day care; ACT NOW; C.C.A. |
| Body Shop, The | BS | ✓ | ✓ | ✓ | ? | ✓ | ✓ | ✓ | No | ? | ? | ACT NOW; U.K. |
| Borden Inc. | BN | ✓ | ✓ | ✓ | ✓ | ✓ | ✓ | ✓ | YesIN | ✓ | ✓ | |

# LARGE COMPANIES

| Product or Company | Abbr. | $ | | | | | | | | | ALERT |
|---|---|---|---|---|---|---|---|---|---|---|---|
| Bristol-Myers Squibb Co. | BMY | ◐ | ✓ | ◐ | ◐ | ✓⊛ | ✓ | YesIN | ◐ | ✓ | infant formula; Workplace Principles; D.C.C.A. |
| CPC International | CPC | ✓+ | ◐ | ✓ | ? | ✓ | ✓ | No | ◐ | ✓ | |
| Cadbury Schweppes p.l.c. | CADB | ? | ? | ? | ✗ | ? | ✓ | YesIN | ? | ? | ⊕; U.K. |
| Campbell Soup | CPB | ✓ | ✓ | ? | ✓ | ✓ | ◐ | No | ◐ | ✓ | on-site day care |
| Carter-Wallace | CAR | ? | ✗ | ◐ | ✗○ | ? | ◐ | No | ? | ? | |
| Celestial Seasonings | CS | ? | ◐ | ✓ | ✓ | ✓ | ✓ | No | ◐ | ✓ | some organic ingredients |
| Chiquita Brands Int'l | CQB | ? | ✓ | ✓ | ◐ | ? | ✓ | No | ✗ | ◐ | D.C.C.A. |
| Church & Dwight | CRCH | ✓+ | ✓ | ◐ | ✓* | ✓ | ✓ | No | ✓ | ✓ | |
| Clorox Co. | CLX | ◐ | ✗ | ✓ | ✓* | ✓ | ✓ | No | ✗ | ✓ | |
| Coca-Cola Company | KO | ◐ | ◐ | ✓ | ? | ✓ | ✓ | Yes | ◐ | ✓ | |
| Colgate-Palmolive | CL | ✓+ | ✓⊛ | ✓ | ✓ | ✓ | ✓ | YesIN | ✓ | ✓ | |

✓ = Top Rating   ◐ = Middle Rating   ✗ = Bottom Rating   ? = Insufficient Information

*For a more detailed explanation see key on page 14*

| Company or Product | Abbr. | $ | ⚥ | ▨ | 🐇 | ✎ | ✊ | 🕊 | No/Yes | ☮ | ALERT |
|---|---|---|---|---|---|---|---|---|---|---|---|
| ConAgra | CAG | ? | ✗ | ✓ | ? | ✗ | ✗ | No | ? | ? | ✗ | safe meat controversy; D.C.C.A.; factory farming |
| Coors Company, Adolph | ACC | ✓+ | ✓ | ✓ | ✗ | ✓ | ✓ | No | ? | ✓ | ✓ | Fair Share |
| Curtice-Burns | CBI | ✓+ | ✓ | ✗ | ✓ | ✓ | ✓ | No | ? | ? | ✓ | |
| Dep Corp. | DEPC | ? | ✓ | ✓ | ✓ | ✓ | ✓ | No | ? | ✓ | ✓ | |
| Dial Corp | G | ? | ? | ✓ | ✓ | ? | ? | No | ? | ? | ? | |
| Dole Food Company | DOL | ✓ | ✓ | ? | ✓ | ✓ | ✗ | No | ✗ | ✓ | ✗ | pesticide sterilization suit |
| Dow Chemical Company | DOW | ✓ | ✓ | ✓ | ✓(®) | ✓ | ✓ | Yes | ✓ | ✓ | ✓ | pesticide steril. suit; nuclear weapons; on-site daycare; makes pesticides |
| Eastman Kodak | EK | ✓ | ✓ | ✓ | ✓(®) | ✓ | ✓ | No | ✓ | ✓ | ✓ | ☢, C.C.A. |
| First Brands | FB | ✓+ | ✗ | ✓ | ✓* | ✗ | ✗ | Yes | ? | ✗ | ✗ | |
| Flowers Industries, Inc. | FLO | ? | ✓ | ? | ✓ | ✓ | ✓ | No | ? | ? | ? | |
| GTE Corporation | GTE | ✓ | ✓ | ✓ | ✓ | ✓ | ✓ | No | ✓ | ✓ | ✓ | nuclear weapons; ☢ |
| General Electric Company | GE | ✗ | ✗ | ? | ✗ | ✗ | ✗ | No | ✗ | ? | ✗ | nuclear weapons; ☢⚛, INFACT boycott |
| General Mills | GIS | ✓+ | ✓ | ✓ | ✓ | ✓ | ✓ | No | ✓ | ✓ | ✓ | C.C.A. |

# LARGE COMPANIES

| Product or Company | Abbr. | $ | ♀ | | | | | | | | ALERT |
|---|---|---|---|---|---|---|---|---|---|---|---|
| Georgia-Pacific | GP | ✗ | ✔ | ? | ? | ✔ | No | ✗ | ? | ? | clearcutting; on-site day care |
| Gerber Products | GEB | ✓ | ✔ | ? | ? | ✗ | Yes | ? | ? | ? | D.C.C.A.; infant formula |
| Gillette | GS | ✓ | ✔ | ✓ | ✔⊛ | ✔ | YesIN | ✓ | ✓ | ✓ | |
| Goya Foods Inc. | GOYA | ? | ? | ? | ? | ? | No | ? | ? | ? | |
| Grand Metropolitan PLC | GMP | ✓ | ✔ | ✔ | ✔ | ✔ | YesIN | ✓ | ✓ | ✓ | 🌐; U.K. |
| Heinz Company, H.J. | HNZ | ✔ | ✓ | ✔ | ✔ | ✓ | No | ✔ | ✓ | ✓ | C.C.A. |
| Hershey Foods Corp. | HSY | ✓ | ✔ | ✓ | ✔* | ✔ | No | ✔ | ✔ | ✔ | on-site day care |
| Hormel & Co., George A. | HRL | ? | ✗ | ✔ | ✗ | ? | No | ? | ? | ? | |
| Int'l Res. & Dev. Corp. | IRDV | ? | ✗ | ✗◯ | ✗ | ✔ | No | ? | ? | ? | |
| James River Corporation | JR | ✓ | ✓ | ✓ | ✔ | ✓ | No | ✗ | ✓ | ✓ | on-site day care |
| John B. Sanfilippo, Inc. | JSAN | ? | ? | ? | ✗ | ? | No | ? | ? | ? | |

✔ = Top Rating  ✓ = Middle Rating  ✗ = Bottom Rating  ? = Insufficient Information

*For a more detailed explanation see key on page 14*

| Company or Product | Abbr. | $ | ♀ | | | | | | | | | ALERT |
|---|---|---|---|---|---|---|---|---|---|---|---|---|
| Johnson & Johnson | JNJ | ✓ | ✓ | ✓ | ✓⊛ | ✓ | ✓ | YesIN | ✓ | ✓ | on-site day care; Workplace Principles |
| Johnson, S.C. & Son | SCJ | ✓+ | ✓ | ✓ | ✓* | ✓ | ✓ | YesIN | ✓ | ✓ | 1st to ban CFCs; on-site day care |
| Johnson Products Co. | JPC | ? | ✓ | ✓ | ✗ | ? | ✓ | No | ? | ? | |
| Kellogg Company | K | ✓ | ✓ | ✓ | ✓* | ✓ | ✓ | YesIN | ✓ | ✓ | C.C.A. |
| Kimberly-Clark Corp. | KMB | ? | ✓ | ✓ | ✗ | ✗ | ? | YesIN | ? | ? | disposable diapers |
| L'Oreal S.A. | LORA | ? | ✓ | ✓ | ✓* | ✓ | ? | Yes | ? | ? | |
| Land O' Lakes Inc. | LAND | ✓+ | ✓ | ✗ | ✓ | ✓ | ✓ | No | ✓ | ✓ | co-op |
| Marcal Paper Mills Inc. | MARC | ? | ✓ | ✓ | ? | ✓ | ✓ | No | ? | ? | |
| Mars, Inc. | MARS | ? | ? | ? | ✓ | ? | ✓ | No | ? | ? | |
| McCormick & Co., Inc. | MCRK | ✓ | ✗ | ? | ✗ | ? | ✗ | No | ? | ? | |
| Mead Corporation | MEA | ? | ✓ | ✓ | ✓ | ✓ | ✓ | No | ✓Ø | ✓ | |
| Melitta Bentz KG | MTA | ? | ✓ | ✓ | ✓ | ✓ | ✓ | No | ✓ | ✓ | |
| Minn. Mining & Mfg. (3M) | MMM | ✓ | ✓ | ✓ | ✓* | ✓ | ✓ | YesIN | ✓ | ✓ | ☢ |

| Product or Company | Abbr. | $ | ♀+ | | | | | | | | | ALERT |
|---|---|---|---|---|---|---|---|---|---|---|---|---|
| Nat'l Grape Co-op Assoc. | GRAP | ? | ? | ? | ? | ✗ | ✓ | No | ? | ? | ? | co-op |
| Nestlé S. A. | NEST | ? | ✓ | ? | ✓* | ✓ | ? | YesIN | ✓ | ? | ? | infant formula; Salv. coffee; ⊕; D.C.C.A.; U.K. |
| Neutrogena Corp. | NGNA | ? | ✓ | ? | ? | ✓ | ? | No | ✗ | ✗ | ? | |
| Ocean Spray | OSC | ? | ✗ | ✓ | ✓ | ✓ | ✓ | No | ✓ | ✓ | ✓ | co-op |
| PepsiCo, Inc. | PEP | ✓ | ✓ | ✓ | ✗ | ✓ | ✓ | Yes | ✓ | ✓ | ✓ | |
| Perdue Farms Inc. | PRDU | ? | ? | ? | ? | ✗ | ✗ | No | ✗ | ? | ✗ | D.C.C.A.; factory frmg.; safe chicken contr. |
| Pet Inc. | PET | ? | ? | ? | ? | ✗ | ? | No | ? | ? | ? | |
| Pfizer Inc. | PFE | ✓ | ✗ | ? | ? | ✗ | ✓ | YesIN | ? | ? | ? | heart valve suits |
| Philip Morris | MO | ? | ✓ | ✓ | ✓ | ✗ | ? | Yes | ? | ? | ? | cigarettes; Salvadoran coffee; Work. Princ. |
| Polaroid Corporation | PRD | ✓ | ✓ | ✓ | ✓ | ✓ | ✓ | No | ✓ | ✓ | ✓ | Workplace Principles; C.C.A. |
| Procter & Gamble | PG | ✓ | ✓ | ✓ | ✓⊛ | ✓ | ✓ | Yes | ✓ | ? | ✓ | disposable diapers; Salvadoran coffee; on-site day care; C.C.A. |

✓ = Top Rating    ✓ = Middle Rating    ✗ = Bottom Rating    ? = Insufficient Information

For a more detailed explanation see key on page 14

Page 111

LARGE COMPANIES

| Company or Product | Abbr. | 💲 | ♀ |  |  |  |  |  |  |  | ▦ | ALERT |
|---|---|---|---|---|---|---|---|---|---|---|---|---|
| Quaker Oats Company | OAT | ✔+ | ✔ | ✔ | ✔ | ✔ | ✔ | ✔ | No | ✔ | ✔ | Fair Share |
| RJR Nabisco, Inc. | RJR | ? | ◑ | ? | ? | ◑ | ✔ | ✖ | Yes | ✖ | ? | cigarettes; D.C.C.A. |
| Ralston Purina Company | RAL | ◑ | ✔ | ✔ | ? | ✔ | ✔ | ✔ | No | ✔ | ✔ | |
| Reckitt & Colman plc | RCP | ? | ? | ? | ? | ◑ | ? | ◑ | YesIN | ? | ✖ | 🌐, U.K. |
| Revlon, Inc. | REVL | ? | ? | ? | ? | ✔ | ? | ✖ | YesIN | ◑ | ? | |
| Reynolds Metals Company | RLM | ✖ | ✖ | ? | ? | ✔ | ✔ | ✔ | No | ◑ | ◑ | |
| Rhone-Poulenc Rorer Inc. | ROR | ? | ◑ | ? | ? | ✔ | ? | ✖ | YesIN | ? | ? | |
| Sandoz Ltd. | SAND | ? | ? | ? | ? | ✔ | ✖ | ✖ | YesIN | ◑ | ? | makes pesticides |
| Sara Lee Corporation | SLE | ◑ | ✔ | ✔ | ✔⊛ | ✔ | ✔ | ✔ | Yes | ✔∅ | ◑ | on-site day care; C.C.A. |
| Schering-Plough | SGP | ✔ | ✔ | ✔ | ✔⊛ | ✔ | ✔ | ✔ | YesIN | ◑ | ◑ | on-site day care; Workplace Principles |
| Scott Paper Company | SPP | ✔ | ✖ | ✔ | ✔* | ✔ | ✔ | ✔ | Yes | ✖ | ✔ | forestry criticized |
| Seagram Company Ltd. | VO | ? | ? | ? | ? | ✖ | ? | ✖ | No | ? | ? | 🌐 |
| SmithKline Beecham plc | BECH | ✖ | ◑ | ✔ | ✖○ | ✔ | ✔ | ✔ | YesIN | ✔∅ | ✔ | 🌐, Work. Princ.; on-site day care; U.K. |

| Product or Company | Abbr. | 💲 | ♀ | | 🐇 | | | | | | ALERT |
|---|---|---|---|---|---|---|---|---|---|---|---|
| Smucker Company, J.M. | SJM | ✔ | ⟋ | ✗ | ✔ | ✔ | ✔ | No | ⟋ | ⟋ | some organic ingredients |
| Source Perrier | SPER | ? | ? | ? | ✔ | ? | ? | No | ? | ? | |
| Tasty Baking Company | TBC | ✔+ | ⟋ | ✗ | ⟋ | ? | ✔ | No | ? | ⟋ | |
| Tillamook Cheese | TILA | ✔+ | ⟋ | ✗ | ✔ | ✔ | ✔ | No | ✔ | ✔ | co-op |
| Tyson Foods, Inc. | TYSN | ? | ✗ | ✗ | ✔ | ✔ | ✔ | No | ⟋ | ✗ | factory farming, safe chicken contr. |
| Unilever PLC | UN | ? | ✗ | ? | ✔* | ✔ | ✔ | YesIN | ⟋ | ? | ⊕; U.K. |
| United Biscuits Hldgs. PLC | UBH | ⟋ | ✗ | ⟋ | ✔ | ✗ | ✔ | No | ? | ⟋ | ⊕; U.K. |
| Universal Foods Corp. | UFC | ? | ✗ | ? | ✔ | ✗ | ✔ | No | ? | ? | |
| Upjohn Company | UPJ | ✔ | ✔ | ✔ | ✔⊛ | ✔ | ✔ | YesIN | ⟋ | ✔ | |
| Warner-Lambert Company | WLA | ✔ | ⟋ | ⟋ | ✗○ | ⟋ | ⟋ | YesIN | ⟋⊘ | ⟋ | on-site day care; Workplace Principles |
| Wrigley Jr. Company, Wm. | WWY | ✗ | ✗ | ? | ⟋ | ⟋ | ⟋ | No | ⟋⊘ | ? | Fair Share |

✔ = Top Rating   ⟋ = Middle Rating   ✗ = Bottom Rating   ? = Insufficient Information

*For a more detailed explanation see key on page 14*

Page 113

LARGE COMPANIES

| Company or Product | Abbr. | $ | ♀ | 🖐 | 🐫 | 🐾 | 🕊 | ⚖ | 🏠 | ALERT |
|---|---|---|---|---|---|---|---|---|---|---|
| **SMALL COMPANIES** | | | | | | | | | | |
| 21st Century Foods* | TFC | ✖ | ✔ | ✔ | ✔ | ✔ | No | ✔ | ✔ | on-site day care |
| Alexandra Avery* | ALEX | ✔+ | ✔ | ✔∅ | ✔ | ✔ | No | ✔ | ✔ | |
| Allens Naturally* | ANY | ✔ | ✔ | ✔∅ | ✔ | ? | No | ✔ | ✔ | |
| Apple & Eve* | APNE | ✔+ | ✔ | ✔∅ | ✔ | ✖ | No | ✔∅ | ? | some organic ingredients |
| Aroma Vera# | AV | ✖ | ✔ | ✔ | ✔ | ✖ | No | ✔ | ✖ | |
| Associated Cooperatives* | ACOP | ? | ? | ✔ | ✖ | ? | No | ? | ? | co-op |
| Aubrey Organics# | AUB | ? | ✔ | ✔ | ✔ | ✔ | No | ? | ✔ | some organic ingredients |
| Aura Cacia* | AURA | ✔+ | ✔ | ✔∅ | ✔ | ✔ | No | ✔ | ✔ | 1% For Peace; on-site day care |
| Autumn-Harp, Inc.* | AUT | ✔+ | ✔ | ✔∅ | ✔ | ✔ | No | ✔ | ✔ | |
| Aveda Corp.# | AVED | ✔ | ✔ | ✔ | ✔ | ✔ | No | ✖ | ✖ | Valdez Principles; ACT NOW |
| Barbara's Bakery, Inc.# | BARB | ✔+ | ✔ | ✔ | ✔ | ✔ | No | ✔ | ✔ | some organic ingredients |
| Body Love Nat. Cosmetics* | BLN | ✔ | ✔ | ✔ | ✔ | ✔ | No | ✔ | ✔ | some organic ingredients |

| Product or Company | Abbr. | 💲 | ♀ | 🚶 | 🐁 | ⚖ | 🕊 | 🌍 | ❓ | ALERT |
|---|---|---|---|---|---|---|---|---|---|---|
| Bumkins International# | BUMK | ? | ? | ? | ✖ | ? | No | ? | ? | |
| Clientele, Inc.# | CTL | ✔+ | ✔ | ? | ✔ | ✔ | No | ✔∅ | ✔ | |
| Desert Essence* | DES | ? | ? | ? | ✖ | ✔ | No | ? | ? | 1% For Peace |
| Earth Care Paper Inc.# | ECP | ✔+ | ✔ | ✖ | ✔ | ✔ | No | ✔ | ✔ | 1% For Peace; ACT NOW; Valdez Principles |
| Earth's Best, Inc.# | EBI | ✔+ | ✖ | ✔ | ✔ | ✔ | No | ✔ | ✔ | 100% organic ingredients |
| Earthrise Company* | RIS | ✔ | ✔ | ✔ | ✔ | ✔ | No | ? | ✔ | |
| Ecco Bella* | ECC | ✔ | ✔ | ✔∅ | ✔ | ✔ | No | ✔ | ✔ | |
| Eden Foods, Inc.# | EDEN | ✔+ | ✔ | ✔ | ✔ | ✔ | No | ✔ | ✔ | some organic ingredients |
| Falcon Trading Co.# | FALC | ? | ✔ | ✖ | ✔ | ✔ | No | ✔ | ✔ | 1% For Peace; some organic ingredients |
| Fantastic Foods Inc.# | FFI | ✔ | ✔ | ✔ | ✔ | ✔ | No | ✔ | ✔ | some organic ingredients |
| Health Valley Nat'l Foods # | HVAL | ? | ? | ? | ✖ | ? | No | ? | ? | some organic ingredients |

✔ = Top Rating  ✐ = Middle Rating  ✖ = Bottom Rating  ? = Insufficient Information

For a more detailed explanation see key on page 14

Page 115

SMALL COMPANIES

| Company or Product | Abbr. | #$ | ♀ | | | | No | | | ◇ | ⊞ | ALERT |
|---|---|---|---|---|---|---|---|---|---|---|---|---|
| Ida Grae Cosmetics* | IDA | ? | ✓ | ✓ | ✓ | ✓ | No | ✓ | | ? | ? | |
| Jason Natural Cosmetics# | JNP | ? | ✓ | ✗ | ✓ | ✓ | No | ✓⊘ | | ✗ | ✓ | |
| Kiss My Face# | KMF | ? | ✓ | ✗ | ✓ | ✓ | No | ✓ | | ✓ | ✓ | |
| Loriva Supreme Foods* | LOR | ✓ | ✓⊘ | ✓ | ✓ | ✓ | No | ✓⊘ | | ? | ? | |
| Mayacamas Fine Foods* | MAYA | ? | ? | ✓ | ✗ | ✓ | No | ? | | ? | ? | |
| Mountain Ocean, Ltd.* | MOUN | ? | ? | ✓ | ? | ✓ | No | ? | | ? | ? | |
| Newman's Own* | NEWO | ✓+ | ✓ | ✓ | ✓ | ✓ | No | ✓ | | ✓ | ✓ | 100% profit to charity; C.C.A. |
| Orjene Natural Cosmetics# | ORJ | ✓+ | ✓ | ✓ | ✗ | ✓ | No | ✓ | | ✓ | ? | |
| Paul Penders Company* | PP | ✓+ | ✓ | ✓⊘ | ✓ | ✓ | No | ✓ | | ✓ | ✓ | 1% For Peace |
| Rachel Perry, Inc.# | RP | ✓+ | ✓ | ✓ | ✗ | ✓ | No | ✓ | | ✗ | ✓ | |
| San-J International Inc.# | SANJ | ✓ | ✓ | ✓ | ✓ | ✓ | No | ✓ | | ✓ | ✓ | |
| Solgar Co., Inc.# | SLGR | ? | ? | ? | ? | ✓ | No | ✓⊘ | | ? | ? | |
| Stonyfield Farms, Inc.# | STON | ? | ✓ | ✓ | ✓ | ✓ | No | ✓ | | ✓ | ✓ | Valdez Principles; ACT-NOW |

| Product or Company | Abbr. | $ | ♀ | | | | | | | | | | | ALERT |
|---|---|---|---|---|---|---|---|---|---|---|---|---|---|---|
| Tom's of Maine# | TOM | ✓+ | ✓ | ✗ | ✓ | ✓ | ✓ | ✓ | No | ✓ | ✓ | ✓ | | |
| Twin Laboratories, Inc.# | TWIN | ? | ? | ? | ✓ | ✓ | ? | ? | No | ? | ? | ? | | |
| Whole Earth Foods# | WHO | ✓+ | ✓ | ✓ | ✓ | ✓ | ✓ | ✓ | No | ? | ✓ | ✓ | | 1% For Peace; some organic ingredients |
| **GAS & OIL COMPANIES** | | | | | | | | | | | | | | |
| Amoco Corp. | AN | ✓ | ✓ | ✓ | ✓ | ✓* | ✓ | ✓ | No | ✓ | ? | ? | | ♣, C.C.A. |
| Atlantic Richfield | ARC | ✓ | ✓ | ✓ | ✓ | ✗ | ✓ | ✗ | No | ✓ | ✓ | ✓ | | ♣ |
| British Petroleum (BP) | BP | ✓ | ✗ | ? | ✓ | ✓* | ✓ | ✓ | YesJS | ✓ | ✓ | ✓ | | foreign-based company; ☢, ♣; U.K. |
| Chevron Corporation | CHV | ✓ | ✗ | ✗ | ✓ | ✓* | ✓ | ✗ | YesJS | ✓ | ✓ | ✗ | | makes pesticides; Work. Princ.; military contracts |
| Exxon Corp. | XON | ✓ | ✓ | ✓ | ? | ? | ✓ | ✗ | No | ✓ | ✓ | ✓ | | oil spill; ♣, D.C.C.A.; on-site day care |
| Marathon | X | ✗ | ✗ | ✗ | ✗ | ? | ✗ | ✗ | Yes | ✓ | ? | ✗ | | D.C.C.A. |
| Mobil Corporation | MOB | ✗ | ✓ | ✗ | ✓ | ✓* | ✓ | ✗ | No | ✓ | ✓ | ✗ | | ♣; Work. Princ.; D.C.C.A. |

✓ = Top Rating  ✓ = Middle Rating  ✗ = Bottom Rating  ? = Insufficient Information

For a more detailed explanation see key on page 14

Page 117

GAS & OIL COMPANIES

## GAS & OIL COMPANIES

| Company or Product | Abbr. | $ | ♀ | 👥 | 🐾 | ✋ | 🌍 | No/Yes | ⚛ | ✗ | ALERT |
|---|---|---|---|---|---|---|---|---|---|---|---|
| Phillips Petroleum Company | P | ✓ | ✔ | ✔ | ✔ | ✔ | ✓ | No | ✔ | ✗ | ✈, on-site day care |
| Royal Dutch/Shell | SC | ? | ? | ? | ? | ✔ | ✔ | YesIS | ✗ | ✓ | ✈, ⊕; pesticide sterilization suit |
| Sun Company, Inc. | SUN | ✔+ | ? | ? | ? | ? | No | ✗ | ? | ? | |
| Texaco Inc. | TX | ? | ✗ | ? | ? | ✓ | ✗ | YesIS | ✗ | ? | ☢, ✈ |
| USX Corporation | X | ✗ | ✗ | ✗ | ? | ✗ | ✗ | Yes | ✗ | ✗ | D.C.C.A. |
| **SUPERMARKETS** | | | | | | | | | | | |
| A&P | GAP | ✔+ | ✔ | ✔ | ✔ | ✔ | ✓ | No | ✓ | ✓ | on-site day care |
| Acme Markets, Inc. | ASC | ? | ? | ? | ? | ✔ | ✔ | No | ✓∅ | ✓ | ? |
| Albertson's Inc. | ABS | ✗ | ✗ | ✔ | ✗ | ✔ | ✓ | No | ✓∅ | ✔ | ? |
| American Stores | ASC | ? | ? | ✔ | ✓ | ✔ | ? | No | ✓∅ | ✓ | ? |
| Big Star Grocery Store | GUC | ? | ? | ✔ | ✗ | ✔ | ✓ | No | ✓ | ? | ? |
| Bruno's Inc. | BRI | ? | ✗ | ✔ | ✗ | ✔ | ? | No | ? | ? | ? |
| Dillon Companies, Inc. | KR | ✔+ | ✔ | ✔ | ✔ | ✓ | ✔ | No | ✔ | ✗ | Fair Share |

| Product or Company | Abbr. | $ | ♀ | | | | | | | | ALERT |
|---|---|---|---|---|---|---|---|---|---|---|---|
| Dominick's Finer Foods | DOM | ? | ? | ? | ? | ✗ | ✓~ | No | ? | ? | |
| Farmer Jack | GAP | ✓+ | ✓ | ✓ | ✓ | ✓ | ✓~ | No | ✓~ | ✓ | on-site day care |
| Food Emporium | GAP | ✓+ | ✓ | ✓ | ✓ | ✓ | ✓~ | No | ✓~ | ✓ | on-site day care |
| Food Fair | BRI | ? | ✗ | ? | ✓ | ✗ | ? | No | ? | ? | |
| Food Lion, Inc. | FL | ? | ✗ | ? | ✓ | ✗ | ? | No | ? | ? | |
| Food World | BRI | ? | ✗ | ? | ✓ | ✗ | ? | No | ? | ? | |
| Foodmax | BRI | ? | ✗ | ? | ✓ | ✗ | ? | No | ? | ? | |
| Fred Meyer, Inc. | MEYR | ? | ✓ | ✗ | ? | ✓~ | ? | No | ✓~ | ✓~ | |
| Giant Eagle | GIA | ? | ? | ? | ? | ✗ | ? | No | ? | ? | |
| Giant Food Inc. | GF | ✓~ | ✓~ | ✓ | ✓ | ✓ | ✓ | No | ✓ | ✓ | |
| Grand Union Company | GUC | ? | ? | ? | ✓ | ✗ | ? | No | ✓~ | ? | |

| ✓ = Top Rating | ✓~ = Middle Rating | ✗ = Bottom Rating | ? = Insufficient Information | Page 119 |
|---|---|---|---|---|

*For a more detailed explanation see key on page 14*

**SUPERMARKETS**

| Company or Product | Abbr. | $ | ♀ | 👥 | 🖐 | 🖼 | 🕊 | | ♲ | ▦ | ALERT |
|---|---|---|---|---|---|---|---|---|---|---|---|
| Gristedes | RED | ? | ? | ? | ? | ✗ | ? | No | ? | ? | |
| H.E. Butt Grocery | HEBG | ? | ? | ? | ? | ✓ | ? | No | ? | ✗ | |
| Jewel Food Stores | ASC | ? | ? | ✓ | ? | ✓ | ? | No | ✓∅ | ✓ | |
| Kohl's Food Stores | GAP | ✓+ | ✓ | ✓ | ? | ✓ | ? | No | ✓ | ✓ | on-site day care |
| Kroger Company | KR | ✓+ | ✓ | ✓ | ? | ✓ | ✓ | No | ✓ | ? | Fair Share |
| Lucky Stores, Inc. | ASC | ? | ? | ✓ | ? | ✓ | ? | No | ✓∅ | ✓ | |
| Pak 'n Save | SAFE | ✓+ | ✓ | ✓ | ? | ✓ | ? | No | ✓ | ✓ | Fair Share |
| Pathmark | SGH | ? | ✓ | ✓ | ? | ✓ | ✓ | No | ✓ | ✓ | Fair Share |
| Pavilions | VON | ? | ✗ | ? | ✓ | ✗ | ✓ | No | ? | ? | removed tobacco |
| Piggly Wiggly Southern | BRI | ? | ✗ | ✓ | ✓ | ✗ | ✓ | No | ? | ? | |
| Publix Supermarkets | PUB | ? | ? | ✓ | ✓ | ✗ | ✓ | No | ✓ | ? | on-site day care |
| Ralph's Grocery Company | RG | ? | ✗ | ? | ? | ✗ | ? | No | ✓ | ? | |
| Red Apple Companies | RED | ? | ? | ? | ? | ✗ | ? | No | ? | ? | |

| Product or Company | Abbr. | | | | | | | | | | ALERT |
|---|---|---|---|---|---|---|---|---|---|---|---|
| Safeway Stores, Inc. | SAFE | ✓+ | ✓ | ✓ | ✓ | ✓ | No | ◔ | | ◔ | Fair Share |
| Skaggs Alpha Beta | ASC | ? | ? | ? | ✓ | ? | No | ◔∅ | ◔ | ? | |
| Smith's Food & Drug | SFD | ✗ | ? | ? | ✓ | ? | No | ? | ◔ | ? | |
| Star Market Co. | ASC | ? | ? | ? | ✓ | ? | No | ◔∅ | ◔ | ? | |
| Stop & Shop Co.'s, Inc. | STOP | ? | ? | ✓ | ? | ◔ | No | ◔ | ◔ | ? | Fair Share |
| Super Fresh | GAP | ✓+ | ✓ | ✓ | ✓ | ✓ | No | ◔ | ◔ | ? | on-site day care |
| Supermkts Gen. Hold. Corp. | SGH | ? | ◔ | ? | ✓ | ✓ | No | ◔ | ◔ | ◔ | Fair Share |
| Vons Companies, Inc. | VON | ? | ✗ | ? | ? | ? | No | ? | ? | ? | |
| Waldbaum's | GAP | ✓+ | ✓ | ✓ | ✓ | ◔ | No | ✓ | ◔ | ✓ | on-site day care |
| Winn-Dixie Stores, Inc. | WIN | ◔ | ? | ✓ | ◔ | ✗ | No | ◔∅ | ? | ? | |

✓ = Top Rating   ◔ = Middle Rating   ✗ = Bottom Rating   ? = Insufficient Information

*For a more detailed explanation see key on page 14*

**SUPERMARKETS**

Page 121

# RATINGS BY PRODUCT

| Company or Product | Abbr. | $ | | | | | | | | ALERT |
|---|---|---|---|---|---|---|---|---|---|---|
| **ALCOHOLIC BEVERAGES** | | | | | | | | | | |
| Asahi | ASA | | | | | | | | | see page 344 for Japanese companies |
| Bass Ale | GUI | | | | | | | | | see page 330 for U.K. ratings |
| Budweiser | BUD | ✔+ | ✓ | | ✔ | ✔ | No | ✔ | ✓ | |
| Busch | BUD | ✔+ | ✓ | | ✔ | ✔ | No | ✔ | ✓ | |
| Carlsberg | BUD | ✔+ | ✓ | | ✔ | ✔ | No | ✔ | ✓ | |
| Coors | ACC | ✔+ | ✓ | | ✔ | ✓ | No | ✔ | ✓ | Fair Share |
| Dos XX | GUI | | | | | | | | | see page 330 for U.K. ratings |
| Extra Gold | ACC | ✔+ | ✓ | | ✔ | ✔ | No | ✔ | ✓ | Fair Share |
| Guinness Stout | GUI | | | | | | | | | see page 330 for U.K. ratings |
| Herman Joseph's | ACC | ✔+ | ✓ | | ✔ | ✔ | No | ✔ | ✓ | Fair Share |
| Keystone | ACC | ✔+ | ✓ | | ✔ | ✔ | No | ✔ | ✓ | Fair Share |
| Killian's Irish Red | ACC | ✔+ | ✓ | | ✔ | ✔ | No | ✔ | ✓ | Fair Share |

| Product or Company | Abbr. | 💲 | ♀ | 👥 | 🐾 | ⚖ | 🌐 | ♻ | 🏠 | ALERT |
|---|---|---|---|---|---|---|---|---|---|---|
| Leinenkugel | MO | ? | ✓ | ? | ✗ | ? | Yes | ? | ? | cigarettes; Salvadoran coffee; Work. Princ. |
| Lite | MO | ? | ✓ | ? | ✗ | ? | Yes | ? | ? | cigarettes; Salvadoran coffee; Work. Princ. |
| Lowenbrau | MO | ? | ✓ | ? | ✗ | ? | Yes | ? | ? | cigarettes; Salvadoran coffee; Work. Princ. |
| Magnum | MO | ? | ✓ | ? | ✗ | ? | Yes | ? | ? | cigarettes; Salvadoran coffee; Work. Princ. |
| Masters | ACC | ✓+ | ⩗ | ✓ | ✓ | ⩗ | No | ⩗ | ⩗ | Fair Share |
| Meister Brau | MO | ? | ✓ | ? | ✗ | ✓ | Yes | ? | ? | cigarettes; Salvadoran coffee; Work. Princ. |
| Michelob | BUD | ✓+ | ⩗ | ✓ | ✓ | ✓ | No | ⩗ | ⩗ | |
| Miller | MO | ? | ✓ | ? | ✗ | ? | Yes | ? | ? | cigarettes; Salvadoran coffee; Work. Princ. |
| Milwaukee's Best | MO | ? | ✓ | ? | ✗ | ? | Yes | ? | ? | cigarettes; Salvadoran coffee; Work. Princ. |
| Moosehead | GUI | | | | | | | | | see page 330 for U.K. ratings |
| Munich Oktoberfest | MO | ? | ✓ | ✓ | ✗ | ? | Yes | ? | ? | cigarettes; Salvadoran coffee; Work. Princ. |

✓ = Top Rating   ⩗ = Middle Rating   ✗ = Bottom Rating   ? = Insufficient Information

For a more detailed explanation see key on page 14

**ALCOHOLIC BEVERAGES**

| Company or Product | Abbr. | $ | ♀ | ✊ | 🐾 | ✎ | ⚖ | 🐰 | ⚛ | ❤ | 🌍 | ALERT |
|---|---|---|---|---|---|---|---|---|---|---|---|---|
| Natural Light | BUD | ✓+ | ✓ | ? | ✓ | ✓ | ✓ | No | ✓ | ✓ | ✓ | |
| Seagram's Wine Coolers | VO | ? | ✗ | ? | ? | ✗ | ? | No | ? | ? | ? | ⊕ |
| Sol | GUI | | | | | | | | | | | see page 330 for U.K. ratings |
| Suntory | SNT | | | | | | | | | | | see page 344 for Japanese companies |
| **BABY FOODS** | | | | | | | | | | | | |
| Beech Nut | RAL | ✓ | ✓ | ✓ | ✓ | ✓ | ✓ | No | ✓ | ✓ | ✓ | |
| Carnation | NEST | ?+ | ✓ | ✓ | ? | ✓* | ✓ | YesIN | ✓ | ? | ? | infant formula; Salv. coffee; ⊕; D.C.C.A.; U.K. |
| Earth's Best# | EBI | ✓+ | ✗ | ✓ | ✓ | ✓ | ✓ | No | ✓ | ✓ | ✓ | 100% organic ingredients |
| Enfamil | BMY | ✓ | ✓ | ✓ | ✓⊛ | ✓ | ✓ | YesIN | ✓ | ✓ | ✓ | infant formula; Workplace Principles; D.C.C.A. |
| First Foods | GEB | ✓ | ✓ | ? | ? | ✗ | ? | Yes | ? | ? | ? | D.C.C.A.; infant formula |
| Gerber | GEB | ✓ | ✓ | ? | ? | ✗ | ? | Yes | ? | ? | ? | D.C.C.A.; infant formula |
| Good Nature | NEST | ? | ✓ | ? | ✓* | ✓ | ✓ | YesIN | ✓ | ? | ? | infant formula; Salv. coffee; ⊕; D.C.C.A.; U.K. |
| Isomil | ABT | ? | ? | ? | ? | ✓⊛ | ✓ | YesIN | ✓ | ✓ | ✓ | infant formula |

| Product or Company | Abbr. | $ | ♀ | | | | | | | ALERT |
|---|---|---|---|---|---|---|---|---|---|---|
| Mead Johnson | BMY | ℐ | ✓ | ℐ | ✓® | ℐ | YesIN | ℐ | ℐ | infant formula; Workplace Principles; D.C.C.A |
| Nursoy | AHP | ✗ | ✓ | ℐ | ✓® | ✓ | Yes | ✓ | ✓ | infant formula |
| Pro Sobee | BMY | ℐ | ✓ | ✓ | ✓® | ✓ | YesIN | ✓ | ✓ | infant formula; Workplace Principles; D.C.C.A |
| Ross Laboratories | ABT | ? | ✓ | ? | ✓® | ✓ | YesIN | ✓ | ✓ | infant formula |
| S-M-A | AHP | ✗ | ✓ | ℐ | ✓® | ✓ | Yes | ✓ | ✓ | infant formula |
| Similac | ABT | ? | ✓ | ? | ✓® | ✓ | YesIN | ✓ | ✓ | infant formula |
| **BABY NEEDS** | | | | | | | | | | |
| A & D Ointment | SGP | ℐ | ✓ | ✓ | ✓® | ✓ | YesIN | ℐ | ✓ | on-site day care; Workplace Principles |
| Autumn Harp* | AUT | ✓+ | ℐ | ℐ⊘ | ✓ | ✓ | No | ✓ | ✓ | |
| Baby Fresh | SPP | ✓ | ✓ | ✓ | ✓* | ✓ | Yes | ℐ | ✓ | forestry criticized |
| Bumkins Cloth Diap.# | BUMK | ? | ? | ? | ✓ | ✗ | No | ? | ? | |

✓ = Top Rating   ℐ = Middle Rating   ✗ = Bottom Rating   ? = Insufficient Information

*For a more detailed explanation see key on page 14*

BABY NEEDS

| Company or Product | Abbr. | $ | ♀ | | | | | | | | | ALERT |
|---|---|---|---|---|---|---|---|---|---|---|---|---|
| Huggies | KMB | ? | ✔ | ✔ | ✘ | ? | YesIN | ✘ | ? | ✔ | | disposable diapers |
| Johnson's Baby Powder | JNJ | ✔ | ✔ | ✔⊛ | ✔ | ✔ | YesIN | ✔ | ? | ✔ | | on-site day care; Workplace Principles |
| Luvs | PG | ✔ | ✔ | ✔⊛ | ✔ | ? | Yes | ✔ | ✔ | ✔ | | disposable diapers; Salvadoran coffee; on-site day care; C.C.A. |
| Nuk | GEB | ✔ | ✔ | ? | ✘ | ? | Yes | ? | ? | ? | | D.C.C.A.; infant formula |
| Pampers | PG | ✔ | ✔ | ✔⊛ | ✔ | ✔ | Yes | ✔ | ✔ | ✔ | | disposable diapers; Salvadoran coffee; on-site day care; C.C.A. |
| **BAKED GOODS: FRESH & REFRIGERATED** | | | | | | | | | | | | |
| Entenmann's | MO | ? | ✔ | ? | ✘ | ✔ | Yes | ? | ? | ? | | cigarettes; Salvadoran coffee; Work. Princ. |
| Freihofer's | MO | ? | ✔ | ? | ✘ | ✔ | Yes | ? | ? | ? | | cigarettes; Salvadoran coffee; Work. Princ. |
| Grands! | GMP | ✔ | ✔ | ✔ | ✔ | ✔ | YesIN | ✔ | ✔ | ✔ | | ⊕, U.K. |
| Hungry Jack | GMP | ✔ | ✔ | ✔ | ✔ | ✔ | YesIN | ✔ | ✔ | ✔ | | ⊕, U.K. |
| Mexican Originals | TYSN | ? | ✘ | ✔ | ✘ | ✘ | No | ✔ | ✘ | ? | | factory farming; safe chicken contr. |
| Oronoque | PET | ? | ? | ✔ | ? | ? | No | ? | ? | ? | | |
| Pop Tarts | K | ✔ | ✔ | ✔* | ✔ | ✔ | YesIN | ✔ | ✔ | ✔ | | C.C.A. |

| Product or Company | Abbr. | 💲 | ♀ | 〰 | 👥 | 🏃 | 🐾 | 🌍 | 🏠 | ⚖ | ❓ | ALERT |
|---|---|---|---|---|---|---|---|---|---|---|---|---|
| **BAKED GOODS: FROZEN** | | | | | | | | | | | | |
| Aunt Fanny's | PET | ? | ? | ? | ? | ✖ | ? | ? | No | ? | ? | |
| Aunt Jemima | OAT | ✔+ | ? | ✔ | ? | ✔ | ✔ | No | ✔ | ⊘ | ? | Fair Share |
| Downyflake | PET | ? | ? | ? | ? | ✖ | ? | ? | No | ? | ? | |
| Eggo | K | ✔ | ✔ | ✔ | ✔* | ✔ | ✔ | YesIN | ✔ | ✔ | ✔ | C.C.A. |
| Fresh 'n Fruity | GIS | ✔+ | ✔ | ✔ | ✔ | ✔ | ✔ | No | ⊘ | ✔ | ✔ | C.C.A. |
| Great Starts | CPB | ✔ | ✔ | ✔ | ? | ✔ | ✔ | No | ⊘ | ⊘ | ⊘ | on-site day care |
| Lender's Bagels | MO | ? | ✔ | ✔ | ? | ✖ | ? | Yes | ? | ? | ? | cigarettes; Salvadoran coffee; Work. Princ. |
| Mrs. Smith's | K | ✔ | ✔ | ✔ | ✔* | ✔ | ✔ | YesIN | ✔ | ✔ | ✔ | C.C.A. |
| Pepperidge Farm | CPB | ✔ | ✔ | ✔ | ? | ✔ | ✔ | No | ⊘ | ✔ | ⊘ | on-site day care |
| Roman Meal | PET | ? | ? | ? | ? | ✖ | ? | ? | No | ? | ? | |

✔ = Top Rating   ⊘ = Middle Rating   ✖ = Bottom Rating   ? = Insufficient Information

*For a more detailed explanation see key on page 14*

**BAKED GOODS: FROZEN**

| Company or Product | Abbr. | $ | ♀ | | | | | | Yes/No | | | ALERT |
|---|---|---|---|---|---|---|---|---|---|---|---|---|
| Sara Lee | SLE | ✔ | ✔ | ✔ | ✔ | ✔ | ✔ | ✔ | Yes | ✔ | ✔ | on-site day care; C.C.A. |
| Toaster Strudel | GMP | ✓ | ✔ | ✔ | ✔ | ✔ | ✔ | ✔ | YesIN | ✓ | ✓ | 🌐, U.K. |
| **BAKING MIXES** | | | | | | | | | | | | |
| Aunt Jemima | OAT | ✔+ | ✔ | ✔ | ✔ | ✔ | ✔ | ✔ | No | ✔ | ✔ | Fair Share |
| Bake Shop | GIS | ✔+ | ✔ | ✔ | ✔ | ✔ | ✔ | ✔ | No | ✓ | ✔ | C.C.A. |
| Bake-a-Bar | GIS | ✔+ | ✔ | ✔ | ✔ | ✔ | ✔ | ✔ | No | ✓ | ✔ | C.C.A. |
| Betty Crocker | GIS | ✔+ | ✔ | ✔ | ✔ | ✔ | ✔ | ✔ | No | ✓ | ✔ | C.C.A. |
| Big Batch | GIS | ✔+ | ✔ | ✔ | ✔ | ✔ | ✔ | ✔ | No | ✓ | ✔ | C.C.A. |
| Bisquick | GIS | ✔+ | ✔ | ✔ | ✔ | ✔ | ✔ | ✔ | No | ✓ | ✔ | C.C.A. |
| Bundt | GMP | ✓ | ✔ | ✔ | ✔ | ✔ | ✔ | ✔ | YesIN | ✓ | ✓ | 🌐, U.K. |
| Cake Lovers Collection | GIS | ✔+ | ✔ | ✔ | ✔ | ✔ | ✔ | ✔ | No | ✓ | ✔ | C.C.A. |
| Choco-Bake | NEST | ? | ? | ✔ | ✔ | ✔* | ✓ | ✔ | YesIN | ? | ? | infant formula; Salv, coffee; 🌐 D.C.C.A.; U.K. |
| Classics | GIS | ✔+ | ✔ | ✔ | ✔ | ✔ | ✔ | ✔ | No | ✓ | ✔ | C.C.A. |

| Product or Company | Abbr. | $ | ♀ | | | | | | | ALERT |
|---|---|---|---|---|---|---|---|---|---|---|
| Duncan Hines | PG | ✓ | ✓ | ✓ | ✓ | ✓(®) | ✓ | Yes | ◐ | ✓ | disposable diapers; Salvadoran coffee; on-site day care; C.C.A. |
| Dutch Maid | K | ✓ | ✓ | ✓ | ✓ | ✓* | ✓ | YesIN | ✓ | ✓ | C.C.A. |
| Flako | OAT | ✓+ | ✓ | ✓ | ✓ | ✓ | ✓ | No | ◐ | ◐ | Fair-Share |
| Hansen Island | K | ✓+ | ✓ | ✓ | ✓ | ✓* | ✓ | YesIN | ✓ | ✓ | C.C.A. |
| Health Valley# | HVAL | ? | ? | ? | ✓ | ✗ | ? | No | ? | ? | some organic ingredients |
| Liqui-Dri Foods, Inc. | OAT | ✓+ | ✓ | ✓ | ✓ | ✓ | ✓ | No | ✓ | ◐ | Fair-Share |
| Microrave | GIS | ✓+ | ✓ | ✓ | ◐ | ✓ | ✓ | No | ◐ | ✓ | C.C.A. |
| Pennant | UN | ? | ✗ | ? | ✓ | ✓* | ✓ | YesIN | ◐ | ? | ⊕; U.K. |
| Pillsbury | GMP | ◐ | ✓ | ◐ | ✓ | ✓ | ✓ | YesIN | ◐ | ◐ | ⊕; U.K. |
| Quick-Rise | UFC | ? | ✗ | ? | ✓ | ✓ | ✗ | No | ✗ | ? | |
| Rustco | TYSN | ? | ✗ | ? | ✓ | ✓ | ✗ | No | ◐ | ✗ | factory farming; safe chicken contr. |

| ✓ = Top Rating | ◐ = Middle Rating | ✗ = Bottom Rating | ? = Insufficient Information | Page 131 |
|---|---|---|---|---|
| | *For a more detailed explanation see key on page 14.* | | Insufficient Information | |

**BAKING MIXES**

| Company or Product | Abbr. | $ | ♀ | ✊ | 🌐 | ⚗ | 🐇 | ☢ No/Yes | ⚖ | 🔫 | ⊞ | ALERT |
|---|---|---|---|---|---|---|---|---|---|---|---|---|
| Snackin' Cakes | GIS | ✓+ | ✓ | ✓ | ✓ | ✓ | ✓ | No | ◔ | ✓ | ✓ | C.C.A. |
| Stir'n Streusel | GIS | ✓+ | ✓ | ✓ | ✓ | ✓ | ✓ | No | ◔ | ✓ | ✓ | C.C.A. |
| Super Moist | GIS | ✓+ | ✓ | ✓ | ✓ | ✓ | ✓ | No | ◔ | ✓ | ✓ | C.C.A. |
| **BAKING NEEDS** | | | | | | | | | | | | |
| Argo | CPC | ◔ | ✓ | ✓ | ✓ | ✓ | ✓ | No | ◔ | ✓ | ✓ | |
| Arm & Hammer | CRCH | ✓+ | ✓ | ◔ | ✓ | ✓* | ✗ | No | ✓ | ✓ | ✓ | |
| Baker's Joy | ACV | ? | ◔ | ? | ◔ | ✗ | ? | No | ? | ? | ✗ | |
| Bakers | MO | ? | ✓ | ✓ | ✗ | ? | ✓ | Yes | ? | ? | ? | cigarettes; Salvadoran coffee; Work. Princ. |
| Baking Magic | MCRK | ✓ | ✗ | ? | ✗ | ? | ✓ | No | ? | ? | ? | |
| Cake-Mate | MCRK | ✓ | ✗ | ? | ✓ | ? | ✓ | No | ? | ? | ? | |
| Calumet | MO | ? | ◔ | ? | ✓ | ? | ✓ | Yes | ? | ? | ? | cigarettes; Salvadoran coffee; Work. Princ. |
| Cream | G | ? | ✓ | ◔ | ✓ | ? | ◔ | No | ? | ? | ? | |
| Davis Baking Powder | RJR | ? | ◔ | ? | ? | ✗ | ◔ | Yes | ✗ | ? | ? | cigarettes; D.C.C.A. |

| Product or Company | Abbr. | $ | ♀ | | | | | | | | ✿ 🏠 | ALERT |
|---|---|---|---|---|---|---|---|---|---|---|---|---|
| Domino | TLP | | | | | | | | | | | see page 330 for U.K. ratings |
| Enticing Delights# | FALC | ? | ✔ | ✘ | ✔ | ✔ | ✔ | No | ✔ | ✔ | ✔ | 1% For Peace; some organic ingredients |
| Frosting Supreme | GMP | ✓ | ✔ | ✔ | ✔ | ✔ | ✔ | YesIN | ✓ | ✓ | ✔ | 🌐; U.K. |
| Hershey's | HSY | ✓ | ✔ | ✔ | ✔* | ✔ | ✔ | No | ✔ | ✔ | ✔ | onsite day care |
| Indian Sun | ACC | ✓ | ✓ | ✔ | ✔ | ✔ | ✔ | No | ✓ | ✓ | ✓ | Fair Share |
| Knox | UN | ? | ✘ | ✘ | ✔* | ✔ | ✔ | YesIN | ✓ | ✓ | ? | 🌐; U.K. |
| Mini-Morsels | GIS | ✓+ | ✔ | ✓ | ✔ | ✔ | ✔ | No | ✓ | ✔ | ✔ | C.C.A. |
| PAM | AHP | ✘ | ✔ | ✔ | ✔(🌐) | ✔ | ✔ | Yes | ✓ | ✔ | ✔ | infant formula |
| Planters | RJR | ? | ✓ | ? | ? | ✘ | ✔ | Yes | ? | ? | ? | cigarettes; D.C.C.A. |
| Rapidrise | RJR | ? | ✓ | ? | ? | ✘ | ✔ | Yes | ? | ? | ? | cigarettes; D.C.C.A. |
| Ready-to-Spread | GIS | ✓+ | ✔ | ✔ | ✔ | ✔ | ✔ | No | ✓ | ✔ | ✔ | C.C.A. |

✔ = Top Rating   ✓ = Middle Rating   ✘ = Bottom Rating   ? = Insufficient Information
*For a more detailed explanation see key on page 14*

| | |
|---|---|
| | Page 133 |

**BAKING NEEDS**

| Company or Product | Abbr. | $ | ♀ | | | | | | | | | | ALERT |
|---|---|---|---|---|---|---|---|---|---|---|---|---|---|
| Red Star | UFC | ? | ✗ | ? | ? | ✓ | ✓ | ✗ | No | ? | ✗ | ? | |
| Stir'n Frost | GIS | ✓+ | ✓ | ? | ✓ | ✓ | ✓ | ✓ | No | ✓ | ✓ | ? | C.C.A. |
| Sugar Twin | ACV | ? | ✗ | ? | ✗ | ✗ | ✓ | ? | No | ? | ✗ | ? | |
| Sure Jell | MO | ? | ✓ | ✓ | ? | ? | ✗ | ? | Yes | ? | ? | ? | cigarettes; Salvadoran coffee; Work. Princ. |
| Toll House Morsels | NEST | ? | ✓ | ? | ✓* | ✓ | ✓ | ✓ | YesIN | ✓ | ? | ? | infant formula; Salv. coffee; 🌍; D.C.C.A.; U.K. |
| Treasures | NEST | ? | ✓ | ? | ✓* | ✓ | ✓ | ✓ | YesIN | ✓ | ? | ? | infant formula; Salv. coffee; 🌍; D.C.C.A.; U.K. |
| **BEANS: CANNED & DRIED** | | | | | | | | | | | | | |
| Beanee-Weenee | OAT | ✓+ | ✓ | ✓ | ✓ | ✓ | ✓ | ✓ | No | ✓ | ✓ | ✓ | Fair Share |
| Casera | CPB | ✓ | ✓ | ✓ | ? | ? | ✓ | ✓ | No | ✓ | ✓ | ✓ | on-site day care |
| Jack Rabbit | CAG | ? | ✗ | ✓ | ? | ? | ✗ | ✗ | No | ? | ? | ✗ | safe meat controversy; D.C.C.A.; factory farming |
| Whole Earth# | WHO | ✓+ | ✓ | ✓ | ✓ | ✓ | ✓ | ✓ | No | ✓ | ✓ | ✓ | 1% For Peace; some organic ingredients |
| **BEVERAGE MIXES** | | | | | | | | | | | | | |
| Cactus Cooler | CADB | ? | ? | ? | ? | ✓ | ✗ | ✓ | YesIN | ? | ? | ? | 🌍; U.K. |

| Product or Company | Abbr. | $ | ♀ | ✊ | 🐾 | ✋ | 🌍 | ⚖ | ♲ | ⌂ | ALERT |
|---|---|---|---|---|---|---|---|---|---|---|---|
| Caribbean Cooler | MO | ? | ✔ | ✔ | ? | ✖ | ? | Yes | ? | ? | cigarettes; Salvadoran coffee; Work. Princ. |
| Coco Lopez | BN | ◐ | ✔ | ✔ | ✔ | ✔ | ◐ | YesIN | ◐ | ✔ | |
| Country Foods | MO | ? | ✔ | ✔ | ? | ✖ | ? | Yes | ? | ? | cigarettes; Salvadoran coffee; Work. Princ. |
| Country Time | MO | ? | ✔ | ✔ | ? | ✖ | ? | Yes | ? | ? | cigarettes; Salvadoran coffee; Work. Princ. |
| Crystal Light | MO | ? | ✔ | ✔ | ? | ✖ | ? | Yes | ? | ? | cigarettes; Salvadoran coffee; Work. Princ. |
| Diet Sun | MO | ? | ✔ | ✔ | ? | ✖ | ? | Yes | ? | ? | cigarettes; Salvadoran coffee; Work. Princ. |
| Ice Teasers | NEST | ? | ? | ✔* | ◐ | ◐ | YesIN | ◐ | ? | ? | infant formula; Salv. coffee; 🌍, D.C.C.A.; U.K. |
| Kool-Aid | MO | ? | ✔ | ✔ | ? | ✖ | ? | Yes | ? | ? | cigarettes; Salvadoran coffee; Work. Princ. |
| Supri | MO | ? | ✔ | ✔ | ? | ✖ | ? | Yes | ? | ? | cigarettes; Salvadoran coffee; Work. Princ. |
| Tang | MO | ? | ✔ | ✔ | ? | ✖ | ? | Yes | ? | ? | cigarettes; Salvadoran coffee; Work. Princ. |
| Wyler's | UN | ? | ✖ | ◐ | ✔* | ✔ | ◐ | YesIN | ◐ | ? | 🌍; U.K. |

✔ = Top Rating   ◐ = Middle Rating   ✖ = Bottom Rating   ? = Insufficient Information

*For a more detailed explanation see key on page 14*

**BEVERAGE MIXES**

## BREAD, TOAST & BREAD PRODUCTS

| Company or Product | Abbr. | $ | | | | | | | | ALERT |
|---|---|---|---|---|---|---|---|---|---|---|
| Arnold | CPC | ✔+ | ✓ | ✔ | ✔ | ✔ | No | ✓ | ✔ | |
| B & M | PET | ? | ? | ? | ✖ | ? | No | ? | ? | |
| Beefsteak | RAL | ✓ | ✔ | ✔ | ✔ | ✓ | No | ✓ | ✓ | |
| Bran'nola | CPC | ✔+ | ✔ | ✔ | ✔ | ✓ | No | ✓ | ✔ | |
| Bread Du Jour | RAL | ✓ | ✔ | ✔ | ✔ | ✓ | No | ✓ | ✓ | |
| Breads International | FLO | ? | ✖ | ? | ✖ | ? | No | ? | ✓ | |
| Brownberry | CPC | ✔+ | ✔ | ✔ | ✔ | ✔ | No | ✓ | ✔ | |
| Cobblestone Mill | FLO | ? | ✖ | ? | ✖ | ? | No | ? | ? | |
| Colonial | BUD | ✔+ | ✔ | ✔ | ✔ | ✔ | No | ✓ | ✓ | |
| Corn Flake Crumbs | K | ✔ | ✔ | ✔* | ✔ | ✔ | YesIN | ✔ | ✔ | C.C.A. |
| Country Hearth | BUD | ✔+ | ✓ | ✔ | ✔ | ✔ | No | ✓ | ✓ | |
| Croutettes | K | ✔ | ✔ | ✔* | ✔ | ✔ | YesIN | ✔ | ✔ | C.C.A. |

| Product or Company | Abbr. | $ | | | | | | | | | ALERT |
|---|---|---|---|---|---|---|---|---|---|---|---|
| Devonsheer | CPC | ✔+ | ✓ | ✔ | ✔ | ✓ | No | ✓ | ✓ | ✓ | |
| Earth Grains | BUD | ✔+ | ✓ | ✔ | ✔ | ✓ | No | ✓ | ✓ | ✓ | |
| Evangeline Maid | FLO | ? | ✖ | ? | ✖ | ? | No | ? | ? | ? | some organic ingredients |
| Fantastic Foods# | FFI | ✔ | ✓ | ✔ | ✔ | ✓ | No | ✔ | ✓ | ✓ | |
| French Quarter | GIS | ✔+ | ✓ | ✔ | ✔ | ✓ | No | ✓ | ✓ | ✔ | C.C.A. |
| Friend's | PET | ? | ? | ? | ? | ? | No | ? | ? | ? | |
| Homepride | RAL | ✓ | ✓ | ✓ | ✓ | ✓ | No | ✓ | ✓ | ✓ | |
| Hometown | FLO | ? | ✖ | ? | ✖ | ? | No | ? | ? | ? | |
| Kangaroo* | DES | ? | ? | ? | ✔ | ✓ | No | ✓/∅ | ? | ? | 1% For Peace |
| Kilpatrick's | BUD | ✔+ | ✓ | ✔ | ✔ | ✔ | No | ✓ | ✓ | ✔ | |
| Levy's | CPC | ✔+ | ✓ | ✔ | ✔ | ✓ | No | ✓ | ✓ | ✔ | |

✔ = Top Rating   ✓ = Middle Rating   ✖ = Bottom Rating   ? = Insufficient Information

*For a more detailed explanation see key on page 14*

Page 137

**BREAD, TOAST & BREAD PRODUCTS**

| Company or Product | Abbr. | $ | ⚥ | ⬚ | ⬚ | ⬚ | ⬚ | ⬚ | ⬚ | ⬚ | ⬚ | ALERT |
|---|---|---|---|---|---|---|---|---|---|---|---|---|
| Nature's Own | FLO | ? | ✗ | ? | ? | ✗ | ? | ? | No | ? | ? | |
| Oatmeal Goodness | RAL | ✓ | ✓ | ✓ | ✓ | ✓ | ✓ | ✓ | No | ✓ | ✓ | |
| Oro Wheat | MO | ? | ✓ | ✓ | ? | ✗ | ✓ | ? | Yes | ? | ? | cigarettes; Salvadoran coffee; Work. Princ. |
| Oven Fry | MO | ? | ✓ | ✓ | ? | ✗ | ✓ | ? | Yes | ? | ? | cigarettes; Salvadoran coffee; Work. Princ. |
| Pepperidge Farm | CPB | ✓ | ✓ | ✓ | ? | ✓ | ✓ | ✓ | No | ✓ | ✓ | on-site day care |
| Rainbo | BUD | ✓+ | ✓ | ✓ | ✓ | ✓ | ✓ | ✓ | No | ✓ | ✓ | |
| Regal Manor | FLO | ? | ✗ | ? | ? | ✗ | ? | ? | No | ? | ? | |
| Rich Grain | FLO | ? | ✗ | ? | ? | ✗ | ? | ✓ | No | ? | ? | |
| Sahara | CPC | ✓+ | ✓ | ✓ | ? | ✓ | ✓ | ✓ | No | ✓ | ? | |
| Salad Crispins | CLX | ✓ | ✗ | ✓ | ✓* | ✓ | ✓ | ✓ | No | ✓ | ✗ | |
| Shake 'n Bake | MO | ? | ✓ | ✓ | ? | ✗ | ✓ | ? | Yes | ? | ? | cigarettes; Salvadoran coffee; Work. Princ. |
| Sprouts 7# | HVAL | ? | ? | ? | ? | ✗ | ? | ? | No | ? | ? | some organic ingredients |
| Stove Top | MO | ? | ✓ | ✓ | ? | ✗ | ✓ | ? | Yes | ? | ? | cigarettes; Salvadoran coffee; Work. Princ. |

| Product or Company | Abbr. | $ | ♀ | | | | | | | | | | ALERT |
|---|---|---|---|---|---|---|---|---|---|---|---|---|---|
| Sunbeam Buttermaid | FLO | ? | ✖ | ? | ? | ? | ✖ | ? | No | ? | ✔ | ✔ | |
| Thomas' | CPC | ✔+ | ◡ | ? | ✔ | ? | ✔ | ? | No | ? | ✔ | ✔ | |
| Toast-r-Cakes | CPC | ✔+ | ◡ | ? | ✔ | ? | ✔ | ◡ | No | ◡ | ✔ | ✔ | |
| Warsaw | FLO | ? | ✖ | ? | ? | ? | ✖ | ? | No | ? | ? | ? | |
| Wonder | RAL | ◡ | ◡ | ✔ | ✔ | ✔ | ✔ | ◡ | No | ◡ | ◡ | ◡ | |
| **BUTTER** | | | | | | | | | | | | | |
| Breakstone's | MO | ? | ✔ | ✔ | ✖ | ✔ | ✖ | ? | Yes | ? | ? | ? | cigarettes; Salvadoran coffee; Work. Princ. |
| Butter Buds | AHP | ✖ | ◡ | ✔ | ✔(*) | ◡ | ✔ | ◡ | Yes | ◡ | ◡ | ◡ | infant formula |
| Land O'Lakes | LAND | ✔+ | ✔ | ✔ | ? | ✔ | ✔ | ◡ | No | ◡ | ✔ | ◡ | co-op |
| Molly McButter | ACV | ? | ✔ | ? | ? | ✖ | ◡ | ? | No | ? | ✖ | ? | |

✔ = Top Rating   ◡ = Middle Rating   ✖ = Bottom Rating   ? = Insufficient Information

*For a more detailed explanation see key on page 14*

| | |
|---|---|
| | Page 139 |

**BUTTER**

| Company or Product | Abbr. | 💲 | | | | | | | | | ALERT |
|---|---|---|---|---|---|---|---|---|---|---|---|
| **CANDY** | | | | | | | | | | | |
| 3 Musketeers | MARS | ? | ? | ? | ? | ✔ | No | ? | ? | ✔ | |
| 5th Avenue | HSY. | ✔ | ? | ? | ✔ | ✔ | No | ✔ | ✔ | ✔ | on-site day care |
| After Eight Dinner Mints | NEST | ? | ✔ | ✔* | ✔ | ✔ | YesIN | ✔ | ? | ? | infant formula; Salv. coffee; ⊕, D.C.C.A.; U.K. |
| Altoids | CAG | ? | ✘ | ? | ✘ | ✘ | No | ? | ? | ✘ | safe meat controversy; D.C.C.A.; factory farming |
| Amurol Products | WWY | ✘ | ✘ | ? | ✔ | ✔ | No | ✔ | ✔ | ? | Fair Share |
| Baby Ruth | NEST | ? | ✔ | ✔* | ✔ | ✔ | YesIN | ✔ | ? | ? | infant formula; Salv. coffee; ⊕, D.C.C.A.; U.K. |
| Bar None | HSY | ✔ | ✔ | ✔ | ✔ | ✔ | No | ✔ | ✔ | ✔ | on-site day care |
| Bit-O-Honey | NEST | ? | ✔ | ✔* | ✔ | ✔ | YesIN | ✔ | ? | ? | infant formula; Salv. coffee; ⊕, D.C.C.A.; U.K. |
| Bonkers | RJR | ? | ✔ | ? | ✘ | ✔ | Yes | ✔ | ? | ? | cigarettes; D.C.C.A. |
| Breathsavers | RJR | ? | ✔ | ? | ✘ | ✔ | Yes | ✔ | ? | ? | cigarettes; D.C.C.A. |
| Butterfinger | NEST | ? | ✔ | ✔* | ✔ | ✔ | YesIN | ✔ | ? | ? | infant formula; Salv. coffee; ⊕, D.C.C.A.; U.K. |
| Cadbury | HSY | ✔ | ✔ | ✔ | ✔ | ✔ | No | ✔ | ✔ | ✔ | on-site day care |

| Product or Company | Abbr. | 💲 | ♀ | 🐱 | ⚙ | ✶ | ⚘ | ⚖ | 🌐 | ⚛ | ♻ | ALERT |
|---|---|---|---|---|---|---|---|---|---|---|---|---|
| Cadbury's Creme Eggs | HSY | ⌀ | ✓ | ✓ | ✓ | ✓* | ✓ | ✓ | No | ✓ | ✓ | on-site day care |
| Callard & Bowser | UBH | ⌀ | ✗ | ✗ | ✗ | ✓ | ✓ | ✓ | No | ? | ? | ⊕, U.K. |
| Campfire | BN | ⌀ | ✓ | ✓ | ✓ | ✓ | ✓ | ⌀ | YesIN | ⌀ | ✓ | |
| Caramel | MO | ? | ✓ | ✗ | ? | ✓ | ? | ? | Yes | ? | ? | cigarettes; Salvadoran coffee; Work. Princ. |
| Caramello | HSY | ⌀ | ✓ | ✓ | ✓ | ✓* | ✓ | ✓ | No | ✓ | ✓ | on-site day care |
| Certs | WLA | ✓ | ⌀ | ✗ | ✗○ | ⌀ | ✓ | ✓ | YesIN⌀ | ? | ⌀ | on-site day care; Workplace Principles |
| Charleston Chew! | WLA | ✓ | ⌀ | ✗ | ✗○ | ⌀ | ✓ | ✓ | YesIN⌀ | ? | ⌀ | on-site day care; Workplace Principles |
| Chunky | NEST | ? | ✓ | ? | ✓* | ⌀ | ✓ | ✓ | YesIN⌀ | ? | ? | infant formula; Salv. coffee; ⊕, D.C.C.A.; U.K. |
| Clorets | WLA | ✓ | ⌀ | ✗ | ✗○ | ⌀ | ✓ | ✓ | YesIN⌀ | ? | ⌀ | on-site day care; Workplace Principles |
| Cobblestone Farm | FLO | ? | ✗ | ? | ? | ? | ? | ✗ | No | ? | ? | |
| Confeti | MO | ? | ✓ | ✗ | ? | ✓ | ? | ? | Yes | ? | ? | cigarettes; Salvadoran coffee; Work. Princ. |

| ✓ = Top Rating | ⌀ = Middle Rating | ✗ = Bottom Rating | ? = Insufficient Information | Page 141 |
|---|---|---|---|---|

For a more detailed explanation see key on page 14

**CANDY**

| Company or Product | Abbr. | $ | ♀ | ⚎ | 🐇 | 🏭 | ⚛ | ☢ | ✡ | ⚖ | ALERT |
|---|---|---|---|---|---|---|---|---|---|---|---|
| Featherweight Diet Pdcts | SAND | ? | ? | ? | ? | ? | ✖ | ? | YesIN | ? | ? | makes pesticides |
| Godiva | CPB | ✔ | ✔ | ✔ | ✔ | ? | ✔ | ✔ | No | ? | ◡ | on-site day care |
| Golden Almond | HSY | ◡ | ✔ | ✔ | ✔ | ✔ | ✔ | ✔ | No | ? | ✔ | on-site day care |
| Goobers | NEST | ? | ✔ | ? | ✔ | ✔* | ◡ | ◡ | YesIN | ? | ? | infant formula; Salv. coffee; ⊕, D.C.C.A.; U.K. |
| Hershey's | HSY | ◡ | ✔ | ✔ | ✔ | ✔ | ✔ | ✔ | No | ✔ | ✔ | on-site day care |
| Junior Mints | WLA | ✔ | ◡ | ✔ | ✔ | ✖○ | ◡ | ✔ | YesIN | ◡∅ | ◡ | on-site day care; Workplace Principles |
| Kit Kat | HSY | ◡ | ✔ | ✔ | ✔ | ✔* | ✔ | ✔ | No | ✔ | ✔ | on-site day care |
| Krackel | HSY | ◡ | ✔ | ✔ | ✔ | ✔* | ✔ | ✔ | No | ✔ | ✔ | on-site day care |
| Kraft | MO | ? | ✔ | ✔ | ✔ | ? | ✖ | ? | Yes | ? | ? | cigarettes; Salvadoran coffee; Work. Princ. |
| Licorice Nips | RJR | ? | ◡ | ◡ | ? | ? | ✖ | ◡ | Yes | ✖ | ? | cigarettes; D.C.C.A. |
| Lifesavers | RJR | ? | ◡ | ◡ | ? | ? | ✖ | ◡ | Yes | ✖ | ? | cigarettes; D.C.C.A. |
| M & M's | MARS | ? | ? | ? | ? | ? | ◡ | ? | No | ? | ✔ | |
| Mars | MARS | ? | ? | ? | ? | ? | ? | ? | No | ? | ✔ | |

| Product or Company | Abbr. | $ | | ♀ | | | | | | ? | | ALERT |
|---|---|---|---|---|---|---|---|---|---|---|---|---|
| Mellow | MO | ? | ✔ | ✔ | ✔ | ✗ | ? | Yes | ? | ? | ? | cigarettes; Salvadoran coffee; Work. Princ. |
| Mentos | WLA | ✔ | ✔ | ✔ | ✓ | ✗○ | ✓ | YesIN | ✓∅ | ? | ✓ | on-site day care; Workplace Principles |
| Milky Way | MARS | ? | ✔ | ? | ? | ✓ | ? | No | ? | ✔ | ? | |
| Mr. Goodbar | HSY | ✓ | ✔ | ✔ | ✔ | ✔* | ✓ | No | ✔ | ✔ | ✔ | on-site day care |
| Nestle | NEST | ? | ✔ | ? | ✔ | ✔* | ✓ | YesIN | ✓ | ✔ | ? | infant formula; Salv. coffee; ⊕, D.C.C.A.; U.K |
| Nibs | HSY | ✓ | ✔ | ✔ | ✔ | ✔* | ✔ | No | ✔ | ✔ | ✔ | on-site day care |
| Oh Henry! | NEST | ? | ✔ | ? | ✔ | ✔* | ✓ | YesIN | ✓ | ✔ | ? | infant formula; Salv. coffee; ⊕, D.C.C.A.; U.K |
| Peter Paul Almond Joy | HSY | ✓ | ✔ | ✔ | ✔ | ✔* | ✔ | No | ✔ | ✔ | ✔ | on-site day care |
| Peter Paul Mounds | HSY | ✓ | ✔ | ✔ | ✔ | ✔* | ✔ | No | ✔ | ✔ | ✔ | on-site day care |
| Pom Poms | WLA | ✔ | ✔ | ✓ | ✔ | ✗○ | ✓ | YesIN | ✓ | ? | ✓ | on-site day care; Workplace Principles |
| Pop Rocks | MO | ? | ✔ | ? | ✔ | ✗ | ? | Yes | ? | ? | ? | cigarettes; Salvadoran coffee; Work. Princ. |

✔ = Top Rating   ✓ = Middle Rating   ✗ = Bottom Rating   ? = Insufficient Information
For a more detailed explanation see key on page 14

Page 143

CANDY

| Company or Product | Abbr. | $ | ♀ | | | | | | | 🏢 | ALERT |
|---|---|---|---|---|---|---|---|---|---|---|---|
| Queen Anne | HSY | ✓ | ✓ | ✓ | ✓* | ✓ | ✓ | No | ✓ | ✓ | on-site day care |
| Raisinets | NEST | ? | ✓ | ? | ? | ✓ | ✓ | YesIN | ✓ | ? | infant formula; Salv. coffee; ⊕, D.C.C.A.; U.K. |
| Rascals | WLA | ✓ | ? | ✓ | ✗○ | ✓ | ✓○ | YesIN | ? | ✓ | on-site day care; Workplace Principles |
| Reed's | WWY | ✗ | ✓ | ✓ | ? | ✓ | ✓∅ | No | ✓∅ | ? | Fair Share |
| Reese's | HSY | ✓ | ✓ | ✓ | ✓* | ✓ | ✓ | No | ✓ | ✓ | on-site day care |
| Rolo | HSY | ✓ | ✓ | ✓ | ✓* | ✓ | ✓ | No | ✓ | ✓ | on-site day care |
| Skittles | MARS | ? | ✓ | ? | ? | ✓ | ✓ | No | ✓ | ? | |
| Skor | HSY | ✓ | ✓ | ✓ | ✓* | ✓ | ✓ | No | ✓ | ✓ | on-site day care |
| Snickers | MARS | ? | ✓ | ? | ? | ✓ | ✓ | No | ✓ | ? | |
| Sno-Caps | NEST | ? | ✓ | ✓ | ✓* | ✓ | ✓ | YesIN | ✓ | ? | infant formula; Salv. coffee; ⊕, D.C.C.A.; U.K. |
| Special Dark | HSY | ✓ | ✓ | ✓ | ? | ✓ | ✓ | No | ✓ | ✓ | on-site day care |
| Starburst | MARS | ? | ✓ | ? | ? | ✓ | ✓ | No | ✓ | ? | |
| Sugar Babies | WLA | ✓ | ✓ | ✓ | ✗○ | ✓ | ✓○ | YesIN | ? | ✓ | on-site day care; Workplace Principles |

| Product or Company | Abbr. | | | | | | | | | | | ALERT |
|---|---|---|---|---|---|---|---|---|---|---|---|---|
| Sugar Daddy | WLA | ✓ | ✓ | ✓ | ✓ | ✓ | ✗○ | ✓ | YesIN | ✓○ | ✓ | on-site day care; Workplace Principles |
| Symphony | HSY | ✓ | ✓ | ✓ | ✓ | ✓ | ✓ | ✓ | No | ✓* | ✓ | on-site day care |
| Terry's | UBH | ✓ | ✓ | ✗ | ✗ | ✓ | ✗ | ? | No | ✓ | ? | 🌐, U.K. |
| Toblerone | MO | ? | ? | ✓ | ✓ | ✓ | ✗ | ? | Yes | ? | ? | cigarettes; Salvadoran coffee; Work. Princ. |
| Twix | MARS | ? | ? | ? | ? | ? | ? | ? | No | ? | ✓ | |
| Whatchamacallit | HSY | ✓ | ✓ | ✓ | ✓ | ✓ | ✓ | ✓ | No | ✓* | ✓ | on-site day care |
| Whitman's Chocolates | PET | ? | ? | ? | ? | ✗ | ✗ | ? | No | ? | ? | |
| Whole Earth# | WHO | ✓+ | ✓ | ✓ | ✓ | ✓ | ✓ | ✓ | No | ? | ✓ | 1% For Peace; some organic ingredients |
| Winter Fresh | WWY | ✗ | ✗ | ? | ? | ✓ | ✓ | ? | No | ✓○ | ? | Fair Share |
| Y&S Twizzlers | HSY | ✓ | ✓ | ✓ | ✓ | ✓ | ✓ | ✓ | No | ✓ | ✓ | on-site day care |
| York Peppermint Patties | HSY | ✓ | ✓ | ✓ | ✓ | ✓ | ✓ | ✓ | No | ✓ | ✓ | on-site day care |

✓ = Top Rating     ✓ = Middle Rating     ✗ = Bottom Rating     ? = Insufficient Information
*For a more detailed explanation see key on page 14*

Page 145

CANDY

| Company or Product | Abbr. | $ | ♀ | | | | | | | | | | ALERT |
|---|---|---|---|---|---|---|---|---|---|---|---|---|---|
| **CEREAL** | | | | | | | | | | | | | |
| All-Bran | K | ✔ | ✔ | ✔ | ✔ | ✔ | ✔* | ✔ | ✔ | YesIN | ✔ | | ✔ | C.C.A. |
| Almond Delight | RAL | ◐ | ✔ | ✔ | ✔ | ✔ | ✔ | | ◐ | No | ◐ | | ◐ | |
| Alpen | WBX | | | | | | | | | | | | | see page 330 for U.K. ratings |
| Alpha-Bits | MO | ? | ✔ | ✔ | ✔ | ✖ | ? | ✔ | ? | Yes | ? | | ? | cigarettes; Salvadoran coffee; Work. Princ. |
| Apple Jacks | K | ✔ | ✔ | ✔ | ✔ | ✔ | ✔* | ✔ | ✔ | YesIN | ✔ | | ✔ | C.C.A. |
| Apple Raisin Crisp | K | ✔ | ✔ | ✔ | ✔ | ✔ | ✔* | ✔ | ✔ | YesIN | ✔ | | ✔ | C.C.A. |
| Barbara's Bakery# | BARB | ✔+ | ◐ | ✔ | ✔ | ✔ | ✔ | ✔ | ◐ | No | ✔ | | ◐ | some organic ingredients |
| Batman | RAL | ◐ | ✔ | ✔ | ✔ | ✔ | ✔ | | ◐ | No | ◐ | | ◐ | |
| Big G | GIS | ✔+ | ✔ | ✔ | ✔ | ✔ | ✔ | ✔ | ✔ | No | ✔ | | ◐ | |
| Bigg Mixx | K | ✔ | ✔ | ✔ | ✔ | ✔ | ✔* | ✔ | ✔ | YesIN | ✔ | | ✔ | C.C.A. |
| Boo Berry | GIS | ✔+ | ✔ | ✔ | ✔ | ✔ | ✔ | ✔ | ✔ | No | ✔ | | ◐ | C.C.A. |
| Bran Buds | K | ✔ | ✔ | ✔ | ✔ | ✔ | ✔* | ✔ | ✔ | YesIN | ✔ | | ✔ | C.C.A. |

| Product or Company | Abbr. | $ | | | | | | | | | ALERT |
|---|---|---|---|---|---|---|---|---|---|---|---|
| Bran Flakes | K | ✔ | ✔ | ✔ | ✔ | ✔* | ✔ | YesIN | ✔ | ✔ | C.C.A. |
| Bran Muffin Crisp | GIS | ✔+ | ✔ | ✔ | ✔ | ✔ | ✔ | No | ✔ | ✔ | C.C.A. |
| Breakfast with Barbie | RAL | ◡ | ✔ | ◡ | ✔ | ✔ | ✔ | No | ◡ | ◡ | C.C.A. |
| Buc Wheats | GIS | ✔+ | ✔ | ✔ | ✔ | ✔ | ✔ | No | ◡ | ✔ | C.C.A. |
| Buckeye | OAT | ✔+ | ✔ | ✔ | ✔ | ✔ | ✔ | No | ✔ | ◡ | Fair-Share |
| Cap'n Crunch | OAT | ✔+ | ✔ | ✔ | ✔ | ✔ | ✔ | No | ◡ | ◡ | Fair-Share |
| Cheerios | GIS | ✔+ | ✔ | ✔ | ✔ | ✔ | ✔ | No | ◡ | ✔ | C.C.A. |
| Chex | RAL | ◡ | ✔ | ◡ | ✔ | ✔ | ✔ | No | ◡ | ◡ | |
| Cinnamon Toast Crunch | GIS | ✔+ | ✔ | ✔ | ✔ | ✔ | ✔ | No | ✔ | ✔ | C.C.A. |
| Circus Fun | GIS | ✔+ | ✔ | ✔ | ✔ | ✔ | ✔ | No | ✔ | ✔ | C.C.A. |
| Clusters | GIS | ✔+ | ✔ | ✔ | ✔ | ✔ | ✔ | No | ✔ | ✔ | C.C.A. |

✔ = Top Rating   ◡ = Middle Rating   ✘ = Bottom Rating   ? = Insufficient Information

*For a more detailed explanation see key on page 14*

Page 147

CEREAL

| Company or Product | Abbr. | 💲 | ♀ | | | 🤝 | | | 🐾 | | ▦ | ALERT |
|---|---|---|---|---|---|---|---|---|---|---|---|---|
| Cocoa Krispies | K | ✓ | ✓ | ✓ | ✓* | ✓ | ✓ | YesIN | ✓ | ✓ | ✓ | C.C.A. |
| Cocoa Puffs | GIS | ✓+ | ✓ | ✓ | ✓ | ✓ | ✓ | No | ✓ | ✓ | ✓ | C.C.A. |
| Common Sense O. Br. | K | ✓ | ✓ | ✓ | ✓* | ✓ | ✓ | YesIN | ✓ | ✓ | ✓ | C.C.A. |
| Cookie Crisp | RAL | ✓ | ✓ | ✓ | ✓ | ✓ | ✓ | No | ✓ | ✓ | ✓ | |
| Corn Flakes | K | ✓ | ✓ | ✓ | ✓* | ✓ | ✓ | YesIN | ✓ | ✓ | ✓ | C.C.A. |
| Corn Pops | K | ✓ | ✓ | ✓ | ✓* | ✓ | ✓ | YesIN | ✓ | ✓ | ✓ | C.C.A. |
| Corn Total | GIS | ✓+ | ✓ | ✓ | ✓ | ✓ | ✓ | No | ✓ | ✓ | ✓ | C.C.A. |
| Count Chocula | GIS | ✓+ | ✓ | ✓ | ✓ | ✓ | ✓ | No | ✓ | ✓ | ✓ | C.C.A. |
| Country Corn Flakes | GIS | ✓+ | ✓ | ✓ | ✓ | ✓ | ✓ | No | ✓ | ✓ | ✓ | C.C.A. |
| Cracklin' Oat Bran | K | ✓+ | ✓ | ✓ | ✓* | ✓ | ✓ | YesIN | ✓ | ✓ | ✓ | C.C.A. |
| Crazy Corn | GIS | ✓+ | ✓ | ✓ | ✓ | ✓ | ✓ | No | ✓ | ✓ | ✓ | C.C.A. |
| Cream of Wheat | RJR | ? | ? | ✗ | ✗ | ? | ✓ | Yes | ? | ? | ? | cigarettes; D.C.C.A. |
| Cremerie Triple Cream | MO | ? | ? | ✓ | ✗ | ? | ? | Yes | ? | ? | ? | cigarettes; Salvadoran coffee; Work, Princ. |

| Product or Company | Abbr. | 💲 | ♀ | ⚥ | ⚕ | 🍼 | ⚖ | Yes/No | ◇ | ⊞ | ALERT |
|---|---|---|---|---|---|---|---|---|---|---|---|
| Crispix | K | ✔ | ✔ | ✔ | ✔ | ✔* | ✔ | YesIN | ✔ | ✔ | C.C.A. |
| Crispy Critters | MO | ? | ✔ | ✔ | ? | ? | ✔ | Yes | ? | ? | cigarettes; Salvadoran coffee; Work. Princ. |
| Crispy Wheats 'n Raisins | GIS | ✔+ | ✔ | ✔ | ✔ | ✔ | ✔ | No | ◐ | ✔ | C.C.A. |
| Croonchy Stars | MO | ? | ✔ | ✔ | ? | ? | ✔ | Yes | ? | ? | cigarettes; Salvadoran coffee; Work. Princ. |
| Donutz | GIS | ✔+ | ✔ | ✔ | ✔ | ✔ | ✔ | No | ◐ | ✔ | C.C.A. |
| E.T. | GIS | ✔+ | ✔ | ✔ | ✔ | ✔ | ✔ | No | ◐ | ✔ | C.C.A. |
| Enticing Delights# | FALC | ? | ✖ | ✔ | ◐ | ✔ | ✔ | No | ✔ | ◐ | 1% For Peace; some organic ingredients |
| Farina | GMP | ◐ | ✔ | ✔ | ✔ | ✔ | ✔ | YesIN | ◐ | ◐ | ⊕; U.K. |
| Fiber One | GIS | ✔+ | ✔ | ✔ | ✔ | ✔ | ✔ | No | ◐ | ✔ | C.C.A. |
| Frankenberry | GIS | ✔+ | ✔ | ✔ | ✔ | ✔ | ✔ | No | ◐ | ✔ | C.C.A. |
| Froot Loops | K | ✔ | ✔ | ✔ | ✔ | ✔* | ✔ | YesIN | ✔ | ✔ | C.C.A. |

✔ = Top Rating  ◐ = Middle Rating  ✖ = Bottom Rating  ? = Insufficient Information

For a more detailed explanation see key on page 14

CEREAL

| Company or Product | Abbr. | $ | | | | | | | | | | ALERT |
|---|---|---|---|---|---|---|---|---|---|---|---|---|
| Frosted Flakes | K | ✓ | ✓ | ✓ | ✓ | ✓* | ✓ | YesIN | ✓ | ✓ | ✓ | C.C.A. |
| Frosted Mini-Wheats | K | ✓ | ✓ | ✓ | ✓ | ✓* | ✓ | YesIN | ✓ | ✓ | ✓ | C.C.A. |
| Frosted Rice Krinkles | MO | ? | ✓ | ✓ | ✓ | ? | ✗ | Yes | ? | ? | ? | cigarettes; Salvadoran coffee; Work. Princ. |
| Fruit & Bran Wheaties | GIS | ✓+ | ✓ | ✓ | ✓ | ✓ | ✓ | No | ✓ | ✓ | ✓ | C.C.A. |
| Fruit & Fibre | MO | ? | ✓ | ✓ | ✓ | ? | ✗ | Yes | ? | ? | ? | cigarettes; Salvadoran coffee; Work. Princ. |
| Fruit & Fitness# | HVAL | ? | ✓ | ? | ✓ | ✓ | ✗ | No | ? | ? | ? | some organic ingredients |
| Fruitful Bran | K | ✓ | ✓ | ✓ | ✓ | ✓* | ✓ | YesIN | ✓ | ✓ | ✓ | C.C.A. |
| Fruity Mshmls. Krsp. | K | ✓ | ✓ | ✓ | ✓ | ✓* | ✓ | YesIN | ✓ | ✓ | ✓ | C.C.A. |
| Ghostbusters | RAL | ✓ | ✓ | ✓ | ✓ | ✓ | ✓ | No | ✓ | ✓ | ✓ | |
| Golden Crisp | MO | ? | ✓ | ✓ | ✓ | ? | ✗ | Yes | ? | ? | ? | cigarettes; Salvadoran coffee; Work. Princ. |
| Golden Grahams | GIS | ✓+ | ✓ | ✓ | ✓ | ✓ | ✓ | No | ✓ | ✓ | ✓ | C.C.A. |
| Grainfield's | WBX | | | | | | | | | | | see page 330 for U.K. ratings |
| Grape-Nuts | MO | ? | ✓ | ✓ | ? | ? | ✗ | Yes | ? | ? | ? | cigarettes; Salvadoran coffee; Work. Princ. |

| Product or Company | Abbr. | $ | ♀ | 👤 | 🐾 | 🐇 | 🌐 | Yes/No | ♻ | 🕊 | ALERT |
|---|---|---|---|---|---|---|---|---|---|---|---|
| Health Valley# | HVAL | ? | ? | ? | ✓ | ✗ | ? | No | ? | ? | ? | some organic ingredients |
| Heartland | PET | ? | ? | ? | ✓ | ✗ | ? | No | ? | ? | ? | |
| Honey Buc Wheat Crisp | GIS | ✓+ | ? | ✓ | ✓ | ✓ | ? | No | ✓ | ✓ | ? | C.C.A. |
| Honey Bunches of Oats | MO | ? | ? | ✓ | ✓ | ✗ | ? | Yes | ? | ? | ? | cigarettes; Salvadoran coffee; Work. Princ. |
| Honey Nut Cheerios | GIS | ✓+ | ? | ✓ | ✓ | ✓ | ? | No | ◐ | ✓ | ? | C.C.A. |
| Honey Nut Crunch | MO | ? | ? | ✓ | ✓ | ✗ | ? | Yes | ? | ? | ? | cigarettes; Salvadoran coffee; Work. Princ. |
| Honey Smacks | K | ✓ | ✓ | ✓ | ✓* | ✓ | ✓ | YesIN | ✓ | ✓ | | C.C.A. |
| Honeycomb | MO | ? | ? | ✓ | ✓ | ✗ | ? | Yes | ? | ? | ? | cigarettes; Salvadoran coffee; Work. Princ. |
| Horizon | MO | ? | ? | ✓ | ✓ | ✗ | ? | Yes | ? | ? | ? | cigarettes; Salvadoran coffee; Work. Princ. |
| Ice Cream Cones | GIS | ✓+ | ? | ✓ | ✓ | ✓ | ? | No | ◐ | ✓ | ✓ | C.C.A. |
| Just Right | K | ✓ | ✓ | ✓ | ✓* | ✓ | ✓ | YesIN | ✓ | ✓ | | C.C.A. |

✓ = Top Rating    ◐ = Middle Rating    ✗ = Bottom Rating    ? = Insufficient Information

*For a more detailed explanation see key on page 14*

| Company or Product | Abbr. | 💲 | ♀ | | | | | | | | ALERT |
|---|---|---|---|---|---|---|---|---|---|---|---|
| Kaboom | GIS | ✓+ | ✓ | ✓ | ✓ | ✓ | ✓ | No | ✓ | ✓ | C.C.A. |
| Kenmei Rice Bran | K | ✓ | ✓ | ✓ | ✓* | ✓ | ✓ | YesIN | ✓ | ✓ | C.C.A. |
| Kix | GIS | ✓+ | ✓ | ✓ | ✓ | ✓ | ✓ | No | ✓ | ✓ | C.C.A. |
| Kretschmer Wheat Grm. | OAT | ✓+ | ✓ | ✓ | ✓ | ✓ | ✓ | No | ✓ | ✓ | Fair Share |
| Life | OAT | ✓+ | ✓ | ✓ | ✓ | ✓ | ✓ | No | ✓ | ✓ | Fair Share |
| Lucky Charms | GIS | ✓+ | ✓ | ✓ | ✓ | ✓ | ✓ | No | ✓ | ✓ | C.C.A. |
| Maypo Oatmeal | AHP | ✗ | ✓ | ✓ | ✓(®) | ● | ✓ | Yes | ✓ | ✓ | infant formula |
| Mother's Rolled Oats | OAT | ✓+ | ✓ | ✓ | ✓ | ✓ | ✓ | No | ✓ | ✓ | Fair Share |
| Muesli | RAL | ✓ | ✓ | ✓ | ✓ | ✓ | ✓ | No | ✓ | ✓ | |
| Muesli | WBX | | | | | | | | | | see page 330 for U.K. ratings |
| Mueslix | K | ✓ | ✓ | ✓ | ✓* | ✓ | ✓ | YesIN | ✓ | ✓ | C.C.A. |
| Nabisco Fruit Wheats | RJR | ? | ? | ? | ✗ | ✗ | ✓ | Yes | ? | ? | cigarettes; D.C.C.A. |
| Nabisco Raisin Bran | RJR | ? | ? | ? | ✗ | ✗ | ✓ | Yes | ? | ? | cigarettes; D.C.C.A. |

| Product or Company | Abbr. | $ | ♀ | | | | | | | ALERT |
|---|---|---|---|---|---|---|---|---|---|---|
| Nintendo Cereals | RAL | ◐ | ✓ | ◐ | ✓ | ✓ | No | ✓ | ◐ |  |
| Nut & Honey Crunch | K | ✓ | ✓ | ✓ | ✓* | ✓ | YesIN | ✓ | ✓ | C.C.A. |
| Nutri-Grain | K | ✓ | ✓ | ✓ | ✓* | ✓ | YesIN | ✓ | ✓ | C.C.A. |
| Oat Bran Options | RAL | ◐ | ✓ | ✓ | ✓ | ◐ | No | ◐ | ◐ |  |
| Oatbake | K | ✓ | ✓ | ✓ | ✓* | ✓ | YesIN | ✓ | ✓ | C.C.A. |
| Oatmeal Raisin Crisp | GIS | ◐+ | ✓ | ✓ | ✓ | ✓ | No | ✓ | ✓ | C.C.A. |
| Oatmeal Swirlers | GIS | ◐+ | ✓ | ✓ | ✓ | ◐ | No | ◐ | ✓ | C.C.A. |
| Oh's | OAT | ◐+ | ✓ | ✓ | ✓ | ✓ | No | ✓ | ◐ | Fair Share |
| Orange Blossom | GIS | ◐+ | ✓ | ✓ | ✓ | ◐ | No | ✓ | ✓ | C.C.A. |
| Orangeola# | HVAL | ◐+ | ? | ? | ✗ | ? | No | ? | ? | some organic ingredients |
| Pac-man | GIS | ◐+ | ✓ | ✓ | ✓ | ◐ | No | ✓ | ✓ | C.C.A. |

✓ = Top Rating   ◐ = Middle Rating   ✗ = Bottom Rating   ? = Insufficient Information

*For a more detailed explanation see key on page 14*

| | |
|---|---|
| | Page 153 |

CEREAL

| Company or Product | Abbr. | 💲 | ♀ | ✕ | 🏃 | 🐇 | 🐦 | ⚛ | | ▦ | ALERT |
|---|---|---|---|---|---|---|---|---|---|---|---|
| Pebbles | MO | ? | ✓ | ✓ | ? | ✓ | ✗ | ? | Yes | ? | ? | cigarettes; Salvadoran coffee; Work. Princ. |
| Post Grape Nuts | MO | ? | ✓ | ✓ | ? | ✓ | ✗ | ? | Yes | ? | ? | cigarettes; Salvadoran coffee; Work. Princ. |
| Post Raisin Bran | MO | ? | ✓ | ✓ | ? | ✓ | ✗ | ? | Yes | ? | ? | cigarettes; Salvadoran coffee; Work. Princ. |
| Product 19 | K | ✓ | ✓ | ✓ | ✓* | ✓ | ✓ | ✓ | YesIN | ✓ | ✓ | C.C.A. |
| Quaker | OAT | ✓+ | ✓ | ✓ | ✓ | ✓ | ✓ | ✓ | No | ✓ | ✓ | Fair Share |
| Quaker 100% Natural | OAT | ✓+ | ✓ | ✓ | ✓ | ✓ | ✓ | ✓ | No | ✓ | ✓ | Fair Share |
| Quaker Oat Squares | OAT | ✓+ | ✓ | ✓ | ✓ | ✓ | ✓ | ✓ | No | ✓ | ✓ | Fair Share |
| Raisin Bran | K | ✓ | ✓ | ✓ | ✓* | ✓ | ✓ | ✓ | YesIN | ✓ | ✓ | C.C.A. |
| Raisin Nut Bran | GIS | ✓+ | ✓ | ✓ | ✓ | ✓ | ✓ | ✓ | No | ✓ | ✓ | C.C.A. |
| Ralston | RAL | ✓ | ✓ | ✓ | ✓ | ✓ | ✓ | ✓ | No | ✓ | ✓ | |
| Real# | HVAL | ? | ? | ✓ | ? | ✓ | ✗ | ? | No | ? | ? | some organic ingredients |
| Rice Krispies | K | ✓ | ✓ | ✓ | ✓* | ✓ | ✓ | ✓ | YesIN | ✓ | ✓ | C.C.A. |
| Rocky Road | GIS | ✓+ | ✓ | ✓ | ✓ | ✓ | ✓ | ✓ | No | ✓ | ✓ | C.C.A. |

| Product or Company | Abbr. | $ | ♀ | | | | | | | | | ALERT |
|---|---|---|---|---|---|---|---|---|---|---|---|---|
| S'More's Crunch | GIS | ✓+ | ✓ | ✓ | ✓ | ✓ | No | ◔ | ✓ | ✓ | | C.C.A. |
| S.W. Graham | K | ✓ | ✓ | ✓ | ✓* | ✓ | YesIN | ✓ | ? | ✓ | | C.C.A. |
| Shredded Wheat | RJR | ? | ? | ? | ✗ | ? | Yes | ✗ | ? | ? | | cigarettes; D.C.C.A. |
| Shredded Wheat Sqrs. | K | ✓ | ✓ | ✓ | ✓* | ✓ | YesIN | ✓ | ✓ | ✓ | | C.C.A. |
| Smurf Magic Berries | MO | ? | ✓ | ✓ | ? | ✗ | Yes | ? | ? | ? | | cigarettes; Salvadoran coffee; Work. Princ. |
| Special K | K | ✓ | ✓ | ✓ | ✓* | ✓ | YesIN | ✓ | ✓ | ✓ | | C.C.A. |
| Spoon Size Shr. Wht. | RJR | ? | ✓ | ? | ? | ✗ | Yes | ✗ | ? | ? | | cigarettes; D.C.C.A. |
| Sun Flakes | RAL | ◔ | ✓ | ✓ | ✓ | ✓ | No | ◔ | ◔ | ◔ | | |
| Super Golden Crisp | MO | ? | ✓ | ✓ | ? | ✗ | Yes | ? | ? | ? | | cigarettes; Salvadoran coffee; Work. Princ. |
| Teenage Mnt. Nj. T. | RAL | ◔ | ✓ | ✓ | ✓ | ✓ | No | ◔ | ◔ | ◔ | | |
| Toasted Oat Rings | GEB | ◔ | ✓ | ✓ | ? | ✗ | Yes | ? | ◔ | ? | | D.C.C.A.; infant formula |

✓ = Top Rating  ◔ = Middle Rating  ✗ = Bottom Rating  ? = Insufficient Information

*For a more detailed explanation see key on page 14*  | **Page 155**

CEREAL

| Company or Product | Abbr. | $ | | | | | | | | | ALERT |
|---|---|---|---|---|---|---|---|---|---|---|---|
| Toasties | MO | ? | ✔ | ✔ | ? | ✖ | ? | Yes | ? | ? | cigarettes; Salvadoran coffee; Work. Princ. |
| Total | GIS | ✔+ | ✔ | ✔ | ✔ | ✔ | ✔ | No | ◔ | ✔ | C.C.A. |
| Total Oatmeal | GIS | ✔+ | ✔ | ✔ | ✔ | ✔ | ✔ | No | ◔ | ✔ | C.C.A. |
| Treat-Pak | MO | ? | ✔ | ✔ | ? | ✖ | ? | Yes | ? | ? | cigarettes; Salvadoran coffee; Work. Princ. |
| Trix | GIS | ✔+ | ✔ | ✔ | ✔ | ✔ | ✔ | No | ◔ | ? | C.C.A. |
| Weetabix | WBX | | | ✔ | ✔ | ✔ | | | | | see page 330 for U.K. ratings |
| Wheat Hearts | GIS | ✔+ | ✔ | ✔ | ✔ | ✔ | | No | ✔ | ✔ | C.C.A. |
| Wheatena | AHP * | ✖ | ◔ | ✔⊛ | ◔ | ✔ | ◔ | Yes | ◔ | ◔ | infant formula |
| Wheaties | GIS | ✔+ | ✔ | ✔ | ✔ | ✔ | ✔ | No | ◔ | ✔ | C.C.A. |
| **CHEESE** | | | | | | | | | | | |
| Aerofil | CAG | ? | ✖ | ◔ | ? | ✖ | ? | No | ? | ✖ | safe meat controversy; D.C.C.A.; factory farming |
| Borden | BN | ◔ | ✔ | ✔ | ✔ | ◔ | ✔ | YesIN | ◔ | ✔ | |
| Butterfly | CAG | ? | ✖ | ◔ | ? | ✖ | ? | No | ? | ✖ | safe meat controversy; D.C.C.A.; factory farming |

| Product or Company | Abbr. | 💲 | ⚥ | 👤 | 🐇 | ⚖ | ☢ | ♻ | ⚙ | ALERT |
|---|---|---|---|---|---|---|---|---|---|---|
| Casino | MO | ? | ✔ | ? | ✗ | ? | Yes | ? | ? | cigarettes; Salvadoran coffee; Work. Princ. |
| Cheese Whip | MO | ? | ✔ | ? | ✗ | ? | Yes | ? | ? | cigarettes; Salvadoran coffee; Work. Princ. |
| Cheez Whiz | MO | ? | ✔ | ? | ✗ | ? | Yes | ? | ? | cigarettes; Salvadoran coffee; Work. Princ. |
| Churny | MO | ? | ✔ | ? | ✗ | ? | Yes | ? | ? | cigarettes; Salvadoran coffee; Work. Princ. |
| Coon | MO | ? | ✔ | ? | ✗ | ? | Yes | ? | ? | cigarettes; Salvadoran coffee; Work. Princ. |
| Country Crock | UN | ? | ✗ | ◐ | ✔ | ◐ | YesIN | ◐ | ? | ⊕, U.K. |
| County Line | CAG | ? | ✗ | ? | ✗ | ✗ | No | ? | ✗ | safe meat controversy; D.C.C.A.; factory farming |
| Cracker Barrel | MO | ? | ✔ | ◐ | ✗ | ◐ | Yes | ? | ? | cigarettes; Salvadoran coffee; Work. Princ. |
| Cream Chief# | TFC | ✗ | ◐ | ✔ | ✔ | ✔ | No | ✔ | ◐ | on-site day care |
| Fisher | BN | ◐ | ✔ | ✔* | ✔ | ✔ | YesIN | ◐ | ✔ | |
| Gardenia | UNG | | | | | | | | | see page 330 for U.K. ratings |

| ✔ = Top Rating | ◐ = Middle Rating | ✗ = Bottom Rating | ? = Insufficient Information | Page 157 |
|---|---|---|---|---|

*For a more detailed explanation see key on page 14*

CHEESE

| Company or Product | Abbr. | $ | ♀ | ⚥ | ✊ | 🜨 | 🐇 | ☢ | ⚛ | 🐾 | ▦ | ALERT |
|---|---|---|---|---|---|---|---|---|---|---|---|---|
| Goldbrick | CAG | ? | ✖ | ✓ | ✖ | ? | ✖ | No | ? | ? | ✖ | safe meat controversy; D.C.C.A.; factory farming |
| Jersey Maid | MO | ? | ✓ | ✓ | ✖ | ? | ✓ | Yes | ? | ? | ? | cigarettes; Salvadoran coffee; Work. Princ. |
| Knudsen | MO | ? | ✓ | ✓ | ✖ | ? | ✓ | Yes | ? | ? | ? | cigarettes; Salvadoran coffee; Work. Princ. |
| Kraft | MO | ? | ✓ | ✓ | ✖ | ? | ✓ | Yes | ? | ? | ? | cigarettes; Salvadoran coffee; Work. Princ. |
| Land O'Lakes | LAND | ✓+ | ✓ | ✓ | ✓ | ? | ✓ | No | ✓ | ✓ | ✓ | co-op |
| Lily Lake | CAG | ? | ✖ | ✓ | ✖ | ? | ✖ | No | ? | ? | ✖ | safe meat controversy; D.C.C.A.; factory farming |
| Maman Luise | MO | ? | ✓ | ✓ | ✓ | ? | ✖ | Yes | ? | ? | ? | cigarettes; Salvadoran coffee; Work. Princ. |
| Meadow Gold | BN | ✓ | ✓ | ✓ | ✓ | ✓ | ✓ | YesN | ✓ | ✓ | ✓ | cigarettes; Salvadoran coffee; Work. Princ. |
| New Dimensions | CAG | ? | ✖ | ✓ | ✖ | ? | ✖ | No | ? | ? | ✖ | safe meat controversy; D.C.C.A.; factory farming |
| Paul Jean Barnett | MO | ? | ✓ | ✓ | ✖ | ? | ✓ | Yes | ? | ? | ? | cigarettes; Salvadoran coffee; Work. Princ. |
| Pauly | CAG | ? | ✖ | ✓ | ✖ | ? | ✖ | No | ? | ? | ✖ | safe meat controversy; D.C.C.A.; factory farming |
| Phila. Cream Cheese | MO | ? | ✓ | ✓ | ✖ | ? | ✓ | Yes | ? | ? | ? | cigarettes; Salvadoran coffee; Work. Princ. |
| Polly-O | MO | ? | ✓ | ✓ | ✖ | ? | ✓ | Yes | ? | ? | ? | cigarettes; Salvadoran coffee; Work. Princ. |

| Product or Company | Abbr. | $ | ♀ | | | | | | | ♻ | ⌂ | ALERT |
|---|---|---|---|---|---|---|---|---|---|---|---|---|
| Red Rooster | MO | ? | ✔ | ✔ | ? | ✖ | ? | Yes | ? | ? | ? | cigarettes; Salvadoran coffee; Work. Princ. |
| Sandwich Mate | BN | ◡ | ✔ | ✔ | ◡ | ✔ | ◡ | YesIN | ◡ | ✔ | ✔ | |
| Select-A-Size | MO | ? | ✔ | ✔ | ? | ✖ | ? | Yes | ? | ? | ? | cigarettes; Salvadoran coffee; Work. Princ. |
| Temp Tee | MO | ? | ✔ | ✔ | ? | ✖ | ? | Yes | ? | ? | ? | cigarettes; Salvadoran coffee; Work. Princ. |
| Tillamook Cheese | TILA | ✔+ | ◡ | ✖ | ✔ | ✔ | ◡ | No | ◡ | ◡ | ✔ | co-op |
| **CHICKEN: CANNED & REFRIGERATED** | | | | | | | | | | | | |
| Bil Mar | SLE | ✔ | ✔ | ✔ | ✔ | ✔ | ✔ | Yes | ✔ | ◡ | ◡ | on-site day care; C.C.A. |
| Butterball | CAG | ? | ✖ | ◡ | ✖ | ✖ | ✖ | No | ? | ✖ | ✖ | safe meat controversy; D.C.C.A.; factory farming |
| Chick 'N Quick | TYSN | ? | ✖ | ? | ✔ | ✖ | ? | No | ◡ | ✖ | ✖ | factory farming, safe chicken contr. |
| Chicken by George | HRL | ? | ✖ | ? | ✖ | ✖ | ? | No | ? | ? | ? | |
| Cornish | TYSN | ? | ✖ | ? | ✔ | ✖ | ? | No | ◡ | ? | ✖ | factory farming, safe chicken contr. |

| ✔ = Top Rating | ◡ = Middle Rating | ✖ = Bottom Rating | ? = Insufficient Information | Page 159 |
|---|---|---|---|---|

*For a more detailed explanation see key on page 14*

**CHICKEN: CANNED & REFRIGERATED**

| Company or Product | Abbr. | $ | | | | | | | | ALERT |
|---|---|---|---|---|---|---|---|---|---|---|
| Country Pride | CAG | ? | ✖ | ? | ? | ✖ | No | ? | ✖ | safe meat controversy; D.C.C.A.; factory farming |
| Flyers | TYSN | ? | ✖ | ? | ✔ | ✖ | No | ? | ✖ | factory farming; safe chicken contr. |
| Golden Farms | CAG | ? | ✖ | ? | ? | ✖ | No | ? | ✖ | safe meat controversy; D.C.C.A.; factory farming |
| Holly Farms | TYSN | ? | ✖ | ? | ✔ | ✖ | No | ? | ✖ | factory farming; safe chicken contr. |
| Mr. Turkey | SLE | ✔ | ✔ | ✔ | ✔ | ✔ | Yes | ✔∅ | ✔ | on-site day care; C.C.A. |
| Perdue | PRDU | ? | ? | ? | ? | ✖ | No. | ✖ | ✖ | D.C.C.A.; factory frmg; safe chicken contr. |
| Shorgood | CAG | ? | ✖ | ✔ | ? | ✖ | No | ? | ✖ | safe meat controversy; D.C.C.A.; factory farming |
| **CLEANSERS & SPONGES FOR HOUSEHOLD USE** | | | | | | | | | | |
| Aerowax | RCP | ? | ? | ? | ✔ | ? | YesIN | ? | ✔ | 🌐; U.K. |
| Airwick | RCP | ? | ? | ? | ✔ | ? | YesIN | ? | ✖ | 🌐; U.K. |
| Ajax | CL | ✔+ | ✔ | ✔⊛ | ✔ | ✔ | YesIN | ✔ | ✔ | |
| Allen's Naturally* | ANY | ✔ | ✔∅ | ✔ | ✔ | ✔ | No | ? | ✔ | |
| Arm & Hammer | CRCH | ✔+ | ✔ | ✔* | ✔ | ✔ | No | ✔ | ✔ | |

| Product or Company | Abbr. | $ | | | | | | | | | | | ALERT |
|---|---|---|---|---|---|---|---|---|---|---|---|---|---|
| Behold | BMY | ✓ | ✓ | ✓ | ✓ | ✓ | ✓⊛ | ✓ | YesIN | ✓ | ✓ | | infant formula; Workplace Principles; D.C.C.A |
| Bowl Brite | BMY | ✓ | ✓ | ✓ | ✓ | ✓ | ✓⊛ | ✓ | YesIN | ✓ | ✓ | | infant formula; Workplace Principles; D.C.C.A |
| Brasso | RCP | ? | ? | ✓ | ? | ✓ | ? | ? | YesIN | ? | ✗ | ? | ⊕, U.K. |
| Brillo | G | ? | ✓ | ? | ✓ | ✗ | ? | ? | No | ? | ? | ? | |
| Brite | SCJ | ✓+ | ✓ | ✓ | ✓ | ✓* | ✓ | ✓ | YesIN | ✓ | ✓ | ✓ | 1st to ban CFCs; on-site day care |
| Bully | RCP | ? | ? | ? | ✓ | ? | ? | ? | YesIN | ? | ✗ | ✓ | ⊕, U.K. |
| Cameo | G | ? | ? | ? | ✓ | ✗ | ? | ? | No | ? | ? | ? | |
| Carpet Fresh | RCP | ? | ? | ✓ | ? | ✓ | ? | ? | YesIN | ? | ✗ | ✓ | ⊕, U.K. |
| Cascade | PG | ✓ | ✓ | ✓ | ✓ | ✓⊛ | ✓ | ✓ | Yes | ✓ | ✓ | ✓ | disposable diapers; Salvadoran coffee; on-site day care; C.C.A. |
| Chore Boy | RCP | ? | ? | ? | ✓ | ? | ? | ? | YesIN | ? | ✗ | ✓ | ⊕, U.K. |
| Cinch | PG | ✓ | ✓ | ✓ | ✓ | ✓⊛ | ✓ | ✓ | Yes | ✓ | ✓ | ✓ | disposable diapers; Salvadoran coffee; on-site day care; C.C.A. |

| ✓ = Top Rating   ✓ = Middle Rating   ✗ = Bottom Rating   ? = Insufficient Information | Page 161 |
|---|---|
| For a more detailed explanation see key on page 14 | |

**CLEANSERS & SPONGES**

| Company or Product | Abbr. | $ | ♀ | ‖ | 🖐 | ✐ | 🐇 | [⌗] | ☮ | 👪 | ALERT |
|---|---|---|---|---|---|---|---|---|---|---|---|
| Clean 'n Clear | SCJ | ✓+ | ✓ | ✓ | ✓ | ✓* | ✓ | YesIN | ✓ | ✓ | 1st to ban CFCs; on-site day care |
| Comet | PG | ✓ | ✓ | ? | ✓ | ✓⊛ | ✓ | Yes | ⦸ | ✓ | disposable diapers; Salvadoran coffee; on-site day care; C.C.A. |
| Crystalaire | RCP | ? | ? | ? | ⦸ | ? | ⦸ | YesIN | ? | ✗ | ⊕, U.K. |
| Dawn | PG | ✓ | ✓ | ? | ✓ | ✓⊛ | ✓ | Yes | ⦸ | ✓ | disposable diapers; Salvadoran coffee; on-site day care; C.C.A. |
| Daylites | ACV | ? | ? | ? | ✗ | ? | ⦸ | No | ? | ? | |
| Depend-O | RCP | ? | ? | ? | ? | ? | ⦸ | YesIN | ? | ⦸ | ⊕, U.K. |
| Dermassage | CL | ✓+ | ✓ | ? | ✓ | ✓(⊛) | ✓ | YesIN | ? | ⦸ | |
| Dow Bathroom Cleaner | DOW | ⦸ | ⦸ | ⦸ | ✓ | ✓⊛ | ⦸ | Yes | ⦸ | ⦸ | pesticide steril. suit; nuclear weapons; on-site day care; makes pesticides |
| Drano | BMY | ⦸ | ⦸ | ⦸ | ✓ | ✓⊛ | ⦸ | YesIN | ⦸ | ⦸ | infant formula; Workplace Principles; D.C.C.A |
| Duster Plus | SCJ | ✓+ | ✓ | ✓ | ✓ | ✓* | ✓ | YesIN | ✓ | ✓ | 1st to ban CFCs; on-site day care |
| Easy Reach | BMY | ⦸ | ⦸ | ⦸ | ✓ | ✓⊛ | ⦸ | YesIN | ⦸ | ⦸ | infant formula; Workplace Principles; D.C.C.A |
| Easy-Off Oven Cleaner | RCP | ? | ? | ? | ✓ | ? | ✓ | YesIN | ✗ | ⦸ | ⊕, U.K. |
| Ecco Bella* | ECC | ✓ | ✓ | ⦸⌀ | ✓ | ✓ | ✓ | No | ✓ | ⦸ | |

| Product or Company | Abbr. | | | | | | | | | | | ALERT |
|---|---|---|---|---|---|---|---|---|---|---|---|---|
| Endust | BMY | ✓ | ✓ | ✓ | ✓ | YesIN | ✓ | ✓ | ✓ | ✓ | ✓ | infant formula; Workplace Principles; D.C.C.A. |
| Ever Fresh | BN | ✓ | ✓ | ✓ | ✓ | YesIN | ✓ | ✓ | ✓ | ✓ | ✓ | |
| Fantastik | DOW | ✓ | ✓ | ✓ | ✓(*) | Yes | ✓ | ✓ | ✓ | ✓ | ✓ | pesticide steril. suit; nuclear weapons; on-site day care; makes pesticides |
| Favor | SCJ | ✓+ | ✓ | ✓ | ✓* | YesIN | ✓ | ✓ | ✓ | ✓ | ✓ | 1st to ban CFCs; on-site day care |
| Fine Wood | SCJ | ✓+ | ✓ | ✓ | ✓* | YesIN | ✓ | ✓ | ✓ | ✓ | ✓ | 1st to ban CFCs; on-site day care |
| Formby | EK | ✓ | ✗ | ✓ | ✓(*) | No | ✓ | ✓ | ✗ | ✓ | ✓ | ♣; C.C.A. |
| Formula 409 | CLX | ✓ | ✓ | ✓ | ✓* | No | ✓ | ✓ | ✓ | ✓ | ✓ | |
| Future | SCJ | ✓+ | ✓ | ✓ | ✓* | YesIN | ✓ | ✓ | ✓ | ✓ | ✓ | 1st to ban CFCs; on-site day care |
| Glade | SCJ | ✓+ | ✓ | ✓ | ✓* | YesIN | ✓ | ✓ | ✓ | ✓ | ✓ | 1st to ban CFCs; on-site day care |
| Glass Plus | DOW | ✓ | ✓ | ✓ | ✓(*) | Yes | ✓ | ✓ | ✓ | ✓ | ✓ | pesticide steril. suit; nuclear weapons; on-site day care; makes pesticides |
| Glass Wax | RCP | ? | ? | ? | ? | YesIN | ? | ✓ | ✗ | ? | ✓ | ⊕; U.K. |

| | |
|---|---|
| ✓ = Top Rating    ✓ = Middle Rating    ✗ = Bottom Rating    ? = Insufficient Information | Page 163 |
| For a more detailed explanation see key on page 14 | |

CLEANSERS & SPONGES

| Company or Product | Abbr. | $ | ♀ | | | | | | | | ALERT |
|---|---|---|---|---|---|---|---|---|---|---|---|
| Glo-Coat | SCJ | ✓+ | ✓ | ✓ | ✓ | YesIN | ✓ | ✓* | ✓ | ✓ | 1st to ban CFCs; on-site day care |
| Glory | SCJ | ✓+ | ✓ | ✓ | ✓ | YesIN | ✓ | ✓* | ✓ | ✓ | 1st to ban CFCs; on-site day care |
| Grease Relief | DOW | (✓) | (✓) | ✓ | ✓ | Yes | ✓ | ✓⊛ | ✓ | (✓) | pesticide steril. suit; nuclear weapons; on-site day care; makes pesticides |
| Handi Wipes | CL | ✓+ | ✓ | ✓ | ✓ | YesIN | ✓ | ✓⊛ | ✓ | ✓ | |
| Ivory Liquid | PG | ✓ | ✓ | ✓ | ✓ | Yes | (✓) | ✓⊛ | ✓ | ✓ | disposable diapers; Salvadoran coffee; on-site day care; C.C.A. |
| Johnson's Wax | SCJ | ✓+ | ✓ | ✓ | ✓ | YesIN | ✓ | ✓* | ✓ | ✓ | 1st to ban CFCs; on-site day care |
| Joy | PG | ✓ | ✓ | ✓ | ✓ | Yes | (✓) | ✓⊛ | ✓ | ✓ | disposable diapers; Salvadoran coffee; on-site day care; C.C.A. |
| Jubilee | SCJ | ✓+ | ✓ | ✓ | ✓ | YesIN | ✓ | ✓* | ✓ | ✓ | 1st to ban CFCs; on-site day care |
| Klean 'n Shine | SCJ | ✓+ | ✓ | ✓ | ✓ | YesIN | ✓ | ✓* | ✓ | ✓ | 1st to ban CFCs; on-site day care |
| Klear | SCJ | ✓+ | ✓ | ✓ | ✓ | YesIN | ✓ | ✓* | ✓ | ✓ | 1st to ban CFCs; on-site day care |
| Kleen Guard | ACV | ? | ✓ | ? | ✓ | No | ? | ✗ | ✓ | ? | |
| Lestoil | PG | ✓ | ✓ | ✓ | ✓ | Yes | (✓) | ✓⊛ | (✓) | ✓ | disposable diapers; Salvadoran coffee; on-site day care; C.C.A. |
| Liquid-Plumr | CLX | (✓) | ✗ | ✓ | ✓ | No | ✗ | ✓* | ✗ | ✓ | |

| Product or Company | Abbr. | $ | | | | | | | | | | ALERT |
|---|---|---|---|---|---|---|---|---|---|---|---|---|
| Love My Carpet | EK | ◐ | ✔ | ◐ | ✔⊛ | ✔ | ✔ | ✔ | No | ◐ | ✔ | 🐱; C.C.A |
| Lysoform | UN | ? | ✖ | ◐ | ✔* | ? | ✔ | ◐ | YesIN | ◐ | ? | 🌐; U.K. |
| Lysol | EK | ◐ | ✔ | ◐ | ✔⊛ | ? | ✔ | ✔ | No | ◐ | ✔ | 🐱; C.C.A |
| Magic Mushroom | RCP | ? | ? | ? | ? | ? | ◐ | ✔ | YesIN | ? | ◐ | 🌐; U.K. |
| Mirwax | EK | ◐ | ✔ | ◐ | ✔⊛ | ✔ | ✔ | ✔ | No | ◐ | ✔ | 🐱; C.C.A |
| Mop & Glow | EK | ◐ | ✔ | ◐ | ✔⊛ | ✔ | ✔ | ✔ | No | ◐ | ✔ | 🐱; C.C.A |
| Mr. Clean | PG | ✔ | ✔ | ◐ | ✔⊛ | ◐ | ✔ | ✔ | Yes | ◐ | ✔ | disposable diapers; Salvadoran coffee; on-site day care; C.C.A |
| Mr. Muscle | BMY | ◐ | ✔ | ◐ | ◐ | ◐ | ◐ | ✔ | YesIN | ◐ | ◐ | infant formula; Workplace Principles; D.C.C.A |
| Mrs. Culver's Sparklers | ACV | ? | ✔ | ✖ | ✖ | ? | ? | ? | No | ✖ | ? | |
| Noxon | RCP | ? | ? | ? | ? | ? | ◐ | ? | YesIN | ✖ | ◐ | 🌐; U.K. |
| O-Cedar | BMY | ◐ | ✔ | ◐ | ✔⊛ | ◐ | ◐ | ✔ | YesIN | ✔ | ◐ | infant formula; Workplace Principles; D.C.C.A |

| ✔ = Top Rating | ◐ = Middle Rating | ✖ = Bottom Rating | ? = Insufficient Information |
|---|---|---|---|

*For a more detailed explanation see key on page 14*

**CLEANSERS & SPONGES**

| Company or Product | Abbr. | 💲 | ♀ | ✊ | 🐇 | 👐 | 👪 | 🌐 | S.Af. | ⚖ | ♲ | ALERT |
|---|---|---|---|---|---|---|---|---|---|---|---|---|
| O-Cell-O | GIS | ✓+ | ✓ | ✓ | ✓ | ✓ | ✓ | No | ✓ | ✓ | ✓ | C.C.A. |
| Old English | RCP | ? | ? | ? | ? | ✓ | ? | YesIN | ? | ✗ | ✓ | 🌐, U.K. |
| Palmolive | CL | ✓+ | ✓ | ✓ | ✓⊛ | ✓ | ✓ | YesIN | ✓ | ✓ | ✓ | |
| Parson's | G | ? | ✓ | ? | ✓ | ✓ | ? | No | ? | ? | ? | |
| Perfex | RCP | ? | ✓ | ? | ? | ✓ | ? | YesIN | ? | ✗ | ✓ | 🌐, U.K. |
| Perk | EK | ◡ | ✗ | ✓ | ✓⊛ | ✓ | ✓ | No | ✓ | ◡ | ✓ | |
| Pine-Sol | CLX | ◡ | ✗ | ✓ | ✓* | ✓ | ✓ | No | ✓ | ✗ | ✓ | ☘, C.C.A. |
| Pledge | SCJ | ✓+ | ✓ | ✓ | ✓* | ✓ | ? | YesIN | ✓ | ✓ | ✓ | 1st to ban CFCs; on-site day care |
| Red Devil | RCP | ? | ? | ? | ? | ✓ | ? | YesIN | ? | ✗ | ✓ | 🌐, U.K. |
| Renuzit | BMY | ◡ | ✓ | ✓ | ✓⊛ | ◡ | ◡ | YesIN | ◡ | ✓ | ✓ | infant formula; Workplace Principles; D.C.C.A. |
| Resolve | EK | ◡ | ✓ | ✓ | ✓⊛ | ✓ | ✓ | No | ◡ | ✓ | ✓ | ☘, C.C.A. |
| Rug Fresh | RCP | ? | ? | ? | ? | ✓ | ? | YesIN | ? | ✗ | ◡ | 🌐, U.K. |
| S.O.S. | BAG | ? | ? | ? | ✗◯ | ✗ | ? | YesIN | ? | ✗ | ? | makes pesticides |

| Product or Company | Abbr. | $ | ♀ | ✊ | 🐇 | 👪 | (info) | ☢ | 🏭 | ALERT |
|---|---|---|---|---|---|---|---|---|---|---|
| Sani-Flush | RCP | ? | ? | ? | ? | YesIN | ? | ✘ | ◐ | 🌐; U.K. |
| Scotch-Brite | MMM | ◐ | ✔ | ✔ | ✔* | YesIN | ◐ | ✔ | ✔ | ✳ |
| Silvo | RCP | ? | ✔ | ? | ? | YesIN | ? | ✘ | ◐ | 🌐; U.K. |
| Sno Bowl | G | ? | ✔ | ◐ | ✔ | No | ✔ | ? | ? | |
| Soft Scrub | CLX | ◐ | ✘ | ✔ | ✔* | No | ✔ | ✘ | ✔ | |
| Spic & Span | PG | ✔ | ✔ | ✔ | ✔⊕ | Yes | ◐ | ✔ | ✔ | disposable diapers; Salvadoran coffee; on-site day care; C.C.A. |
| Step Saver | SCJ | ✔+ | ✔ | ✔ | ✔* | YesIN | ✔ | ✔ | ✔ | 1st to ban CFCs; on-site day care |
| Stick Ups | RCP | ? | ? | ? | ? | YesIN | ? | ✘ | ◐ | 🌐; U.K. |
| Sun Light | UN | ? | ✘ | ◐ | ✔* | YesIN | ◐ | ◐ | ? | 🌐; U.K. |
| Tackle | CLX | ◐ | ✘ | ✔ | ✔* | No | ✔ | ✘ | ✔ | |
| Tilex | CLX | ◐ | ✘ | ✔ | ✔* | No | ✔ | ✘ | ✔ | |

✔ = Top Rating  ◐ = Middle Rating  ✘ = Bottom Rating  ? = Insufficient Information

*For a more detailed explanation see key on page 14*

**CLEANSERS & SPONGES**

| Company or Product | Abbr. | 💲 | ♀+ | ⚥ | ✊ | 🐾 | 👥 | ☢ | 🏭 | ⚖ | 🏠 | ALERT |
|---|---|---|---|---|---|---|---|---|---|---|---|---|
| Top Job | PG | ✓ | ✓ | ✓ | ✓(*) | ✓ | ✓ | Yes | ✓ | ✓ | ✓ | disposable diapers; Salvadoran coffee; on-site day care; C.C.A. |
| Tough Act | DOW | ✓ | ✓ | ✓ | ✓(*) | ✓ | ✓ | Yes | ✓ | ✓ | ✓ | pesticide steril. suit; nuclear weapons; on-site day care; makes pesticides |
| Vanish | BMY | ✓ | ✓ | ✓ | ✓(*) | ✓ | ? | YesIN | ✓ | ✓ | ✓ | infant formula; Workplace Principles; D.C.C.A. |
| Windex | BMY | ✓ | ✓ | ✓ | ✓(*) | ✓ | ? | YesIN | ✓ | ✓ | ✓ | infant formula; Workplace Principles; D.C.C.A. |
| Wizard | RCP | ? | ? | ? | ? | ✓ | ? | YesIN | ? | ✗ | ✓ | 🌐; U.K. |
| Woolite | RCP | ? | ? | ? | ? | ✓ | ? | YesIN | ? | ✗ | ✓ | 🌐; U.K. |
| Zud Rust & Stain Remover | RCP | ? | ? | ? | ? | ✓ | ? | YesIN | ? | ✗ | ✓ | 🌐; U.K. |
| **COCOA & MILK MODIFIERS** | | | | | | | | | | | | |
| Alba | HNZ | ✓ | ✓ | ✓ | ✓ | ✓ | ✓ | No | ✓ | ✓ | ✓ | C.C.A |
| Hershey's | HSY | ✓ | ✓ | ? | ✓* | ✓ | ✓ | No | ✓ | ✓ | ✓ | on-site day care |
| Ovaltine | SAND | ? | ? | ? | ? | ✗ | ? | YesIN | ? | ? | ? | makes pesticides |
| Quik | NEST | ? | ✓ | ✓ | ✓* | ✓ | ✓ | YesIN | ? | ? | ? | infant formula; Salv. coffee; 🌐, D.C.C.A.; U.K. |
| Swiss Miss | CAG | ? | ✗ | ? | ? | ✗ | ✗ | No | ✗ | ? | ✗ | safe meat controversy; D.C.C.A.; factory farming |

| Product or Company | Abbr. | 💲 | ♀ | (icons →) | | | | | | | | | ALERT |
|---|---|---|---|---|---|---|---|---|---|---|---|---|---|
| Weight Watchers | HNZ | ✔ | ✔ | ✔ | ✔ | ✔ | ✔ | No | ✓ | ✔ | ✓ | | C.C.A. |
| **COFFEE** | | | | | | | | | | | | | |
| Brim | MO | ? | ✖ | ✔ | ? | ✔ | ✔ | Yes | ? | ? | ? | | cigarettes; Salvadoran coffee; Work. Princ. |
| Bustelo | ALP | ✖ | ✓ | ✔ | ✖ | ✔ | ✔ | Yes | ✓ | ✓ | ✓ | | ⊕; U.K. |
| Continental Coffee | OAT | ✔+ | ✔ | ✓ | ✔ | ✔ | ✔ | No | ✓ | ✓ | ✔ | | Fair Share |
| Eight O'Clock | GAP | ✔+ | ✔ | ✔ | ✔ | ✔ | ✔ | No | ✓ | ✓ | ✔ | | on-site day care |
| Folgers | PG | ✔ | ✔ | ✔ | ✔✱ | ✖ | ✔ | Yes | ✓ | ✔ | ✔ | | disposable diapers; Salvadoran coffee; on-site day care; C.C.A. |
| General Foods Int'l Cof | MO | ? | ✔ | ✔ | ? | ✖ | ✔ | Yes | ? | ? | ? | | cigarettes; Salvadoran coffee; Work. Princ. |
| Gevalia | MO | ? | ✔ | ✔ | ? | ✖ | ✔ | Yes | ? | ? | ? | | cigarettes; Salvadoran coffee; Work. Princ. |
| Hag | MO | ? | ✔ | ✔ | ? | ✖ | ✔ | Yes | ? | ? | ? | | cigarettes; Salvadoran coffee; Work. Princ. |
| High Point | PG | ✔ | ✔ | ✔ | ✔✱ | ✖ | ✔ | Yes | ✓ | ✔ | ✔ | | disposable diapers; Salvadoran coffee; on-site day care; C.C.A. |

✔ = Top Rating  ✓ = Middle Rating  ✖ = Bottom Rating  ? = Insufficient Information

*For a more detailed explanation see key on page 14*

Page 169

COFFEE

| Company or Product | Abbr. | # | ♀ |  |  |  |  |  |  |  |  | ALERT |
|---|---|---|---|---|---|---|---|---|---|---|---|---|
| Kava | BN | ✓ |  | ✓ | ✓ | ✓ | ✓ | YesIN | ✓ | ✓ | ✓ |  |
| Lyons | ALP | ✗ | ✓ | ✓ | ✓ | ✓ | ✓ | Yes | ✓ |  | ✓ | ⊕; U.K. |
| Martinson | ALP | ✗ | ✓ | ✓ | ✓ | ✓ | ✓ | Yes | ✓ |  | ✓ | ⊕; U.K. |
| Maryland Club/Btrnt Cof. | PG | ✓ | ✓ | ✓ | ✓ | ✓⊕ | ✓ | Yes | ✓ | ✓ | ✓ | disposable diapers; Salvadoran coffee; on-site day care; C.C.A. |
| Master Blend | MO | ? | ✓ | ✓ | ? | ✓ | ✗ | Yes | ? | ? | ✓ | cigarettes; Salvadoran coffee; Work. Princ. |
| Maxim | MO | ? | ✓ | ✓ | ? | ✓ | ✗ | Yes | ? | ? | ✓ | cigarettes; Salvadoran coffee; Work. Princ. |
| Maxwell House | MO | ? | ✓ | ✓ | ? | ✓ | ✗ | Yes | ? | ? | ✓ | cigarettes; Salvadoran coffee; Work. Princ. |
| Medaglia D'Oro | ALP | ✗ | ✓ | ✓ | ✓ | ✓ | ✓ | Yes | ✓ | ✓ | ✓ |  |
| Melitta | MTA | ? | ? | ✓ | ? | ✓ | ✓ | No | ✓ | ✓ | ✓ |  |
| Nescafe | NEST | ? | ? | ✓ | ✓* | ? | ✓ | YesIN | ✓ | ? | ? | infant formula; Salv. coffee; ⊕, D.C.C.A.; U.K. |
| Postum | MO | ? | ✓ | ✓ | ? | ✓ | ✗ | Yes | ? | ? | ✓ | cigarettes; Salvadoran coffee; Work. Princ. |
| Sanka | MO | ? | ✓ | ? | ? | ✓ | ✗ | Yes | ? | ? | ✓ | cigarettes; Salvadoran coffee; Work. Princ. |
| Savarin | ALP | ✗ | ✓ | ✓ | ✓ | ✓ | ✓ | Yes | ✓ | ✓ | ✓ | ⊕; U.K. |

| Product or Company | Abbr. | $ | ♀ | | | | | | | | ALERT |
|---|---|---|---|---|---|---|---|---|---|---|---|
| Taster's Choice | NEST | ? | ✓ | ? | ✓* | ✓ | YesIN | ✓ | ? | ? | infant formula; Salv. coffee; ⊕ D.C.C.A.; U.K. |
| Yuban | MO | ? | ✓ | ✗ | ? | ? | Yes | ? | ? | ? | cigarettes; Salvadoran coffee; Work. Princ. |

## COLD & COUGH REMEDIES

| Product or Company | Abbr. | $ | ♀ | | | | | | | | ALERT |
|---|---|---|---|---|---|---|---|---|---|---|---|
| 4-Way Nasal Spray | BMY | ✓ | ✓ | ✓ | ✓⊛ | ✓ | YesIN | ✓ | ✓ | ✓ | infant formula; Workplace Principles; D.C.C.A. |
| Afrin | SGP | ✓ | ✓ | ✓ | ✓⊛ | ✓ | YesIN | ✓ | ✓ | ✓ | on-site day care; Workplace Principles |
| Benylin | WLA | ✓ | ✓ | ✓ | ✗○ | ✓ | YesIN✓∅ | ✓ | ? | ✓ | on-site day care; Workplace Principles |
| Chloraseptic | PG | ✓ | ✓ | ✓ | ✓⊛ | ✓ | Yes | ✓ | ✓ | ✓ | disposable diapers; Salvadoran coffee; on-site day care; C.C.A. |
| Comtrex | BMY | ✓ | ✓ | ✓ | ✓⊛ | ✓ | YesIN | ✓ | ✓ | ✓ | infant formula; Workplace Principles; D.C.C.A. |
| Congestac | BECH | ✗ | ✓ | ✓ | ✗○ | ✓ | YesIN✓∅ | ✓ | ✓ | ✓ | ⊕; Work. Princ.; on-site day care; U.K. |
| Coricidin | SGP | ✓ | ✓ | ✓ | ✓⊛ | ✓ | YesIN | ✓ | ✓ | ✓ | on-site day care; Workplace Principles |
| Dorcol | SAND | ? | ? | ? | ? | ✗ | YesIN | ? | ? | ? | makes pesticides |

✓ = Top Rating   ✓ = Middle Rating   ✗ = Bottom Rating   ? = Insufficient Information

*For a more detailed explanation see key on page 14*

Page 171

COLD & COUGH REMEDIES

| Company or Product | Abbr. | $ | ⚥ | | | | | | | | | ALERT |
|---|---|---|---|---|---|---|---|---|---|---|---|---|
| Dristan | AHP | ✗ | ✓ | ✓ | ✓ | ✓(*) | ✓ | Yes | ✓ | ✓ | | infant formula |
| Drixoral | SGP | ✓ | ✔ | ✓ | ✔ | ✔(*) | ✔ | YesIN | ✓ | ✓ | | on-site day care; Workplace Principles |
| Duration | SGP | ✓ | ✔ | ✓ | ✔ | ✔(*) | ✔ | YesIN | ✓ | ✓ | | on-site day care; Workplace Principles |
| Formula 44 | PG | ✔ | ✔ | ✓ | ✔ | ✔(*) | ✔ | Yes | ✔ | ✔ | | disposable diapers; Salvadoran coffee; on-site day care; C.C.A. |
| Halls | WLA | ✔ | ✓ | ✗ | ✗ | ○ | ✓ | YesIN | ? | ✓ | | on-site day care; Workplace Principles |
| Hold | BECH | ✗ | ✓ | ✗ | ✗ | ○ | ✔ | YesIN | ✓∅ | ✔ | | 🌐, Work. Princ.; on-site day care; U.K. |
| Luden's | HSY | ✓ | ✔ | ✔ | ✔ | ✔* | ✔ | No | ✔ | ✓ | | on-site day care |
| N'ICE | BECH | ✗ | ✓ | ✔ | ✗ | ○ | ✔ | YesIN | ✓∅ | ✔ | | 🌐, Work. Princ.; on-site day care; U.K. |
| Nyquil | PG | ✔ | ✔ | ✔ | ✔ | ✔(*) | ✔ | Yes | ✔ | ✔ | | disposable diapers; Salvadoran coffee; on-site day care; C.C.A. |
| Resolve | DOW | ✓ | ✔ | ✓ | ✔ | ✔(*) | ✔ | Yes | ✓ | ✓ | | pesticide steril. suit; nuclear weapons; on-site day care; makes pesticides |
| Sinex | PG | ✔ | ✔ | ✔ | ✔ | ✔(*) | ✔ | Yes | ✔ | ✔ | | disposable diapers; Salvadoran coffee; on-site day care; C.C.A. |
| St. Joseph's | SGP | ✓ | ✔ | ✓ | ✔ | ✔(*) | ✓ | YesIN | ✓ | ✓ | | on-site day care; Workplace Principles |
| Sucrets | BECH | ✗ | ✓ | ✔ | ✗ | ○ | ✔ | YesIN | ✓∅ | ✔ | | 🌐, Work. Princ.; on-site day care; U.K. |

| Product or Company | Abbr. | $ | | | | | | | | | | ALERT |
|---|---|---|---|---|---|---|---|---|---|---|---|---|
| Theraflu | SAND | ? | ? | ? | ? | ✖ | ? | YesIN | ✓ | ? | ? | makes pesticides |
| Triaminic Syrup | SAND | ? | ? | ? | ? | ✖ | ? | YesIN | ✓ | ? | ? | makes pesticides |
| Triaminicol | SAND | ? | ? | ? | ? | ✖ | ? | YesIN | ✓ | ? | ? | makes pesticides |
| Ursinus | SAND | ? | ? | ? | ? | ✖ | ? | YesIN | ✓ | ? | ? | makes pesticides |
| Vicks Throat Drops | PG | ✓ | ✓ | ✓ | ✓⊛ | ✓ | ✓ | Yes | ✓ | ✓ | ✓ | disposable diapers; Salvadoran coffee; on-site day care; C.C.A. |
| Vicks Vaporub | PG | ✓ | ✓ | ✓ | ✓⊛ | ✓ | ✓ | Yes | ✓ | ✓ | ✓ | disposable diapers; Salvadoran coffee; on-site day care; C.C.A. |
| **CONDIMENTS** | | | | | | | | | | | | |
| Bama | BN | ✓ | ✓ | ✓ | ✓ | ✓ | ✓ | YesIN | ✓ | ✓ | ✓ | |
| Best Foods | CPC | ✓+ | ✓ | ✓ | ✓ | ✓ | ✓ | No | ✓ | ✓ | ✓ | |
| Diablo | AHP | ✖ | ✓ | ✓ | ✓⊛ | ✓ | ✓ | Yes | ✓ | ✓ | ✓ | infant formula |
| Eden# | EDEN | ✓+ | ✓ | ✓ | ✓ | ✓ | ✓ | No | ✓ | ✓ | ✓ | some organic ingredients |

✓ = Top Rating    ✖ = Bottom Rating    ? = Insufficient Information

✓ = Middle Rating

*For a more detailed explanation see key on page 14*

Page 173

**CONDIMENTS**

| Company or Product | Abbr. | 💲 | ♀ | | | 🐇 | | | Yes/No | ⚛ | ▦ | ALERT |
|---|---|---|---|---|---|---|---|---|---|---|---|---|
| French's | RCP | ? | ? | ? | ? | ? | ✓ | ? | YesN | ? | ✓ | ⊕, U.K. |
| Grey Poupon | RJR | ? | ✓ | ? | ? | ✗ | ✓ | ? | Yes | ✗ | ? | cigarettes; D.C.C.A. |
| Gulden's Mustard | AHP | ✗ | ✓ | ✓ | ? | ✓(®) | ✓ | ✓ | Yes | ✓ | ✓ | infant formula |
| Hain | PET | ? | ? | ? | ? | ✗ | ? | ? | No | ? | ? | |
| Health Valley# | HVAL | ? | ? | ? | ✓ | ✗ | ? | ? | No | ? | ? | some organic ingredients |
| Heinz | HNZ | ✓ | ✓ | ✓ | ✓ | ✓ | ✓ | ? | No | ✓ | ✓ | |
| Hellmann's | CPC | ✓+ | ? | ✓ | ✓ | ✗ | ✓ | ? | No | ✓ | ✓ | C.C.A. |
| Hunt's | CAG | ? | ✗ | ? | ? | ✗ | ? | ? | No | ? | ✗ | safe meat controversy; D.C.C.A.; factory farming |
| Kraft | MO | ? | ✓ | ? | ? | ✗ | ? | ? | Yes | ? | ? | cigarettes; Salvadoran coffee; Work. Princ. |
| Mi Secrito | PET | ? | ? | ? | ? | ✗ | ? | ? | No | ? | ? | |
| Miracle Whip | MO | ? | ✓ | ? | ? | ✗ | ? | ? | Yes | ? | ? | cigarettes; Salvadoran coffee; Work. Princ. |
| Regina | RJR | ? | ✓ | ? | ? | ✓ | ? | ? | Yes | ✗ | ? | cigarettes; D.C.C.A. |
| Spicy Brown | AHP | ✗ | ✓ | ✓ | ? | ✓(®) | ✓ | ✓ | Yes | ✓ | ✓ | infant formula |

| Product or Company | Abbr. | $ | ♀ | | | | | | | | ALERT |
|---|---|---|---|---|---|---|---|---|---|---|---|
| Whole Earth# | WHO | ✔+ | ✔ | ✔ | ✔ | ✔ | No | ? | ✔ | | 1% For Peace; some organic ingredients |
| **COOKIES** | | | | | | | | | | | |
| 21st Century Foods* | TFC | ✖ | ✔ | ✔ | ✔ | ✔ | No | ? | ✔ | | on-site day care |
| Almost Home | RJR | ? | ✔ | ? | ? | ✖ | Yes | ? | ? | | cigarettes;D.C.C.A |
| Barnum's Animals | RJR | ? | ✔ | ? | ? | ✖ | Yes | ? | ? | | cigarettes;D.C.C.A |
| Chip-A-Roos | RJR | ? | ✔ | ? | ? | ✖ | Yes | ? | ? | | cigarettes;D.C.C.A |
| Chips Ahoy | RJR | ? | ✔ | ? | ? | ✖ | Yes | ? | ? | | cigarettes;D.C.C.A |
| Deluxe Grahams | UBH | ✔ | ✔ | ✔ | ✔ | ✖ | No | ? | ? | | ⊕,U.K. |
| Fig Newtons | RJR | ? | ✔ | ? | ? | ✖ | Yes | ? | ? | | cigarettes;D.C.C.A |
| Fudge Stripes | UBH | ✔ | ✔ | ✔ | ✔ | ✖ | No | ? | ? | | ⊕,U.K. |
| Giggles | RJR | ? | ✔ | ? | ? | ✖ | Yes | ? | ? | | cigarettes;D.C.C.A |

✔ = Top Rating    ✓ = Middle Rating    ✖ = Bottom Rating    ? = Insufficient Information

*For a more detailed explanation see key on page 14*

COOKIES

# COOKIES

| Company or Product | Abbr. | $ | | | | | | | | | ALERT |
|---|---|---|---|---|---|---|---|---|---|---|---|
| Grandma's | PEP | ✓ | ✓ | ✓ | ✓ | ? | ✓ | Yes | ✓ | ✓ | |
| Health Valley# | HVAL | ? | ? | ? | ✗ | ? | ? | No | ? | ? | some organic ingredients |
| Keebler Soft Batch | UBH | ✓ | ✗ | ✓ | ✗ | ✓ | ✓ | No | ? | ? | 🌐, U.K. |
| Lorna Doone | RJR | ? | ✓ | ✗ | ? | ✗ | ✓ | Yes | ? | ? | cigarettes; D.C.C.A. |
| Mallomars | RJR | ? | ✓ | ✗ | ? | ✗ | ✓ | Yes | ✗ | ? | cigarettes; D.C.C.A. |
| McVitie's | UBH | ✓ | ✗ | ✗ | ✓ | ✗ | ✓ | No | ? | ? | 🌐, U.K. |
| Newtons | RJR | ? | ✓ | ? | ? | ✗ | ✓ | Yes | ✗ | ? | cigarettes; D.C.C.A. |
| Nilla | RJR | ? | ✓ | ? | ? | ✗ | ✓ | Yes | ✗ | ? | cigarettes; D.C.C.A. |
| Nutter Butter | RJR | ? | ✓ | ? | ? | ✗ | ✓ | Yes | ✗ | ? | cigarettes; D.C.C.A. |
| Oreos | RJR | ? | ✓ | ? | ? | ✗ | ✓ | Yes | ✗ | ? | cigarettes; D.C.C.A. |
| Pepperidge Farm | CPB | ✓ | ✓ | ✓ | ✓ | ✓ | ✓ | No | ✓ | ✓ | on-site day care |
| Teddy Grahams | RJR | ? | ? | ? | ? | ✗ | ✓ | Yes | ✗ | ? | cigarettes; D.C.C.A. |

# COSMETICS & SKIN CARE AIDS

| Product or Company | Abbr. | $ | ♀ | ⚛ | | | | | | | | ALERT |
|---|---|---|---|---|---|---|---|---|---|---|---|---|
| **COSMETICS & SKIN CARE AIDS** | | | | | | | | | | | | |
| Acid Mantle Cream | SAND | ? | ? | ? | ? | ✗ | ? | YesIN | ✓ | ? | ? | makes pesticides |
| Acnomel | BECH | ✗ | ✓ | ✗○ | ✓ | ✓ | ✓ | YesIN | ✓∅ | ✓ | ✓ | ⊕; Work. Princ.; on-site day care; U.K. |
| Acrasil | ACV | ? | ✓ | ? | ✗ | ✗ | ? | No | ? | ✗ | ? | |
| Air Spun | PFE | ✓ | ✗ | ? | ? | ✗ | ✓ | YesIN | ✗ | ? | ? | heart valve suits |
| Alexandra Avery* | ALEX | ✓+ | ✓ | ✓∅ | ✓ | ✓ | ✓ | No | ✓ | ✓ | ✓ | |
| Allercreme | IRDV | ? | ✗ | ? | ✗○ | ✗ | ? | No | ? | ✓ | ? | |
| Almay | REVL | ? | ? | ✓ | ✓ | ✗ | ? | YesIN | ✓ | ? | ✓ | |
| Anbesol | AHP | ✗ | ✓ | ✓(*) | ✓ | ✓ | ✓ | Yes | ✓ | ✓ | ✓ | infant formula |
| Aqua Care | BECH | ✗ | ✓ | ✗○ | ✓ | ✓ | ✓ | YesIN | ✓∅ | ✓ | ✓ | ⊕; Work. Princ.; on-site day care; U.K. |
| Aroma Lotion* | BLN | ✓ | ✓ | ✓ | ✓ | ✓ | ✓ | No | ✓ | ✓ | ✓ | some organic ingredients |

✓ = Top Rating    ✓ = Middle Rating    ✗ = Bottom Rating    ? = Insufficient Information

*For a more detailed explanation see key on page 14*

COSMETICS & SKIN CARE AIDS

| Company or Product | Abbr. | $ | ♀+ | | | | | | Yes/No | | | | ALERT |
|---|---|---|---|---|---|---|---|---|---|---|---|---|---|
| Aroma Vera# | AV | ✘ | ✔ | ✔ | ✔ | ✔ | ✔ | ✘ | No | ✔ | ◐ | ✘ | |
| Autumn Harp* | AUT | ✔+ | ◐ | ✔∅ | ✔ | ✔ | ✔ | ✔ | No | ✔ | ✘ | ✔ | Valdez Principles; ACT NOW |
| Aveda# | AVED | ✔ | ◐ | ✔ | ✔ | ✔ | ◐ | ✔ | No | ✔ | ✔ | ✔ | |
| Aveeno | SCJ | ✔+ | ✔ | ✔ | ✔* | ✔ | ✔ | ✔ | YesIN | ✔ | ✘ | ✔ | 1st to ban CFCs; on-site day care |
| Avocado Oils# | ORJ | ✔+ | ✔ | ✔ | ✔ | ✔ | ✔ | ✘ | No | ◐ | ◐ | ? | |
| Avon | AVP | ✔+ | ✔ | ✔ | ✔ | ✔ | ◐ | ◐ | No | ◐ | ✔ | ✔ | on-site day care; C.C.A. |
| Bain de Soleil | PG | ✔ | ✔ | ✔ | ✔(*) | ✔ | ✔ | ◐ | Yes | ◐ | ✔ | ✔ | disposable diapers; Salvadoran coffee; on-site day care; C.C.A. |
| Beyond | ACV | ? | ? | ? | ✘ | ◐ | ? | ? | No | ? | ✘ | ? | |
| Bicozene | SAND | ? | ? | ? | ? | ✘ | ? | ? | YesIN | ◐ | ? | ? | makes pesticides |
| Bill Blass | REVL | ? | ? | ? | ✔ | ✘ | ? | ? | YesIN | ◐ | ? | ? | |
| Biotherm | LORA | ? | ? | ✔ | ✔* | ✔ | ? | ? | Yes | ? | ? | ? | |
| Block-Out | CAR | ? | ✘ | ✔ | ✘◯ | ✔ | ◐ | ? | No | ◐ | ✘ | ? | |
| Body Shop, The | BS | ◐ | ? | ✔ | ✔ | ✔ | ✔ | ✔ | No | ✔ | ? | ? | ACT NOW; U.K. |

| Product or Company | Abbr. | 💲 | ♀ | ⛏ | 🐇 | 🕊 | 🏠 | | 🌍 | ⚕ | ALERT |
|---|---|---|---|---|---|---|---|---|---|---|---|
| Carme | IRDV | ? | ✗ | ? | ✗○ | ✗ | ? | No | ? | ? | |
| Chicogo | UN | ? | ✗ | ? | ✓* | ✓ | ✓ | YesIN | ✓ | ? | 🌐; U.K. |
| Clarion Cosmetics | PG | ✓ | ✓ | ✓ | ✓⊛ | ✓ | ✓ | Yes | ✓ | ✓ | disposable diapers; Salvadoran coffee; on-site day care; C.C.A. |
| Clear Skin II | AVP | ✓+ | ✓ | ✓ | ✓ | ✓ | ✓ | No | ✓ | ✓ | on-site day care; C.C.A. |
| Clearasil | PG | ✓ | ✓ | ✓ | ✓⊛ | ✓ | ✓ | Yes | ✓ | ✓ | disposable diapers; Salvadoran coffee; on-site day care; C.C.A. |
| Clientele# | CTL | ✓+ | ✓ | ✓ | ✓ | ✓ | ✓ | No | ✓∅ | ✓ | |
| Complex 15 | SGP | ✓ | ✓ | ✓ | ✓⊛ | ✓ | ✓ | YesIN | ✓ | ✓ | on-site day care; Workplace Principles |
| Compound W | AHP | ✗ | ✓ | ✓ | ✓⊛ | ✓ | ✓ | Yes | ✓ | ✓ | infant formula |
| Coppertone | SGP | ✓ | ✓ | ✓ | ✓⊛ | ✓ | ✓ | YesIN | ✓ | ✓ | on-site day care; Workplace Principles |
| Coty '24' Lipsticks | PFE | ✓ | ✗ | ? | ? | ✗ | ✓ | YesIN | ? | ? | heart valve suits |
| Country Roads | IRDV | ? | ✗ | ? | ✗○ | ✗ | ? | No | ? | ? | |

✓ = Top Rating    ✓ = Middle Rating    ✗ = Bottom Rating    ? = Insufficient Information

*For a more detailed explanation see key on page 14*

**COSMETICS & SKIN CARE AIDS**

# COSMETICS & SKIN CARE AIDS

| Company or Product | Abbr. | 💲 | ♀ | ✦ | 🐰 | ✦ | (Yes/No) | ✦ | ✦ | 🕊 | 🏢 | ALERT |
|---|---|---|---|---|---|---|---|---|---|---|---|---|
| Cover Girl Cosmetics | PG | ✓ | ✓ | ✓ | ✓/®(*) | ✓ | Yes | ✓ | ✓ | ✓ | ✓ | disposable diapers; Salvadoran coffee; on-site day care; C.C.A. |
| Curel | SCJ | ✓+ | ✓ | ✓ | ✓* | ✓ | YesIN | ✓ | ✓ | ✓ | ✓ | 1st to ban CFCs; on-site day care |
| Cutex | UN | ? | ✗ | ✓ | ✓* | ✓ | YesIN | ✓ | ? | ✓ | ? | 🌐; U.K. |
| Cuticura | DEPC | ? | ✓ | ✓ | ✓ | ✓ | No | ? | ✓ | ✓ | ✓ | |
| Daily Revival | AVP | ✓+ | ✓ | ✓ | ✓ | ✓ | No | ✓ | ✓ | ✓ | ✓ | on-site day care; C.C.A. |
| Derma Fresh | ACV | ? | ✓ | ? | ✗ | ? | No | ? | ✗ | ? | ✗ | |
| Desitin | PFE | ✓ | ✗ | ? | ? | ✗ | YesIN | ✓ | ? | ? | ? | heart valve suits |
| DiRinse Cold Cream | PG | ✓ | ✓ | ✓ | ✓/® | ✓ | Yes | ✓ | ✓ | ✓ | ✓ | disposable diapers; Salvadoran coffee; on-site day care; C.C.A. |
| Dr. Scholl | SGP | ✓ | ✓ | ✓ | ✓/® | ✓ | YesIN | ✓ | ✓ | ✓ | ✓ | on-site day care; Workplace Principles |
| Dream Glo | KAO | | | ✓ | | | | | | | ✓ | see page 344 for Japanese companies |
| Dry & Clear | AHP | ✗ | ✓ | ✓ | ✓/® | ✓ | Yes | ✓ | ✓ | ✓ | ✓ | infant formula |
| DuBarry | IRDV | ? | ✗ | ? | ✗/○ | ✗ | No | ? | ? | ? | ? | |
| Ecco Bella* | ECC | ✓ | ✓ | ✓/○ | ✓ | ✓ | No | ✓ | ✓ | ✓ | ✓ | |

| Product or Company | Abbr. | 💲 | ♀ | 🐾 | 🐇 | ✋ | (rating) | ⭐ | ⌖ | ALERT |
|---|---|---|---|---|---|---|---|---|---|---|
| Elizabeth Arden | UN | ? | ✘ | ✓ | ✔* | ✓ | YesIN | ✓ | ? | 🌐, U.K. |
| Eversoft | KAO | | | | | | | | | see page 344 for Japanese companies |
| Fisher-Price | SCJ | ✔+ | ✔ | ✔ | ✔* | ✔ | YesIN | ✔ | ✔ | 1st to ban CFCs; on-site day care |
| Fostex | BMY | ✓ | ✔ | ? | ✔⊛ | ✔ | YesIN | ✔ | ✓ | infant formula; Workplace Principles; D.C.C.A. |
| Halston | REVL | ? | ? | ✔ | ✔ | ? | YesIN | ? | ? | |
| Ida Grae* | IDA | ? | ✔ | ✔ | ✔ | ✔ | No | ✔ | ? | |
| Jafra | GS | ✓ | ✔ | ✔⊛ | ✔ | ✔ | YesIN | ✓ | ✔ | |
| Jason Natural# | JNP | ? | ✓ | ✘ | ✔ | ✔ | No | ✓⊘ | ✘ | |
| Jergens | KAO | | | | | | | | | see page 344 for Japanese companies |
| Johnson's Swabs | JNJ | ✔ | ✔ | ✔⊛ | ✔ | ✔ | YesIN | ✔ | ✔ | on-site day care; Workplace Principles |
| Juniper Tonic Masge Oil* | BLN | ✔ | ✔ | ✔ | ✔ | ✔ | No | ✔ | ✓ | some organic ingredients |

✔ = Top Rating   ✓ = Middle Rating   ✘ = Bottom Rating   ? = Insufficient Information

*For a more detailed explanation see key on page 14*

**COSMETICS& SKIN CARE AIDS**

Page 181

# COSMETICS & SKIN CARE AIDS

| Company or Product | Abbr. | $ | ♀ | ⚥ | ◻ | ◻ | ◻ | ◻ | No/Yes | ◻ | ? | ALERT |
|---|---|---|---|---|---|---|---|---|---|---|---|---|
| Kangaroo* | DES | ? | | | ? | ✓ | ✗ | ✓ | No | ✓∅ | ? | ? | 1% For Peace |
| Kao | KAO | | | | | | | | | | | | see page 344 for Japanese companies |
| Keri Lotion | BMY | ✓ | ✓ | ✓ | ✓⊛ | ✓ | ✓ | ✓ | YesIN | ✓ | ✓ | ✓ | infant formula; Workplace Principles; D.C.C.A. |
| Kiss My Face# | KMF | ? | ✓ | ✓ | ✓ | ✓ | ? | ✓ | No | ✓ | ✓ | ? | |
| L'Oreal | LORA | ? | ✓ | ✓ | ✓* | ✓ | ? | ✓ | Yes | ? | ? | ? | |
| Lancome | LORA | ? | ✓ | ✓ | ✓* | ✓ | ? | ✓ | Yes | ? | ? | ? | |
| Lip Sense* | AUT | ✓+ | ✓∅ | ✓ | ✓ | ✓ | ✓ | ✓ | No | ✓ | ✓ | ✓ | |
| Lip Trip* | MOUN | ? | ? | ? | ✓ | ✓ | ? | ? | No | ? | ? | ? | |
| Lubriderm | WLA | ✓ | ✓ | ✓ | ✗○ | ✓ | ✓ | ✓ | YesIN | ✓ | ✓∅ | ✓ | on-site day care; Workplace Principles |
| Mandarin Magic# | AUB | ? | ✓ | ? | ✓ | ✓ | ✓ | ✓ | No | ? | ? | ? | some organic ingredients |
| Max Factor | PG | ✓ | ✓ | ✓ | ✓⊛ | ✓ | ✓ | ✓ | Yes | ✓ | ✓ | ✓ | disposable diapers; Salvadoran coffee; on-site day care; C.C.A. |
| MoistureWear | PG | ✓ | ✓ | ✓ | ✓⊛ | ✓ | ✓ | ✓ | Yes | ✓ | ✓ | ✓ | disposable diapers; Salvadoran coffee; on-site day care; C.C.A. |
| Moisturel | BMY | ✓ | ✓ | ✓ | ✓⊛ | ✓ | ✓ | ✓ | YesIN | ✓ | ✓ | ✓ | infant formula; Workplace Principles; D.C.C.A. |

| Product or Company | Abbr. | $ | ♀ | | | | | | | | | | ALERT |
|---|---|---|---|---|---|---|---|---|---|---|---|---|---|
| Natural Lips# | AUB | ? | ✔ | ✔ | ✔ | ✔ | ✔ | ? | No | ✔ | ? | ✔ | some organic ingredients |
| Nature's Family | DEPC | ? | ✔ | ◐ | ◐ | ◐ | ✔ | ? | No | ? | ? | ◐ | |
| Neutrogena | NGNA | ? | ◐ | ? | ? | ? | ? | ◐∅ | No | ✖ | ? | ? | |
| Noxzema | PG | ✔ | ✔ | ✔ | ✔◉ | ✔ | ✔ | ◐ | Yes | ◐ | ✔ | ✔ | disposable diapers; Salvadoran coffee; on-site day care; C.C.A. |
| Oil of Olay | PG | ✔ | ✔ | ✔ | ✔◉ | ✔ | ✔ | ◐ | Yes | ◐ | ✔ | ✔ | disposable diapers; Salvadoran coffee; on-site day care; C.C.A. |
| Old Spice | PG | ✔ | ✔ | ✔ | ✔◉ | ✔ | ✔ | ◐ | Yes | ✔ | ✔ | ✔ | disposable diapers; Salvadoran coffee; on-site day care; C.C.A. |
| Orjene Nat. Cosmetics# | ORJ | ✔+ | ✔ | ✔ | ✔ | ✖ | ✔ | ◐ | No | ✔ | ✔ | ? | |
| PHiso-Derm | EK | ◐ | ✔ | ✔ | ✔◉ | ✔ | ✔ | ◐ | No | ◐ | ✔ | ◐ | ♣ C.C.A. |
| Paul Penders* | PP | ✔+ | ✔ | ◐∅ | ✔ | ✔ | ✔ | ◐ | No | ✔ | ✔ | ◐ | 1% For Peace |
| Pond's | UN | ? | ✖ | ◐ | ✔* | ◐ | ✔ | ◐ | YesIN | ◐ | ◐ | ? | ⊕, U.K. |
| Porcelana | DEPC | ? | ◐ | ◐ | ◐ | ◐ | ◐ | ? | No | ? | ◐ | ◐ | |

✔ = Top Rating   ◐ = Middle Rating   ✖ = Bottom Rating   ? = Insufficient Information

*For a more detailed explanation see key on page 14*

**COSMETICS & SKIN CARE AIDS**

| Company or Product | Abbr. | $ | | | | | | YesIN | | | | ALERT |
|---|---|---|---|---|---|---|---|---|---|---|---|---|
| PreSun | BMY | ✓ | ✓ | ✓ | ✓⊛ | ✓ | ✓ | YesIN | ✓ | ✓ | ✓ | infant formula; Workplace Principles; D.C.C.A. |
| Q-Tips | UN | ? | ✗ | ✓ | ✓* | ✗ | ✓ | YesIN | ✓ | ✓ | ? | ⊕, U.K. |
| Rachel Perry# | RP | ✓+ | ✗ | ✓ | ✓ | ✗ | ✗ | No | ✗ | ✗ | ✓ | |
| Rain Tree | PG | ✓ | ✓ | ✓ | ✓⊛ | ✓ | ✓ | Yes | ✓ | ✓ | ✓ | disposable diapers; Salvadoran coffee; on-site day care; C.C.A. |
| Revlon | REVL | ? | ? | ✓ | ✓ | ? | ✓ | YesIN | ✓ | ? | ? | |
| Rhuli | SCJ | ✓+ | ✓ | ✓ | ✓* | ✓ | ✓ | YesIN | ✓ | ✓ | ✓ | 1st to ban CFCs; on-site day care |
| Rimmel | UN | ? | ✗ | ✓ | ✓* | ✓ | ✓ | YesIN | ✓ | ✓ | ? | ⊕, U.K. |
| Roux | REVL | ? | ? | ✓ | ✓ | ? | ✗ | YesIN | ✓ | ? | ? | |
| Sea & Ski | CAR | ? | ✗ | ✓ | ✗◯ | ? | ✗ | No | ? | ✗ | ? | |
| Sea Breeze | BMY | ✓ | ✓ | ✓ | ✓⊛ | ✓ | ✓ | YesIN | ✓ | ✓ | ✓ | infant formula; Workplace Principles; D.C.C.A. |
| Shade | SGP | ✓ | ✓ | ✓ | ✓⊛ | ✓ | ✓ | YesIN | ✓ | ✓ | ✓ | on-site day care; Workplace Principles |
| Shiseido | SHI | | | | | | | | | | | see page 344 for Japanese companies |
| Skin Trip* | MOUN | ? | ? | ✓ | ✗ | ? | ✗ | No | ? | ? | ? | |

| Product or Company | Abbr. | 💲 | ♀ | | | | | | | | | ALERT |
|---|---|---|---|---|---|---|---|---|---|---|---|---|
| Skin-So-Soft | AVP | ✔+ | ✔ | ✔ | ✔ | ✔ | No | ✓ | ✔ | ✔ | ✔ | on-site day care; C.C.A. |
| Soft Sense | SCJ | ✔+ | ✔ | ✔ | ✔* | ✔ | YesIN | ✔ | ✔ | ? | ✔ | 1st to ban CFCs; on-site day care |
| Solgar Company# | SLGR | ? | ? | ? | ? | ? | No | ✓∅ | ✔ | ? | ? | |
| Stri-Dex | EK | ✓ | ✔ | ✔ | ✔(®) | ✔ | No | ✓ | ✔ | ✓ | ✔ | ♻, C.C.A. |
| Sun Seekers | AVP | ✔+ | ✔ | ✔ | ✔ | ✔ | No | ✓ | ✔ | ✔ | ✔ | on-site day care; C.C.A. |
| Sundown | JNJ | ✔ | ✔ | ✔ | ✔(®) | ✔ | YesIN | ✔ | ✔ | ✔ | ✔ | on-site day care; Workplace Principles |
| Tropical Blend | SGP | ✓ | ✔ | ✓∅ | ✔(®) | ✔ | YesIN | ✓ | ✔ | ✓ | ✓ | on-site day care; Workplace Principles |
| Ultra Care* | AUT | ✔+ | ✔ | ✓ | ✔* | ✔ | No | ✔ | ✔ | ✔ | ✔ | |
| Vaseline | UN | ? | ✗ | ✓ | ✔* | ✔ | YesIN | ✓ | ✓ | ? | ? | ⊕ U.K. |
| Vit-A-Skin Cream# | ORJ | ✔+ | ✔ | ✔ | ✔ | ✗ | No | ✔ | ✔ | ? | ✔ | |
| Water Babies | SGP | ✓ | ✔ | ✔ | ✔(®) | ✔ | YesIN | ✓ | ✔ | ✓ | ✓ | on-site day care; Workplace Principles |

✔ = Top Rating    ✓ = Middle Rating    ✗ = Bottom Rating    ? = Insufficient Information

*For a more detailed explanation see key on page 14*

**COSMETICS & SKIN CARE AIDS**

Page 185

| Company or Product | Abbr. | $ | ♀ | (minorities) | (icon) | (animal) | (icon) | (Yes/No) | (icon) | (iiii) | ALERT |
|---|---|---|---|---|---|---|---|---|---|---|---|
| Wondra | PG | ✔ | ✔ | ✔ | ✔⊛ | ✔ | ✔ | Yes | ✔ | ✔ | disposable diapers; Salvadoran coffee; on-site day care; C.C.A. |
| Youth Garde | AHP | ✖ | ✔ | ✔ | ✔⊛ | ✔ | ✔ | Yes | ✔ | ✔ | infant formula |
| ZINKA | SGP | ✔ | ✔ | ✔ | ✔⊛ | ✔ | ✔ | YesIN | ✔ | ✔ | on-site day care; Workplace Principles |
| **CRACKERS** | | | | | | | | | | | |
| Barbara's Bakery# | BARB | ✔+ | ✔ | ✔ | ✔ | ✔ | ✔ | No | ✔ | ✔ | some organic ingredients |
| Better Cheddars | RJR | ? | ✔ | ? | ✖ | ✖ | ✔ | Yes | ? | ? | cigarettes; D.C.C.A. |
| Carr's | UBH | ✔ | ✔ | ? | ✔ | ✔ | ✔ | No | ? | ? | 🌐, U.K. |
| Cheese Nips | RJR | ? | ✔ | ? | ✖ | ✖ | ✔ | Yes | ? | ? | cigarettes; D.C.C.A. |
| Chibs | UBH | ✔ | ✔ | ✖ | ✖ | ✔ | ✔ | No | ? | ✔ | 🌐, U.K. |
| Chico-San | HNZ | ✔ | ✔ | ✔ | ✔ | ✔ | ✔ | No | ✔ | ✔ | C.C.A. |
| Classic | RJR | ? | ✔ | ? | ✔ | ✖ | ✔ | Yes | ✔ | ? | cigarettes; D.C.C.A. |
| Flowers | FLO | ? | ✔ | ? | ? | ✖ | ? | No | ? | ? | |
| Gold Label | BUD | ✔+ | ✔ | ✔ | ✔ | ✔ | ✔ | No | ✔ | ✔ | |

| Product or Company | Abbr. | 💲 | ♀ | 🖐 | ✊ | 🌐 | ♻ | | | ALERT |
|---|---|---|---|---|---|---|---|---|---|---|
| Health Valley# | HVAL | ? | ? | ✓ | ✖ | ? | No | ? | ? | some organic ingredients |
| Honey Maid | RJR | ? | ◐ | ? | ✖ | ◐ | Yes | ✖ | ? | cigarettes;D.C.C.A. |
| Pepperidge Farm | CPB | ✓ | ✓ | ✓ | ✓ | ◐ | No | ◐ | ◐ | on-site day care |
| Premium | RJR | ? | ◐ | ? | ✖ | ◐ | Yes | ✖ | ? | cigarettes;D.C.C.A. |
| Ritz | RJR | ? | ◐ | ? | ✖ | ◐ | Yes | ✖ | ? | cigarettes;D.C.C.A. |
| Ry Krisp | RAL | ◐ | ✓ | ✓ | ✓ | ◐ | No | ◐ | ◐ | |
| Sociables | RJR | ? | ◐ | ? | ✖ | ◐ | Yes | ✖ | ? | cigarettes;D.C.C.A. |
| Sunflower | RJR | ? | ◐ | ✖ | ✖ | ◐ | Yes | ✖ | ? | cigarettes;D.C.C.A. |
| Town House | UBH | ◐ | ✖ | ✓ | ✖ | ◐ | No | ? | ? | 🌐;U.K. |
| Triscuit | RJR | ? | ◐ | ? | ✖ | ◐ | Yes | ✖ | ? | cigarettes;D.C.C.A. |
| Uneeda | RJR | ? | ◐ | ? | ✖ | ◐ | Yes | ✖ | ? | cigarettes;D.C.C.A. |

✓ = Top Rating    ◐ = Middle Rating    ✖ = Bottom Rating    ? = Insufficient Information

For a more detailed explanation see key on page 14

**CRACKERS**

| Company or Product | Abbr. | 💲 | 👩 | 🧑 | 🐾 | ✊ | ☢ | 🐇 | 🌐 | ⊞ | 🕊 | ALERT |
|---|---|---|---|---|---|---|---|---|---|---|---|---|
| Wasa Crispbread | SAND | ? | ? | ? | ? | ✖ | ? | ? | YesIN | ✓ | ? | makes pesticides |
| Waverly | RJR | ? | ? | ? | ? | ✖ | ? | ✓ | Yes | ✖ | ? | cigarettes; D.C.C.A. |
| Wheat Thins | RJR | ? | ✓ | ? | ? | ✖ | ? | ✓ | Yes | ✖ | ? | cigarettes; D.C.C.A. |
| Wheatables | UBH | ✓ | ✖ | ✖ | ✓ | ✖ | ✓ | ✓ | No | ? | ? | 🌐, U.K. |
| Wheatsworth | RJR | ? | ✓ | ? | ? | ✖ | ? | ✓ | Yes | ✖ | ? | cigarettes; D.C.C.A. |
| Zesta | UBH | ✓ | ✖ | ✖ | ✓ | ✖ | ✓ | ✓ | No | ? | ? | 🌐, U.K. |
| **DENTAL CARE NEEDS** | | | | | | | | | | | | |
| Act | JNJ | ✓ | ✓ | ✓ | ✓® | ✓ | ✓ | ✓ | YesIN | ✓ | ✓ | on-site day care; Workplace Principles |
| Benzodent | PG | ✓ | ✓ | ✓ | ✓® | ✓ | ✓ | ✓ | Yes | ✓ | ✓ | disposable diapers; Salvadoran coffee; on-site day care; C.C.A. |
| Binaca | RCP | ? | ? | ? | ? | ✓ | ✓ | ? | YesIN | ? | ✓ | 🌐, U.K. |
| Cepacol | DOW | ✓ | ✓ | ✓ | ✓® | ✓ | ✓ | ✓ | Yes | ✓ | ✓ | pesticide steril. suit; nuclear weapons; on-site daycare; makes pesticides |
| Colgate | CL | ✓+ | ✓ | ✓ | ✓® | ✓ | ✓ | ✓ | YesIN | ✓ | ✓ | |
| Complete | PG | ✓ | ✓ | ✓ | ✓® | ✓ | ✓ | ✓ | Yes | ✓ | ✓ | disposable diapers; Salvadoran coffee; on-site day care; C.C.A. |

| Product or Company | Abbr. | 💲 | ♀ | ☮ | ⚖ | 🌍 | 🐰 | ⚛ | ♻ | ALERT |
|---|---|---|---|---|---|---|---|---|---|---|
| Efferdent | WLA | ✓ | ✓ | ✓ | ✗○ | ✓ | YesIN ✓∅ | ? | ✓ | on-site day care; Workplace Principles |
| Fasteeth | PG | ✓ | ✓ | ✓ | ✓⊛ | ✓ | Yes | ✓ | ✓ | disposable diapers; Salvadoran coffee; on-site day care; C.C.A. |
| Fixodent | PG | ✓ | ✓ | ✓ | ✓⊛ | ✓ | Yes | ✓ | ✓ | disposable diapers; Salvadoran coffee; on-site day care; C.C.A. |
| Flourigard | CL | ✓+ | ✓ | ✓ | ✓⊛ | ✓ | YesIN | ✓ | ✓ | |
| Kleenite | PG | ✓ | ✓ | ✓ | ✓⊛ | ✓ | Yes | ✓ | ✓ | disposable diapers; Salvadoran coffee; on-site day care; C.C.A. |
| Lavoris | DEPC | ? | ✓ | ✓ | ✓ | ✓ | No | ? | ✓ | |
| Listerine | WLA | ✓ | ✓ | ✓ | ✗○ | ✓ | YesIN ✓∅ | ? | ✓ | on-site day care; Workplace Principles |
| Listermint | WLA | ✓ | ✓ | ✓ | ✗○ | ✓ | YesIN ✓∅ | ? | ✓ | on-site day care; Workplace Principles |
| Plax | PFE | ✓ | ✗ | ✗ | ? | ✗ | YesIN ✗ | ? | ? | heart valve suits |
| Scope | PG | ✓ | ✓ | ✓ | ✓⊛ | ✓ | Yes | ✓ | ✓ | disposable diapers; Salvadoran coffee; on-site day care; C.C.A. |
| Signal | UN | ? | ✗ | ? | ✓* | ✓ | YesIN | ✓ | ? | 🌐 U.K. |

✓ = Top Rating   Ⅴ = Middle Rating   ✗ = Bottom Rating   ? = Insufficient Information

*For a more detailed explanation see key on page 14*

**DENTAL CARE NEEDS**

| Company or Product | Abbr. | $ | ♀ | 👥 | 🐾 | ✊ | ⊛ | 📋 | S.Af. | 🕊 | ⚖ | 👨‍👩‍👧 | ALERT |
|---|---|---|---|---|---|---|---|---|---|---|---|---|---|
| **Sudden Action** | AHP | ✗ | ✓ | ✓ | | ✓ | ✓ | ✓ | Yes | ✓ | ✓ | ✓ | infant formula |
| **DEODORANTS** | | | | | | | | | | | | | |
| Aftate | SGP | ✓ | ✓ | ✓ | ✓ | ✓ | ✓⊛ | ✓ | YesIN | ✓ | ✓ | ✓ | on-site day care; Workplace Principles |
| Alexandra Avery* | ALEX | ✓+ | ✓ | ✓∅ | ✓ | ✓ | ✓ | ✓ | No | ✓ | ✓ | ✓ | |
| Ammens | BMY | ✓ | ✗ | ✓ | ✓ | ✓ | ✓⊛ | ✓ | YesIN | ✓ | ✓ | ✓ | infant formula; Workplace Principles; D.C.C.A. |
| Arrid | CAR | ? | ? | ✓ | ✓ | ✗○ | ✗ | ? | No | ? | ✗ | ? | |
| Ban | BMY | ✓ | ✓ | ✓ | ✓ | ✓ | ✓⊛ | ✓ | YesIN | ✓ | ✓ | ✓ | infant formula; Workplace Principles; D.C.C.A. |
| Calm | ACV | ? | ✓ | ✓ | ? | ✓ | ✗ | ✓ | No | ✓ | ✗ | ? | |
| Consort | ACV | ? | ✓ | ? | ✓ | ✓ | ✗ | ✓ | No | ? | ✗ | ? | |
| Cool Confidence | AVP | ✓+ | ✓ | ✓ | ✓ | ✓ | ✓ | ✓ | No | ✓ | ✓ | ✓ | on-site day care; C.C.A. |
| Dry & Natural | ACV | ? | ✓ | ? | ✓ | ✓ | ✗ | ✓ | No | ? | ✗ | ? | |
| Dry Idea | GS | ✓ | ✓ | ✓ | ✓ | ✓ | ✓⊛ | ✓ | YesIN | ✓ | ✓ | ✓ | |
| Dry World | ACV | ? | ✓ | ? | ✓ | ✓ | ✗ | ✓ | No | ? | ✗ | ? | |

| Product or Company | Abbr. | $ | | | | | | | | | ALERT |
|---|---|---|---|---|---|---|---|---|---|---|---|
| Dryad | KAO | | | | | | | | | | see page 344 for Japanese companies |
| Fancy Feet | AVP | ✔+ | ✔ | ✔ | ✔ | ✔ | ? | No | ✔ | ✔ | on-site day care; C.C.A. |
| Feelin' Fresh | AVP | ✔+ | ✔ | ✔ | ✔ | ✔ | ? | No | ✔ | ✔ | on-site day care; C.C.A. |
| Foot Guard | GS | ◡ | ◡ | ✔ | ✔ | ✔* | ✔ | YesIN | ✔ | ✔ | |
| Gillette | GS | ◡ | ◡ | ✔ | ✔ | ✔* | ✔ | YesIN | ✔ | ✔ | |
| HI & DRI | REVL | ? | ? | ✔ | ✔ | ? | ✔ | YesIN | ? | ✔ | |
| Kangaroo* | DES | ? | ? | ? | ? | ◡ | ✔ | No | ? | ? | 1% For Peace |
| Lady's Choice | CAR | ? | ✖ | ◯ | ◡ | ? | ✖ | No | ? | ✖ | |
| Lotrimin AF | SGP | ◡ | ✔ | ✔ | ✔* | ✔ | ✔ | YesIN | ✔ | ✔ | on-site day care; Workplace Principles |
| Mitchum | REVL | ? | ? | ? | ✔ | ✖ | ? | YesIN | ? | ? | |
| Mum | BMY | ◡ | ✔ | ✔ | ✔* | ◡ | ✔ | YesIN | ✔ | ✔ | infant formula; Workplace Principles; D.C.C.A. |

✔ = Top Rating    ◡ = Middle Rating    ✖ = Bottom Rating    ? = Insufficient Information

For a more detailed explanation see key on page 14

Page 191

DEODORANTS

# DEODORANTS

| Company or Product | Abbr. | $ | | | | | | Yes/No | | | | ALERT |
|---|---|---|---|---|---|---|---|---|---|---|---|---|
| Natrel | GS | ◑ | ✓ | ✓ | ✓* | ✓ | ✓ | YesIN | ◑ | ✓ | ✓ | |
| Old Spice | PG | ✓ | ✓ | ✓ | ✓* | ✓ | ✓ | Yes | ✓ | ✓ | ✓ | disposable diapers; Salvadoran coffee; on-site day care; C.C.A. |
| On Duty 24 Plus | AVP | ✓+ | ✓ | ✓ | ✓ | ✓ | ✓ | No | ◑ | ✗ | ✓ | on-site day care; C.C.A. |
| Right Guard | GS | ◑ | ◑ | ✓ | ✓* | ✓ | ✓ | YesIN | ◑ | ✓ | ✓ | |
| Second Chance | ACV | ? | ? | ◑ | ✗ | ◑ | ? | No | ? | ✗ | ? | |
| Secret | PG | ✓ | ✓ | ✓ | ✓* | ✓ | ✓ | Yes | ◑ | ✓ | ✓ | disposable diapers; Salvadoran coffee; on-site day care; C.C.A. |
| Shower to Shower | JNJ | ✓ | ✓ | ✓ | ✓* | ✓ | ✓ | YesIN | ✓ | ✓ | ✓ | on-site day care; Workplace Principles |
| So Dry | ACY | ◑ | ? | ✗ | ✗○ | ✓ | ? | YesIN | ✗ | ? | ? | makes pesticides; D.C.C.A.; nuclear weapons |
| Soft & Dri | GS | ◑ | ✓ | ✓ | ✓* | ✓ | ✓ | YesIN | ◑ | ✓ | ✓ | |
| Sure | PG | ✓ | ✓ | ✓ | ✓* | ✓ | ✓ | Yes | ◑ | ✓ | ✓ | disposable diapers; Salvadoran coffee; on-site day care; C.C.A. |
| Tickle | BMY | ◑ | ◑ | ✓ | ✓ | ◑ | ✓ | YesIN | ◑ | ✓ | ◑ | infant formula; Workplace Principles; D.C.C.A. |
| Tinactin | SGP | ◑ | ◑ | ✓ | ✓* | ✓ | ✓ | YesIN | ◑ | ✓ | ◑ | on-site day care; Workplace Principles |
| Tom's of Maine# | TOM | ✓+ | ✓ | ✗ | ✓ | ✓ | ✓ | No | ✓ | ✓ | ✓ | |

| Product or Company | Abbr. | $ | ♀ | | | | | | | | | ALERT |
|---|---|---|---|---|---|---|---|---|---|---|---|---|
| Tussy | EK | ✓ | ✓ | ✔ | ✔ | ✔ | ✔ | No | ✓ | ✔ | ✔ | ⚡ C.C.A |

## DESSERTS: REFRIGERATED & FROZEN

| Product or Company | Abbr. | $ | ♀ | | | | | | | | | ALERT |
|---|---|---|---|---|---|---|---|---|---|---|---|---|
| Ambrosia | CPC | ✓ | ✓ | ✓ | ✓ | ✓ | ✓ | No | ✓ | ✓ | ✔ | |
| Ben & Jerry's | B&J | ✔+ | ✔+ | ✔ | ✔ | ✔ | ✓ | No | ✓ | ✔ | ✔ | 1% For Peace; on-site day care; ACT NOW; C.C.A. |
| Birds | MO | ? | ✔ | ✔ | ✔ | ✘ | ? | Yes | ? | ✔ | ? | cigarettes; Salvadoran coffee; Work. Princ. |
| Bon Bons | NEST | ? | ✔ | ? | ✔* | ✓ | ✓ | YesIN | ? | ? | ? | infant formula; Salv. coffee; ⊕; D.C.C.A.; U.K. |
| Borden | BN | ✓ | ✔ | ✔ | ✔ | ✔ | ✓ | YesIN | ✓ | ✔ | ✔ | |
| Breyer's | MO | ? | ✔ | ✔ | ? | ✘ | ? | Yes | ? | ? | ? | cigarettes; Salvadoran coffee; Work. Princ. |
| Comet Cups | RJR | ? | ✓ | ✓ | ? | ✘ | ✓ | Yes | ? | ? | ? | cigarettes; D.C.C.A. |
| Comstock | CBI | ✔+ | ✓ | ✘ | ✔ | ✔ | ✓ | No | ? | ✔ | ✓ | |
| Cool Whip | MO | ? | ✔ | ✔ | ? | ✘ | ? | Yes | ? | ? | ? | cigarettes; Salvadoran coffee; Work. Princ. |

✔ = Top Rating   ✓ = Middle Rating   ✘ = Bottom Rating   ? = Insufficient Information

*For a more detailed explanation see key on page 14*

**DESSERTS: REFRIGERATED & FROZEN**

Page 193

| Company or Product | Abbr. | $ | ♀ | | | | | | | | ALERT |
|---|---|---|---|---|---|---|---|---|---|---|---|
| Cover Farms | MO | ? | ✔ | ✔ | ? | ✖ | ? | Yes | ? | ? | cigarettes; Salvadoran coffee; Work. Princ. |
| D-Zerta | MO | ? | ✔ | ✔ | ? | ✖ | ? | Yes | ? | ? | cigarettes; Salvadoran coffee; Work. Princ. |
| Dove | MARS | ? | ? | ? | ? | ✓ | ? | No | ✔ | ? | |
| Dream Whip | MO | ? | ✔ | ✔ | ? | ✖ | ? | Yes | ? | ? | cigarettes; Salvadoran coffee; Work. Princ. |
| Eagle Brand | BN | ✓ | ✔ | ✔ | ✔ | ✔ | ✓ | YesIN | ✓ | ✔ | |
| Easy As Pie | K | ✔ | ✔ | ✔ | ✔* | ✔ | ✔ | YesIN | ✔ | ✔ | C.C.A. |
| Foremost | MO | ? | ✔ | ✔ | ? | ✖ | ? | Yes | ? | ? | cigarettes; Salvadoran coffee; Work. Princ. |
| Fruit-Line | UN | ? | ✖ | ✓ | ✔* | ✔ | ✓ | YesIN | ✓ | ? | 🌐, U.K. |
| Fruitage | SJM | ✔ | ✔ | ✓ | ✔ | ✔ | ✓ | No | ✓ | ✓ | some organic ingredients |
| Frusen Gladje | MO | ? | ✔ | ✔ | ? | ✖ | ? | Yes | ? | ? | cigarettes; Salvadoran coffee; Work. Princ. |
| Gold Bond | UN | ? | ✖ | ✔ | ✔* | ✔ | ✓ | YesIN | ✓ | ? | 🌐, U.K. |
| Gold Rush | GIS | ✔+ | ✔ | ✔ | ✔ | ✔ | ✔ | No | ✓ | ✔ | C.C.A. |
| Good Humor | UN | ? | ✖ | ✓ | ✔* | ✔ | ✓ | YesIN | ✓ | ? | 🌐, U.K. |

| Product or Company | Abbr. | $ | ♀+ | | | | | | | | ALERT |
|---|---|---|---|---|---|---|---|---|---|---|---|
| Haagen-Dazs | GMP | ✓ | ✔ | ✔ | ✔ | ✔ | YesIN | ✓ | ✓ | ✓ | 🌐; U.K. |
| Handi-Snacks | MO | ? | ✔ | ✗ | ✔ | ? | Yes | ? | ? | ? | cigarettes; Salvadoran coffee; Work. Princ. |
| Hunt's Snack Pack | CAG | ? | ✗ | ✗ | ✓ | ? | No | ? | ? | ✗ | safe meat controversy; D.C.C.A.; factory farming |
| Jell-O | MO | ? | ✔ | ✗ | ✔ | ? | Yes | ? | ? | ? | cigarettes; Salvadoran coffee; Work. Princ. |
| La Creme | PET | ? | ? | ✗ | ? | ? | No | ? | ? | ? | |
| Lyons | ALP | ✗ | ✓ | ✓ | ✔ | ✔ | Yes | ✓ | ✓ | ✓ | |
| Magic Shell | SJM | ✔ | ✗ | ✓ | ✓ | ✔ | No | ✔ | ✓ | ✓ | some organic ingredients |
| McMillan's | PET | ? | ? | ? | ✗ | ? | No | ? | ? | ? | |
| Minimilk | UN | ? | ✓ | ✓ | ✓ | ✓* | YesIN | ✓ | ✓ | ✓ | 🌐; U.K. |
| Minute Tapioca | MO | ? | ✔ | ✓ | ? | ? | Yes | ? | ? | ? | cigarettes; Salvadoran coffee; Work. Princ. |
| My*T*Fine | RJR | ? | ✓ | ? | ✗ | ✓ | Yes | ✗ | ? | ? | cigarettes; D.C.C.A. |

| ✔ = Top Rating | ✓ = Middle Rating | ✗ = Bottom Rating | ? = Insufficient Information |
|---|---|---|---|

*For a more detailed explanation see key on page 14*

**DESSERTS: REFRIGERATED & FROZEN**

| Company or Product | Abbr. | $ | ♀ | | | | | | | ALERT |
|---|---|---|---|---|---|---|---|---|---|---|
| Nice 'n Light | MO | ? | ✓ | ✓ | ? | ✗ | Yes | ? | ? | cigarettes; Salvadoran coffee; Work. Princ. |
| Nutrifil | CAG | ? | ✗ | ? | ? | ✗ | No | ? | ✗ | safe meat controversy; D.C.C.A.; factory farming |
| Olde Fashioned Recipe | BN | ✓ | ✓ | ✓ | ✓ | ✓ | YesIN | ✓ | ✓ | |
| Pet Whip | PET | ? | ? | ? | ? | ✗ | No | ? | ? | |
| Pet-Ritz | PET | ? | ? | ? | ? | ✗ | No | ? | ? | |
| Pie in Minutes | K | ✓ | ✓ | ✓ | ✓* | ✓ | YesIN | ✓ | ✓ | C.C.A |
| Polar B'ar | MO | ? | ✓ | ✓ | ? | ✗ | Yes | ? | ? | cigarettes; Salvadoran coffee; Work. Princ. |
| R.W. Snyder Foods | OAT | ✓+ | ✓ | ✓ | ? | ✓ | No | ✓ | ✓ | Fair Share |
| Reddi-Wip | CAG | ? | ✗ | ? | ? | ✗ | No | ? | ✗ | safe meat controversy; D.C.C.A.; factory farming |
| Richardson | OAT | ✓+ | ✓ | ✓ | ? | ✓ | No | ✓ | ✓ | Fair Share |
| Rondos | MARS | ? | ? | ? | ? | ? | No | ? | ✓ | |
| Royal | RJR | ? | ✓ | ? | ✓ | ✓ | Yes | ✗ | ? | cigarettes; D.C.C.A. |
| Sealtest | MO | ? | ? | ? | ? | ✗ | Yes | ? | ? | cigarettes; Salvadoran coffee; Work. Princ. |

| Product or Company | Abbr. | $ | ⚥ | | | | | (Animal Testing) | | | ALERT |
|---|---|---|---|---|---|---|---|---|---|---|---|
| Snowkist | GIS | ✓+ | ✓ | ✓ | ✓ | ✓ | ✓ | No | ✓ | ✓ | C.C.A. |
| Special Additions | GMP | ⌣ | ✓ | ✓ | ✓ | ✓ | ✓ | YesIN | ⌣ | ⌣ | 🌐; U.K. |
| Special Recipe | SJM | ✓ | ✗ | ⌣ | ✓ | ⌣ | ⌣ | No | ✓ | ⌣ | some organic ingredients |
| Squeezit | GIS | ✓+ | ✓ | ✓ | ✓ | ✓ | ✓ | No | ✓ | ✓ | C.C.A. |
| Stater Bros. | MO | ? | ✗ | ? | ✗ | ? | ? | Yes | ? | ? | cigarettes; Salvadoran coffee; Work. Princ. |
| Thank You Brand | CBI | ✓+ | ✗ | ⌣ | ✓ | ✓ | ⌣ | No | ✓ | ⌣ | |
| Tillamook Cheese | TILA | ✓+ | ✗ | ⌣ | ✓ | ✓ | ✓ | No | ⌣ | ✓ | co-op |
| Tropical Pops | GIS | ✓+ | ✓ | ✓ | ✓ | ✓ | ✓ | No | ✓ | ✓ | C.C.A. |
| Turtles | BN | ⌣ | ⌣ | ✓ | ✓ | ⌣ | ⌣ | YesIN | ⌣ | ✓ | |
| Viva | BN | ⌣ | ⌣ | ✓ | ✓ | ⌣ | ⌣ | YesIN | ⌣ | ✓ | |
| Weight Watchers | HNZ | ✓ | ⌣ | ✓ | ✓ | ✓ | ⌣ | No | ✓ | ⌣ | C.C.A. |

✓ = Top Rating   ⌣ = Middle Rating   ✗ = Bottom Rating   ? = Insufficient Information

*For a more detailed explanation see key on page 14*

**DESSERTS: REFRIGERATED & FROZEN**

## DIETARY SUPPLEMENTS

| Company or Product | Abbr. | $ | ♀ | (min) | (anml) | (comm) | (fam) | (wkpl) | (disc) | (envt) | ALERT |
|---|---|---|---|---|---|---|---|---|---|---|---|
| Amino 75# | SLGR | ? | ? | ? | ✗ | ? | ? | No | ? | ? | |
| Bugs Bunny | BAG | ? | ? | ✗ | ✗ | ? | ? | YesIN | ✗ | ? | makes pesticides |
| Centrum | ACY | ✓ | ✗ | ✓⊘ | ✗ | ? | ? | YesIN | ✗ | ? | makes pesticides; D.C.C.A.; nuclear weapons |
| Diet Ayds | DEPC | ? | ✓ | ✓ | ✓ | ✓ | ? | No | ? | ✓ | |
| Earthrise* | RIS | ✓ | ✓ | ✓ | ✓ | ✓ | ✓ | No | ✓ | ✓ | |
| Flinstones | BAG | ? | ? | ✗○ | ✗ | ✓ | ? | YesIN | ✗ | ? | makes pesticides |
| Formula VM-75# | SLGR | ? | ? | ? | ✓ | ✓ | ? | No | ✓⊘ | ? | |
| Geritol | BECH | ✗ | ✓ | ✗○ | ✓ | ✓ | ✓ | YesIN | ✓⊘ | ✓ | ⊕; Work. Princ.; on-site day care; U.K. |
| Max EPA# | SLGR | ? | ? | ? | ✗ | ✓ | ? | No | ✓⊘ | ? | |
| Myadec | WLA | ✓ | ✓ | ✗○ | ✓ | ✓ | ✓ | YesIN | ✓⊘ | ✓ | on-site day care; Workplace Principles |
| Nature's Herbs# | TWIN | ? | ? | ✓ | ✗ | ✓ | ? | No | ? | ? | |
| Nutrament | BMY | ✓ | ✓ | ✓⊛ | ✓ | ✓ | ✓ | YesIN | ✓ | ✓ | infant formula; Workplace Principles; D.C.C.A. |

| Product or Company | Abbr. | $ | ♀ | | | | | | | | ALERT |
|---|---|---|---|---|---|---|---|---|---|---|---|
| One-A-Day | BAG | ? | ? | ✖○ | ✖ | ? | YesIN | ✖ | ? | ? | makes pesticides |
| Poly Vi-Sol Vitamins | BMY | ⊘ | ✔ | ✔⊛ | ⊘ | ⊘ | YesIN | ⊘ | ✔ | ⊘ | infant formula; Workplace Principles; D.C.C.A. |
| Popeye Vitamins | BECH | ✖ | ? | ✖○ | ✔ | ⊘ | YesIN⊘ | ✔ | ✔ | ⊘ | 🌐, Work. Princ; on-site day care; U.K. |
| Stressgard | BAG | ? | ? | ✖○ | ✖ | ? | YesIN | ✖ | ? | ? | makes pesticides |
| Theragran | BMY | ⊘ | ✔ | ✔⊛ | ⊘ | ⊘ | YesIN | ✔ | ✔ | ⊘ | infant formula; Workplace Principles; D.C.C.A. |
| Twin Labs# | TWIN | ? | ? | ✔ | ✖ | ? | No | ? | ? | ? | |
| Unicap Vitamins | UPJ | ✔ | ✔ | ✔⊛ | ✔ | ✔ | YesIN | ⊘ | ✔ | ✔ | |
| **DIGESTIVE AIDS** | | | | | | | | | | | |
| Alka-Seltzer | BAG | ? | ? | ✖○ | ✖ | ? | YesIN | ✖ | ? | ? | makes pesticides |
| Amer. Home Remedy | BAG | ? | ? | ✖○ | ✖ | ? | YesIN | ✖ | ? | ? | makes pesticides |
| Bromo-Seltzer | WLA | ✔ | ⊘ | ✖○ | ⊘ | ✔ | YesIN⊘ | ⊘ | ? | ⊘ | on-site day care; Workplace Principles |

| | | |
|---|---|---|
| ✔ = Top Rating ⊘ = Middle Rating ✖ = Bottom Rating ? = Insufficient Information | | Page 199 |
| For a more detailed explanation see key on page 14 | | |

**DIGESTIVE AIDS**

| Company or Product | Abbr. | $ | ⚥ | 🤝 | 🐇 | ⚛ | 🌐 | ALERT |
|---|---|---|---|---|---|---|---|---|
| Citrucel | DOW | ⊘ | ✓ | ✓ | ✓(*) | ✓ | Yes | ✓ | pesticide steril. suit; nuclear weapons; on-site day care; makes pesticides |
| Correctol | SGP | ⊘ | ✓ | ✓ | ✓(*) | ✓ | YesIN | ✓ | on-site day care; Workplace Principles |
| DI-GEL | SGP | ⊘ | ✓ | ✓ | ✓(*) | ✓ | YesIN | ✓ | on-site day care; Workplace Principles |
| Dilantin | WLA | ✓ | ✓ | ✓ | ✗○ | ○ | YesIN✓∅ | ? | on-site day care; Workplace Principles |
| Exlax | SAND | ? | ? | ? | ? | ✗ | YesIN | ? | makes pesticides |
| Feen-A-Mint | SGP | ⊘ | ✓ | ✓ | ✓(*) | ✓ | YesIN | ✓ | on-site day care; Workplace Principles |
| Fiber Con | ACY | ⊘ | ✗ | ? | ✗○ | ✗ | YesIN | ? | makes pesticides; D.C.C.A.; nuclear weapons |
| Gasex | SAND | ? | ? | ? | ○ | ✗ | YesIN | ? | makes pesticides |
| Gelusil | WLA | ✓ | ✓ | ✓ | ✗○ | ○ | YesIN✓∅ | ? | on-site day care; Workplace Principles |
| Imodium A-D | JNJ | ✓ | ✓ | ✓ | ✓(*) | ✓ | YesIN | ✓ | on-site day care; Workplace Principles |
| Kaopectate | UPJ | ✓ | ✓ | ? | ✓(*) | ✓ | YesIN | ✓ | on-site day care; Workplace Principles |
| Maalox | ROR | ? | ○ | ? | ? | ✗ | YesIN | ? | |
| Metamucil | PG | ✓ | ✓ | ✓ | ✓(*) | ✓ | Yes | ✓ | disposable diapers; Salvadoran coffee; on-site day care; C.C.A. |

| Product or Company | Abbr. | $ | | | | | | | | | | | ALERT |
|---|---|---|---|---|---|---|---|---|---|---|---|---|---|
| Momentum | AHP | ✖ | ✔ | ✔ | ✔ | ✔ | ✔(*) | ✔ | Yes | ✔ | ✔ | infant formula |
| Peptic Ulcer treatment | BECH | ✖ | 🌐 | ✔ | ✔ | ✖○ | ✔ | YesIN | ✔∅ | ✔ | 🌐, Work. Princ.; on-site day care; U.K. |
| Pepto-Bismol | PG | ✔ | ✔ | ✔ | ✔ | ✔(*) | ✔ | Yes | ✔ | ✔ | disposable diapers; Salvadoran coffee; on-site day care; C.C.A. |
| Phillips Milk of Magnesia | EK | ✔ | ✔ | ✔ | ✔ | ✔(*) | ✔ | No | ✔ | ✔ | ⚡, C.C.A. |
| Remegel | WLA | ✔ | ✔ | ✔ | ✔ | ✖○ | ✔ | YesIN | ✔∅ | ? | on-site day care; Workplace Principles |
| Rolaids | WLA | ✔ | ✔ | ✔ | ✔ | ✖○ | ✔ | YesIN | ✔∅ | ? | on-site day care; Workplace Principles |
| **FEMININE HYGIENE** | | | | | | | | | | | | |
| Always | PG | ✔ | ✔ | ✔ | ✔ | ✔(*) | ✔ | Yes | ✔ | ✔ | disposable diapers; Salvadoran coffee; on-site day care; C.C.A. |
| Answer 2 | CAR | ? | ✖ | ✔ | ✔ | ✖○ | ? | No | ? | ? | |
| Carefree | JNJ | ✔ | ✔ | ✔ | ✔ | ✔(*) | ✔ | YesIN | ✔ | ✔ | on-site day care; Workplace Principles |
| FDS | ACV | ? | ✖ | ? | ✔ | ✖ | ? | No | ? | ✖ | |

✔ = Top Rating  ✓ = Middle Rating  ✖ = Bottom Rating  ? = Insufficient Information
*For a more detailed explanation see key on page 14*

Page 201

FEMININE HYGIENE

| Company or Product | Abbr. | $ | ♀ | | | | | | | | | ALERT |
|---|---|---|---|---|---|---|---|---|---|---|---|---|
| Kotex | KMB | ? | ✔ | ✔ | ✖ | ✖ | ? | YesIN | ✖ | ? | ? | disposable diapers |
| Lightdays | KMB | ? | ✔ | ✔ | ✖ | ✖ | ? | YesIN | ✖ | ? | ? | disposable diapers |
| Massengill | BECH | ✖ | ✖ | ✔ | ✔ | ✖○ | ✔ | YesIN | ✔○ | ✔ | ✔ | 🌐, Work. Princ.; on-site day care; U.K. |
| Mischief | CAR | ? | ✔ | ✔ | ? | ✖○ | ? | No | ? | ✖ | ? | |
| Neet | RCP | ? | ✔ | ✔ | ? | ✔ | ✔ | YesIN | ? | ✖ | ✔ | 🌐, U.K. |
| New Freedom | KMB | ? | ✔ | ✔ | ✖ | ✖ | ? | YesIN | ✖ | ? | ? | disposable diapers |
| Security | KMB | ? | ✔ | ✔ | ✖ | ✖ | ? | YesIN | ✖ | ? | ? | disposable diapers |
| Simplique | KMB | ? | ✔ | ✔ | ✖ | ✖ | ? | YesIN | ✖ | ? | ? | disposable diapers |
| Stayfree | JNJ | ✔ | ✔ | ✔ | ✔/✱ | ✔ | ✔ | YesIN | ✔ | ✔ | ✔ | on-site day care; Workplace Principles |
| Sure & Natural | JNJ | ✔ | ✔ | ✔ | ✔/✱ | ✔ | ✔ | YesIN | ✔ | ✔ | ✔ | on-site day care; Workplace Principles |
| o.b. | JNJ | ✔ | ✔ | ✔ | ✔/✱ | ✔ | ✔ | YesIN | ✔ | ✔ | ✔ | on-site day care; Workplace Principles |

**FIRST AID**

| Band— | JPI | | | | | | | YesIN | | | | |

| Product or Company | Abbr. | $ | | | | | | | | | | ALERT |
|---|---|---|---|---|---|---|---|---|---|---|---|---|
| Bactine | BAG | ? | ✔ | ✔ | ? | ✖○ | ✖ | ? | YesIN | ✖ | ? | makes pesticides |
| Band Aid | JNJ | ✔ | ✔ | ✔ | ✔ | ✔⊛ | ✔ | ✔ | YesIN | ? | ✔ | on-site day care; Workplace Principles |
| Campho-Phenique | EK | ◡ | ✔ | ✔ | ✔ | ✔⊛ | ✔ | ✔ | No | ◡ | ✔ | ✦ C.C.A. |
| Hydrogen Peroxide | WLA | ✔ | ✔ | ✔ | ✔ | ✖○ | ◡ | ✔ | YesIN | ✔∅ | ? | on-site day care; Workplace Principles |
| Johnson & Johnson | JNJ | ◡ | ✔ | ✔ | ✔ | ✔⊛ | ✔ | ✔ | YesIN | ✔ | ✔ | on-site day care; Workplace Principles |
| Micropore | MMM | ◡ | ✔ | ✔ | ✔ | ◡* | ✔ | ✔ | YesIN | ◡ | ✔ | ❀ |
| Mycitracin | UPJ | ✔ | ✔ | ✔ | ✔ | ✔⊛ | ✔ | ✔ | YesIN | ◡ | ✔ | |
| Solarcaine | SGP | ◡ | ✔ | ✔ | ✔ | ✔⊛ | ✔ | ✔ | YesIN | ◡ | ◡ | on-site day care; Workplace Principles |
| **FISH: CANNED & REFRIGERATED** | | | | | | | | | | | | |
| De Jeans | BN | ◡ | ✔ | ✔ | ✔ | ✔ | ✔ | ◡ | YesIN | ◡ | ✔ | |
| Doxsee | BN | ◡ | ✔ | ✔ | ✔ | ✔ | ✔ | ◡ | YesIN | ◡ | ✔ | |

✔ = Top Rating   ◡ = Middle Rating   ✖ = Bottom Rating   ? = Insufficient Information

For a more detailed explanation see key on page 14

FIRST AID

| Company or Product | Abbr. | $ | ♀ | ⚥ | 🐾 | 🌐 | (policy) | ✡ | 🏠 | ALERT |
|---|---|---|---|---|---|---|---|---|---|---|
| Harris | BN | ◑ | ✔ | ✔ | ✔ | ◑ | YesIN | ◑ | ✔ | |
| Louis Kemp | MO | ? | ✔ | ? | ✖ | ? | Yes | ? | ? | cigarettes; Salvadoran coffee; Work. Princ. |
| Orleans | BN | ◑ | ✔ | ✔ | ✔ | ◑ | YesIN | ◑ | ✔ | |
| Pride Of Alaska | NSK | | | | | | | | | see page 344 for Japanese companies |
| Snow's | BN | ◑ | ✔ | ✔ | ✔ | ◑ | YesIN | ◑ | ✔ | |
| StarKist | HNZ | ✔ | ✔ | ◑ | ✔ | ◑ | No | ✔ | ◑ | C.C.A. |
| **FLOUR** | | | | | | | | | | |
| Action | ADM | ✖ | ✖ | ✖ | ? | ✖ | No | ? | ? | |
| Ardex 550 | ADM | ✖ | ✖ | ✖ | ? | ✖ | No | ? | ? | |
| Bakemaster | ADM | ✖ | ✖ | ✖ | ? | ✖ | No | ? | ? | |
| Commander | ADM | ✖ | ✖ | ✖ | ? | ✖ | No | ? | ? | |
| Cream Loaf | ADM | ✖ | ✖ | ✖ | ? | ✖ | No | ? | ? | |
| Drifted Snow | GIS | ✔ | ✔ | ✔ | ✔ | ◑ | No | ✔ | ✔ | C.C.A. |

| Product of Company | ADDL. | | | | | | | | | | | ALERT |
|---|---|---|---|---|---|---|---|---|---|---|---|---|
| Eden# | EDEN | ✔+ | ✔ | ? | ✔ | ✔ | ✔ | ✔ | No | ✔ | ✔ | some organic ingredients |
| Empress | ADM | ✘ | ✘ | ? | ✘ | ✘ | ✘ | ? | No | ✘ | ? | |
| Freedom | ADM | ✘ | ✘ | ? | ✘ | ✘ | ✘ | ? | No | ✘ | ? | |
| Gigantic | ADM | ✘ | ✘ | ? | ✘ | ✘ | ✘ | ? | No | ✘ | ? | |
| Gold Medal | GIS | ✔ | ✔ | ✔ | ✔ | ✔ | ✔ | ✔ | No | ◔ | ✔ | C.C.A. |
| Great Caesar | ADM | ✘ | ✘ | ? | ✘ | ✘ | ✘ | ? | No | ✘ | ? | |
| Husky | ADM | ✘ | ✘ | ? | ✘ | ✘ | ✘ | ? | No | ✘ | ? | |
| King Midas | CAG | ? | ◔ | ? | ✘ | ✘ | ✘ | ✘ | No | ? | ✘ | safe meat controversy; D.C.C.A.; factory farming |
| Kitchen-Tested | GIS | ✔+ | ✔ | ✔ | ✔ | ✔ | ✔ | ✔ | No | ◔ | ✔ | C.C.A. |
| La Pina | GIS | ✔+ | ✔ | ✔ | ✔ | ✔ | ✔ | ✔ | No | ◔ | ✔ | C.C.A. |
| Larabees Best | ADM | ✘ | ✘ | ? | ✘ | ✘ | ✘ | ? | No | ✘ | ? | |

| | |
|---|---|
| ✔ = Top Rating ◔ = Middle Rating ✘ = Bottom Rating ? = Insufficient Information<br>*For a more detailed explanation see key on page 14* | Page 205 |

**FLOUR**

| Company or Product | Abbr. | 💲 | ♀ | | | | | | | | ALERT |
|---|---|---|---|---|---|---|---|---|---|---|---|
| Maplesota | ADM | ✖ | ✖ | ? | ? | ✖ | ? | No | ? | ? | |
| Minneapolis Best | ADM | ✖ | ✖ | ? | ? | ✖ | ? | No | ? | ? | |
| Miss Minneapolis | ADM | ✖ | ✖ | ? | ? | ✖ | ? | No | ? | ? | |
| Mother's Best | CAG | ? | ✖ | ⌒ | ? | ✖ | ✖ | No | ? | ✖ | safe meat controversy; D.C.C.A.; factory farming |
| Myti Strong | ADM | ✖ | ✖ | ? | ? | ✖ | ? | No | ✖ | ? | |
| NW Special | ADM | ✖ | ✖ | ? | ? | ✖ | ? | No | ? | ? | |
| Quaker | OAT | ✓+ | ✓ | ✓ | ✓ | ✓ | ✓ | No | ✓ | ⌒ | Fair Share |
| Red Brand | GIS | ✓+ | ✓ | ✓ | ✓ | ✓ | ✓ | No | ⌒ | ✓ | C.C.A. |
| Silver Ribbon | GIS | ✓+ | ✓ | ✓ | ✓ | ✓ | ✓ | No | ⌒ | ✓ | C.C.A. |
| Softasilk | GIS | ✓+ | ✓ | ✓ | ✓ | ✓ | ✓ | No | ⌒ | ✓ | C.C.A. |
| Spartan | ADM | ✖ | ✓ | ? | ✖ | ✖ | ? | No | ✖ | ? | |
| Sperry | GIS | ✓+ | ✓ | ✓ | ? | ✓ | ✓ | No | ⌒ | ✓ | C.C.A. |
| Sweetheart | ADM | ✖ | | | | | | | | | |

| Product or Company | Abbr. | 💲 | [icon] | [icon] | [icon] | [icon] | [icon] | [icon] | [icon] | [icon] | [icon] | ALERT |
|---|---|---|---|---|---|---|---|---|---|---|---|---|
| Sunfed | ADM | ✖ | ✖ | ? | ? | ✖ | ? | No | ✖ | ? | ? | |
| Sunloaf | ADM | ✖ | ✖ | ? | ? | ✖ | ? | No | ✖ | ? | ? | |
| Washburn's Special | GIS | ✔+ | ✔ | ✔ | ✔ | ✔ | ✔ | No | ◔ | ✔ | ✔ | C.C.A. |
| White Deer | GIS | ✔+ | ✔ | ✔ | ✔ | ✔ | ✔ | No | ◔ | ✔ | ✔ | C.C.A. |
| White Lily | TYSN | ? | ✖ | ? | ✖ | ✖ | ✖ | No | ◔ | ? | ✖ | factory farming; safe chicken contr. |
| Wondra | GIS | ✔+ | ✔ | ✔ | ✔ | ✔ | ✔ | No | ◔ | ✔ | ✔ | C.C.A. |
| **FRAGRANCES** | | | | | | | | | | | | |
| Anais Anais | LORA | ? | ✔ | ✔ | ◔ | ✔* | ? | Yes | ✔ | ? | ? | |
| Aroma Oil* | BLN | ✔ | ✔ | ✔ | ✔ | ✔ | ✔ | No | ✔ | ✔ | ◔ | some organic ingredients |
| Avon | AVP | ✔+ | ✔ | ◔ | ✔ | ✔ | ✔ | No | ◔ | ✔ | ✔ | on-site day care; C.C.A. |
| Body Shop, The | BS | ◔ | ✔ | ◔ | ◔ | ✔ | ✔ | No | ✔ | ? | ✔ | ACT NOW; U.K. |

✔ = Top Rating ◔ = Middle Rating ✖ = Bottom Rating ? = Insufficient Information

For a more detailed explanation see key on page 14

FRAGRANCES

| Company or Product | Abbr. | $ | ⚥+ | | | | | | | ▦ | ALERT |
|---|---|---|---|---|---|---|---|---|---|---|---|
| Brut 33 | UN | ? | ✖ | √ | ✓* | ✓ | ? | YesIN | √ | ? | 🌐, U.K. |
| Cacharel | LORA | ? | ✓ | √ | ✓* | √ | ? | Yes | ? | ? | |
| Cover Girl | PG | ✓ | ✓ | ✓ | ✓⊛ | ✓ | ✓ | Yes | ✓ | ✓ | disposable diapers; Salvadoran coffee; on-site day care; C.C.A. |
| Emeraude | PFE | √ | ✖ | ? | ? | ✖ | √ | YesIN | ? | ? | heart valve suits |
| Giorgio Armani | LORA | ? | ✓ | √ | ✓* | √ | ? | Yes | ? | ? | |
| Gloria Vanderbilt | LORA | ? | ✓ | √ | ✓* | √ | ? | Yes | ? | ? | |
| Guy Laroche | LORA | ? | ✓ | √ | ✓* | √ | ? | Yes | ? | ? | |
| Hero | UN | ? | ✖ | √ | ✓* | ✓ | √ | YesIN | √ | ? | 🌐, U.K. |
| Iron | PFE | √ | ✖ | ? | ? | ✖ | √ | YesIN | ? | ? | heart valve suits |
| L'Effleur | PFE | √ | ✖ | ? | ? | ✖ | √ | YesIN | ? | ? | heart valve suits |
| Lady Stetson | PFE | √ | ✖ | ? | ? | ✖ | √ | YesIN | ? | ? | heart valve suits |
| Musk for Men | PFE | √ | ✖ | ? | ? | ✖ | √ | YesIN | ? | ? | heart valve suits |
| Paloma Picasso | LORA | ? | ✓ | √ | ✓* | √ | ? | Yes | ? | ? | |

| Product or Company | Abbr. | 💲 | ♀ | ⚥ | 🐇 | 🏠 | 👥 | ℹ️ | ▢ | ⊞ | ALERT |
|---|---|---|---|---|---|---|---|---|---|---|---|
| Preferred Stock | PFE | ✓ | ✗ | ? | ✗ | ✓ | YesIN | ? | ? | | heart valve suits |
| Ralph Lauren | LORA | ? | ✓ | ✓* | ✓ | ? | Yes | ? | ? | | |
| Sand & Sable | PFE | ✓ | ✗ | ? | ✗ | ✓ | YesIN | ? | ? | | heart valve suits |
| Stetson | PFE | ✓ | ✗ | ? | ✗ | ✓ | YesIN | ? | ? | | heart valve suits |
| **FRUIT: CANNED, DRIED, FRESH & FROZEN** | | | | | | | | | | | |
| Bird's Eye | MO | ? | ✓ | ? | ✗ | ✗ | Yes | ? | ? | | cigarettes; Salvadoran coffee; Work. Princ. |
| Cabana | DOL | ✓ | ✓ | ? | ✓ | ✓ | No | ✓ | ✗ | | pesticide sterilization suit |
| Calypso | CBI | ✓+ | ✓ | ✗ | ✓ | ✓ | No | ? | ✓ | | |
| Chico | CQB | ? | ✓ | ✓ | ✓ | ✓ | No | ✓ | ✓ | | D.C.C.A. |
| Chiquita | CQB | ? | ✓ | ✓ | ✓ | ✓ | No | ✓ | ✓ | | D.C.C.A. |
| Deana | TYSN | ? | ✗ | ? | ✗ | ✗ | No | ? | ✗ | | factory farming; safe chicken contr. |

✓ = Top Rating    ✓ = Middle Rating    ✗ = Bottom Rating    ? = Insufficient Information

*For a more detailed explanation see key on page 14*

Page 209

**FRUIT: CANNED, DRIED, FRESH & FROZEN**

| Company or Product | Abbr. | $ | ♀ | ‼ | 🐰 | ◻ | S.Afr. | ◻ | ◻ | ▦ | ALERT |
|---|---|---|---|---|---|---|---|---|---|---|---|
| Dole | DOL | ✔ | ✓ | ? | ✔ | ✓ | No | ✘ | ✓ | ✘ | pesticide sterilization suit |
| Fruit 'n Juice | DOL | ✔ | ✓ | ? | ✔ | ✓ | No | ✘ | ✓ | ✘ | pesticide sterilization suit |
| Fruit Classics | GEB | ✓ | ✔ | ? | ? | ✘ | Yes | ? | ? | ? | D.C.C.A.; infant formula |
| Geobe | TYSN | ? | ✘ | ? | ✔ | ✘ | No | ✓ | ? | ✘ | factory farming; safe chicken contr. |
| Mott's | CADB | ? | ? | ? | ? | ✘ | YesIN | ? | ? | ? | 🌐; U.K. |
| Ocean Spray | OSC | ✔ | ✘ | ? | ✔ | ✓ | No | ✓ | ✓ | ✓ | co-op |
| Stilwell | FLO | ? | ? | ? | ? | ? | No | ? | ? | ? | |
| Sun Giant | DOL | ✔ | ✔ | ? | ✔ | ✓ | No | ✘ | ✓ | ✘ | pesticide sterilization suit |
| Tropic Isle | CBI | ✔+ | ✘ | ✘ | ✔ | ✔ | No | ? | ✔ | ✓ | |
| **GASOLINE & CAR SUPPLIES** | | | | | | | | | | | |
| 3-in-One | RCP | ? | ? | ? | ? | ✓ | YesIN | ? | ✘ | ✓ | 🌐; U.K. |
| ARCO | ARC | ✓ | ✓ | ✓ | ✘ | ✓ | No | ✔ | ✔ | ✓ | ✈ |
| Amoco | AN | ✓ | ✔ | ✔ | ✔* | ✓ | No | ✓ | ? | ? | ↓ C C A |

| Product or Company | Abbr. | 💲 | ♀ | 👥 | ✊ | 🐾 | 🕊 | ⌂ | ▦ | ALERT |
|---|---|---|---|---|---|---|---|---|---|---|
| BP America | BP | ◐ | ✗ | ? | ✓ | ✓ | YesIS | ✗ | ✓ | ⊕, ☀, ✈, U.K. |
| Chevron | CHV | ◐ | ✗ | ✓ | ✓ | ✓ | YesIS | ✗ | ✗ | makes pesticides; Work. Princ.; ✈ |
| Exxon | XON | ◐ | ◐ | ? | ✓ | ◐ | No | ✗ | ✗ | oil spill; ✈; D.C.C.A.; on-site day care |
| Marathon | X | ◐ | ✗ | ? | ✗ | ✗ | Yes | ? | ✗ | D.C.C.A. |
| Mobil | MOB | ✗ | ✗ | ◐✓* | ✓ | ✓ | No | ✗ | ✗ | ✈, Work. Princ.; D.C.C.A. |
| Phillips 66 | P | ◐ | ◐ | ✓ | ◐ | ✓ | No | ✓ | ✗ | |
| Prestone Hi-Temp | FB | ✓+ | ✗ | ✓* | ✓ | ✓ | Yes | ✗ | ◐ | ✈; on-site day care |
| STP | FB | ✓+ | ✗ | ✓* | ◐ | ✓ | Yes | ✗ | ◐ | |
| Shell | SC | ? | ? | ? | ✓ | ✓ | YesIS | ✓ | ◐ | ✈, ⊕; pesticide sterilization suit |
| Simoniz | FB | ✓+ | ✗ | ✓* | ✓ | ✓ | Yes | ✗ | ◐ | |
| Sunoco | SUN | ✓+ | ? | ? | ✗ | ✗ | No | ? | ? | ✈ |

✔ = Top Rating    ◐ = Middle Rating    ✗ = Bottom Rating    ? = Insufficient Information

*For a more detailed explanation see key on page 14*

GASOLINE & CAR SUPPLIES

| Company or Product | Abbr. | $ | ♀ | | | | | | | | | ALERT |
|---|---|---|---|---|---|---|---|---|---|---|---|---|
| Texaco | TX | ? | ✗ | ? | ? | ✓ | ? | YesIS | ✗ | ? | ? | ❋; ✦ |
| USX | X | ✗ | ✗ | ✗ | ? | ✗ | ✗ | Yes | ✗ | ? | ✗ | D.C.C.A. |
| **GUM** | | | | | | | | | | | | |
| All Pro | GIS | ✓+ | ✗ | ✓ | ✓ | ✓ | ✓ | No | ✓ | ✓ | ✓ | C.C.A. |
| Big Red | WWY | ✗ | ✗ | ? | ? | ? | ? | No | ✓○ | ✓ | ? | Fair Share |
| Bubble Yum | RJR | ? | ? | ? | ✗ | ✗ | ? | Yes | ✗ | ? | ? | cigarettes; D.C.C.A. |
| Bubblicious | WLA | ✓ | ✓ | ✓ | ✗○ | ✓ | ✓ | YesIN | ✓○ | ? | ✓ | on-site day care; Workplace Principles |
| Carefree | RJR | ? | ✓ | ? | ? | ✗ | ? | Yes | ✗ | ? | ? | cigarettes; D.C.C.A. |
| Chewels | WLA | ✓ | ✓ | ✓ | ✗○ | ✓ | ✓ | YesIN | ✓○ | ? | ✓ | on-site day care; Workplace Principles |
| Chiclets | WLA | ✓ | ✓ | ✓ | ✗○ | ✓ | ✓ | YesIN | ✓○ | ? | ✓ | on-site day care; Workplace Principles |
| Dentyne | WLA | ✓ | ✓ | ✓ | ✗○ | ✓ | ✓ | YesIN | ✓○ | ? | ✓ | on-site day care; Workplace Principles |
| Doublemint | WWY | ✗ | ✗ | ? | ? | ✓ | ✓ | No | ✓○ | ? | ? | Fair Share |
| Extra Sugarfree Gum | WWY | ✗ | ✗ | ? | ? | ✗ | ✓ | No | ✓○ | ? | ? | Fair Share |

# GUM

| Product or Company | Abbr. | $ | ♀ | | | | | No/Yes | | ▦ | ALERT |
|---|---|---|---|---|---|---|---|---|---|---|---|
| Freedent | WWY | ✖ | ? | | ? | ✓ | ? | No | ✓ | ? | Fair Share |
| Freshen-Up | WLA | ✓ | ✓ | ✖○ | ✓ | ✓ | ✓ | YesIN | ? | ✓ | on-site day care; Workplace Principles |
| Hot Flash Camera Gum | GIS | ✓+ | ✓ | ✓ | ✓ | ✓ | ✓ | No | ✓ | ✓ | C.C.A. |
| Hubba Bubba | WWY | ✖ | ✖ | ? | ? | ? | ? | No | ✓○ | ? | Fair Share |
| Juicy Fruit | WWY | ✓ | ✓ | ? | ✓ | ? | ? | No | ✓○ | ? | Fair Share |
| Overhead Smash | GIS | ✓+ | ✓ | ✓ | ✓ | ✓ | ✓ | No | ✓ | ✓ | C.C.A. |
| Sticklets | WLA | ✓ | ✓ | ✖○ | ✓ | ✓ | ✓ | YesIN | ? | ✓ | on-site day care; Workplace Principles |
| Strawberries'n Cream | GIS | ✓+ | ✓ | ✓ | ✓ | ✓ | ✓ | No | ✓ | ✓ | C.C.A. |
| Trebor Wine Gums | CADB | ? | ? | ? | ✓ | ✖ | ? | YesIN | ? | ? | 🌐, U.K. |
| Trident | WLA | ✓ | ✓ | ✖○ | ✓ | ✓ | ✓ | YesIN | ? | ✓ | on-site day care; Workplace Principles |
| Wrigley's | WWY | ✖ | ✖ | ? | ? | ? | ? | No | ✓○ | ? | Fair Share |

✓ = Top Rating   ✓ = Middle Rating   ✖ = Bottom Rating   ? = Insufficient Information

For a more detailed explanation see key on page 14

Page 213

## HAIR CARE NEEDS

| Company or Product | Abbr. | $ | ▪ | ▪ | ▪ | ▪ | ▪ | ▪ | ▪ | ▪ | ▪ | ALERT |
|---|---|---|---|---|---|---|---|---|---|---|---|---|
| Adorn | GS | ✓ | ✓ | ✔ | ✔ | ✔ | ✔* | ✔ | YesIN | ✓ | ✔ | |
| Alberto VO5 | ACV | ? | ✔ | ✔ | ✔ | ✓ | ✗ | ? | No | ? | ✗ | |
| Aubrey Organics# | AUB | ? | ? | ✔ | ✓ | ✔ | ✔ | ✔ | No | ✔ | ? | some organic ingredients |
| Aveda# | AVED | ✔ | ✔ | ✔ | ✔ | ✔ | ✔ | ✔ | No | ✔ | ✔ | Valdez Principles; ACT NOW |
| Body Shop, The | BS | ✓ | ✔ | ✓ | ✔ | ✔ | ✗ | ✓ | No | ? | ? | ACT NOW; U.K. |
| Breck | G | ? | ✔ | ✓ | ✓ | ✓ | ✗ | ? | No | ? | ? | |
| Clairol | BMY | ✓ | ✔ | ✓ | ✔ | ✓ | ✔* | ✓ | YesIN | ✓ | ✔ | infant formula; Workplace Principles; D.C.C.A. |
| Clear Difference | GS | ✓ | ✔ | ✔ | ✔ | ✔ | ✔* | ✔ | YesIN | ✔ | ✔ | |
| Clientele# | CTL | ✔+ | ✔ | ? | ✔ | ✔ | ✗ | ✔ | No | ✓ | ✔ | |
| Command | ACV | ? | ✔ | ? | ✔ | ✗ | ✔* | ? | No | ✗ | ? | |
| Condition | BMY | ✓ | ✔ | ✓ | ✔ | ✓ | ✔* | ✓ | YesIN | ✓ | ✔ | infant formula; Workplace Principles; D.C.C.A. |
| Consort | ACV | ? | ✔ | ? | ✗ | ? | ✗ | ? | No | ✗ | ? | |

| Product or Company | Abbr. | $ | | | | | | | | | | ALERT |
|---|---|---|---|---|---|---|---|---|---|---|---|---|
| Crystal Clear | ACV | | ? | ✔ | ? | ? | No | ✗ | ? | ✗ | ? | |
| Dep | DEPC | | ? | ✓ | ✓ | ✓ | No | ✓ | ✓ | ✓ | ✓ | |
| Dippity-Do | GS | ✓ | ✓ | ✓ | ✔(*) | ✓ | YesIN | ✔ | ✓ | ✔ | ✓ | |
| Epic Waves | GS | ✓ | ✓ | ✓ | ✔(*) | ✓ | YesIN | ✔ | ✓ | ✔ | ✓ | |
| European Naturals | ACV | | ? | ✓ | ✗ | ? | No | ✓ | ? | ✗ | ? | |
| Final Net | BMY | ✓ | ✓ | ✔(*) | ✗ | ✓ | YesIN | ✓ | ✔ | ✓ | ? | infant formula; Workplace Principles; D.C.C.A. |
| Flex | REVL | ? | ? | ✓ | ✔ | ? | YesIN | ✓ | ✓ | ? | ? | |
| For Brunettes Only | ACV | | ? | ✓ | ✗ | ? | No | ✓ | ? | ✗ | ? | |
| Gelee | ACV | | ? | ✓ | ✗ | ? | No | ✓ | ? | ✗ | ? | |
| Get Set | ACV | | ? | ✓ | ✗ | ? | No | ✓ | ? | ✗ | ? | |
| Instant Beauty | BMY | ✓ | ✓ | ✔(*) | ✓ | ✓ | YesIN | ✓ | ✔ | ✓ | ✓ | infant formula; Workplace Principles; D.C.C.A. |

✔ = Top Rating    ✓ = Middle Rating    ✗ = Bottom Rating    ? = Insufficient Information

For a more detailed explanation see key on page 14

HAIR CARE NEEDS

Page 215

| Company or Product | Abbr. | $ | ♀ | | | | | | | | ALERT |
|---|---|---|---|---|---|---|---|---|---|---|---|
| L'Oreal | LORA | ? | ✓ | ✓ | ✓* | ✓ | ? | Yes | ? | ? | |
| L.A. Looks | DEPC | ? | ✓ | ✓ | ✓ | ✓ | ✓ | No | ? | ✓ | |
| Lancome | LORA | ? | ✓ | ✓ | ✓* | ✓ | ? | Yes | ? | ? | |
| Lit | DEPC | ? | ✓ | ✓ | ✓ | ✓ | ✓ | No | ? | ✓ | |
| Loving Care | BMY | ✓ | ✓ | ✓ | ✓⊛ | ✓ | ✓ | YesIN | ✓ | ✓ | infant formula; Workplace Principles; D.C.C.A. |
| Miss Breck | ACY | ✓ | ✗ | ? | ✗○ | ✗ | ? | YesIN | ? | ? | makes pesticides; D.C.C.A.; nuclear weapons |
| Miss Clairol | BMY | ✓ | ✓ | ✓ | ✓⊛ | ✓ | ✓ | YesIN | ✓ | ✓ | infant formula; Workplace Principles; D.C.C.A. |
| New Dawn | ACV | ? | ✓ | ? | ✗ | ✗ | ? | No | ✗ | ? | |
| Nice 'N Easy | BMY | ✓ | ✓ | ✓ | ✓⊛ | ✓ | ✓ | YesIN | ✓ | ✓ | infant formula; Workplace Principles; D.C.C.A. |
| Ogilvie | EK | ✓ | ✓ | ✓ | ✓⊛ | ✓ | ✓ | No | ✓ | ✓ | ♣; C.C.A. |
| Pantene | PG | ✓ | ✗ | ✓ | ✓⊛ | ✓ | ✓ | Yes | ✓ | ✓ | disposable diapers; Salvadoran coffee; on-site day care; C.C.A. |
| Rave | UN | ? | ✓ | ✓ | ✓* | ✓ | ✓ | YesIN | ✓ | ? | ⊕, U.K. |
| Rinse Away | ACV | ? | ? | ✗ | ✗ | ✗ | ? | No | ✗ | ? | |

| Product or Company | Abbr. | 💲 | ♀ | ✊ | ⚛ | 🐰 | 🌍 | | ⚖ | 🕊 | ⚕ | ALERT |
|---|---|---|---|---|---|---|---|---|---|---|---|---|
| Second Chance | ACV | ? | ✔ | ? | ✖ | ✓ | ? | No | ? | ✖ | ? | |
| Style Hairspray | DOW | ✓ | ✔ | ✓ | ✔® | ✔ | ✓ | Yes | ✓ | ✔ | ✓ | pesticide steril. suit; nuclear weapons; on-site day care; makes pesticides |
| Sudden Beauty | AHP | ✖ | ✔ | ✓ | ✔® | ✓ | ✓ | Yes | ✓ | ✓ | ✓ | infant formula |
| The Natural One | ACV | ? | ✔ | ? | ✖ | ✓ | ? | No | ? | ✖ | ? | |
| Toni Lightwaves | GS | ✓ | ✔ | ✓ | ✔® | ✓ | ✔ | YesIN | ✓ | ✔ | ✓ | |
| Tres Spray | ACV | ? | ✔ | ? | ✖ | ✓ | ? | No | ? | ✖ | ? | |
| Ultress | BMY | ✓ | ✔ | ✓ | ✔® | ✓ | ✔ | YesIN | ✓ | ✔ | ✓ | infant formula; Workplace Principles; D.C.C.A. |
| Vidal Sassoon | PG | ✔ | ✔ | ✔ | ✔® | ✔ | ✔ | Yes | ✓ | ✔ | ✓ | disposable diapers; Salvadoran coffee; on-site day care; C.C.A. |
| Vitalis | BMY | ✓ | ✔ | ✓ | ✔® | ✓ | ✔ | YesIN | ✓ | ✔ | ✓ | infant formula; Workplace Principles; D.C.C.A. |
| White Rain | GS | ✓ | ✓ | ✓ | ✔® | ✓ | ✔ | YesIN | ✓ | ✔ | ✓ | |

✔ = Top Rating   ✓ = Middle Rating   ✖ = Bottom Rating   ? = Insufficient Information

For a more detailed explanation see key on page 14

| | Page 217 |
|---|---|

**HAIR CARE NEEDS**

| Company or Product | Abbr. | $ | ♀ | O | ☪ | 🐇 | ⚒ | 🐁 | ⬟ | 🏭 | ALERT |
|---|---|---|---|---|---|---|---|---|---|---|---|
| **JAMS, JELLIES & FRUIT SPREADS** | | | | | | | | | | | |
| Autumn Harvest | SJM | ✔ | ✓ | ✗ | ✔ | ✔ | ✔ | No | ✔ | ✓ | some organic ingredients |
| Bama | BN | ✓ | ✔ | ✔ | ✔ | ✔ | ✓ | YesIN | ✓ | ✔ | |
| Crosse & Blackwell | NEST | ? | ✔ | ? | ✔* | ✓ | ✔ | YesIN | ? | ? | infant formula; Salv. coffee; ⊕, D.C.C.A.; U.K. |
| Dickinson's | SJM | ✔ | ✔ | ✗ | ✔ | ✔ | ✔ | No | ✓ | ✓ | some organic ingredients |
| Dutch Girl | SJM | ✔ | ✔ | ✗ | ✔ | ✔ | ✔ | No | ✔ | ✓ | some organic ingredients * |
| Elsenham | SJM | ✔ | ✔ | ✗ | ✔ | ✔ | ✔ | No | ✔ | ✓ | some organic ingredients |
| Good Morning | SJM | ✔ | ✔ | ✗ | ✔ | ✔ | ✔ | No | ✔ | ✓ | some organic ingredients |
| Health Valley# | HVAL | ? | ? | ? | ✔ | ✗ | ? | No | ? | ? | some organic ingredients |
| Home Brands | CAG | ✗ | ✗ | ? | ✗ | ✗ | ✔ | No | ? | ✗ | safe meat controversy; D.C.C.A.; factory farming |
| Laura Secord | CPB | ✔ | ✓ | ✓ | ? | ✔ | ✓ | No | ✓ | ✓ | on-site day care |
| Light | SJM | ✔ | ✔ | ✗ | ✔ | ✔ | ✔ | No | ✔ | ✓ | some organic ingredients |
| Lite & Fruity | BN | ✓ | ✔ | ✔ | ✔ | ✔ | ✓ | YesIN | ✓ | ✔ | |

| Product or Company | Abbr. | 💲 | 👤 | 🐇 | 🌿 | 🌍 | ☮ | ⚖ | 🏢 | ALERT |
|---|---|---|---|---|---|---|---|---|---|---|
| Lost Acres | SJM | ✔ | ✓ | ✘ | ✔ | ✔ | No | ✓ | ✓ | some organic ingredients |
| Mary Ellen | SJM | ✔ | ✓ | ✘ | ✔ | ✔ | No | ✓ | ✓ | some organic ingredients |
| Purely Fruit | SJM | ✔ | ✓ | ✘ | ✔ | ✔ | No | ✓ | ✓ | some organic ingredients |
| Santa Cruz Natural | SJM | ✔ | ✓ | ✘ | ✔ | ✔ | No | ✓ | ✓ | some organic ingredients |
| Simply Fruit | SJM | ✔ | ✓ | ✘ | ✔ | ✔ | No | ✓ | ✓ | some organic ingredients |
| Slenderella | SJM | ✔ | ✓ | ✘ | ✔ | ✔ | No | ✓ | ✓ | some organic ingredients |
| Smucker's | SJM | ✔ | ✓ | ✘ | ✔ | ✔ | No | ✓ | ✓ | some organic ingredients |
| Whole Earth# | WHO | ✔+ | ✓ | ✓ | ✔ | ✓ | No | ? | ✓ | 1% For Peace; some organic ingredients |
| **JUICES & DRINKS: FROZEN** | | | | | | | | | | |
| Bacardi | KO | ✓ | ✓ | ? | ✔ | ✓ | Yes | ✓ | ? | |
| Bright & Early | KO | ✓ | ✓ | ? | ✔ | ✓ | Yes | ✓ | ? | |

✔ = Top Rating   ✓ = Middle Rating   ✘ = Bottom Rating   ? = Insufficient Information

*For a more detailed explanation see key on page 14*

| | Page 219 |
|---|---|

**JUICES & DRINKS: FROZEN**

| Company or Product | Abbr. | $ | ♀ | ‖ | 🐾 | ✎ | 👥 | (S.A.) | ⚖ | ❤ | ▦ | ALERT |
|---|---|---|---|---|---|---|---|---|---|---|---|---|
| **Dole** | DOL | ✓ | ? | ? | ✓ | ✗ | ✗ | No | ✗ | ✓ | ✗ | pesticide sterilization suit |
| **Five Alive** | KO | ◐ | ✓ | ✓ | ? | ✓ | ✓ | Yes | ✓ | ◐ | ? | |
| **Health Valley#** | HVAL | ? | ? | ? | ✓ | ✗ | ? | No | ? | ✓ | ? | some organic ingredients |
| **Minute Maid** | KO | ◐ | ✓ | ✓ | ✓ | ✓ | ✓ | Yes | ✓ | ◐ | ? | |
| **Squeeze Fresh** | KO | ◐ | ✓ | ✓ | ? | ✓ | ✓ | Yes | ✓ | ◐ | ? | |
| JUICES, JUICE DRINKS & CONCENTRATES | | | | | | | | | | | | |
| **Apple & Eve\*** | APNE | ✓+ | ✓∅ | ✓ | ✓ | ✓ | ✓ | No | ✓ | ? | ? | some organic ingredients |
| **Ardmore Farms** | OAT | ✓+ | ✓ | ✓ | ✓ | ✓ | ✓ | No | ✓ | ✓ | ✓ | Fair Share |
| **Bali Fruit Drinks** | CADB | ? | ? | ? | ? | ✗ | ? | YesIN | ? | ? | ? | ⊕, U.K. |
| **Campbell's** | CPB | ✓ | ✓ | ✓ | ? | ✓ | ✓ | No | ✓ | ✓ | ✓ | on-site day care |
| **Chiquita** | CQB | ? | ? | ◐ | ◐ | ✓ | ◐ | No | ✓ | ✓ | ✓ | D.C.C.A. |
| **Citrus Hill** | PG | ✓ | ✓ | ✓ | ✓(*) | ✓(®) | ✓ | Yes | ✓ | ✓ | ✓ | disposable diapers; Salvadoran coffee; on-site day care; C.C.A. |
| **Clamato** | CADB | ? | ? | ✓ | ✓ | ✗ | ✗ | YesIN | ? | ? | ? | ⊕, U.K. |

| Product or Company | Abbr. | 💲 | 👥 | 🐾 | ⚖ | 🕊 | 🌐 | | 🏛 | ⬛ | ALERT |
|---|---|---|---|---|---|---|---|---|---|---|---|
| Dole | DOL | ✔ | ◐ | ? | ✔ | ◐ | ✔ | No | ✖ | ✖ | pesticide sterilization suit |
| Five Alive | KO | ◐ | ✔ | ✔ | ✔ | ✔ | ✔ | Yes | ✔ | ◐ | ? |
| Fruit Boxes | MO | ? | ✔ | ? | ✖ | ? | ✔ | Yes | ? | ? | cigarettes; Salvadoran coffee; Work. Princ. |
| Fruit Juicer | GIS | ✔+ | ✔ | ✔ | ✔ | ✔ | ✔ | No | ◐ | ✔ | C.C.A. |
| Fruit Squeez | GIS | ✔+ | ✔ | ✔ | ✔ | ✔ | ✔ | No | ◐ | ✔ | C.C.A. |
| Gatorade | OAT | ✔+ | ✔ | ✔ | ✔ | ✔ | ✔ | No | ✔ | ◐ | Fair Share |
| Hawaiian Punch | PG | ✔ | ✔ | ✔(⊛) | ✔ | ✔ | ✔ | Yes | ◐ | ✔ | disposable diapers; Salvadoran coffee; on-site day care; C.C.A. |
| Hi-C | KO | ◐ | ✔ | ? | ? | ✔ | ✔ | Yes | ✔ | ? | |
| Hollywood | PET | ? | ? | ? | ✖ | ? | ✖ | No | ? | ? | |
| Juice and More | GEB | ◐ | ✔ | ? | ✖ | ? | ✖ | Yes | ? | ? | D.C.C.A.; infant formula |
| Juicy Juice | NEST | ? | ✔ | ? | ✔* | ◐ | ◐ | YesN | ◐ | ? | infant formula; Salv. coffee; ⊕, D.C.C.A.; U.K. |

✔ = Top Rating  ◐ = Middle Rating  ✖ = Bottom Rating  ? = Insufficient Information

*For a more detailed explanation see key on page 14*

## JUICES, JUICE DRINKS & CONCENTRATES

| Company or Product | Abbr. | | | | | | | | | | | | | ALERT |
|---|---|---|---|---|---|---|---|---|---|---|---|---|---|---|
| La Famosa | BN | ✓ | ✓ | ✓ | ✓ | ✓ | ✓ | ✓ | YesIN | ✓ | ✓ | ✓ | ✓ | |
| Libby's | NEST | ? | ✓ | ? | ✓ | ✓ | ✓* | ✓ | YesIN | ✓ | ? | ? | ✓ | infant formula; Salv. coffee; ⊕, D.C.C.A.; U.K. |
| Lincoln | PG | ✓ | ✓ | ✓ | ✓ | ✓ | ✓(⊛) | ✓ | Yes | ✓ | ✓ | ✓ | ✓ | disposable diapers; Salvadoran coffee; on-site day care; C.C.A. |
| Minute Maid | KO | ✓ | ✓ | ? | ✓ | ? | ? | ✓ | Yes | ✓ | ✓ | ? | ? | |
| Mott's | CADB | ? | ? | ? | ✗ | ✓ | ✓ | ✓ | YesIN | ? | ✓ | ? | ? | ⊕, U.K. |
| Newman's Own* | NEWO | ✓+ | ✓∅ | ✓ | ✗ | ✓ | ✓ | ✓ | No | ✓ | ✓ | ✓ | ✓ | 100% profit to charity; C.C.A. |
| Nice & Natural | SJM | ✓ | ✓ | ✗ | ? | ✓ | ✓ | ✓ | No | ✓ | ✓ | ✓ | ✓ | some organic ingredients |
| Ocean Spray | OSC | ✓ | ✓ | ? | ✓ | ✓ | ✓ | ✓ | No | ✓ | ✓ | ✓ | ✓ | co-op |
| Power Ade | KO | ✓ | ✓ | ✓ | ✓ | ✓ | ✓ | ✓ | Yes | ✓ | ✓ | ✓ | ? | |
| ReaLemon/ReaLime | BN | ✓ | ✓ | ✓ | ✓ | ✓ | ✓ | ✓ | YesIN | ✓ | ✓ | ✓ | ✓ | |
| Red Cheek | CADB | ? | ? | ? | ✗ | ✓ | ✓ | ✓ | YesIN | ? | ✓ | ? | ? | ⊕, U.K. |
| Speas Farm | PG | ✓ | ✓ | ✓ | ✓ | ✓ | ✓(⊛) | ✓ | Yes | ✓ | ✓ | ✓ | ✓ | disposable diapers; Salvadoran coffee; on-site day care; C.C.A. |
| Squeeze It | GIS | ✓+ | ✓ | ✓ | ✓ | ✓ | ✓ | ✓ | No | ✓ | ✓ | ✓ | ✓ | C.C.A. |

# JUICES, JUICE DRINKS & CONCENTRATES

| Product or Company | Addr. | | | | | | | Yes/No | | | ALERT |
|---|---|---|---|---|---|---|---|---|---|---|---|
| Strawberry Falls | MO | ? | ✔ | ✔ | ✗ | ? | ? | Yes | ? | ? | cigarettes; Salvadoran coffee; Work. Princ. |
| Sun Sip | PG | ✔ | ✔ | ✔(*) | ✔ | ✔ | ✔ | Yes | ✔ | ✔ | disposable diapers; Salvadoran coffee; on-site day care; C.C.A. |
| Sunkist | RJR | ? | ? | ? | ✓ | ✓ | ? | Yes | ✗ | ? | cigarettes; D.C.C.A. |
| Sunny Delight | PG | ✔ | ✔ | ✔(*) | ✔ | ✔ | ✔ | Yes | ✓ | ✔ | disposable diapers; Salvadoran coffee; on-site day care; C.C.A. |
| Texsun | PG | ✔ | ✔ | ✔(*) | ✔ | ✔ | ✔ | Yes | ✔ | ✔ | disposable diapers; Salvadoran coffee; on-site day care; C.C.A. |
| R.W. Knudsen | SJM | ✔ | ✗ | ✓ | ✔ | ✔ | ✔ | No | ✔ | ✓ | some organic ingredients |
| Tropi | CAG | ? | ✗ | ? | ? | ✗ | ✗ | No | ? | ✗ | safe meat controversy; D.C.C.A.; factory farming |
| Tropicana | VO | ? | ✗ | ? | ? | ✔ | ? | No | ? | ? | ⊕ |
| V8 | CPB | ✔ | ✔ | ? | ? | ✔ | ✔ | No | ✓ | ✓ | on-site day care |
| Welch's | GRAP | ? | ? | ? | ? | ? | ✗ | No | ? | ? | co-op |
| Whole Earth# | WHO | ✔+ | ✓ | ✓ | ✔ | ✓ | ✓ | No | ✓ | ✔ | 1% For Peace; some organic ingredients |

| ✔ = Top Rating | ✓ = Middle Rating | ✗ = Bottom Rating | ? = Insufficient Information | Page 223 |
|---|---|---|---|---|

*For a more detailed explanation see key on page 14*

| Company or Product | Abbr. | $ | | | | | | | | | | | ALERT |
|---|---|---|---|---|---|---|---|---|---|---|---|---|---|
| Winter Hill | PG | ✓ | ✗ | ✓ | ✓ | ✓(*) | ✓ | | Yes | ✓ | ✓ | | disposable diapers; Salvadoran coffee; on-site day care; C.C.A. |
| Wyler's | MO | ? | ✓ | ✓ | ✓ | ? | ✗ | | Yes | ? | ? | | cigarettes; Salvadoran coffee; Work. Princ. |
| Yukijirushi | SNB | | | | | | | | | | | | see page 344 for Japanese companies |
| **LAUNDRY SUPPLIES** | | | | | | | | | | | | | |
| All | UN | ? | ✓ | ✗ | ✓ | ✓ | ✓* | ✓ | YesIN | ✓ | ✓ | ? | 🌐 U.K. |
| Allen's Naturally* | ANY. | ✓ | ✓ | ✓ | ✓⊘ | ✓ | ✓ | ? | No | ✓ | ✓ | ? | |
| Ariel | PG | ✓+ | ✓ | ✓ | ✓ | ✓(*) | ✓ | ✓ | Yes | ✓ | ✓ | ✓ | disposable diapers; Salvadoran coffee; on-site day care; C.C.A. |
| Arm & Hammer | CRCH | ✓ | ✓ | ? | ✓ | ✓* | ✓ | ✓ | No | ✓ | ✓ | ✓ | |
| Biz | PG | ✓ | ✓ | ✓ | ✓ | ✓(*) | ✓ | ✓ | Yes | ✓ | ✓ | ✓ | disposable diapers; Salvadoran coffee; on-site day care; C.C.A. |
| Bold | PG | ✓ | ✓ | ✓ | ✓ | ✓(*) | ✓ | ✓ | Yes | ✓ | ✓ | ✓ | disposable diapers; Salvadoran coffee; on-site day care; C.C.A. |
| Borateem | G | ? | ✓ | ✗ | ✓ | ✓ | ✗ | ? | No | ? | ? | ? | |
| Borax | G | ? | ✓ | ✗ | ✓ | ✓ | ✗ | ? | No | ? | ? | ? | |
| Bounce | PG | ✓ | ✓ | ✓ | ✓ | ✓(*) | ✓ | ✓ | Yes | ✓ | ✓ | ✓ | disposable diapers; Salvadoran coffee; on-site |

# LAUNDRY SUPPLIES

| Product or Company | Abbr. | 💲 | ♀ | ◐ | 🖐 | 🐫 | 🐇 | | ⊕ | ♻ | ALERT |
|---|---|---|---|---|---|---|---|---|---|---|---|
| Cheer | PG | ✓ | ✓ | ✓ | ✓ | ✓⊛ | ✓ | Yes | ◒ | ✓ | disposable diapers; Salvadoran coffee; on-site day care; C.C.A. |
| Clorox | CLX | ◒ | ✗ | ✗ | ✓ | ✓* | ✓ | No | ✓ | ✓ | |
| Clorox 2 | CLX | ◒ | ✗ | ✗ | ✓ | ✓* | ✓ | No | ✗ | ✓ | |
| Delicate Cycle | KAO | | | | | | ◒ | | ◒ | | see page 344 for Japanese companies |
| Downy | PG | ✓ | ✓ | ✓ | ✓ | ✓⊛ | ✓ | Yes | ◒ | ✓ | disposable diapers; Salvadoran coffee; on-site day care; C.C.A. |
| Dreft | PG | ✓ | ✓ | ✓ | ✓ | ✓⊛ | ✓ | Yes | ◒ | ✓ | disposable diapers; Salvadoran coffee; on-site day care; C.C.A. |
| Dynamo | CL | ✓+ | ✓ | ✓ | ✓ | ✓⊛ | ◒ | YesIN | ✓ | ✓ | |
| Easy Wash | RCP | ? | ? | ? | ? | ? | ◒ | YesIN ? | ✗ | ◒ | ⊕, U.K. |
| Easy-On | RCP | ? | ? | ? | ? | ? | ◒ | YesIN ? | ✗ | ◒ | ⊕, U.K. |
| Era | PG | ✓ | ✓ | ✓ | ✓ | ✓⊛ | ✓ | Yes | ◒ | ✓ | disposable diapers; Salvadoran coffee; on-site day care; C.C.A. |
| Fab | CL | ✓+ | ✓ | ✓ | ✓ | ✓⊛ | ✓ | YesIN | ✓ | ✓ | |

✔ = Top Rating    ◒ = Middle Rating    ✗ = Bottom Rating    ? = Insufficient Information

*For a more detailed explanation see key on page 14*

## LAUNDRY SUPPLIES

| Company or Product | Abbr. | $ | ♀ | | | | | | | | | | ALERT |
|---|---|---|---|---|---|---|---|---|---|---|---|---|---|
| Final Touch | UN | ? | ✗ | ◐ | ? | ◐ | ◐ | ◐ | YesIN | ◐ | ◐ | ? | 🌐 U.K. |
| Fresh Start | CL | ✓+ | ✓ | ◐ | ✓ | ✓* | ✓ | ✓ | YesIN | ✓ | ✓ | ✓ | |
| Gain | PG | ✓ | ◐ | ✓ | ✓ | ✓⊛ | ✓ | ✓ | Yes | ◐ | ✓ | ✓ | disposable diapers; Salvadoran coffee; on-site day care; C.C.A. |
| Ivory Snow | PG | ✓ | ◐ | ✓ | ✓ | ✓⊛ | ✓ | ✓ | Yes | ◐ | ✓ | ✓ | disposable diapers; Salvadoran coffee; on-site day care; C.C.A. |
| Javex | BMY | ◐ | ◐ | ◐ | ✓ | ✓⊛ | ✓ | ◐ | YesIN | ◐ | ✓ | ◐ | infant formula; Workplace Principles; D.C.C.A. |
| K2r | DOW | ◐ | ◐ | ✓ | ✓ | ✓⊛ | ✓ | ✓ | Yes | ◐ | ✓ | ◐ | pesticide steril. suit; nuclear weapons; on-site day care; makes pesticides |
| Lavender Sachet | RCP | ? | ✓ | ? | ? | ? | ✓ | ◐ | YesIN | ? | ✗ | ◐ | 🌐 U.K. |
| Lemon Dash | PG | ✓ | ◐ | ✓ | ✓ | ✓⊛ | ✓ | ✓ | Yes | ◐ | ✓ | ✓ | disposable diapers; Salvadoran coffee; on-site day care; C.C.A. |
| Niagara | CPC | ✓+ | ◐ | ✓ | ✓ | ✓ | ◐ | ✗ | No | ◐ | ✗ | ? | |
| Oxydol | PG | ✓ | ◐ | ✓ | ✓ | ✓⊛ | ✓ | ✓ | Yes | ◐ | ✓ | ✓ | disposable diapers; Salvadoran coffee; on-site day care; C.C.A. |
| Purex | G | ? | ◐ | ✓ | ✓ | ✓ | ? | ✗ | No | ? | ? | ? | |
| Shout | SCJ | ✓+ | ✓ | ✓ | ✓ | ✓* | ✓ | ✓ | YesIN | ✓ | ✓ | ✓ | 1st to ban CFCs; on-site day care |
| Snowy | RCP | ? | ? | ? | ? | ? | ◐ | ? | YesIN | ✗ | ✗ | ◐ | 🌐 U.K. |

| Product or Company | Abbr. | $ | ♀ | ✊ | ⚥ | 🐰 | ☢ | 🌍 | 🤝 | ♻ | ⚖ | ALERT |
|---|---|---|---|---|---|---|---|---|---|---|---|---|
| Snuggle | UN | ? | ✗ | ✓ | ✓ | ✓ | ✔* | ✓ | YesN | ✓ | ? | 🌐; U.K. |
| Solo | PG | ✓ | ✓ | ✓ | ✓ | ✓ | ✔⊛ | ✓ | Yes | ✓ | ✓ | disposable diapers; Salvadoran coffee; on-site day care; C.C.A. |
| Spray 'n Starch | DOW | ✓ | ✓ | ✓ | ✓ | ✓ | ✔⊛ | ✓ | Yes | ✓ | ✓ | pesticide steril. suit; nuclear weapons; on-site day care; makes pesticides |
| Spray 'n Wash | DOW | ✓ | ✓ | ✓ | ✓ | ✓ | ✔⊛ | ✓ | Yes | ✓ | ✓ | pesticide steril. suit; nuclear weapons; on-site day care; makes pesticides |
| Static-Guard | ACV | ? | ✗ | ? | ✓ | ? | ✗ | ✓ | No | ✗ | ? | |
| Surf | UN | ? | ✗ | ✓ | ✓ | ✓ | ✔* | ✓ | YesN | ✓ | ? | 🌐; U.K. |
| Texize | DOW | ✓ | ✓ | ✓ | ✓ | ✓ | ✔⊛ | ✓ | Yes | ✓ | ✓ | pesticide steril. suit; nuclear weapons; on-site day care; makes pesticides |
| Tide | PG | ✓ | ✓ | ✓ | ✓ | ✓ | ✔⊛ | ✓ | Yes | ✓ | ✓ | disposable diapers; Salvadoran coffee; on-site day care; C.C.A. |
| Vivid | DOW | ✓ | ✓ | ✓ | ✓ | ✓ | ✔⊛ | ✓ | Yes | ✓ | ✓ | pesticide steril. suit; nuclear weapons; on-site day care; makes pesticides |
| Wisk | UN | ? | ✗ | ✓ | ✓ | ✓ | ✔* | ✓ | YesN | ✓ | ? | 🌐; U.K. |
| Woolite | RCP | ? | ? | ? | ? | ? | ? | ✓ | YesN | ✓ | ✓ | 🌐; U.K. |

✔ = Top Rating    ✓ = Middle Rating    ✗ = Bottom Rating    ? = Insufficient Information

*For a more detailed explanation see key on page 14*

| | |
|---|---|
| | Page 227 |

**LAUNDRY SUPPLIES**

| Company or Product | Abbr. | $ | ♀ | [icon] | [icon] | [icon] | [icon] | [Yes/No] | [icon] | [icon] | ALERT |
|---|---|---|---|---|---|---|---|---|---|---|---|
| Yes | DOW | ✓ | ✓ | ✓ | ✓ | ✓(*) | ✓ | Yes | ✓ | ✓ | pesticide steril. suit; nuclear weapons; on-site day care; makes pesticides |
| **MARGARINE** | | | | | | | | | | | |
| Baker's Blend | RJR | ? | ✓ | ? | ✗ | ? | ✗ | Yes | ? | ? | cigarettes; D.C.C.A. |
| Blue Bonnet | RJR | ? | ✓ | ? | ✗ | ? | ✗ | Yes | ? | ? | cigarettes; D.C.C.A. |
| Chiffon | MO | ? | ✓ | ✓ | ✗ | ? | ✗ | Yes | ? | ? | cigarettes; Salvadoran coffee; Work. Princ. |
| Countryside Spread | MO | ? | ✓ | ✓ | ✗ | ? | ✗ | Yes | ? | ? | cigarettes; Salvadoran coffee; Work. Princ. |
| Fleischmann's | RJR | ? | ✓ | ? | ✗ | ? | ✗ | Yes | ? | ? | cigarettes; D.C.C.A. |
| Good Luck | UN | ? | ✓ | ✓ | ✓ | ✓* | ✓ | YesN | ✓ | ? | 🌐, U.K. |
| I Can't Believe It's Not Btr | UN | ? | ✓ | ✓ | ✓ | ✓* | ✓ | YesN | ✓ | ? | 🌐, U.K. |
| Imperial | UN | ? | ✓ | ✓ | ✓ | ✓* | ✓ | YesN | ✓ | ? | 🌐, U.K. |
| Mazola | CPC | ✓+ | ✗ | ✓ | ✓ | ✓* | ✗ | No | ✓ | ✓ | |
| Parkay | MO | ? | ✓ | ✓ | ✓ | ✓* | ✓ | Yes | ? | ? | cigarettes; Salvadoran coffee; Work. Princ. |
| Promise | UN | ? | ✓ | ✓ | ✓ | ✓* | ✓ | YesN | ✓ | ? | 🌐, U.K. |

| Product or Company | Abbr. | $ | ♀ | | | | | | | ALERT |
|---|---|---|---|---|---|---|---|---|---|---|
| Shedd's Spread | UN | ? | ✖ | ✓ | ✓ | ✓ | YesIN | ✓ | ? | ⊕; U.K. |
| Sun Valley | UN | ? | ✖ | ✓ | ✓* | ✓ | YesIN | ✓ | ? | ⊕; U.K. |
| Touch Of Butter | MO | ? | ✓ | ✓ | ? | ✖ | Yes | ? | ? | cigarettes; Salvadoran coffee; Work. Princ. |
| Yukijirushi | SNB | | | | | | | | | see page 344 for Japanese companies |
| **MEAT: CANNED & REFRIGERATED** | | | | | | | | | | |
| Armour | CAG | ? | ✖ | ✓ | ✓ | ✖ | No | ? | ✖ | safe meat controversy; D.C.C.A.; factory farming |
| Armour Star | G | ? | ✓ | ✓ | ? | ? | No | ? | ? | |
| Ball Park | SLE | ✓ | ✓ | ✓ | ✓ | ✓ | Yes | ✓ | ✓ | on-site day care; C.C.A. |
| Brookfield | CAG | ? | ✖ | ✓ | ? | ✖ | No | ? | ✖ | safe meat controversy; D.C.C.A.; factory farming |
| Brown 'n' Serve | CAG | ? | ✖ | ✓ | ? | ✖ | No | ? | ✖ | safe meat controversy; D.C.C.A.; factory farming |
| Bryan | SLE | ✓ | ✓ | ✓ | ✓ | ✓ | Yes | ✓ | ✓ | on-site day care; C.C.A. |

✓ = Top Rating   ✓ = Middle Rating   ✖ = Bottom Rating   ? = Insufficient Information

*For a more detailed explanation see key on page 14*

Page 229

**MEAT: CANNED & REFRIGERATED**

# MEAT: CANNED & REFRIGERATED

| Company or Product | Abbr. | $ | ♀ | ⚇ | 🔔 | 🐕 | 🐾 | Yes/No | ⬡ | ⊞ | ALERT |
|---|---|---|---|---|---|---|---|---|---|---|---|
| Bun Length | MO | ? | ✔ | ? | ✗ | ? | ? | Yes | ? | ? | cigarettes; Salvadoran coffee; Work. Princ. |
| Dinner Bell | CQB | ? | ✔ | ✗ | ✔ | ✔ | ✗ | No | ✔ | ✔ | D.C.C.A. |
| Dinty Moore | HRL | ? | ✗ | ? | ✔ | ✔ | ? | No | ? | ? | |
| E-Z Cut | CQB | ? | ✔ | ✔ | ✔ | ✗ | ✗ | No | ✔ | ✔ | D.C.C.A. |
| Gold Leaf | TYSN | ? | ✗ | ? | ✔ | ✔ | ✗ | No | ✔ | ✗ | factory farming; safe chicken contr. |
| Grillmaster | SLE | ✔ | ✔ | ✔ | ✔ | ✔ | ✔∅ | Yes | ✔ | ✔∅ | on-site day care; C.C.A. |
| Harkers | TYSN | ? | ✗ | ? | ✔ | ✔ | ✗ | No | ✔ | ? | factory farming; safe chicken contr. |
| Henry House | TYSN | ? | ✗ | ? | ✔ | ✔ | ✗ | No | ✔ | ? | factory farming; safe chicken contr. |
| Hi-Brand Foods | SLE | ✔ | ✔ | ✔ | ✔ | ✔ | ✔∅ | Yes | ✔ | ✔ | on-site day care; C.C.A. |
| Hillshire Farm | SLE | ✔ | ✔ | ✔ | ✔ | ✔ | ✔∅ | Yes | ✔ | ✔ | on-site day care; C.C.A. |
| Hormel | HRL | ? | ✗ | ? | ✔ | ✗ | ✔ | No | ? | ? | |
| Hunter | CQB | ? | ✔ | ✔ | ✔ | ✔ | ? | No | ✔ | ✔ | D.C.C.A. |
| Jesse Jones | GIS | ✔+ | ✔ | ✔ | ✔ | ✔ | ✔ | No | ✔ | ✔ | C.C.A. |

| Product or Company | Abbr. | | | | | | | | | | ALERT |
|---|---|---|---|---|---|---|---|---|---|---|---|
| Jimmy Dean | SLE | ✔ | ✔ | ✔ | ✔ | ✔ | Yes | ✓∅ | ✔ | ✓ | on-site day care; C.C.A. |
| John Morrell | CQB | ? | ✔ | ✔ | ✔ | ? | No | ✗ | ✔ | ✓ | D.C.C.A. |
| Kahn's | SLE | ✔ | ✔ | ✔ | ✔ | ✔ | Yes | ✓∅ | ✔ | ✓ | on-site day care; C.C.A. |
| Kretschmar | CQB | ? | ✔ | ✔ | ✔ | ? | No | ✗ | ✔ | ✓ | D.C.C.A. |
| Krey | CQB | ? | ✔ | ✔ | ✔ | ? | No | ✗ | ✔ | ✓ | D.C.C.A. |
| Lean'N Crisp | ADM | ✗ | ✗ | ? | ? | ✗ | No | ✗ | ? | ✓ | |
| Liguria | CQB | ? | ✔ | ✔ | ✔ | ✓ | No | ✗ | ✔ | ✓ | D.C.C.A. |
| Louis Rich | MO | ? | ✗ | ✔ | ? | ✗ | Yes | ? | ? | ? | cigarettes; Salvadoran coffee; Work. Princ. |
| Mary Kitchen | HRL | ? | ✗ | ✔ | ✔ | ✗ | No | ? | ? | ? | |
| Mosey's | CQB | ? | ✔ | ✔ | ✔ | ✓ | No | ✗ | ✔ | ✓ | D.C.C.A. |
| Nathan's Famous | CQB | ? | ✔ | ✔ | ✔ | ✓ | No | ✗ | ✔ | ✓ | D.C.C.A. |

✔ = Top Rating    ✓ = Middle Rating    ✗ = Bottom Rating    ? = Insufficient Information

*For a more detailed explanation see key on page 14*

MEAT: CANNED & REFRIGERATED

| Company or Product | Abbr. | $ |  |  |  |  |  |  |  |  |  | ALERT |
|---|---|---|---|---|---|---|---|---|---|---|---|---|
| Oscar Mayer | MO | ? | ✓ | ✓ | ? | ✗ | ? | Yes | ? | ✓ | ? | cigarettes;Salvadoran coffee; Work. Princ. |
| Partridge | CQB | ? | ✓ | ✓ | ✓ | ✓ | ? | No | ? | ✓ | ✓ | D.C.C.A. |
| Peyton's | CQB | ? | ✓ | ✓ | ✓ | ✓ | ? | No | ? | ✓ | ✓ | D.C.C.A. |
| Pork Classics | CQB | ? | ✓ | ✓ | ✓ | ✓ | ? | No | ? | ✓ | ✓ | D.C.C.A. |
| Rath Black Hawk | CQB | ? | ✓ | ✓ | ✓ | ✓ | ? | No | ? | ✓ | ✓ | D.C.C.A. |
| Rodeo | CQB | ? | ✓ | ✓ | ✓ | ✓ | ? | No | ? | ✓ | ✓ | D.C.C.A. |
| SPAM | HRL | ? | ✗ | ✓ | ✓ | ✗ | ? | No | ? | ? | ? |  |
| Scott Peterson | CQB | ? | ✓ | ✓ | ✓ | ✓ | ? | No | ? | ✓ | ✓ | D.C.C.A. |
| Sizzlean | CAG | ? | ✗ | ✓ | ? | ✗ | ✗ | No | ? | ? | ✗ | safe meat controversy; D.C.C.A.; factory farming |
| Surrey Farm | CAG | ? | ✗ | ✓ | ? | ✗ | ✗ | No | ? | ? | ✗ | safe meat controversy; D.C.C.A.; factory farming |
| Swift Premium | CAG | ? | ✗ | ✓ | ? | ✗ | ✗ | No | ? | ? | ✗ | safe meat controversy; D.C.C.A.; factory farming |
| Tobin's First Prize | CQB | ? | ✓ | ✓ | ✓ | ✓ | ? | No | ? | ✓ | ✓ | D.C.C.A. |
| Underwood | PET | ? | ✓ | ? | ? | ✗ | ? | No | ? | ✓ | ? |  |

| Product or Company | Abbr. | 💲 | ♀ | ✋ | 🍴 | 👥 | 🐇 | ⚛ | ALERT |
|---|---|---|---|---|---|---|---|---|---|
| Weaver | TYSN | ? | ✖ | ? | ✓ | No | ? | ✖ | factory farming; safe chicken contr. |
| **MILK: CANNED & POWDERED** | | | | | | | | | |
| Carnation | NEST | ? | ✖ | ? | ✓* | YesIN | ✓ | ? | infant formula; Salv. coffee; ⊕, D.C.C.A.; U.K. |
| Carousel | MO | ? | ✓ | ✓ | ? | Yes | ? | ? | cigarettes; Salvadoran coffee; Work. Princ. |
| Coffeetwin | MO | ? | ✓ | ✓ | ? | Yes | ? | ? | cigarettes; Salvadoran coffee; Work. Princ. |
| Cremora | BN | ✓ | ✓ | ✓ | ✓ | YesIN | ✓ | ✓ | |
| Dairymate | PET | ? | ? | ? | ✖ | No | ? | ? | |
| Eagle Brand | BN | ✓ | ✓ | ✓ | ✓ | YesIN | ✓ | ✓ | |
| KLIM | BN | ✓ | ✓ | ✓ | ✓ | YesIN | ✓ | ✓ | |
| Magnolia Brand | BN | ✓ | ✓ | ✓ | ✓ | YesIN | ✓ | ✓ | |
| Mil-Lait | CAG | ? | ✓ | ? | ✖ | No | ? | ✖ | safe meat controversy; D.C.C.A.; factory farming |

✔ = Top Rating    ✓ = Middle Rating    ✖ = Bottom Rating    ? = Insufficient Information    Page 233

*For a more detailed explanation see key on page 14*

**MILK: CANNED & POWDERED**

| Company or Product | Abbr. | $ | ♀ | | | | | | | | | ALERT |
|---|---|---|---|---|---|---|---|---|---|---|---|---|
| **N-Rich** | CAG | ? | ✖ | ✔ | ? | ✖ | ✖ | No | ? | ✖ | ✖ | safe meat controversy; D.C.C.A.; factory farming |
| **PET** | PET | ? | ? | ? | ? | ✖ | ? | No | ? | ? | ? | |
| **Party Time** | MO | – | ✔ | ? | ✔ | ✖ | ? | Yes | ? | ? | ? | cigarettes; Salvadoran coffee; Work. Princ. |
| **Sanalac** | CAG | ? | ✖ | ✔ | ? | ✖ | ✖ | No | ? | ? | ✖ | safe meat controversy; D.C.C.A.; factory farming |
| **PAIN/DISCOMFORT RELIEVERS** | | | | | | | | | | | | |
| **Advil** | AHP | ✖ | ✔ | ✔ | ✔(*) | ✔ | ✔ | Yes | ✔ | ✔ | ✔ | infant formula |
| **Anacin** | AHP | ✖ | ✔ | ✔ | ✔(*) | ✔ | ✔ | Yes | ✔ | ✔ | ✔ | infant formula |
| **Anbesol** | AHP | ✖ | ✔ | ✔ | ✔(*) | ✔ | ✔ | Yes | ✔ | ✔ | ✔ | infant formula |
| **Anusol** | WLA | ✔ | ✔ | ✔ | ✖○ | ✔ | ✔ | YesIN | ✔∅ | ✔ | ✔ | on-site day care; Workplace Principles |
| **Aroma Vera#** | AV | ? | ✔ | ✔ | ✔ | ✖ | ✖ | No | ✔ | ✔ | ✖ | |
| **Bantron** | DEPC | ? | ✔ | ✔ | ✔ | ✔ | ✔ | No | ? | ✔ | ✔ | |
| **Bayer** | EK | ✔ | ✔ | ✔ | ✔(*) | ✔ | ✔ | No | ✔ | ✔ | ✔ | ♣, C.C.A. |
| **Ben Gay** | PFE | ✔ | ✖ | ? | ? | ✖ | ✔ | YesIN | ✖ | ? | ? | heart valve suits |

| Product or Company | Abbr. | | | | | | | | | ALERT |
|---|---|---|---|---|---|---|---|---|---|---|
| Benadryl | WLA | ✓ | ✓ | ✓ | ✗○ | ✓ | YesIN | ✓⊘ | ? | on-site day care; Workplace Principles |
| Bonine | PFE | ✓ | ✗ | ? | ? | ✗ | YesIN | ✗ | ? | heart valve suits |
| Bufferin | BMY | ✓ | ✓ | ✓ | ✓⊛ | ✓ | YesIN | ✓ | ✓ | infant formula; Workplace Principles; D.C.C.A |
| Caladryl | WLA | ✓ | ✓ | ✓ | ✗○ | ✓ | YesIN | ✓⊘ | ? | on-site day care; Workplace Principles |
| Cama Arthritis Pain Rel. | SAND | ? | ? | ? | ? | ? | YesIN | ✓ | ? | makes pesticides |
| Chlor-Trimeton | SGP | ✓ | ✓ | ✓ | ✓⊛ | ✓ | YesIN | ✓ | ✓ | on-site day care; Workplace Principles |
| Clear Eyes | ABT | ? | ✓ | ? | ✓⊛ | ✓ | YesIN | ✓ | ✓ | infant formula |
| Cortaid | UPJ | ✓ | ✓ | ✓ | ✓⊛ | ✓ | YesIN | ✓ | ✓ | |
| Datril | BMY | ✓ | ✓ | ✓ | ✓⊛ | ✓ | YesIN | ✓ | ✓ | infant formula; Workplace Principles; D.C.C.A |
| Excedrin | BMY | ✓ | ✓ | ✓ | ✓⊛ | ✓ | YesIN | ✓ | ✓ | infant formula; Workplace Principles; D.C.C.A |
| Feldene | PFE | ✓ | ✗ | ? | ? | ✗ | YesIN | ✗ | ? | heart valve suits |

✔ = Top Rating   ✔ = Middle Rating   ✗ = Bottom Rating   ? = Insufficient Information

*For a more detailed explanation see key on page 14*

| | Page 235 |
|---|---|

**PAIN/DISCOMFORT RELIEVERS**

# PAIN/DISCOMFORT RELIEVERS

| Company or Product | Abbr. | 💲 | ♀ | | ✽ | | | | | | ALERT |
|---|---|---|---|---|---|---|---|---|---|---|---|
| Gyne-Lotrimin | SGP | ○ | ✓ | ✓ | ✓✽ | ✓ | YesIN | ○ | ✓ | ✓ | on-site day care; Workplace Principles |
| Heet | AHP | ✗ | ✓ | ○ | ✓✽ | ✓ | Yes | ○ | ✓ | ✓ | infant formula |
| Medipren | JNJ | ✓ | ✓ | ✓ | ✓✽ | ✓ | YesIN | ✓ | ○ | ✓ | on-site day care; Workplace Principles |
| Midol | EK | ○ | ✓ | ✓ | ✓✽ | ✓ | No | ○ | ✓ | ✓ | ✈ C.C.A. |
| Mineral Ice | BMY | ○ | ✓ | ○ | ✓✽ | ○ | YesIN | ○ | ✓ | ✓ | infant formula; Workplace Principles; D.C.C.A. |
| Motrin IB | UPJ | ✓ | ✓ | ✓ | ✓✽ | ✓ | YesIN | ✓ | ✓ | ✓ | |
| Murine | ABT | ? | ✓ | ? | ✓✽ | ✓ | YesIN | ✓ | ✓ | ✓ | infant formula |
| Norwich Aspirin | PG | ✓ | ✓ | ✓ | ✓✽ | ✓ | Yes | ✓ | ✓ | ✓ | disposable diapers; Salvadoran coffee; on-site day care; C.C.A. |
| Nuprin | BMY | ○ | ✓ | ○ | ✓✽ | ✓ | YesIN | ○ | ✓ | ✓ | infant formula; Workplace Principles; D.C.C.A. |
| Ocuclear | SGP | ○ | ✓ | ○ | ✓✽ | ✓ | YesIN | ○ | ✓ | ✓ | on-site day care; Workplace Principles |
| Panadol | EK | ○ | ✓ | ✓ | ✓✽ | ✓ | No | ○ | ✓ | ✓ | ✈ C.C.A. |
| Percogesic | PG | ✓ | ✓ | ✓ | ✓✽ | ✓ | Yes | ✓ | ✓ | ✓ | disposable diapers; Salvadoran coffee; on-site day care; C.C.A. |
| Preparation H | AHP | ✗ | ✓ | ✗ | ✓✽ | ✓ | Yes | ○ | ✓ | ○ | infant formula |

# PAIN/DISCOMFORT RELIEVERS

| Product or Company | Abbr. | $ | ♀ | ⚇ | ⚖ | 🐪 | ✋ | ☢ | ♻ | ⚎ | ALERT |
|---|---|---|---|---|---|---|---|---|---|---|---|
| Primatene | AHP | ✖ | ✔ | ◊ | ✔ | ◊⊛ | ✔ | Yes | ◊ | ◊ | infant formula |
| Rid | PFE | ◊ | ✖ | ? | ✔ | ? | ◊ | YesIN | ✖ | ? | heart valve suits |
| Serenity | JNJ | ✔ | ✔ | ✔ | ✔ | ✔⊛ | ✔ | YesIN | ✔ | ✔ | on-site day care; Workplace Principles |
| Sine-Aid | JNJ | ✔ | ✔ | ✔ | ✔ | ✔⊛ | ✔ | YesIN | ✔ | ✔ | on-site day care; Workplace Principles |
| Sinutab | WLA | ✔ | ◊ | ✔ | ✔ | ✖◯ | ◊ | YesIN | ✔∅ | ? | on-site day care; Workplace Principles |
| St. Joseph's | SGP | ◊ | ✔ | ✔ | ✔ | ✔⊛ | ✔ | YesIN | ✔ | ◊ | on-site day care; Workplace Principles |
| Synephrine | EK | ◊ | ◊ | ◊ | ✔ | ✔⊛ | ✔ | No | ◊ | ◊ | ✈, C.C.A. |
| Trendar | AHP | ✖ | ✔ | ✔ | ✔ | ✔⊛ | ◊ | Yes | ◊ | ◊ | infant formula |
| Triaminic | SAND | ? | ? | ? | ? | ? | ? | YesIN | ◊ | ? | makes pesticides |
| Triaminicin | SAND | ? | ? | ? | ? | ? | ✖ | YesIN | ◊ | ? | makes pesticides |
| Tronolane | ABT | ? | ✔ | ? | ◊ | ✔⊛ | ✔ | YesIN | ✔ | ◊ | infant formula |

✔ = Top Rating  ◊ = Middle Rating  ✖ = Bottom Rating  ? = Insufficient Information

*For a more detailed explanation see key on page 14*

Page 237

| Company or Product | Abbr. | $ | ⚥ | 🔫 | 🖐 | 🐇 | Yes/No | ? | 🏠 | ALERT |
|---|---|---|---|---|---|---|---|---|---|---|
| Tucks | WLA | ✓ | ✓ | ✓ | ✗○ | ✓ | YesIN | ? | ✓ | on-site day care; Workplace Principles |
| Tylenol | JNJ | ✓ | ✓ | ✓ | ✓⊛ | ✓ | YesIN | ✓ | ✓ | on-site day care; Workplace Principles |
| Vanquish | EK | ◐ | ✓ | ✓ | ✓⊛ | ✓ | No | ◐ | ✓ | ☘; C.C.A. |
| Visine | PFE | ◐ | ✗ | ? | ? | ✗ | YesIN | ? | ? | heart valve suits |
| **PAPER & PLASTIC PRODUCTS** | | | | | | | | | | |
| American | SPP | ✓ | ✓ | ✓ | ✓* | ✓ | Yes | ◐ | ✓ | forestry criticized |
| Angel Soft | GP | ✗ | ✓ | ✓ | ? | ✓ | No | ? | ? | clearcutting; on-site day care |
| Attends | PG | ✓ | ✓ | ✓ | ✓⊛ | ✓ | Yes | ✓ | ✓ | disposable diapers; Salvadoran coffee; on-site day care; C.C.A. |
| Aurora | JR | ◐ | ✗ | ◐ | ✗ | ◐ | No | ◐ | ◐ | on-site day care |
| Baggies | MOB | ✗ | ✓ | ✓ | ✓* | ✓ | No | ✗ | ✗ | ☘; Work. Princ.; D.C.C.A. |
| Banner | PG | ✓ | ✓ | ✓ | ✓⊛ | ✓ | Yes | ◐ | ✓ | disposable diapers; Salvadoran coffee; on-site day care; C.C.A. |
| Basic | KMB | ? | ✓ | ✓ | ✗ | ✗ | YesIN | ✗ | ? | disposable diapers |
| Big 'n Thirsty | GP | ✗ | ✓ | ✓ | ? | ◐ | No | ✗ | ? | clearcutting; on-site day care |

| Product or Company | Abbr. | | | | | | | | | ALEKT |
|---|---|---|---|---|---|---|---|---|---|---|
| Bolt | JR | ◐ | ✓ | ✗ | ✓ | ✓ | No | ✓ | ✓ | on-site day care |
| Bounty | PG | ✓ | ✓ | ✓⊛ | ✓ | ✓ | Yes | ✓ | ✓ | disposable diapers; Salvadoran coffee; on-site day care; C.C.A. |
| Brawny | JR | ◐ | ✓ | ✗ | ✓ | ✓ | No | ✓ | ◐ | on-site day care |
| Charmin | PG | ✓ | ✓ | ✓⊛ | ✓ | ✓ | Yes | ✓ | ✓ | disposable diapers; Salvadoran coffee; on-site day care; C.C.A. |
| Chubs | EK | ◐ | ✓ | ✓⊛ | ✓ | ◐ | No | ✓ | ✓ | 🐟; C.C.A. |
| Clout | KMB | ? | ✓ | ✗ | ✓ | ? | YesIN | ✗ | ? | disposable diapers |
| Coronet | GP | ✗ | ✓ | ? | ✓ | ✓ | No | ✗ | ? | clearcutting, on-site day care |
| Cottonelle | SPP | ✓ | ✓ | ✓* | ✓ | ✓ | Yes | ✗ | ✓ | forestry criticized |
| Cut-Rite | RLM | ✗ | ✗ | ✓ | ◐ | ✓ | No | ◐ | ◐ | |
| Delta | GP | ✗ | ✓ | ✓ | ✓ | ✓ | No | ✗ | ? | clearcutting; on-site day care |
| Depend | KMB | ? | ? | ✗ | ✗ | ? | YesIN | ✗ | ? | disposable diapers |

| | | | | |
|---|---|---|---|---|
| ✓ = Top Rating | ◐ = Middle Rating | ✗ = Bottom Rating | ? = Insufficient Information | |

*For a more detailed explanation see key on page 14*

| | |
|---|---|
| PAPER & PLASTIC PRODUCTS | Page 239 |

# PAPER & PLASTIC PRODUCTS

| Company or Product | Abbr. | 💲 | ♀ | ⚕ | ‖ | ✍ | 🐾 | ☠ | ♻ | ALERT |
|---|---|---|---|---|---|---|---|---|---|---|
| Dixie | JR | ✓ | ✗ | ✓ | ✓ | ✓ | ✓ | No | ✓ | on-site day care |
| Earth Care Comp. Paper# | ECP | ✓+ | ✗ | ✓ | ✓ | ✓ | ✓ | No | ✓ | 1% For Peace; ACT NOW; Valdez Principles |
| Earth Care Copy Paper# | ECP | ✓+ | ✗ | ✓ | ✓ | ✓ | ✓ | No | ✓ | 1% For Peace; ACT NOW; Valdez Principles |
| Earth Care Gift Wrap# | ECP | ✓+ | ✗ | ✓ | ✓ | ✓ | ✓ | No | ✓ | 1% For Peace; ACT NOW; Valdez Principles |
| Earthnote Cards# | ECP | ✓+ | ✗ | ✓ | ✓ | ✓ | ✓ | No | ✓ | 1% For Peace; ACT NOW; Valdez Principles |
| Earthnote Stationary# | ECP | ✓+ | ✗ | ✓ | ✓ | ✓ | ✓ | No | ✓ | 1% For Peace; ACT NOW; Valdez Principles |
| Flair | GP | ✗ | ✓ | ? | ✗ | ✓ | ✓ | No | ? | clearcutting; on-site day care |
| Gala | JR | ✓ | ✗ | ✗ | ✗ | ✓ | ✓ | No | ✓ | on-site day care |
| Georgia-Pacific | GP | ✗ | ✓ | ? | ✗ | ✓ | ✓ | No | ? | clearcutting; on-site day care |
| Glad | FB | ✓+ | ✗ | ✓* | ✓ | ✓ | ✓ | Yes | ✓ | |
| Gladlock | FB | ✓+ | ✗ | ✓* | ✓ | ✓ | ✓ | Yes | ✗ | |
| Handi-Wrap | DOW | ✓ | ✓ | ✓⊛ | ✓ | ✓ | ✓ | Yes | ✓ | pesticide steril. suit; nuclear weapons; on-site day care; makes pesticides |
| Handle-Tie | FB | ✓+ | ✗ | ✓* | ✓ | ✓ | ✗ | Yes | ✗ | |

| Product or Company | Abbr. | $ | | | | | | | | | ALERT |
|---|---|---|---|---|---|---|---|---|---|---|---|
| Hefty | MOB | ✗ | ✓ | ✓ | ✓* | ✓ | No | ✗ | ✓ | ✗ | ✈ Work. Princ.; D.C.C.A. |
| Hi-Dri | KMB | ? | ✓ | ✓ | ✗ | ? | YesIN | ✗ | ? | ? | disposable diapers |
| Kleenex | KMB | ? | ✓ | ✓ | ✗ | ? | YesIN | ✗ | ? | ? | disposable diapers |
| Marcal | MARC | ? | ✓ | ✗ | ✓ | ✓ | No | ✓ | ? | ? | |
| Marcal ECO | MARC | ? | ✓ | ✓ | ✓ | ✓ | No | ✓ | ? | ? | |
| Mead | MEA | ? | ✓ | ✓ | ? | ✓ | No | ✓∅ | ✓ | | |
| Melitta | MTA | ? | ? | ✓ | ✓ | ✓ | No | ✓ | ✓ | | |
| Minimum Impact Paper# | ECP | ✓+ | ✓ | ✗ | ✓ | ✓ | No | ✓ | ✓ | | 1% For Peace; ACT NOW; Valdez Principles |
| Mr. Big | GP | ✗ | ✗ | ? | ✓ | ✗ | No | ✗ | ? | | clearcutting; on-site day care |
| Nice 'n Soft | JR | ✓ | ✓ | ✗ | ✓ | ✓ | No | ✗ | ✓ | | on-site day care |
| Northern | JR | ✓ | ✓ | ✗ | ✓ | ✓ | No | ✗ | ✓ | | on-site day care |

✔ = Top Rating   ✓ = Middle Rating   ✗ = Bottom Rating   ? = Insufficient Information

*For a more detailed explanation see key on page 14*

| | |
|---|---|
| PAPER & PLASTIC PRODUCTS | Page 241 |

| Company or Product | Abbr. | $ | ⚥ | 🐾 | 🌎 | ⚛ | ◻ | ◻ | ALERT |
|---|---|---|---|---|---|---|---|---|---|
| PaperMaid | JR | ✓ | ✓ | ✗ | ✓ | ✓ | No | ✓ | on-site day care |
| Post-It | MMM | ✓ | ✗ | ✓ | ✓ | ✓* | YesIN | ✓ | ☢ |
| Puffs | PG | ✓ | ✓ | ✓ | ✓ | ✓(®) | Yes | ✓ | disposable diapers; Salvadoran coffee; on-site day care; C.C.A. |
| Reynold's Wrap | RLM | ✗ | ✗ | ✗ | ✓ | ✓ | No | ✓ | |
| Saran Wrap | DOW | ✓ | ✓ | ✓ | ✓ | ✓(®) | Yes | ✓ | pesticide steril. suit; nuclear weapons; on-site day care; makes pesticides |
| ScotTowels | SPP | ✓ | ✓ | ✓ | ✓ | ✓* | Yes | ✓ | forestry criticized |
| Scott | SPP | ✓ | ✓ | ✓ | ✓ | ✓* | Yes | ✓ | forestry criticized |
| Scotties | SPP | ✓ | ✓ | ✓ | ✓ | ✓* | Yes | ✓ | forestry criticized |
| Sealwrap | BN | ✓ | ✓ | ✓ | ✓ | ✓ | YesIN | ✓ | |
| Soft 'N Pretty | SPP | ✓ | ✓ | ✓ | ✓ | ✓* | Yes | ✓ | forestry criticized |
| Soft-Ply | GP | ✗ | ✗ | ✓ | ? | ? | No | ? | clearcutting; on-site day care |
| Softex | GP | ✗ | ✗ | ✓ | ? | ? | No | ? | clearcutting; on-site day care |
| Softique | KMB | ? | ✓ | ✗ | ? | ✗ | YesIN | ? | disposable diapers |

# PAPER & PLASTIC PRODUCTS

| Product or Company | Abbr. | $ | ⚥ | ▣ | ▣ | ▣ | (Yes/No) | ▣ | ▣ | ▣ | ALERT |
|---|---|---|---|---|---|---|---|---|---|---|---|
| Sparkle | GP | ✖ | ✔ | ✔ | ? | ✔ | No | ✖ | ? | ? | clearcutting; on-site day care |
| Spill-Mate | JR | ✔ | ✖ | ✔ | ✔ | ✔ | No | ✖ | ✔ | ✔ | on-site day care |
| Summit | PG | ✔ | ✔ | ✔⊛ | ✔ | ✔ | Yes | ✔ | ✔ | ✔ | disposable diapers; Salvadoran coffee; on-site day care; C.C.A. |
| Tuff-N-Tidy | GP | ✖ | ✔ | ? | ✔ | ✔ | No | ✖ | ? | ✔ | clearcutting; on-site day care |
| Vanity Fair | JR | ✔ | ✖ | ✖ | ✔ | ✔ | No | ✖ | ✔ | ✔ | on-site day care |
| Viva | SPP | ✔ | ✔ | ✔* | ✔ | ✔ | Yes | ✖ | ✔ | ✔ | forestry criticized |
| Wash 'N Dry | CL | ✔+ | ✔ | ✔⊛ | ✔ | ✔ | Yes/N | ✔ | ✔ | ✔ | |
| Wet Ones | EK | ✔ | ✔ | ✔⊛ | ✔ | ✔ | No | ✖ | ✔ | ✔ | ♠, C.C.A. |
| White Cloud | PG | ✔ | ✔ | ✔⊛ | ✔ | ✔ | Yes | ✔ | ✔ | ✔ | disposable diapers; Salvadoran coffee; on-site day care; C.C.A. |
| Zee | JR | ✔ | ✖ | ✖ | ✔ | ✔ | No | ✖ | ✔ | ✔ | on-site day care |
| Ziploc | DOW | ✔ | ✔ | ✔⊛ | ✔ | ✔ | Yes | ✔ | ✔ | ✔ | pesticide steril. suit; nuclear weapons; on-site day care; makes pesticides |

✔ = Top Rating    ✓ = Middle Rating    ✖ = Bottom Rating    ? = Insufficient Information

*For a more detailed explanation see key on page 14*

| Company or Product | Abbr. | $ | ⚥ | | | | | | Yes/No | | | | ALERT |
|---|---|---|---|---|---|---|---|---|---|---|---|---|---|
| **PASTA** | | | | | | | | | | | | | |
| ABC-123 | AHP | ✖ | ✓ | ✓ | ✓ | ✓(⊛) | ✓ | Yes | ✓ | ✓ | ✓ | ✓ | infant formula |
| American Beauty | HSY | ✓ | ✓ | ✓ | ✓ | ✓* | ✓ | No | ✓ | ✓ | ✓ | ✓ | on-site day care |
| Anthony's | BN | ✓ | ✓ | ✓ | ✓ | ✓ | ✓ | YesIN | ✓ | ✓ | ✓ | ✓ | |
| Beef-O-Getti | AHP | ✖ | ✓ | ✓ | ✓ | ✓(⊛) | ✓ | Yes | ✓ | ✓ | ✓ | ✓ | infant formula |
| Beefaroni | AHP | ✖ | ✓ | ✓ | ✓ | ✓(⊛) | ✓ | Yes | ✓ | ✓ | ✓ | ✓ | infant formula |
| Bravo | BN | ✓ | ✓ | ✓ | ✓ | ✓ | ✓ | YesIN | ✓ | ✓ | ✓ | ✓ | |
| Buitoni | NEST | ? | ✓ | ? | ✓ | ✓* | ✓ | YesIN | ✓ | ? | ✓ | ? | infant formula; Salv. coffee; ⊕; D.C.C.A.; U.K. |
| Catelli | BN | ✓ | ✓ | ✓ | ✓ | ✓ | ✓ | YesIN | ✓ | ✓ | ✓ | ✓ | |
| Contadina | NEST | ? | ✓ | ? | ✓ | ✓* | ✓ | YesIN | ✓ | ? | ✓ | ? | infant formula; Salv. coffee; ⊕; D.C.C.A.; U.K. |
| Creamette | BN | ✓ | ✓ | ✓ | ✓ | ✓* | ✓ | YesIN | ✓ | ✓ | ✓ | ✓ | |
| Delmonico | HSY | ✓ | ✓ | ✓ | ✓ | ✓ | ✓ | No | ✓ | ✓ | ✓ | ✓ | on-site day care |
| Di Giorno | MO | ? | ✓ | ✓ | ? | ? | ✖ | Yes | ? | ? | ? | ? | cigarettes; Salvadoran coffee; Work. Princ. |

| Product or Company | Abbr. | $ | | | | | | | | ALERT |
|---|---|---|---|---|---|---|---|---|---|---|
| **Dutch Maid** | BN | ◑ | ✔ | ✔ | ✔ | ✔ | YesIN | ✔ | ✔ | |
| **Ecco Bella*** | ECC | ✔ | ✔ | ✔ | ✔₀ | ✔ | No | ✔ | ◑ | |
| **Eden#** | EDEN | ✔+ | ✔ | ✔ | ✔ | ✔ | No | ✔ | ✔ | some organic ingredients |
| **Enticing Delights#** | FALC | ? | ✖ | ◑ | ✔ | ✔ | No | ◑ | ◑ | 1% For Peace; some organic ingredients |
| **Fantastic Foods#** | FFI | ✔ | ✔ | ✔ | ✔ | ✔ | No | ◑ | ◑ | some organic ingredients |
| **Franco-American** | CPB | ✔ | ✔ | ? | ✔ | ✔ | No | ✔ | ◑ | on-site day care |
| **Gioia** | BN | ◑ | ✔ | ✔ | ✔ | ✔ | YesIN | ◑ | ✔ | |
| **Globe A-1** | BN | ◑ | ✔ | ✔ | ✔ | ✔ | YesIN | ✔ | ✔ | |
| **Gooch Foods** | ADM | ✖ | ? | ? | ✖ | ? | No | ? | ? | |
| **Goodman's** | BN | ◑ | ✔ | ✔ | ✔ | ✔ | YesIN | ✔ | ✔ | |
| **Health Valley#** | HVAL | ? | ? | ? | ✖ | ? | No | ? | ? | some organic ingredients |

✔ = Top Rating   ◑ = Middle Rating   ✖ = Bottom Rating   ? = Insufficient Information
For a more detailed explanation see key on page 14.

Page 245

PASTA

| Company or Product | Abbr. | $ | ♀ | | | | | | | | ALERT |
|---|---|---|---|---|---|---|---|---|---|---|---|
| Herb's Homestyle Pasta# | EDEN | ✔+ | ✔ | ✔ | ✔ | ✔ | ✔ | No | ✔ | ✔ | some organic ingredients |
| International Noodles | GIS | ✔+ | ✔ | ✔ | ✔ | ✔ | ✔ | No | ⟋ | ✔ | C.C.A. |
| La Rosa | ADM | ✘ | ✘ | ? | ? | ✘ | ? | No | ✔ | ? | |
| Light 'N Fluffy | HSY | ⟋ | ✔ | ✔ | ✔* | ✔ | ✔ | No | ✔ | ✔ | on-site day care |
| Luxury | BN | ⟋ | ✔ | ✔ | ⟋ | ✔ | ⟋ | YesIN | ✔ | ⟋ | |
| Martha Gooch | ADM | ✘ | ✘ | ? | ? | ✘ | ? | No | ✘ | ? | |
| Mayacamas* | MAYA | ? | ? | ? | ? | ✔ | ? | No | ? | ? | |
| Merlino's | BN | ⟋ | ✔ | ✔ | ✔ | ✔ | ⟋ | YesIN | ⟋ | ✔ | |
| Mini Bites | AHP | ✘ | ✔ | ⟋ | ✔® | ✔ | ⟋ | Yes | ⟋ | ✔ | infant formula |
| Mrs. Grass | BN | ⟋ | ✔ | ✔ | ✔ | ✔ | ⟋ | YesIN | ⟋ | ✔ | |
| Mueller's | CPC | ✔+ | ✔ | ✔ | ✔ | ✔ | ⟋ | No | ⟋ | ✔ | |
| New Mill | BN | ⟋ | ✔ | ✔ | ✔ | ✔ | ⟋ | YesIN | ⟋ | ✔ | |
| Noodle Roni | OAT | ✔+ | ✔ | ✔ | ✔ | ✔ | ✔ | No | ✔ | ⟋ | Fair Share |

| Product or Company | Abbr. | | | | | | | | | | | | ALERT |
|---|---|---|---|---|---|---|---|---|---|---|---|---|---|
| Pacific Gardens* | ACOP | ? | ✔ | ? | ? | ✔ | ✖ | No | ? | ? | ? | ? | co-op |
| Pastamania | HSY | ◡ | ✔ | ◡ | ✔ | ✔* | ✔ | No | ✔ | ✔ | ✔ | ? | on-site day care |
| Pennsylvania Dutch | BN | ◡ | ✔ | ✔ | ✔ | ✔ | ◡ | YesIN | ◡ | ✔ | ✔ | ✔ | |
| Perfection | HSY | ◡ | ✔ | ✔ | ✔ | ✔* | ✔ | No | ◡ | ✔ | ✔ | ✔ | on-site day care |
| Prince | BN | ◡ | ✔ | ✔ | ✔ | ✔ | ✔ | YesIN | ◡ | ✔ | ✔ | ✔ | |
| Procino-Rossi (P&R) | HSY | ◡ | ✔ | ✔ | ✔ | ✔* | ✔ | No | ◡ | ✔ | ✔ | ✔ | on-site day care |
| R&F | BN | ◡ | ✔ | ✔ | ✔ | ✔ | ✔ | YesIN | ◡ | ✔ | ✔ | ✔ | |
| Red Cross | BN | ◡ | ✔ | ✔ | ✔ | ✔ | ✔ | YesIN | ◡ | ✔ | ✔ | ✔ | |
| Roller Coasters | AHP | ✖ | ✔ | ◡ | ✔ | ✔⊛ | ✔ | Yes | ◡ | ◡ | ✔ | ◡ | infant formula |
| Ronco | BN | ◡ | ✔ | ◡ | ✔ | ✔ | ✔ | YesIN | ◡ | ✔ | ✔ | ✔ | |
| Ronzoni | HSY | ◡ | ✔ | ◡ | ✔ | ✔* | ✔ | No | ◡ | ✔ | ✔ | ✔ | on-site day care |

✔ = Top Rating   ◡ = Middle Rating   ✖ = Bottom Rating   ? = Insufficient Information

*For a more detailed explanation see key on page 14*

PASTA

# PEANUT BUTTER & OTHER SPREADS

| Company or Product | Abbr. | 💲 | ♀ | ✊ | 🐇 | 🏃 | 🐾 | ☮ | ⚖ | ▦ | ALERT |
|---|---|---|---|---|---|---|---|---|---|---|---|
| **Russo** | ADM | ✖ | ✔ | ? | ✖ | ? | ✔ | ✖ | No | ✖ | ? | |
| **San Giorgio** | HSY | ✔ | ✔ | ✔ | ✔ | ✔* | ✔ | ✔ | No | ✔ | ✔ | on-site day care |
| **Skinner** | HSY | ✔ | ✔ | ✔ | ✔ | ✔* | ✔ | ✔ | No | ✔ | ✔ | on-site day care |
| **Suzy Wan** | MO | ? | ✔ | ✔ | ✔ | ? | ✖ | ? | Yes | ? | ? | cigarettes; Salvadoran coffee; Work. Princ. |
| **Vimco** | BN | ✔ | ✔ | ✔ | ✔ | ✔ | ✔ | ✔ | YesN | ✔ | ✔ | |
| **Zooroni** | AHP | ✖ | ✔ | ✔ | ✔ | ✔⊛ | ✔ | ✔ | Yes | ✔ | ✔ | infant formula |

## PEANUT BUTTER & OTHER SPREADS

| | | | | | | | | | | | |
|---|---|---|---|---|---|---|---|---|---|---|---|
| **21st Century Foods\*** | TFC | ✖ | ✔ | ✔ | ✔ | ✔ | ✔ | ✔ | No | ✔ | ✔ | on-site day care |
| **Choko Butter** | GOYA | ? | ? | ? | ? | ? | ✖ | ? | No | ? | ? | |
| **Evon** | JSAN | ? | ? | ? | ✔ | ✔ | ✖ | ? | No | ? | ? | |
| **Goober** | SJM | ✔ | ✔ | ✔ | ✔ | ✔ | ✔ | ✔ | No | ✔ | ✔ | some organic ingredients |
| **Jif** | PG | ✔ | ✔ | ✔ | ✔⊛ | ✔ | ✔ | ✔ | Yes | ✔ | ✔ | disposable diapers; Salvadoran coffee; on-site day care; C.C.A. |
| **Laura Scudder's** | BN | ✔ | ✔ | ✔ | ✔ | ✔ | ✔ | YesN | ✔ | ✔ | |

| Product or Company | Abbr. | | | | | | | | | | ALERT! |
|---|---|---|---|---|---|---|---|---|---|---|---|
| Loriva Supreme* | LOR | ✔ | ✔ | ✔/∅ | ✔ | ✔ | ✔ | No | ✔ | ? | |
| Marmite | CPC | ✔+ | ✔ | ✔ | ✔ | ✔ | ✔ | No | ✔/∅ | ✔ | |
| Natural Peanut Butter | SJM | ✔ | ✔ | ✗ | ✔ | ✔ | ✔ | No | ✔ | ✔ | some organic ingredients |
| Peter Pan | CAG | ? | ✗ | ? | ✗ | ✔ | ✗ | No | ? | ✗ | safe meat controversy; D.C.C.A.; factory farming |
| Protein Aide Prod.* | LOR | ✔ | ✔ | ✔/∅ | ✔ | ✔ | ✔ | No | ✔/∅ | ? | |
| Skippy | CPC | ✔+ | ✔ | ✔ | ✔ | ✔ | ✔ | No | ✔ | ✔ | |
| Super Krunch | MO | ? | ✗ | ✔ | ✗ | ? | ? | Yes | ? | ? | cigarettes; Salvadoran coffee; Work. Princ. |
| Tinker Bell | CAG | ? | ✗ | ✔ | ✗ | ? | ? | No | ? | ✗ | safe meat controversy; D.C.C.A.; factory farming |
| Whole Earth# | WHO | ✔+ | ✔ | ✔ | ✔ | ✔ | ✔ | No | ✔ | ✔ | 1% For Peace; some organic ingredients |
| **PET FOOD & PET PRODUCTS** | | | | | | | | | | | |
| 9 Lives | HNZ | ✔ | ✔ | ✔ | ✔ | ✔ | ✔ | No | ✔ | ✔ | C.C.A. |

✔ = Top Rating  ✓ = Middle Rating  ✗ = Bottom Rating  ? = Insufficient Information

*For a more detailed explanation see key on page 14*

Page 249

**PEANUT BUTTER & OTHER SPREADS**

| Company or Product | Abbr. | 💲 | ♀ | ⊆ | 🐇 | | | No/Yes | ? | ✗ | ALERT |
|---|---|---|---|---|---|---|---|---|---|---|---|
| ANF | CAG | ? | ✗ | ✓ | ? | ✗ | ✗ | No | ? | ✗ | safe meat controversy; D.C.C.A; factory farming |
| Alley Kat | RAL | ✓ | ✓ | ✓ | ✓ | ✓ | ✓ | No | ✓ | ✓ | |
| Alpo | GMP | ✓ | ✓ | ✓ | ✓ | ✓ | ✓ | YesIN | ✓ | ✓ | 🌐, U.K. |
| Amore | HNZ | ✓ | ✓ | ✓ | ✓ | ✓ | ✓ | No | ✓ | ✓ | C.C.A. |
| Beggin' Strips | RAL | ✓ | ✓ | ✓ | ✓ | ✓ | ✓ | No | ✓ | ✓ | |
| Benji's Moist & Chunky | RAL | ✓ | ✓ | ✓ | ✓ | ✓ | ✓ | No | ✓ | ✓ | |
| Blue Mountain | GMP | ✓ | ✓ | ✓ | ✓ | ✓ | ✓ | YesIN | ✓ | ✓ | 🌐, U.K. |
| Bonkers | CAG | ? | ✗ | ✓ | ? | ✗ | ✗ | No | ? | ✗ | safe meat controversy; D.C.C.A; factory farming |
| Bonz | RAL | ✓ | ✓ | ✓ | ✓ | ✓ | ✓ | No | ✓ | ✓ | |
| Butcher Brand | GMP | ✓ | ✓ | ✓ | ✓ | ✓ | ✓ | YesIN | ✓ | ✓ | 🌐, U.K. |
| Butcher's Blend | RAL | ✓ | ✓ | ✓ | ✓ | ✓ | ✓ | No | ✓ | ✓ | |
| Cat Menu | RAL | ✓ | ✓ | ✓ | ✓ | ✓ | ✓ | No | ✓ | ✓ | |
| Cheese... | RAL | ✓ | ✓ | ✓ | ✓ | ✓ | ✓ | No | ✓ | ✓ | |

| Product or Company | Abbr. | | | | | | | | | | | ALERT |
|---|---|---|---|---|---|---|---|---|---|---|---|---|
| Chef's Blend | NEST | ? | ✔ | ✔ | ✔ | ✔* | ✔ | YesIN | ✔ | ? | ? | infant formula; Salv. coffee; ⊕; D.C.C.A.; U.K |
| Chuck Wagon | RAL | ◖ | ✔ | ✔ | ✔ | ✔ | ✔ | No | ✔ | ◖ | ✔ | |
| Come 'N Get It | NEST | ? | ✔ | ✔ | ✔ | ✔* | ✔ | YesIN | ✔ | ? | ✔ | infant formula; Salv. coffee; ⊕; D.C.C.A.; U.K |
| Control | CLX | ✗ | ✔ | ✔ | ✔ | ✔ | ✔ | No | ✔ | ✗ | ✔ | |
| Doggie Bag | GIS | ✔+ | ✔ | ✔ | ✔ | ✔ | ✔ | No | ✔ | ✔ | ✔ | C.C.A |
| Ecco Bella* | ECC | ✔ | ✔ | ◖∅ | ✔ | ✔ | ◖ | No | ◖ | ◖ | ◖ | |
| Fancy Feast | NEST | ? | ✔ | ? | ✔ | ✔* | ✔ | YesIN | ◖ | ? | ? | infant formula; Salv. coffee; ⊕; D.C.C.A.; U.K |
| Field 'n Farm | RAL | ◖ | ✔ | ✔ | ✔ | ✔ | ✔ | No | ✔ | ◖ | ✔ | |
| Fresh Feliners | CL | ✔+ | ✔ | ✔ | ✔ | ✔⊛ | ✔ | YesIN | ✔ | ✔ | ✔ | |
| Fresh Step | CLX | ✗ | ✔ | ✔ | ✔ | ✔* | ✔ | No | ✗ | ✔ | ✔ | |
| Friskies | NEST | ? | ✔ | ✔ | ✔ | ✔* | ✔ | YesIN | ◖ | ? | ? | infant formula; Salv. coffee; ⊕; D.C.C.A.; U.K |

✔ = Top Rating    ◖ = Middle Rating    ✗ = Bottom Rating    ? = Insufficient Information

*For a more detailed explanation see key on page 14*

| | |
|---|---|
| | Page 251 |

**PET FOOD & PET PRODUCTS**

| Company or Product | Abbr. | $ | ♀+ | 🐇 | 🐁 | 🖐 | 🐾 | ⦂ | ♻ | ▦ | ALERT |
|---|---|---|---|---|---|---|---|---|---|---|---|
| Gaines Cycle | OAT | ✓+ | ✓ | ✓ | ✓ | ✓ | No | ✓ | ✓ | ✓ | FairShare |
| Grand Gourmet | NEST | ? | ✓ | ? | ✓* | ✓ | YesIN | ✓ | ? | ? | infant formula; Salv. coffee; ⊕; D.C.C.A.; U.K. |
| Gravy Train | OAT | ✓+ | ✓ | ✓ | ✓ | ✓ | No | ✓ | ✓ | ✓ | FairShare |
| Grrravy | RAL | ✓ | ✓ | ✓ | ✓ | ✓ | No | ✓ | ✓ | ✓ | |
| Happy Cat | RAL | ✓ | ✓ | ✓ | ✓ | ✓ | No | ✓ | ✓ | ✓ | |
| Hearty Chews | RAL | ✓ | ✓ | ✓ | ✓ | ✓ | No | ✓ | ✓ | ✓ | |
| Hill's | CL | ✓+ | ✓ | ✓ | ✓⊛ | ✓ | YesIN | ✓ | ✓ | ✓ | |
| Jerky | HNZ | ✓ | ✓ | ✓ | ✓ | ✓ | No | ✓ | ✓ | ✓ | C.C.A. |
| Jim Dandy | GMP | ✓ | ✓ | ✓ | ✓ | ✓ | YesIN | ✓ | ✓ | ✓ | ⊕, U.K. |
| Kal Kan | MARS | ? | ? | ? | ? | ? | No | ✓ | ✓ | ? | |
| Ken-L Ration | OAT | ✓+ | ✓ | ✓ | ✓ | ✓ | No | ✓ | ✓ | ✓ | FairShare |
| Kibbles 'N Bits | OAT | ✓+ | ✓ | ✓ | ✓ | ✓ | No | ✓ | ✓ | ✓ | FairShare |
| King Kuts | OAT | ✓ | ✓ | ✓ | ✓ | ✓ | No | ✓ | ✓ | ✓ | FairShare |

| Product or Company | Addr. | | | | | | | | | | | ALERT |
|---|---|---|---|---|---|---|---|---|---|---|---|---|
| Kit 'N Kaboodle | RAL | ~ | ✓ | ✓ | ✓ | ✓ | ~ | No | ✓ | ~ | ~ | |
| Litter Green | CLX | ~ | ✗ | ✓ | ✓ | ✓* | ✓ | No | ✓ | ✗ | ✓ | |
| Lucky Dog | RAL | ~ | ✓ | ✓ | ✓ | ✓ | ~ | No | ✓ | ~ | ~ | |
| Marathon | GMP | ~ | ✓ | ✓ | ✓ | ✓ | ✓ | YesIN | ~ | ~ | ~ | 🌐, U.K. |
| Meaty Bone | HNZ | ✓ | ~ | ✓ | ✓ | ✓ | ~ | No | ✓ | ✓ | ~ | C.C.A. |
| Meow Mix | RAL | ~ | ✓ | ✓ | ✓ | ✓ | ~ | No | ~ | ~ | ~ | |
| Milk Bone | RJR | ? | ? | ✗ | ✓ | ~ | ✓ | Yes | ✗ | ? | ? | cigarettes; D.C.C.A. |
| Organimals# | AUB | ? | ✓ | ✓ | ✓ | ✓ | ✓ | No | ✓ | ? | ✓ | some organic ingredients |
| Pounce | OAT | ✓+ | ✓ | ✓ | ✓ | ✓ | ✓ | No | ✓ | ~ | ~ | Fair Share |
| Pup-Peroni | OAT | ✓+ | ✓ | ✓ | ✓ | ✓ | ✓ | No | ✓ | ~ | ~ | Fair Share |
| Purina | RAL | ~ | ✓ | ✓ | ✓ | ✓ | ~ | No | ~ | ~ | ~ | |

✓ = Top Rating    ~ = Middle Rating    ✗ = Bottom Rating    ? = Insufficient Information

*For a more detailed explanation see key on page 14*

**PET FOOD & PET PRODUCTS**

| Company or Product | Abbr. | 💲 | 👤 | 🐾 | 🐇 | 🌐 | 🏭 | 🏢 | ALERT |
|---|---|---|---|---|---|---|---|---|---|
| Puss 'N Boots | OAT | ✓+ | ✓ | ✓ | ✓ | ✓ | No | ✓ | ✓ | Fair Share |
| Recipe | HNZ | ✓ | ✓ | ✓ | ✓ | ✓ | No | ✓ | ✓ | C.C.A. |
| Ribz | RAL | ✓ | ✓ | ✓ | ✓ | ✓ | No | ✓ | ✓ | |
| Rival | CAG | ? | ✗ | ? | ? | ✗ | No | ? | ✗ | safe meat controversy; D.C.C.A.; factory farming |
| Sergeants | CAG | ? | ✗ | ? | ? | ✗ | No | ? | ✗ | safe meat controversy; D.C.C.A.; factory farming |
| Sheba | MARS | ? | ? | ? | ? | ? | No | ✓ | ? | |
| Smart Cat | RAL | ✓ | ✓ | ✓ | ✓ | ✓ | No | ✓ | ✓ | |
| Special Dinners | RAL | ✓ | ✓ | ✓ | ✓ | ✓ | No | ✓ | ✓ | |
| Tender Vittles | RAL | ✓ | ✓ | ✓ | ✓ | ✓ | No | ✓ | ✓ | |
| Thrive | RAL | ✓ | ✓ | ✓ | ✓ | ✓ | No | ✓ | ✓ | |
| Unique | RAL | ✓ | ✓ | ✓ | ✓ | ✓ | No | ✓ | ✓ | |
| Whisker Lickin's | RAL | ✓ | ✓ | ✓ | ✓ | ✓ | No | ✓ | ✓ | |

| Product or Company | Abbr. | 💲 | ⚥ | ♻ | 🐾 | 🌍 | ⚛ | | | | ALERT |
|---|---|---|---|---|---|---|---|---|---|---|---|
| **PICKLES & RELISHES** | | | | | | | | | | | |
| Claussen | MO | ? | ✔ | ? | ✔ | ✖ | ? | Yes | ? | ? | cigarettes; Salvadoran coffee; Work. Princ. |
| Early California | CPB | ✔ | ✔ | ✔ | ? | ✔ | ? | No | ✔ | ◡ | on-site day care |
| Goya | GOYA | ? | ? | ? | ? | ✖ | ? | No | ? | ? | |
| Kraft Horseradish | MO | ? | ✔ | ? | ✔ | ✖ | ? | Yes | ? | ? | cigarettes; Salvadoran coffee; Work. Princ. |
| Vlasic | CPB | ✔ | ✔ | ? | ✔ | ✔ | ? | No | ✔ | ◡ | on-site day care |
| **POTATOES: FROZEN** | | | | | | | | | | | |
| Crispy Browns | CAG | ? | ✖ | ? | ✔ | ✖ | ? | No | ? | ✖ | safe meat controversy; D.C.C.A.; factory farming |
| Garden Gourmet | GMP | ◡ | ✔ | ✔ | ✔ | ✔ | ◡ | YesIN | ◡ | ✔ | 🌐, U.K. |
| Inland Valley | UFC | ? | ✖ | ? | ✔ | ✖ | ◡ | No | ? | ✖ | |
| Ore Ida | HNZ | ✔ | ✔ | ✔ | ✔ | ✔ | ◡ | No | ✔ | ◡ | C.C.A. |

✔ = Top Rating    ◡ = Middle Rating    ✖ = Bottom Rating    ? = Insufficient Information

*For a more detailed explanation see key on page 14*

Page 255

**POTATOES: FROZEN**

| Company or Product | Abbr. | $ | ♀ | ○ | ○ | ○ | ○ | ○ | ○ | ○ | ○ | ALERT |
|---|---|---|---|---|---|---|---|---|---|---|---|---|
| Tiny Taters | MO | ? | ✓ | ? | ? | ✗ | ? | ? | Yes | ? | ? | cigarettes; Salvadoran coffee; Work. Princ. |
| **PREPARED FOODS** | | | | | | | | | | | | |
| Aji-Co | AJI | | | | | | | | | | | see page 344 for Japanese companies |
| B & M | PET | ? | ? | ? | ✓ | ✗ | ✓ | ✓ | No | ? | ? | |
| Burrito Grande | HRL | ? | ✗ | ✓ | ✓ | ✗ | ✓ | ✓ | No | ? | ? | |
| Campbell's | CPB | ✓ | ✓ | ✓ | ? | ✓ | ✓ | ✓ | No | ✓ | ✓ | on-site day care |
| Chef Boyardee | AHP | ✗ | ✓ | ✓ | ✓⊛ | ✓ | ✓ | ✓ | Yes | ✓ | ✓ | infant formula |
| Cook Off | AHP | ✗ | ✓ | ✓ | ✓⊛ | ✓ | ✓ | ✓ | Yes | ✓ | ✓ | infant formula |
| Country Store | BN | ✓ | ✓ | ✓ | ✓ | ✓ | ✓ | ✓ | YesN | ✓ | ✓ | |
| Country Style | AHP | ✗ | ✗ | ✓ | ✓⊛ | ✓ | ✓ | ✓ | Yes | ✓ | ✓ | infant formula |
| Dennison's | AHP | ✗ | ✗ | ✓ | ✓⊛ | ✗ | ✓ | ✓ | Yes | ✓ | ✓ | infant formula |
| Egg Beaters | RJR | ? | ✗ | ? | ? | ✗ | ✗ | ✗ | Yes | ? | ? | cigarettes; D.C.C.A. |
| El Charrito | BUD | ✓+ | ✓ | ✓ | ✓ | ✓ | ✓ | ✗ | No | ✓ | ✓ | |

| Product or Company | Abbr. | | | | | | | | | | | ALERT |
|---|---|---|---|---|---|---|---|---|---|---|---|---|
| Fantastic Foods# | FFI | ✔ | ✔ | ✔ | ✔ | ✔ | ✔ | No | ✔ | ✔ | ✔ | some organic ingredients |
| Franco-American | CPB | ✔ | ? | ? | ✔ | ✔ | ? | No | ✔ | ✔ | ✔ | on-site day care |
| Friend's | PET | ? | ? | ? | ? | ✘ | ? | No | ? | ? | ? | |
| Gebhardt | CAG | ? | ✘ | ✔ | ? | ✘ | ✘ | No | ? | ? | ✘ | safe meat controversy; D.C.C.A.; factory farming |
| Goya | GOYA | ? | ? | ? | ? | ✘ | ? | No | ? | ? | ? | |
| Grande Dinners | BUD | ✔+ | ✔ | ✔ | ✔ | ✔ | ✔ | No | ✔ | ✔ | ✔ | |
| Hamburger Fixin's | CAG | ? | ✘ | ✔ | ? | ✘ | ? | No | ? | ? | ✘ | safe meat controversy; D.C.C.A.; factory farming |
| Hamburger Helper | GIS | ✔+ | ✔ | ✔ | ✔ | ✔ | ✔ | No | ✔ | ✔ | ✔ | C.C.A. |
| Health Valley# | HVAL | ? | ? | ✔ | ✔ | ✔ | ? | No | ✔ | ? | ✔ | some organic ingredients |
| Iron Kettle | AHP | ✘ | ✔ | ✔ | ✔(®) | ✔ | ✔ | Yes | ✔ | ✔ | ✔ | infant formula |
| Knorr Instant Potatoes | CPC | ✔+ | ✔ | ✔ | ✔ | ✔ | ✔ | No | ✔ | ✔ | ✔ | |

| | | | |
|---|---|---|---|
| ✔ = Top Rating | ✔ = Middle Rating | ✘ = Bottom Rating | ? = Insufficient Information |

*For a more detailed explanation see key on page 14*

Page 257

PREPARED FOODS

| Company or Product | Abbr. | $ | ♀ | ⚥ | 🐾 | 🎗 | ⚛ | 🌐 | 🕊 | ℹ | ALERT |
|---|---|---|---|---|---|---|---|---|---|---|---|
| Kraft | MO | ? | ✔ | ✔ | ? | ✖ | ? | Yes | ? | ? | cigarettes; Salvadoran coffee; Work. Princ. |
| La Choy | CAG | ? | ✖ | ? | ✖ | ✖ | ✖ | No | ? | ✖ | safe meat controversy; D.C.C.A.; factory farming |
| Lunch Bucket | G | ? | ✔ | ? | ✔ | ✖ | ? | No | ? | ? | |
| Macaroni & Cheese | MO | ? | ✔ | ✔ | ? | ✖ | ? | Yes | ? | ? | cigarettes; Salvadoran coffee; Work. Princ. |
| Mrs. Giles | CPB | ✔ | ✔ | ✔ | ? | ✔ | ✔ | No | ✔ | ✔ | on-site day care |
| Not-So-Sloppy-Joe | HRL | ? | ✖ | ? | ? | ✖ | ? | No | ? | ? | |
| Old El Paso | PET | ? | ? | ? | ? | ? | ? | No | ? | ? | |
| Oriental Classics | GIS | ✔+ | ✔ | ? | ✔ | ✔ | ✔ | No | ✔ | ✔ | C.C.A. |
| Ortega | RJR | ? | ✔ | ? | ? | ✖ | ✔ | Yes | ✖ | ? | cigarettes; D.C.C.A. |
| Orval Kent | PET | ? | ? | ? | ? | ✖ | ? | No | ? | ? | |
| Pancho Villa | PET | ? | ? | ? | ? | ✖ | ? | No | ? | ? | |
| Pillsbury's Inst. Potatoes | GMP | ✔ | ✔ | ✔ | ✔ | ✔ | ✔ | YesN | ✔ | ✔ | 🌐 U.K. |
| Pizza Pockets | CAG | ? | ✖ | ✖ | ✖ | ✔ | ? | No | ? | ✖ | safe meat controversy; D.C.C.A.; factory farming |

| Product or Company | Abbr. | $ | | | | | | | | | ALERT |
|---|---|---|---|---|---|---|---|---|---|---|---|
| Pizzabake | GIS | ✔+ | ✔ | ✔ | ✔ | ✔ | ✔ | No | ✔ | ✔ | C.C.A. |
| Potato Buds | GIS | ✔+ | ✔ | ✔ | ✔ | ✔ | ✔ | No | ◐ | ✔ | C.C.A. |
| Potato Medleys | GIS | ✔+ | ✔ | ✔ | ✔ | ✔ | ✔ | No | ◐ | ✔ | C.C.A. |
| Progresso | PET | ? | ? | ? | ? | ? | ✔ | No | ? | ? | |
| Rudy's Farm | SLE | ✔ | ✔ | ✔ | ✔ | ✔ | ✔ | Yes | ◐∅ | ◐ | on-site day care; C.C.A. |
| Sloppy Joe Bake | GIS | ✔+ | ✔ | ✔ | ✔ | ✔ | ✔ | No | ◐ | ✔ | C.C.A. |
| Standard Meats | SLE | ✔ | ✔ | ✔ | ✔ | ✔ | ✔ | Yes | ◐∅ | ◐ | on-site day care; C.C.A. |
| Suddenly Salad | GIS | ✔+ | ✔ | ✔ | ✔ | ✔ | ✔ | No | ◐ | ✔ | C.C.A. |
| Tuna Helper | GIS | ✔+ | ✔ | ✔ | ✔ | ✔ | ✔ | No | ◐ | ✔ | C.C.A. |
| Van Camp's | OAT | ✔+ | ✔ | ✔ | ✔ | ✔ | ✔ | No | ✔ | ◐ | Fair Share |
| Velveeta Shells & Cheese | MO | ? | ? | ? | ✘ | ? | ? | Yes | ✔ | ? | cigarettes; Salvadoran coffee; Work. Princ. |

✔ = Top Rating   ◐ = Middle Rating   ✘ = Bottom Rating   ? = Insufficient Information

For a more detailed explanation see key on page 14

**PREPARED FOODS**

| Company or Product | Abbr. | $ | | | | | | | | | | ALERT |
|---|---|---|---|---|---|---|---|---|---|---|---|---|
| West Virginia | SLE | ✓ | ✓ | ✓ | ✓ | ✓ | ✓ | Yes | ✓∅ | ✓ | ✓ | on-site day care; C.C.A. |
| Whole Earth# | WHO | ✓+ | ✓ | ? | ✓ | ✓ | ✓ | No | ? | ✓ | ✓ | 1% For Peace; some organic ingredients |
| Wolf | OAT | ✓+ | ✓ | ✓ | ✓ | ✓ | ✓ | No | ✓ | ✓ | ✓ | Fair Share |
| **PREPARED FOODS: FROZEN** | | | | | | | | | | | | |
| A La Carte | MO | ? | ✓ | ✓ | ✓ | ? | ✗ | Yes | ? | ? | ? | cigarettes; Salvadoran coffee; Work. Princ. |
| Applause | MO | ? | ✓ | ✓ | ✓ | ? | ✗ | Yes | ? | ? | ? | cigarettes; Salvadoran coffee; Work. Princ. |
| Armour Classics | CAG | ? | ✗ | ✓ | ✓ | ? | ✗ | No | ? | ? | ✗ | safe meat controversy; D.C.C.A.; factory farming |
| Aunt Jemima | OAT | ✓+ | ✓ | ✓ | ✓ | ✓ | ✓ | No | ✓ | ✓ | ✓ | Fair Share |
| Banquet | CAG | ? | ✗ | ✓ | ✓ | ? | ✗ | No | ? | ? | ✗ | safe meat controversy; D.C.C.A.; factory farming |
| Bluebox | MO | ? | ✓ | ✓ | ✓ | ? | ✗ | Yes | ? | ✓ | ? | cigarettes; Salvadoran coffee; Work. Princ. |
| Brighton's | BUD | ✓+ | ✓ | ✓ | ✓ | ✓ | ✓ | No | ✓ | ✓ | ✓ | |
| Budget Gourmet | MO | ? | ✓ | ✓ | ✓ | ? | ✗ | Yes | ? | ? | ? | cigarettes; Salvadoran coffee; Work. Princ. |
| Celeste | OAT | ✓+ | ✓ | ✓ | ✓ | ✓ | ✓ | No | ✓ | ? | ✓ | Fair Share |

| Product or Company | Abbr. | | | | | | | | | | | | ALERT |
|---|---|---|---|---|---|---|---|---|---|---|---|---|---|
| Chicken Originals | TYSN | ? | ✖ | ? | ✔ | ✖ | ✖ | ? | No | ✓ | ? | ✖ | factory farming; safe chicken contr. |
| Chun King | CAG | ? | ✖ | ✓ | ? | ✖ | ✖ | ✔ | No | ? | ? | ✖ | safe meat controversy; D.C.C.A.; factory farming |
| Classic | GMP | ✓ | ✔ | ✔ | ✔ | ✔ | ✔ | ✔ | YesIN | ✓ | ✓ | ✓ | ⊕, U.K. |
| Culinova | MO | ? | ✔ | ✔ | ? | ✖ | ? | ? | Yes | ? | ? | ? | cigarettes; Salvadoran coffee; Work. Princ. |
| Day-Lee Food | NPM | | | | | | | | | | | | see page 344 for Japanese companies |
| Dutch Harbor | NSK | | | | | | | | | | | | see page 344 for Japanese companies |
| Fresh Creations | MO | ? | ✔ | ✔ | ? | ✖ | ✔ | ✔ | Yes | ? | ? | ? | cigarettes; Salvadoran coffee; Work. Princ. |
| Fresh-bake | GIS | ✔+ | ✔ | ✔ | ✔ | ✔ | ✔ | ✔ | No | ✓ | ✔ | ✔ | C.C.A. |
| Frozen Singles | HRL | ? | ✖ | ✔ | ✔ | ✖ | ✔ | ? | No | ? | ? | ✔ | |
| Golden West | MCRK | ✔ | ✖ | ✖ | ✔ | ✖ | ✔ | ✔ | No | ? | ? | ✔ | |
| Gorton's | GIS | ✔+ | ✔ | ✔ | ✔ | ✔ | ✔ | ✔ | No | ✓ | ✔ | ✔ | C.C.A. |

✔ = Top Rating  ✓ = Middle Rating  ✖ = Bottom Rating  ? = Insufficient Information

*For a more detailed explanation see key on page 14*

| PREPARED FOODS: FROZEN | | Page 261 |

| Company or Product | Abbr. | 💲 | ♀ | 👥 | 🐇 | 🌍 | ✊ | 🏳️ | 👪 | ⚛ | 🏭 | ALERT |
|---|---|---|---|---|---|---|---|---|---|---|---|---|
| Gourmet Selection | TYSN | ? | ✖ | ✔ | ? | ✔ | ✖ | No | ✔ | ? | ✖ | factory farming; safe chicken contr. |
| Jeno's | GMP | ✔ | ✔ | ? | ✔ | ✖ | ? | YesIN | ✔ | ✔ | ✔ | 🌐 U.K. |
| Kraft Entrees | MO | ? | ✔ | ✔ | ? | ✔ | ✖ | Yes | ? | ? | ? | cigarettes; Salvadoran coffee; Work. Princ. |
| Le Menu | CPB | ✔ | ✔ | ✔ | ? | ✔ | ✔ | No | ✔ | ✔ | ✔ | on-site day care |
| Lean Cuisine | NEST | ? | ✔ | ? | ✔* | ✔ | ✔ | YesIN | ✔ | ? | ? | infant formula; Salv. coffee; 🌐; D.C.C.A.; U.K. |
| Moore's | CLX | ✔ | ✖ | ✔ | ✔* | ✔ | ✔ | No | ✔ | ✖ | ✔ | |
| Morton | CAG | ? | ✖ | ✔ | ? | ✖ | ✔ | No | ✔ | ? | ✖ | safe meat controversy; D.C.C.A.; factory farming |
| Mrs. Paul's | CPB | ✔ | ✔ | ✔ | ? | ✔ | ✔ | No | ✔ | ? | ✔ | on-site day care |
| New Traditions | HRL | ? | ✖ | ? | ? | ✔ | ? | No | ✔ | ? | ? | |
| Papa Dion's | BUD | ✔+ | ✔ | ✔ | ✔ | ✔ | ✔ | No | ✔ | ? | ✔ | |
| Pasta Accents | GMP | ✔ | ✔ | ✔ | ✔ | ✔ | ✔ | YesIN | ✔ | ✔ | ✔ | 🌐 U.K. |
| Patio | CAG | ? | ✖ | ? | ? | ✖ | ✖ | No | ✔ | ? | ✖ | safe meat controversy; D.C.C.A.; factory farming |
| Pepperidge Farm | CPB | ✔ | ✔ | ✔ | ? | ✔ | ✔ | No | ✔ | ? | ✔ | on-site day care |

| Product or Company | Abbr. | 💲 | ♀ | ✊ | 🌍 | 🐇 | | ☮ | ⚕ | ALERT |
|---|---|---|---|---|---|---|---|---|---|---|
| Quick Cuts | TYSN | ? | ✖ | ? | ✔ | ✖ | No | ✔ | ? | ✖ | factory farming; safe chicken contr. |
| Quick to Fix | TYSN | ✔ | ✖ | ? | ✔ | ✖ | No | ✔ | ? | ✖ | factory farming; safe chicken contr. |
| Souper Combo | CPB | ✔ | ✔ | ✔ | ? | ✔ | No | ✔ | ✔ | ✔ | on-site day care |
| Steak-Umm | HNZ | ✔ | ✔ | ✔ | ✔ | ✔ | No | ✔ | ✔ | ✔ | C.C.A. |
| Stouffer's | NEST | ? | ✔ | ? | ✔* | ✔ | Yes|N | ✔ | ? | ? | infant formula; Salv. coffee; ⊕; D.C.C.A.; U.K. |
| Swanson | CPB | ✔ | ✔ | ? | ✔ | ✔ | No | ✔ | ✔ | ✔ | on-site day care |
| Taste O' Sea | CAG | ? | ✖ | ? | ? | ✖ | No | ? | ? | ✖ | safe meat controversy; D.C.C.A.; factory farming |
| Tasty Bird | TYSN | ? | ✖ | ? | ✔ | ✖ | No | ✔ | ✔ | ✖ | factory farming; safe chicken contr. |
| The Gourmet | MO | ? | ✔ | ✔ | ✔ | ✖ | Yes | ? | ? | ? | cigarettes; Salvadoran coffee; Work. Princ. |
| Tombstone | MO | ? | ✔ | ✔ | ✖ | ✖ | Yes | ? | ? | ? | cigarettes; Salvadoran coffee; Work. Princ. |
| Top Shelf | HRL | ? | ✖ | ✔ | ✔ | ✖ | No | ? | ? | ? | |

✔ = Top Rating    ⌣ = Middle Rating    ✖ = Bottom Rating    ? = Insufficient Information

*For a more detailed explanation see key on page 14*

| | |
|---|---|
| PREPARED FOODS: FROZEN | Page 263 |

| Company or Product | Abbr. | 💲 | ♀ | 🧑 | 🐰 | 🏃 | | | | | ALERT |
|---|---|---|---|---|---|---|---|---|---|---|---|
| Totino's | GMP | ✓ | ✓ | ✓ | ✓ | ✓ | YesIN | ✓ | ✓ | | ⊕, U.K. |
| Tyson | TYSN | ? | ✗ | ? | ✓ | ✗ | No | ✓ | ✗ | | factory farming; safe chicken contr. |
| Universal | NSK | | | | | | | | | | see page 344 for Japanese companies |
| Van De Kamp's | PET | ? | ✗ | ? | ? | ✗ | No | ? | ? | | |
| Weaver | TYSN | ? | ✗ | ? | ✓ | ✗ | No | ? | ✗ | | factory farming; safe chicken contr. |
| Weight Watchers | HNZ | ✓ | ✓ | ✓ | ✓ | ✓ | No | ✓ | ✓ | | C.C.A. |
| Yukijirushi | SNB | | | | | | | | | | see page 344 for Japanese companies |
| **RICE & RICE DISHES** | | | | | | | | | | | |
| Country Inn | MARS | ? | ? | ? | ? | ✓ | No | ✓ | ? | | |
| Falcon Trading# | FALC | ? | ✗ | ✓ | ✓ | ✓ | No | ✓ | ✓ | | 1% For Peace; some organic ingredients |
| Fantastic Foods# | FFI | ✓ | ✓ | ✓ | ✓ | ✓ | No | ✓ | ✓ | | some organic ingredients |
| Golden Grain | OAT | ✓+ | ✓ | ✓ | ✓ | ✓ | No | ✓ | ✓ | | Fair Share |
| Minute Rice | MO | ? | ? | ? | ✗ | ? | Yes | ? | ? | | cigarettes; Salvadoran coffee; Work. Princ. |

| Product or Company | Abbr. | 💲 | | | | | | | | | | ALERT |
|---|---|---|---|---|---|---|---|---|---|---|---|---|
| Pantry Express | GMP | ⋁ | | | ✓ | ✓ | ✓ | ✓ | YesIN | ⋁ | ⋁ | ⊕, U.K. |
| Pillsbury | GMP | ⋁ | | | ✓ | ✓ | ✓ | ✓ | YesIN | ⋁ | ⋁ | ⊕, U.K. |
| Rice-A-Roni | OAT | ⋁+ | | ✓ | ✓ | ✓ | ✓ | ✓ | No | ✓ | ⋁ | Fair Share |
| Savory Classics | OAT | ⋁+ | | ✓ | ✓ | ✓ | ✓ | ✓ | No | ✓ | ⋁ | Fair Share |
| Uncle Ben's | MARS | ? | | ? | ? | ? | ⋁ | ? | No | ✓ | ? | |
| **SALAD DRESSINGS** | | | | | | | | | | | | |
| Bernstein's | CBI | ⋁+ | | ⋁ | ✓ | ? | ✓ | ✓ | No | ? | ⋁ | |
| Catalina | MO | ? | | ✓ | ✗ | ✓ | ✓ | ? | Yes | ? | ? | cigarettes; Salvadoran coffee; Work. Princ. |
| Classic Herb | MO | ? | | ✓ | ✗ | ✓ | ✓ | ? | Yes | ? | ? | cigarettes; Salvadoran coffee; Work. Princ. |
| Conzelo | MO | ? | | ✓ | ✗ | ✓ | ✓ | ? | Yes | ? | ? | cigarettes; Salvadoran coffee; Work. Princ. |
| Good Seasons | MO | ? | | ✓ | ✗ | ✓ | ✓ | ? | Yes | ? | ? | cigarettes; Salvadoran coffee; Work. Princ. |

✓ = Top Rating  ⋁ = Middle Rating  ✗ = Bottom Rating  ? = Insufficient Information

*For a more detailed explanation see key on page 14*

Page 265

**SALAD DRESSINGS**

| Company or Product | Abbr. | $ | ♀ | | | | | | | | ALERT |
|---|---|---|---|---|---|---|---|---|---|---|---|
| Hidden Valley Ranch | CLX | ✓ | ✗ | ✓ | ✓* | ✓ | ✓ | No | ✗ | ✓ | |
| Kraft | MO | ? | ? | ✓ | ? | ✓ | ? | Yes | ? | ? | cigarettes; Salvadoran coffee; Work. Princ. |
| Loriva Supreme* | LOR | ✓ | ✓ø | ✓ | ? | ✓ | ✓ | No | ✓ø | ? | |
| Marie's | CPB | ✓ | ✓ | ✓ | ? | ✓ | ✓ | No | ✓ | ✓ | on-site day care |
| Mayacamas* | MAYA | ? | ? | ✓ | ✓ | ✗ | ✓ | No | ? | ? | |
| Newman's Own* | NEWO | ✓+ | ✓ø | ✓ | ✓ | ✓ | ✓ | No | ✓ | ✓ | 100% profit to charity; C.C.A. |
| Protein Aide Prod.* | LOR | ✓ | ✓ø | ✓ | ? | ✓ | ? | No | ✓ø | ? | |
| Seven Seas | MO | ? | ✗ | ✓ | ? | ✗ | ✓ | Yes | ✓ | ? | cigarettes; Salvadoran coffee; Work. Princ. |
| Take Heart | CLX | ✓ | ✓ | ✓ | ✓* | ✓ | ✓ | No | ✓ | ✗ | |
| Thousand Island | MO | ? | ✗ | ✓ | ✗ | ✓ | ? | Yes | ? | ? | cigarettes; Salvadoran coffee; Work. Princ. |
| Vegetarian Pate# | TFC | ✗ | ✓ | ✓ | ✓ | ✓ | ✓ | No | ✓ | ✓ | on-site day care |
| Weight Watchers | HNZ | ✓ | ✓ | ✓ | ✓ | ✓ | ✓ | No | ✓ | ✓ | C.C.A. |
| Whole Earth# | WHO | ✓+ | ✓ | ✓ | ✓ | ✓ | ✓ | No | ? | ✓ | 1% For Peace; some organic ingredients |

| Product or Company | Abbr. | 💲 | ⚥ | | | | | | | | ALERT |
|---|---|---|---|---|---|---|---|---|---|---|---|
| Wishbone | UN | ? | ✖ | ✓ | ✓ | ✓ | YesIN | ✓ | ✓ | ? | 🌐; U.K. |
| **SALT, SEASONINGS & SPICES** | | | | | | | | | | | |
| ADOBO | UN | ? | ✖ | ✓ | ✓* | ✓ | YesIN | ✓ | ✓ | ? | 🌐; U.K. |
| Accent | PET | ? | ? | ? | ✓* | ✖ | No | ? | ? | ? | |
| Adolph's Meat Tend. | UN | ? | ✖ | ✓ | ✓* | ✓ | YesIN | ✓ | ✓ | ? | 🌐; U.K. |
| All Purpose# | HVAL | ? | ? | ? | ✓ | ✖ | No | ? | ? | ? | some organic ingredients |
| Bac-O-Bits | GIS | ✓+ | ✓ | ✓ | ✓ | ✓ | No | ✓ | ✓ | ✓ | C.C.A. |
| Chili-Quick | CAG | ? | ✖ | ✓ | ? | ✖ | No | ✖ | ? | ? | safe meat controversy; D.C.C.A.; factory farming |
| Durkee | RCP | ? | ✓ | ✓ | ✓ | ✓ | YesIN | ✓ | ✖ | ✓ | |
| El Molino | BN | ✓ | ✓ | ✓ | ✓ | ✓ | YesIN | ✓ | ✓ | ✓ | 🌐; U.K. |
| Evon's | JSAN | ? | ? | ? | ✓ | ✓ | No | ? | ? | ? | |

✓ = Top Rating    ✓ = Middle Rating    ✖ = Bottom Rating    ? = Insufficient Information

*For a more detailed explanation see key on page 14*

**SALT, SEASONINGS & SPICES**

| Company or Product | Abbr. | 💲 | ⚥ | ♨ | 🐇 | 🕊 | 🌐 | ☪ | 🐾 | ☮ | ⚔ | ALERT |
|---|---|---|---|---|---|---|---|---|---|---|---|---|
| Instead-of-Salt# | HVAL | ? | ? | ? | ✔ | ✖ | ? | No | ? | ? | ? | some organic ingredients |
| Lawry's | UN | ? | ✖ | ♥ | ✔* | ✔ | ✔ | YesIN | ♥ | ♥ | ? | 🌐, U.K. |
| Little Pancho | BN | ♥ | ✔ | ✔ | ✔ | ✔ | ✔ | YesIN | ♥ | ✔ | ✔ | |
| Makin' Cajun | MO | ? | ✔ | ✔ | ? | ✖ | ? | Yes | ? | ? | ? | cigarettes; Salvadoran coffee; Work. Princ. |
| Mamacita Sofrito | GOYA | ? | ? | ? | ? | ✖ | ? | No | ? | ? | ? | |
| McCormick | MCRK | ✔ | ✖ | ✔ | ✔ | ✖ | ? | No | ? | ? | ? | |
| Mrs. Dash | ACV | ? | ? | ✖ | ✖ | ♥ | ? | No | ? | ✖ | ? | |
| Parsley Patch | MCRK | ✔ | ✖ | ✔ | ✔ | ✖ | ? | No | ? | ? | ? | |
| Sa-son' Ac'cent | PET | ? | ? | ✔ | ? | ✖ | ? | No | ? | ? | ? | |
| Schilling | MCRK | ✔ | ✖ | ✔ | ✔ | ✖ | ? | No | ? | ? | ? | |
| Season-All | MCRK | ✔ | ✖ | ✔ | ✔ | ✖ | ? | No | ? | ? | ? | |
| Vegetable Supreme | MCRK | ✔ | ✖ | ✔ | ✔ | ✖ | ? | No | ? | ? | ? | |

## SAUCES & GRAVY

| Product or Company | Abbr. | $ | | | | | Yes/No | | | | ALERT |
|---|---|---|---|---|---|---|---|---|---|---|---|
| **A-1** | RJR | ? | ? | ✓ | ✗ | ? | Yes | ✗ | ? | ? | cigarettes;D.C.C.A. |
| **Aunt Millie's** | BN | ✓ | ✓ | ✓ | ✓ | ✓ | YesIN | ✓ | ✓ | ✓ | |
| **Bennett's** | BN | ✓ | ✓ | ✓ | ✓ | ✓ | YesIN | ✓ | ✓ | ✓ | |
| **Bull's Eye** | MO | ? | ? | ✓ | ✗ | ✗ | Yes | ? | ? | ? | cigarettes; Salvadoran coffee; Work. Princ. |
| **Charco-it'** | ACV | ? | ? | ✓ | ? | ✓ | No | ✗ | ? | ? | |
| **Chi-Chi's** | HRL | ? | ? | ✗ | ✗ | ✓ | No | ? | ? | ? | |
| **Chicken Helper** | GIS | ✓+ | ✓ | ✓ | ✓ | ✓ | No | ✓ | ✓ | ✓ | |
| **Classico** | BN | ✓ | ✓ | ✓ | ✓ | ✓ | YesIN | ✓ | ✓ | ✓ | C.C.A. |
| **Compliment** | PET | ? | ? | ? | ? | ✗ | No | ? | ? | ? | |
| **El Caldero** | PET | ? | ? | ? | ? | ✗ | No | ? | ? | ? | |

✓ = Top Rating   ✓ = Middle Rating   ✗ = Bottom Rating   ? = Insufficient Information

For a more detailed explanation see key on page 14

SAUCES & GRAVY

| Company or Product | Abbr. | $ | ⚥ | 🐷 | 🐰 | 🌍 | ☢ | ✊ | 🏳️ | ALERT |
|---|---|---|---|---|---|---|---|---|---|---|
| El Molino | BN | ✔ | ✔ | ✔ | ✔ | ✔ | YesIN | ✔ | ✔ | |
| Fantastic Foods# | FFI | ✔ | ✔ | ✔ | ✔ | ✔ | No | ✔ | ✔ | some organic ingredients |
| G. Washington's | AHP | ✘ | ✔ | ✔ | ✔(®) | ✔ | Yes | ✔ | ✔ | infant formula |
| Hunt's | CAG | ? | ✔ | ? | ✘ | ✔ | No | ? | ✘ | safe meat controversy; D.C.C.A.; factory farming |
| K.C. Masterpiece | CLX | ✔ | ✔ | ✔* | ✔ | ✔ | No | ✔ | ✔ | |
| Kikkoman | KIK | | | | | | | | | see page 344 for Japanese companies |
| Kitchen Bouquet | CLX | ✔ | ✘ | ✔* | ✔ | ✔ | No | ✘ | ✔ | |
| Knorr | CPC | ✔ | ✔ | ? | ✔ | ✔ | No | ✔ | ✔ | |
| La Croix | CPB | ✔ | ✔ | ? | ✔ | ✔ | No | ✔ | ✔ | on-site day care |
| Las Palmas | PET | ? | ? | ? | ✔ | ? | No | ? | ? | |
| Lea and Perrins | BSN | | | | | | | | | see page 330 for U.K. ratings |
| Magic Touch | CAG | ? | ✘ | ? | ✘ | ✘ | No | ? | ✘ | safe meat controversy; D.C.C.A.; factory farming |
| Manwich | CAG | ? | ✘ | ? | ✘ | ✘ | No | ? | ✘ | safe meat controversy; D.C.C.A.; factory farming |

| Product or Company | Abbr. | 💲 | ⚥ | 👥 | 🐾 | 🐇 | ✊ | 🌐 | ☢ | ⬡ | ▦ | ALERT |
|---|---|---|---|---|---|---|---|---|---|---|---|---|
| Mayacamas* | MAYA | ? | ? | ? | ? | ✔ | ✖ | ? | No | ? | ? | |
| Milani 1890 | ACV | ? | ✔ | ? | ✖ | ? | ? | ? | No | ✖ | ? | |
| Newman's Own* | NEWO | ✔+ | ✔ | ✔/∅ | ✔ | ✔ | ✔ | ✔ | No | ✖ | ? | 100% profit to charity; C.C.A. |
| Ocean Spray | OSC | ✔ | ✖ | ? | ✔ | ✔ | ✔ | ✔ | No | ✔ | ✔ | co-op |
| Old Smokehouse | HRL | ? | ✖ | ? | ✔ | ✖ | ? | ✔ | No | ✔ | ? | |
| Open Pit | CPB | ✔ | ✔ | ✔ | ? | ✔ | ✔ | ✔ | No | ✔ | ✔ | on-site day care |
| Pacific Gardens* | ACOP | ? | ✔ | ? | ✔ | ✖ | ? | ✔ | No | ? | ? | co-op |
| Prego | CPB | ✔ | ✔ | ✔ | ? | ✔ | ✔ | ✔ | No | ✔ | ✔ | on-site day care |
| Ragu | UN | ? | ✔ | ✔ | ✔* | ✔ | ✔ | ✔ | YesN | ✔ | ? | 🌐, U.K. |
| San-J International# | SANJ | ✔ | ✔ | ✔ | ✔ | ✔ | ✔ | ✔ | No | ✔ | ✔ | |
| Smokehouse | HRL | ? | ✖ | ? | ✔ | ✖ | ? | ✔ | No | ? | ? | |

✔ = Top Rating  ✓ = Middle Rating  ✖ = Bottom Rating  ? = Insufficient Information
For a more detailed explanation see key on page 14

## SAUCES & GRAVY

| Company or Product | Abbr. | 💲 | ♀ | ✊ | ⚖ | 🐾 | 🐇 | ♻ | ⌂ | ALERT |
|---|---|---|---|---|---|---|---|---|---|---|
| Suzi Wan | MARS | ? | ? | ? | ? | ? | No | ? | ? | |
| Thick 'N Spicy | MO | ? | ✔ | ✔ | ? | ✖ | Yes | ? | ? | cigarettes; Salvadoran coffee; Work. Princ. |
| Vlasic | CPB | ✔ | ✔ | ✔ | ? | ✔ | No | ✔ | ✔ | on-site day care |
| Whole Earth# | WHO | ✔+ | ✔ | ◐ | ✔ | ◐ | No | ? | ◐ | 1% For Peace; some organic ingredients |
| **SHAMPOOS & CONDITIONERS** | | | | | | | | | | |
| Afro-Sheen | JPC | ? | ◐ | ✔ | ? | ◐ | No | ? | ? | |
| Agree | SCJ | ✔+ | ✔ | ✔ | ✔* | ✔ | YesIN | ✔ | ✔ | 1st to ban CFCs; on-site day care |
| Alberto VO5 | ACV | ? | ✔ | ✔ | ✖ | ◐ | No | ? | ? | |
| Alexandra Avery* | ALEX | ✔+ | ◐∅ | ✔ | ✔ | ✔ | No | ✔ | ✔ | |
| Apple Pectin | DOW | ◐ | ✔ | ✔⊛ | ✔ | ✔ | Yes | ◐ | ◐ | pesticide steril. suit; nuclear weapons; on-site day care; makes pesticides |
| Aubrey Organics# | AUB | ? | ✔ | ✔ | ✔ | ✔ | No | ✔ | ✔ | some organic ingredients |
| Autumn Harp* | AUT | ✔+ | ◐∅ | ✔ | ✔ | ✔ | No | ✔ | ✔ | |
| Aveda# | AVED | ✔ | ✔ | ✔ | ◐ | ✔ | No | ✖ | ✔ | Valdez Principles; ACT NOW |

| Product or Company | Abbr. | $ | | | | | | | | | ALERT |
|---|---|---|---|---|---|---|---|---|---|---|---|
| Body On Tap | BMY | ✓ | ✓ | ✓ | ✓ | ✓⊛ | ✓ | YesIN | ✓ | ✓ | infant formula; Workplace Principles; D.C.C.A. |
| Body Shop, The | BS | ✓ | ✓ | ? | ✓ | ✓ | ✓ | No | ? | ? | ACT NOW; U.K. |
| Bonsandt | IRDV | ? | ✗ | ? | ✗ | ✗○ | ? | No | ? | ? | |
| Breck | G | ? | ? | ✓ | ✓ | ✓ | ? | No | ? | ? | |
| Carne | IRDV | ? | ✗ | ? | ✗ | ✗○ | ? | No | ? | ? | |
| Clairol | BMY | ✓ | ✓ | ✓ | ✓ | ✓⊛ | ✓ | YesIN | ✓ | ✓ | infant formula; Workplace Principles; D.C.C.A. |
| Clean & Clear | REVL | ? | ? | ✓ | ✓ | ✗ | ✓ | YesIN | ? | ? | |
| Clientele# | CTL | ✓+ | ✓ | ✓ | ✓ | ✓ | ✓ | No | ✓∅ | ✓ | |
| Condition | BMY | ✓ | ✓ | ✓ | ✓ | ✓⊛ | ✓ | YesIN | ✓ | ✓ | infant formula; Workplace Principles; D.C.C.A. |
| Crystal Clear | ACV | ? | ✓ | ? | ✗ | ✗ | ? | No | ✗ | ? | |
| Denorex | AHP | ✗ | ✓ | ✓ | ✓ | ✓⊛ | ✓ | Yes | ✓ | ✓ | infant formula |

✓ = Top Rating    ✓ = Middle Rating    ✗ = Bottom Rating    ? = Insufficient Information

*For a more detailed explanation see key on page 14*

SHAMPOOS & CONDITIONERS

| Company or Product | Abbr. | $ | ♀ | | | | | | | | ALERT |
|---|---|---|---|---|---|---|---|---|---|---|---|
| Dimension | UN | ? | ✖ | ✓ | | ✓* | ✖ | YesIN | ✓ | ? | 🌐; U.K. |
| Elastin | IRDV | ? | ✖ | ? | ? | ✖○ | ✖ | No | ? | ? | |
| Faberge | UN | ? | ✖ | ✓ | ? | ✓* | ✓ | YesIN | ✓ | ? | 🌐; U.K. |
| Fisher-Price | SCJ | ✓+ | ✓ | ✓ | ✓ | ✓* | ✓ | YesIN | ✓ | ✓ | 1st to ban CFCs; on-site day care |
| Flex | REVL | ? | ? | ? | ✖ | ✓ | ✖ | YesIN | ? | ? | |
| Fresh Hold | BMY | ✓ | ✓ | ✓ | ✓ | ✓⊛ | ✓ | YesIN | ✓ | ✓ | infant formula; Workplace Principles; D.C.C.A. |
| Gee, Your Hair Smells Trfc | KAO | | | | | | | | | | see page 344 for Japanese companies |
| Halsa | SCJ | ✓+ | ✓ | ✓ | ✓ | ✓* | ✓ | YesIN | ✓ | ✓ | 1st to ban CFCs; on-site day care |
| Head & Shoulders | PG | ✓ | ✓ | ✓ | ✓ | ✓⊛ | ✓ | Yes | ✓ | ✓ | disposable diapers; Salvadoran coffee; on-site day care; C.C.A. |
| Herbal Essence | BMY | ✓ | ✓ | ✓ | ✓ | ✓⊛ | ✓ | YesIN | ✓ | ✓ | infant formula; Workplace Principles; D.C.C.A. |
| Heritage | ACY | ✓ | ✖ | ? | ✖ | ✖○ | ✓ | YesIN | ? | ? | makes pesticides; D.C.C.A.; nuclear weapons |
| Infusium 23 | BMY | ✓ | ✓ | ✓ | ✓ | ✓⊛ | ✓ | YesIN | ✓ | ✓ | infant formula; Workplace Principles; D.C.C.A. |
| Ivory Shampoo | PG | ✓ | ✓ | ✓ | ✓ | ✓⊛ | ✓ | Yes | ✓ | ✓ | disposable diapers; Salvadoran coffee; on-site day care; C.C.A. |

| Product or Company | Abbr. | $ | ♀ | ◼ | ◼ | ◼ | ◼ | ◼ (animal testing) | ◼ | ◼ | ◼ | ◼ | ALERT |
|---|---|---|---|---|---|---|---|---|---|---|---|---|---|
| Jason Natural# | JNP | ? | 🗸 | ✖ | 🗸 | 🗸 | 🗸 | No | 🗸∅ | ✖ | 🗸 | 🗸 | |
| Johnson's Baby Shamp. | JNJ | 🗸 | 🗸 | 🗸 | 🗸⊛ | ✖ | 🗸 | YesIN | 🗸∅ | 🗸 | 🗸 | 🗸 | on-site day care; Workplace Principles |
| Jojoba Farms* | IRDV | ? | 🗸 | ✖ | ✖◯ | ? | ✖ | No | ? | ? | ? | 🗸 | |
| Kangaroo* | DES | ? | 🗸 | ✖ | ? | ? | ✖ | No | 🗸∅ | ? | ? | 🗸 | 1% For Peace |
| Keep Clear | AVP | 🗸+ | 🗸 | 🗸 | 🗸 | 🗸 | 🗸 | No | 🗸 | 🗸 | 🗸 | 🗸 | on-site day care; C.C.A. |
| L'Oreal | LORA | ? | ? | 🗸 | 🗸* | ? | 🗸 | Yes | 🗸 | ? | ? | ? | |
| La Maur | DOW | 🗸 | 🗸 | 🗸 | 🗸⊛ | 🗸 | 🗸 | Yes | 🗸 | 🗸 | 🗸 | 🗸 | pesticide steril. suit; nuclear weapons; on-site day care; makes pesticides |
| Lancome | LORA | ? | 🗸 | 🗸 | 🗸* | ? | 🗸 | Yes | 🗸 | ? | ? | ? | |
| Liberesse | ACV | ? | 🗸 | ✖ | 🗸 | ? | 🗸 | No | ? | ? | ✖ | 🗸 | |
| Lustrasilk | GS | 🗸 | 🗸 | 🗸 | 🗸⊛ | 🗸 | 🗸 | YesIN | 🗸∅ | 🗸 | 🗸 | 🗸 | |
| Mandarin Magic# | AUB | ? | 🗸 | 🗸 | 🗸 | 🗸 | 🗸 | No | 🗸 | ? | 🗸 | 🗸 | some organic ingredients |

🗸 = Top Rating    ✓ = Middle Rating    ✖ = Bottom Rating    ? = Insufficient Information
*For a more detailed explanation see key on page 14*

| Company or Product | Abbr. | 💲 | ♀ | 🧑 | 🐰 | 🌿 | ⚖ | 👶 | YesIN/No | ♻ | ♻ | ALERT |
|---|---|---|---|---|---|---|---|---|---|---|---|---|
| Men's Stock# | AUB | ? | ✓ | ✓ | ✓ | ✓ | ✓ | No | ✓ | ? | ✓ | some organic ingredients |
| Milk Creek | IRDV | ? | ✗ | ? | ✗○ | ? | ? | No | ? | ? | ? | |
| Mink | GS | ✓ | ✓ | ✓ | ✓⊛ | ✓ | ✓ | YesIN | ✓ | ✓ | ✓ | |
| Mountain Herbery | IRDV | ? | ✗ | ? | ✗○ | ? | ? | No | ? | ? | ? | |
| Mountain Ocean* | MOUN | ? | ? | ? | ✓ | ✗ | ? | No | ? | ? | ? | |
| Neutro Balance | CL | ✓+ | ✓ | ✓ | ✓⊛ | ✓ | ✓ | YesIN | ✓ | ✓ | ✓ | |
| Neutrogena | NGNA | ? | ? | ? | ? | ? | ? | No | ✓⊘ | ✗ | ? | |
| New Image | ACY | ✓ | ✓ | ? | ✗○ | ✗ | ? | YesIN | ? | ? | ? | makes pesticides; D.C.C.A.; nuclear weapons |
| Orjene Natural# | ORJ | ✓+ | ✓ | ✓ | ✓ | ✓ | ✗ | No | ✓ | ✓ | ✓ | |
| Pantene | PG | ✓ | ✓ | ✓ | ✓⊛ | ✓ | ✓ | Yes | ✓ | ✓ | ✓ | disposable diapers; Salvadoran coffee; on-site day care; C.C.A. |
| Perm Soft | DOW | ✓ | ✓ | ✓ | ✓⊛ | ✓ | ✓ | Yes | ✓ | ✓ | ✓ | pesticide steril. suit; nuclear weapons; on-site day care; makes pesticides |
| Pert Plus | PG | ✓ | ✓ | ✓ | ✓⊛ | ✓ | ✓ | Yes | ✓ | ✓ | ✓ | disposable diapers; Salvadoran coffee; on-site day care; C.C.A. |
| Prell | PG | ✓ | ✓ | ✓ | ✓⊛ | ✓ | ✓ | Yes | ✓ | ✓ | ✓ | disposable diapers; Salvadoran coffee; on-site day care; C.C.A. |

| Product or Company | Abbr. | $ | | | | | | | | | | | ALERT |
|---|---|---|---|---|---|---|---|---|---|---|---|---|---|
| Prescription | BMY | ◓ | ✔ | ✔ | ◓ | ✔ | ✔✽ | ✔ | YesIN | ◓ | ✔ | ✔ | infant formula; Workplace Principles; D.C.C.A. |
| Progaine Shampoo | UPJ | ✔ | ✔ | ✔ | ✔ | ✔ | ✔✽ | ✔ | YesIN | ◓ | ✔ | ✔ | |
| Salon Formula | DEPC | ? | ◓ | ◓ | ? | ◓ | ✔ | ◓ | No | ? | ◓ | ◓ | |
| Selsun Blue | ABT | ? | ✔ | ✔ | ? | ◓ | ✔✽ | ✔ | YesIN | ✔ | ✔ | ◓ | infant formula |
| Silkience | GS | ◓ | ✔ | ✔ | ◓ | ✔ | ✔✽ | ✔ | YesIN | ◓ | ✔ | ◓ | |
| Silver Lights | AVP | ✔+ | ✔ | ✔ | ◓ | ✔ | ✔ | ✔ | No | ◓ | ✔ | ✔ | on-site day care; C.C.A. |
| Simply Brilliant | AVP | ✔+ | ✔ | ✔ | ◓ | ✔ | ✔ | ✔ | No | ◓ | ✔ | ✔ | on-site day care; C.C.A. |
| Sleepy Hollow Botanical | IRDV | ? | ✗ | ✔ | ? | ✗◯ | ✔ | ✗ | No | ? | ? | ? | |
| Soft Essentials | AVP | ✔+ | ✔ | ✔ | ◓ | ✔ | ✔ | ✔ | No | ◓ | ✔ | ✔ | on-site day care; C.C.A. |
| Spring Feeling | KAO | | | | | | | | | | | | see page 344 for Japanese companies |
| Squeek | KAO | | | | | | | | | | | | see page 344 for Japanese companies |

✔ = Top Rating  ◓ = Middle Rating  ✗ = Bottom Rating  ? = Insufficient Information

For a more detailed explanation see key on page 14

**SHAMPOOS & CONDITIONERS**

Page 277

| Company or Product | Abbr. | $ | ♀ | ☺ | ✊ | 🐇 | 🌍 | 🕊 | ⚛ | 🍼 | ⚖ | ⚕ | ALERT |
|---|---|---|---|---|---|---|---|---|---|---|---|---|---|
| **Strictly Professional** | ACV | ? | ? | ✔ | ✔ | ✘ | ✔ | ? | No | ? | ✘ | ✘ | ? | |
| **Subdue** | ACV | ? | ? | ✔ | ✔ | ✘ | ✔ | ? | No | ? | ✘ | ✘ | ✔ | |
| **Textra** | DOW | ✔ | ✔ | ✔ | ✔(*) | ✔ | ✔ | ✔ | Yes | ✔ | ✔ | ✔ | ✔ | pesticide steril. suit; nuclear weapons; on-site day care; makes pesticides |
| **Thrive** | ACV | ✔ | ? | ✘ | ✘○ | ✘ | ✔ | ? | YesIN | ✘ | ? | ? | ? | makes pesticides; D.C.C.A.; nuclear weapons |
| **Timoteï** | UN | ? | ✔ | ✔ | ✔* | ✔ | ✔ | ✔ | YesIN | ✔ | ✔ | ✔ | ? | 🌐, U.K. |
| **Tom's of Maine#** | TOM | ✔+ | ✘ | ✔ | ✔ | ✔ | ✔ | ✔ | No | ✘ | ✔ | ✔ | ✔ | |
| **Tresemme** | ACV | ? | ? | ✔ | ✘ | ✔ | ✔ | ✔ | No | ? | ? | ✘ | ? | |
| **Trespac** | ACV | ? | ? | ✔ | ✘ | ✔ | ✔ | ✔ | No | ? | ? | ✘ | ? | |
| **Vidal Sassoon** | PG | ✔ | ✔ | ✔ | ✔(*) | ✔ | ✔ | ✔ | Yes | ✔ | ✔ | ✔ | ✔ | disposable diapers; Salvadoran coffee; on-site day care; C.C.A. |
| **White Rain** | GS | ✔ | ✔ | ✔ | ✔(*) | ✔ | ✔ | ✔ | YesIN | ✔ | ✔ | ✔ | ✔ | |
| **SHAVING NEEDS** | | | | | | | | | | | | | | |
| **Aqua-Velva** | BECH | ✘ | ✔ | ✔ | ✘○ | ✔ | ✔ | ✔ | YesIN | ✔/∅ | ✔ | ✔ | ✔ | 🌐, Work. Princ.; on-site day care; U.K. |
| **Atra** | GS | ✔ | ✔ | ✔ | ✔(*) | ✔ | ✔ | ✔ | YesIN | ✔ | ✔ | | | |

| Product or Company | Abbr. | | | | | | | | | ALERT |
|---|---|---|---|---|---|---|---|---|---|---|
| Barbasol | PPE | 𝒱 | ✗ | ? | ? | ✗ | YesIN | ✗ | ? | heart valve suits |
| Body Shop, The | BS | 𝒱 | ✓ | 𝒱 | ✓ | 𝒱 | No | ✓ | ? | ACT NOW; U.K. |
| Brut 33 | UN | ? | ✗ | 𝒱 | ✓* | ✓ | YesIN | 𝒱 | ? | ⊕; U.K. |
| Colgate | CL | ✓+ | ✓ | ✓ | ✓⊛ | ✓ | YesIN | ✓ | ✓ | |
| Daisy | GS | 𝒱 | 𝒱 | 𝒱 | ✓⊛ | 𝒱 | YesIN | 𝒱 | ✓ | |
| Edge Gel | SCJ | ✓+ | ✓ | ✓ | ✓* | ✓ | YesIN | ✓ | ✓ | 1st to ban CFCs; on-site day care |
| Flic | GS | 𝒱 | 𝒱 | 𝒱 | ✓⊛ | 𝒱 | YesIN | 𝒱 | ✓ | |
| Foamy | GS | 𝒱 | 𝒱 | 𝒱 | ✓⊛ | ✓ | YesIN | ✓ | ✓ | |
| Gillette | GS | 𝒱 | 𝒱 | 𝒱 | ✓⊛ | 𝒱 | YesIN | 𝒱 | ✓ | |
| Good News! | GS | 𝒱 | 𝒱 | 𝒱 | ✓ | ✓ | YesIN | 𝒱 | ✓ | |
| Jason Natural# | JNP | ? | 𝒱 | ✗ | ✓ | 𝒱 | No | 𝒱⊘ | ✓ | |

| ✓ = Top Rating | 𝒱 = Middle Rating | ✗ = Bottom Rating | ? = Insufficient Information | Page 279 |
|---|---|---|---|---|

*For a more detailed explanation see key on page 14*

**SHAVING NEEDS**

| Company or Product | Abbr. | $ | ♀ | ⚖ | 👥 | 🏭 | 🐇 | ☣ | ☢ | ALERT |
|---|---|---|---|---|---|---|---|---|---|---|
| Nair | CAR | ? | ✗ | ✓ | ⊘ | ✗○ | ? | No | ✗ | ? | |
| Night Spice | ACY | ✓ | ✗ | ✗ | ? | ✗○ | ? | Yes | ✗ | ? | makes pesticides; D.C.C.A.; nuclear weapons |
| Old Spice | PG | ✓ | ✓ | ✓ | ✓⊛ | ✓ | ✓ | Yes | ✓⊘ | ✓ | disposable diapers; Salvadoran coffee; on-site day care; C.C.A. |
| Palmolive | CL | ✓+ | ✓ | ✓ | ✓⊛ | ✓ | ✓ | YesIN | ✓ | ✓ | |
| Personal Touch | WLA | ✓ | ✓ | ✓ | ✗○ | ✓ | ✓ | YesIN | ✓⊘ | ✓ | on-site day care; Workplace Principles |
| Schick | WLA | ✓ | ✓ | ✓ | ✗○ | ✓ | ✓ | YesIN | ✓⊘ | ✓ | on-site day care; Workplace Principles |
| Shimmy Shins | ACV | ? | ✓ | ? | ✗ | ✓ | ? | No | ✗ | ? | |
| Soft Sense | SCJ | ✓+ | ✓ | ✓ | ✓* | ✓ | ✓ | YesIN | ✓ | ✓ | 1st to ban CFCs; on-site day care |
| Trac II | GS | ✓ | ✓ | ✓ | ✓⊛ | ✓ | ✓ | YesIN | ✓ | ✓ | |
| Ultrasmooth | BMY | ✓ | ✓ | ✓ | ✓⊛ | ✓ | ✓ | YesIN | ✓ | ✓ | infant formula; Workplace Principles; D.C.C.A. |
| Williams Lectric Shave | BECH | ✓ | ✓ | ✗○ | ✓ | ✓ | ✓ | YesIN | ✓⊘ | ✓ | 🌐, Work. Princ.; on-site day care; U.K. |
| **SHORTENINGS & OILS** | | | | | | | | | | | |
| Adflex | ADM | ✗ | ✗ | ? | ? | ✗ | ? | No | ✗ | ? | |

| Product or Company | Addr. | | | | | | | | | | ALERT |
|---|---|---|---|---|---|---|---|---|---|---|---|
| Archer's | ADM | ✖ | ✖ | ? | ✖ | ? | No | ✖ | ? | ? | |
| Crisco | PG | ✔ | ✔ | ? | ✔⊛ | ✔ | Yes | ✔ | ✔ | ? | disposable diapers; Salvadoran coffee; on-site day care; C.C.A. |
| Don Quijote | GOYA | ? | ? | ? | ? | ? | No | ✖ | ? | ? | |
| E-Z Chef | MO | ? | ✔ | ? | ✖ | ? | Yes | ✖ | ? | ? | cigarettes; Salvadoran coffee; Work. Princ. |
| Good As Gold | ADM | ✖ | ✖ | ? | ✖ | ? | No | ✖ | ? | ? | |
| Hain | PET | ? | ? | ? | ? | ? | No | ✔ | ? | ? | |
| Hollywood | PET | ? | ? | ? | ? | ? | No | ✖ | ? | ? | |
| Loriva Supreme* | LOR | ✔ | ⊘ | ⊘ | ✔ | ✔ | No | ⊘ | ? | ? | |
| Mazola | CPC | ✔+ | ✔ | ⊘ | ✔ | ✔ | No | ⊘ | ✔ | ✔ | |
| Protein Aide Prod.* | LOR | ✔ | ⊘ | ⊘ | ✔ | ✔ | No | ⊘ | ? | ? | |
| Puritan Oil | PG | ✔ | ✔ | ✔⊛ | ✔ | ✔ | Yes | ⊘ | ✔ | ✔ | disposable diapers; Salvadoran coffee; on-site day care; C.C.A. |

| ✔ = Top Rating | ⊘ = Middle Rating | ✖ = Bottom Rating | ? = Insufficient Information | Page 281 |
|---|---|---|---|---|

*For a more detailed explanation see key on page 14*

---

**SHORTENINGS & OILS**

| Company or Product | Abbr. | $ | ⚥ | ❘Ⲕ | 🏇 | 🐇 | 💉 | ☢ | ⚛ | ⌂ | ⊞ | ALERT |
|---|---|---|---|---|---|---|---|---|---|---|---|---|
| Sunlite | CAG | ? | ✖ | ✖ | ✓ | ? | ✖ | ✓ | No | ? | ✖ | safe meat controversy; D.C.C.A.; factory farming |
| Wesson | CAG | ? | ✖ | ✖ | ✓ | ? | ✖ | ✓ | No | ? | ✖ | safe meat controversy; D.C.C.A.; factory farming |
| **SLEEPING AIDS** | | | | | | | | | | | | |
| No-Doz | BMY | ✓ | ✓ | ✓ | ✓(*) | ✓ | ✖ | ✓ | YesIN | ✓ | ✓ | infant formula; Workplace Principles; D.C.C.A. |
| Sleep-Eze | AHP | ✖ | ✓ | ✓ | ✓(*) | ✓ | ✖ | ✓ | Yes | ✓ | ✓ | infant formula |
| Sominex 2 | BECH | ✖ | ✓ | ✓ | ✖○ | ✓ | ✓ | ✓ | YesIN ✓∅ | ✓ | ✓ | 🌐; Work. Princ.; on-site day care; U.K. |
| Unisom | PFE | ✓ | ✖ | ? | ? | ✖ | ✖ | ? | YesIN | ✖ | ? | heart valve suits |
| Vivarin | BECH | ✖ | ✓ | ✓ | ✖○ | ✓ | ✓ | ✓ | YesIN ✓∅ | ? | ✓ | 🌐; Work. Princ.; on-site day care; U.K. |
| **SNACKS** | | | | | | | | | | | | |
| Andy Capp | GIS | ✓+ | ✓ | ✓ | ✓ | ✓ | ✓ | ✖ | No | ✓ | ✓ | |
| Apple Bakes# | HVAL | ? | ? | ? | ✓ | ? | ✖ | ? | No | ? | ? | some organic ingredients |
| Bac-On-Snaps | CAG | ? | ✖ | ✓ | ? | ✖ | ✖ | ✖ | No | ✖ | ✖ | safe meat controversy; D.C.C.A.; factory farming |
| Bahsen's Bakery# | BABR | | | | | | | | | | | |

| Product or Company | Abbr. | 💲 | 🐱 | | | | | Yes/No | | | ALERT |
|---|---|---|---|---|---|---|---|---|---|---|---|
| Barrel O' Fun | BN | ◡ | ✓ | ✓ | ✓ | ✓ | ◡ | YesIN | ✓ | ✓ | |
| BeeBo | FLO | ? | ✗ | ? | ? | ? | ? | No | ? | ? | |
| Berry Bears | GIS | ✓+ | ✓ | ✓ | ✓ | ✓ | ✓ | No | ✓ | ✓ | C.C.A. |
| Betcha Bacon | GIS | ✓+ | ✓ | ✓ | ✓ | ✓ | ✓ | No | ✓ | ✓ | C.C.A. |
| Blue Bird | FLO | ? | ✗ | ? | ? | ? | ? | No | ? | ? | |
| Boppers | GIS | ✓+ | ✓ | ✓ | ✓ | ✓ | ✓ | No | ✓ | ✓ | C.C.A. |
| Break Cakes | BUD | ✓+ | ◡ | ✓ | ✓ | ✓ | ◡ | No | ◡ | ✓ | |
| Buckeye | BN | ◡ | ✓ | ✓ | ✓ | ◡ | ✓ | YesIN | ✓ | ✓ | |
| Bugles | GIS | ✓+ | ✓ | ✓ | ✓ | ✓ | ✓ | No | ✓ | ✓ | C.C.A. |
| Cain's | BN | ◡ | ✓ | ✓ | ✓ | ◡ | ◡ | YesIN | ◡ | ✓ | |
| Cape Cod | BUD | ✓+ | ◡ | ✓ | ✓ | ✓ | ✓ | No | ✓ | ◡ | |

✓ = Top Rating    ◡ = Middle Rating    ✗ = Bottom Rating    ? = Insufficient Information
*For a more detailed explanation see key on page 14*

**SNACKS**

| Company or Product | Abbr. | $ | ⚥ | 👤 | 🐇 | 🌍 | ⚖ | (Yes/No) | ☢ | ⬡⬡⬡ | ALERT |
|---|---|---|---|---|---|---|---|---|---|---|---|
| Chee-tos | PEP | ⌣ | ✓ | ✓ | ? | ✓ | ✓ | Yes | ⌣ | ⌣ | |
| Cheez Links | MO | ? | ? | ✓ | ? | ✗ | ? | Yes | ? | ? | cigarettes; Salvadoran coffee; Work. Princ. |
| Chesty | BN | ⌣ | ✓ | ✓ | ? | ✓ | ⌣ | YesIN | ? | ✓ | |
| Christie | RJR | ? | ? | ✓ | ? | ✗ | ⌣ | Yes | ? | ? | cigarettes; D.C.C.A. |
| Clover Club | BN | ⌣ | ✓ | ✓ | ? | ✓ | ⌣ | YesIN | ⌣ | ✓ | |
| Clover Ridge | MO | ? | ✓ | ? | ? | ✗ | ? | Yes | ? | ? | cigarettes; Salvadoran coffee; Work. Princ. |
| Combos | MARS | ? | ? | ? | ? | ⌣ | ? | No | ? | ? | |
| Corn Diggers | RJR | ? | ⌣ | ? | ✓ | ✗ | ⌣ | Yes | ✗ | ? | cigarettes; D.C.C.A. |
| Cornies | BN | ⌣ | ✓ | ✓ | ✓ | ✓ | ✓ | YesIN | ⌣ | ✓ | |
| Cracker Jack | BN | ⌣ | ✓ | ✓ | ✓ | ✓ | ✓ | YesIN | ⌣ | ✓ | |
| Crane's | BN | ⌣ | ✓ | ✓ | ✓ | ✓ | ✓ | YesIN | ⌣ | ✓ | |
| Crispy Thins | BUD | ✓+ | ✓ | ✓ | ⌣ | ✗ | ✓ | No | ⌣ | ⌣ | |
| | RJR | ? | ⌣ | ? | ? | ✗ | ⌣ | Yes | ? | ? | cigarettes; D.C.C.A. |

| Product or Company | | | | | | | | | | | | |
|---|---|---|---|---|---|---|---|---|---|---|---|---|
| Crunch 'n Munch | AHP | ✗ | ✓ | ✔ | ✔(✴) | ✔ | ✔ | Yes | ✓ | ✓ | infant formula |
| Dandy Bar | GIS | ✔+ | ✔ | ✔ | ✔ | ✔ | ✔ | No | ✔ | ✔ | C.C.A. |
| Date Bakes# | HVAL | ? | ? | ? | ✗ | ? | ? | No | ? | ? | some organic ingredients |
| Delta Gold | PEP | ✓ | ✔ | ? | ✔ | ✔ | ✓ | Yes | ✓ | ✓ | |
| Dipsy Doodles | BN | ✓ | ✔ | ✔ | ✔ | ✓ | ✓ | YesIN | ✓ | ✔ | |
| Dole | DOL | ✔ | ✓ | ? | ✔ | ✗ | ✗ | No | ✓ | ✗ | pesticide sterilization suit |
| Doo Dads | RJR | ? | ✓ | ? | ? | ✓ | ✗ | Yes | ✗ | ? | cigarettes; D.C.C.A. |
| Doritos | PEP | ✓ | ✔ | ? | ✔ | ✔ | ✔ | Yes | ✔ | ✔ | |
| Durkee | RCP | ? | ? | ? | ✔ | ? | ✓ | YesIN | ✗ | ✓ | 🌐,U.K. |
| Dux | GOYA | ? | ? | ? | ✔ | ? | ? | No | ? | ? | |
| Eagle Snacks | BUD | ✔+ | ✓ | ✔ | ✔ | ✔ | ✔ | No | ✓ | ✓ | |

✔ = Top Rating   ✓ = Middle Rating   ✗ = Bottom Rating   ? = Insufficient Information

*For a more detailed explanation see key on page 14*

SNACKS

| Company or Product | Abbr. | $ | ⚲ | | | | | | | | | ALERT |
|---|---|---|---|---|---|---|---|---|---|---|---|---|
| Eden# | EDEN | ✔+ | ✔ | ✔ | ✔ | ✔ | ✔ | No | ✔ | ✔ | | some organic ingredients |
| El Dorado | BN | ✓ | | | | ✓ | ✓ | YesIN | ✓ | | | |
| Enticing Delights# | FALC | ? | ✔ | ✘ | ✔ | ✔ | ✔ | No | ✔ | ✓ | | 1% For Peace; some organic ingredients |
| Evon | JSAN | ? | ? | ? | ? | ✘ | ? | No | ? | ? | | |
| Fiddle Faddle | SAND | ? | ? | ? | ? | ✘ | ? | YesIN | ? | ? | | makes pesticides |
| Fisher Nuts | PG | ✔ | ✔ | ✔ | ✔(*) | ✔ | ✔ | Yes | ✓ | ✔ | | disposable diapers; Salvadoran coffee; on-site day care; C.C.A. |
| Fritos | PEP | ✓ | ✔ | ✔ | ? | ✔ | ✔ | Yes | ✓ | ✓ | | |
| Fruit & Fitness# | HVAL | ? | ? | ? | ✘ | ✔ | ✔ | No | ? | ? | | some organic ingredients |
| Fruit Corners | GIS | ✔+ | ✔ | ✔ | ✔ | ✔ | ✔ | No | ✓ | ✔ | | C.C.A. |
| Fruit Harvest | GIS | ✔+ | ✔ | ✔ | ✔ | ✔ | ✔ | No | ✓ | ✔ | | C.C.A. |
| Fruit Roll-Ups | GIS | ✔+ | ✔ | ✔ | ✔ | ✔ | ✔ | No | ✓ | ✔ | | C.C.A. |
| Fruit Slush | UN | ? | ✓ | ✔ | ✔ | ✔* | ✓ | YesIN | ✓ | ? | | 🌐 U.K. |
| | GIS | | ✘ | ✓ | | | | No | | | | |

| Product or Company | Abbr. | $ | ⚥ | | | | | | | | | ALERT |
|---|---|---|---|---|---|---|---|---|---|---|---|---|
| FunYuns | PEP | ◑ | ✔ | ✔ | ? | ✔ | ✔ | ✔ | Yes | ◑ | ✔ | |
| Geiser's | BN | ◑ | ✔ | ✔ | ✔ | ✔ | ✔ | ◑ | YesIN | ◑ | ✔ | |
| Granola Dipps | OAT | ✔+ | ✔ | ✔ | ✔ | ✔ | ✔ | ✔ | No | ✔ | ✔ | Fair Share |
| Guy's | BN | ◑ | ✔ | ✔ | ✔ | ✔ | ◑ | ✔ | YesIN | ◑ | ✔ | |
| Hain | PET | ? | ? | ? | ? | ✖ | ? | ◑ | No | ? | ? | |
| Hawaiian Kettle | BUD | ✔+ | ◑ | ✔ | ? | ✔ | ✔ | ◑ | No | ◑ | ◑ | |
| Hostess | RAL | ◑ | ✔ | ✔ | ✔ | ✔ | ◑ | ◑ | No | ◑ | ◑ | |
| Humpty Dumpty | BN | ◑ | ✔ | ✔ | ✔ | ✔ | ✔ | ◑ | YesIN | ✔ | ✔ | |
| Jays | BN | ◑ | ✔ | ✔ | ✔ | ✔ | ✔ | ◑ | YesIN | ◑ | ✔ | |
| Jiffy Pop | AHP | ✖ | ✔ | ◑ | ✔⊛ | ✔ | ✔ | ◑ | Yes | ◑ | ◑ | infant formula |
| KAS | BN | ◑ | ✔ | ✔ | ✔ | ✔ | ✔ | ◑ | YesIN | ◑ | ✔ | |

✔ = Top Rating  ◑ = Middle Rating  ✖ = Bottom Rating  ? = Insufficient Information
*For a more detailed explanation see key on page 14*

**SNACKS**

| Company or Product | Abbr. | $ | ⚥ | | | | | | | | | ALERT |
|---|---|---|---|---|---|---|---|---|---|---|---|---|
| KP Lower Fat | UBH | ✓ | ✗ | ✗ | ✓ | ✓ | ✗ | No | ? | ? | ? | ⊕, U.K. |
| Kitty Clover | BN | ✓ | ✓ | ✓ | ✓ | ✓ | ✓ | YesIN | ✓ | ✓ | ✓ | |
| Krunchers! | BN | ✓ | ✓ | ✓ | ✓ | ✓ | ✓ | YesIN | ✓ | ✓ | ✓ | |
| Kudos | MARS | ? | ? | ? | ? | ✓ | ? | No | ? | ? | ✓ | |
| La Famous | BN | ✓ | ✓ | ✓ | ✓ | ✓ | ✓ | YesIN | ✓ | ✓ | ✓ | |
| Laura Scudder's | BN | ✓ | ✓ | ✓ | ✓ | ✓ | ✓ | YesIN | ✓ | ✓ | ✓ | |
| Lay's | PEP | ✓ | ✓ | ✓ | ? | ✓ | ✓ | Yes | ✓ | ✓ | ✓ | |
| Light & Crunchy | GIS | ✓+ | ✓ | ✓ | ✓ | ✓ | ✗ | No | ✓ | ✓ | ✓ | C.C.A. |
| Loriva Supreme* | LOR | ✓ | ✓Ø | ? | ? | ✓ | ✓ | No | ✓Ø | ? | ? | |
| Mister Salty | RJR | ? | ✗ | ✗ | ✗ | ✓ | ✓ | Yes | ✗ | ? | ? | cigarettes; D.C.C.A. |
| Mohawk | MO | ? | ✓ | ✗ | ✓ | ✓ | ? | Yes | ? | ? | ? | cigarettes; Salvadoran coffee; Work. Princ. |
| Moore's | BN | ✓ | ✓ | ✓ | ✓ | ✓ | ✓ | YesIN | ✓ | ✓ | ✓ | |
| Munchos | PEP | ✓ | ✓ | ✓ | ? | ✓ | ✓ | Yes | ✓ | ✓ | ✓ | |

| Product or Company | Abbr. | $ | [icon] | [icon] | [icon] | [icon] | [icon] | [icon] | [icon] | [icon] | ALERT |
|---|---|---|---|---|---|---|---|---|---|---|---|---|
| Nacho Sticks | GIS | ✓+ | ✓ | ✓ | ✓ | ✓ | No | ✓ | ✓ | ✓ | | C.C.A. |
| Nalley's | CBI | ✓+ | ◐ | ✗ | ? | ✓ | No | ? | ◐ | ◐ | | |
| Nature Valley | GIS | ✓+ | ✓ | ✓ | ✓ | ✓ | No | ✓ | ✓ | ✓ | | C.C.A. |
| New York Deli | BN | ◐ | ✓ | ✓ | ◐ | ✓ | YesIN | ◐ | ◐ | ◐ | | |
| Newman's Own* | NEWO | ✓+ | ◐⊘ | ✓ | ✓ | ✓ | No | ✓ | ◐ | ✓ | | 100% profit to charity; C.C.A. |
| O'Boisies | UBH | ◐ | ✗ | ✓ | ? | ✓ | No | ? | ? | ◐ | | 🌐; U.K. |
| O'Grady's | PEP | ◐ | ✓ | ✓ | ? | ✓ | Yes | ◐ | ✓ | ◐ | | |
| O-Ke-Doke | BN | ◐ | ✓ | ✓ | ✓ | ◐ | YesIN | ◐ | ◐ | ✓ | | |
| Orville Redenbacher's | CAG | ? | ✗ | ? | ? | ✗ | No | ? | ✗ | ✗ | | safe meat controversy; D.C.C.A.; factory farming |
| Pacific Gardens* | ACOP | ? | ? | ? | ✓ | ✓ | No | ? | ? | ? | | co-op |
| Peanut Butter Boppers | GIS | ✓+ | ✓ | ✓ | ✓ | ✓ | No | ◐ | ✓ | ✓ | | C.C.A. |

✓ = Top Rating   ◐ = Middle Rating   ✗ = Bottom Rating   ? = Insufficient Information

*For a more detailed explanation see key on page 14*

Page 289

**SNACKS**

| Company or Product | Abbr. | $ | ♀ | 👤 | ✊ | ❓ | 🐾 | ⚖ | ▦ | ▦ | ⊕ | ALERT |
|---|---|---|---|---|---|---|---|---|---|---|---|---|
| Pepe's | CAG | ? | ✖ | ✔ | ? | ✖ | ✖ | ? | No | ? | ✖ | safe meat controversy; D.C.C.A.; factory farming |
| Pepitos | BN | ✔ | ✔ | ✔ | ✔ | ✔ | ✔ | ✔ | YesIN | ✔ | ✔ | |
| Planter's | RJR | ? | ✔ | ? | ✔ | ✖ | ✖ | ? | Yes | ? | ? | cigarettes; D.C.C.A. |
| Pop Secret | GIS | ✔ | ✔ | ✔ | ✔ | ✔ | ✔ | ✔ | No | ✔ | ✔ | C.C.A. |
| Poppycocks | SAND | ? | ? | ✔ | ? | ✖ | ? | ✖ | YesIN | ? | ? | makes pesticides |
| Pringles | PG | ✔ | ✔ | ✔✔⊛ | ✔ | ✔ | ✔ | ✔ | Yes | ✔ | ✔ | disposable diapers; Salvadoran coffee; on-site day care; C.C.A. |
| Protein Aide Prod.* | LOR | ✔+ | ✔∅ | ✔ | ✔ | ✔ | ✔ | ✔ | No | ✔∅ | ? | |
| Pudding Roll-ups | GIS | ✔+ | ✔ | ✔ | ✔ | ✔ | ✔ | ✔ | No | ✔ | ✔ | C.C.A. |
| Raisin Bakes# | HVAL | ? | ? | ✔ | ? | ✖ | ? | ✔ | No | ? | ? | some organic ingredients |
| Ranch Fries | BN | ✔ | ✔ | ✔ | ✔ | ✔ | ✔ | ✔ | YesIN | ✔ | ✔ | |
| Real McCoy | UBH | ✔ | ✔ | ✖ | ✔ | ✔ | ✖ | ? | No | ? | ? | ⊕; U.K. |
| Red Seal | BN | ✔ | ✔ | ✔ | ✔ | ✔ | ✔ | ✔ | YesIN | ✔ | ✔ | |
| Rold Gold | PEP | ✔ | ✔ | ? | ✔ | ✔ | ✔ | ? | Yes | ✔ | ✔ | |

| Product or Company | Abbr. | 💲 | ♀ | ⚥ | 🐾 | 🌍 | | ⚛ | 🏠 | ⚕ | ALERT |
|---|---|---|---|---|---|---|---|---|---|---|---|
| Ruffles | PEP | ◡ | ✓ | ✓ | ✓ | ✓ | Yes | ◡ | ✓ | ◡ | |
| Salsa Rio | PEP | ◡ | ✓ | ? | ✓ | ✓ | Yes | ◡ | ✓ | ◡ | |
| Seyferts | BN | ◡ | ✓ | ✓ | ✓ | ◡ | YesIN | ✓ | ✓ | ✓ | |
| Shark Bites | GIS | ✓+ | ✓ | ✓ | ✓ | ✓ | No | ◡ | ✓ | ✓ | C.C.A. |
| Shreddies | RJR | ? | ? | ? | ✗ | ✗ | Yes | ? | ? | ? | cigarettes; D.C.C.A. |
| Smartfood | PEP | ◡ | ✓ | ✓ | ✓ | ✓ | Yes | ◡ | ✓ | ◡ | |
| Snackin' Fruit | GIS | ✓+ | ✓ | ? | ✓ | ✓ | No | ◡ | ✓ | ✓ | C.C.A. |
| Snacktime | BN | ◡ | ✓ | ✓ | ✓ | ◡ | YesIN | ◡ | ✓ | ✓ | |
| Snyder | CBI | ✓+ | ✗ | ✓ | ✓ | ◡ | No | ◡ | ? | ◡ | |
| Summit | MARS | ? | ? | ? | ? | ◡ | No | ? | ◡ | ? | |
| Sunkist | UN | ? | ✗ | ✓* | ✓ | ◡ | YesIN | ◡ | ◡ | ? | 🌐, U.K. |

✓ = Top Rating  ◡ = Middle Rating  ✗ = Bottom Rating  ? = Insufficient Information

For a more detailed explanation see key on page 14

Page 291

SNACKS

| Company or Product | Abbr. | $ | ♀ | ⊕ | 🐾 | ✿ | 🕊 | | | | | ALERT |
|---|---|---|---|---|---|---|---|---|---|---|---|---|
| **TastyKake** | TBC | ✔+ | ✔ | ✖ | ✔ | ✔ | ✔ | No | ? | ? | ✔ | |
| **Tor-Ticos** | BN | ✔ | ✔ | ✔ | ✔ | ✔ | ✔ | YesIN | ✔ | ✔ | ✔ | |
| **Tostitos** | PEP | ✔ | ✔ | ✔ | ✔ | ? | ✔ | Yes | ✔ | ✔ | ✔ | |
| **Wacky Fruit** | RJR | ? | ? | ✖ | ? | ✖ | ✔ | Yes | ✔ | ? | ? | cigarettes; D.C.C.A. |
| **Walker's Crisps** | RJR | ? | ? | ✖ | ? | ✖ | ✔ | Yes | ✔ | ? | ? | cigarettes; D.C.C.A. |
| **Whipps** | OAT | ✔ | ✔ | ✔ | ✔ | ✔ | ✔ | No | ✔ | ✔ | ✔ | Fair Share |
| **Whole Earth#** | WHO | ✔+ | ✔ | ✔ | ✔ | ✔ | ✔ | No | ? | ✔ | ✔ | 1% For Peace; some organic ingredients |
| **Wise** | BN | ✔ | ✔ | ✔ | ✔ | ✔ | ✔ | YesIN | ✔ | ✔ | ✔ | |
| **SOAPS: HAND & BATH** | | | | | | | | | | | | |
| **Actibath** | KAO | | | | | | | | | | | see page 344 for Japanese companies |
| **Alexandra Avery\*** | ALEX | ✔+ | ✔ | ✔⊘ | ✔ | ✔ | ✔ | No | ✔ | ✔ | ✔ | |
| **Allen's Naturally\*** | ANY | ✔ | ✔ | ✔⊘ | ✔ | ? | ✔ | No | ✔ | ✔ | ? | |
| **Amazing Grains\*** | BLN | ✔ | ✔ | ✔ | ✔ | ✔ | ✔ | No | ✔ | ✔ | ✔ | some organic ingredients |

| Product or Company | Abbr. | 💲 | | | | | | | | | ALERT |
|---|---|---|---|---|---|---|---|---|---|---|---|
| Aroma Oil* | BLN | ✔ | ✔ | ✔ | ✔ | ✔ | ✔ | No | ✔ | ✓ | some organic ingredients |
| Aroma Vera# | AV | ✗ | ✗ | ✓ | ✗ | ✗ | ✗ | No | ✓ | ✗ | |
| Aura Cacia* | AURA | ✔+ | ✓ | ✓ø | ✔ | ✔ | ✔ | No | ✓ | ✓ | 1% For Peace; on-site day care |
| Avon | AVP | ✔+ | ✔ | ✔ | ✔ | ✔ | ✔ | No | ✓ | ✔ | on-site day care; C.C.A. |
| Body Shop, The | BS | ✓ | ✔ | ? | ✔ | ✔ | ✔ | No | ? | ? | ACT NOW; U.K. |
| Boraxo | G | ? | ✔ | ✓ | ✗ | ✔ | ? | No. | ? | ? | |
| Camay | PG | ✔ | ✔ | ? | ✔ | ✔® | ✔ | Yes | ✓ | ✔ | disposable diapers; Salvadoran coffee; on-site day care; C.C.A. |
| Caress | UN | ? | ✗ | ✓ | ✓ | ✔* | ✔ | YesIN | ✓ | ? | 🌐, U.K. |
| Caribee | UN | ? | ✗ | ✓ | ✓ | ✔* | ✔ | YesIN | ✓ | ? | 🌐, U.K. |
| Cashmere Bouquet | CL | ✔+ | ✔ | ✔ | ✔ | ✔® | ✔ | YesIN | ✓ | ✔ | |
| Clear Complexion | KAO | | | | | | | | | | see page 344 for Japanese companies |

✔ = Top Rating   ✓ = Middle Rating   ✗ = Bottom Rating   ? = Insufficient Information

For a more detailed explanation see key on page 14

| Company or Product | Abbr. | $ | ♀ | | | | | | Yes/No | | | | ALERT |
|---|---|---|---|---|---|---|---|---|---|---|---|---|---|
| Coast | PG | ✓ | ✓ | ✓ | ✓ | ✓⊛ | ✓ | ✓ | Yes | ◔ | ✓ | ✓ | disposable diapers; Salvadoran coffee; on-site day care; C.C.A. |
| Cuticura | DEPC | ? | | | | ✓ | | ◔ | No | ? | | ◔ | |
| Daily Revival | AVP | ✓+ | ✓ | ✓ | ✓ | ✓ | ✓ | ✓ | No | ◔ | | ✓ | on-site day care; C.C.A. |
| Dial | G | ? | | ◔ | ✓ | ✓ | ✗ | ? | No | ? | ? | ? | |
| Direct Action | KAO | | | | | | | | | | | | see page 344 for Japanese companies |
| Dove | UN | ? | ✗ | | ◔ | ✓* | ◔ | ✓ | YesIN | ◔ | ✓ | ? | ⊕, U.K. |
| Feelin' Fresh | AVP | ✓+ | ✓ | ◔ | ✓ | ✓ | ◔ | ✓ | No | | ◔ | ✓ | on-site day care; C.C.A. |
| Fiesta | KAO | | | | | | | | | | | | see page 344 for Japanese companies |
| Gentle Touch | KAO | | | | | | | | | | | | see page 344 for Japanese companies |
| Herbal Facial Steams* | BLN | ✓ | ✓ | ✓ | ✓ | ✓ | ✓ | ✓ | No | ✓ | ✓ | ◔ | some organic ingredients |
| Irish Spring | CL | ✓+ | ✓ | ✓ | ✓ | ✓⊛ | ✓ | ✓ | YesIN | ◔ | ✓ | ✓ | |
| Ivory | PG | ✓ | ✓ | ✓ | ✓ | ✓⊛ | ✓ | ✓ | Yes | ◔ | ✓ | ✓ | disposable diapers; Salvadoran coffee; on-site day care; C.C.A. |
| Jason Natural# | JNP | ? | ◔ | | ✗ | ✓ | ✗ | ✓ | No | ✓∅ | | ✓ | |

| Product or Company | Abbr. | | | | | | | | | | ALERT |
|---|---|---|---|---|---|---|---|---|---|---|---|
| Jergens | KAO | | | | | | | | | ✔ | see page 344 for Japanese companies |
| Kirk's | PG | ✔ | ✔ | ✔ | ✔(*) | ✔ | Yes | ✓ | ✔ | ✔ | disposable diapers; Salvadoran coffee; on-site day care; C.C.A. |
| Kiss My Face# | KMF | ? | ✔ | ✔ | ✔ | ✔ | No | ✔ | ✔ | ✓ | |
| Lava | PG | ✔ | ✔ | ✔ | ✔(*) | ✔ | Yes | ✓ | ✔ | ✔ | disposable diapers; Salvadoran coffee; on-site day care; C.C.A. |
| Loanda | IRDV | ? | ✗ | ✔ | ○ | ✗ | No | ? | ? | ? | |
| Love Mitts* | BLN | ✔ | ✔ | ✔ | ✔ | ✔ | No | ✔ | ✔ | ✓ | some organic ingredients |
| Lux | UN | ? | ✗ | ✓ | ✔* | ✓ | YesIN | ✓ | ✓ | ? | 🌐; U.K. |
| Mr. Bubble | RCP | ? | ? | ? | ? | ? | YesIN | ? | ✗ | ✓ | 🌐; U.K. |
| Naturally Exotic* | AURA | ✔+ | ✔ | ✔ | ✔ | ✓0 | No | ✔ | ✔ | ✓ | 1% For Peace; on-site day care |
| Nature Scents | KAO | | | | | | | | | ✗ | see page 344 for Japanese companies |
| Neutrogena | NGNA | ? | ✓ | ✓ | ? | ? | No | ✓0 | ✗ | ? | |

✔ = Top Rating  ✓ = Middle Rating  ✗ = Bottom Rating  ? = Insufficient Information
For a more detailed explanation see key on page 14

**SOAPS: HAND & BATH**

# SOAPS: HAND & BATH

| Company or Product | Abbr. | $ | | | | | | | | | | | ALERT |
|---|---|---|---|---|---|---|---|---|---|---|---|---|---|
| On Duty 24 Plus | AVP | ✓+ | ✓ | ✓ | ✓ | ✓ | ✓ | ✓ | No | ✓ | ✓ | ✓ | on-site day care; C.C.A. |
| Orjene Natural# | ORJ | ✓+ | ✓ | ✓ | ✓ | ✓ | ✗ | ✓ | No | ✓ | ✓ | ? | |
| Palmolive | CL | ✓+ | ✓ | ✓ | ✓⊛ | ✓ | ✓ | ✓ | YesIN | ✓ | ✓ | ✓ | |
| Paul Penders* | PP | ✓+ | ✓ | ✓∅ | ✓ | ✓ | ✗ | ✓ | No | ✓ | ✓ | ✓ | 1% For Peace |
| Pure & Natural | G | ? | ? | ✓ | ✓ | ✗ | ? | ✓ | No | ? | ? | ? | |
| Rosa Mosqueta# | AUB | ? | ✓ | ✓ | ✓ | ✓ | ✓ | ✓ | No | ✓ | ? | ✓ | some organic ingredients |
| Safeguard | PG | ✓ | ✓ | ✓ | ✓⊛ | ✓ | ✓ | ✓ | Yes | ✓ | ✓ | ✓ | disposable diapers; Salvadoran coffee; on-site day care; C.C.A. |
| Sandcastle Arthpy.* | AURA | ✓+ | ✓ | ✓ | ✓ | ✓ | ✓ | ✓ | No | ✓ | ✓ | ✓ | 1% For Peace; on-site day care |
| Shield | UN | ? | ? | ✓ | ✓* | ✓ | ✓ | ✓ | YesIN | ✓ | ? | ? | ⊕, U.K. |
| Softsoap | CL | ✓+ | ✓ | ✓ | ✓⊛ | ✓ | ✓ | ✓ | YesIN | ✓ | ✓ | ✓ | |
| Taoge# | SLGR | ? | ? | ? | ✗ | ? | ✗ | ? | No | ? | ? | ? | |
| Tone | G | ? | ✓ | ✓ | ✓ | ✓ | ✓ | ? | No | ✓ | ? | ? | |
| Woodbury | KAO | | | | | | | | | | | | see page 344 for Japanese companies |

| Product or Company | Abbr. |  |  |  |  |  |  |  |  |  | ALERT |
|---|---|---|---|---|---|---|---|---|---|---|---|
| Zest | PG | ✔ | ✔ | ✔ | ✔⊛ | ✔ | ✔ | Yes | ✓ | ✔ | disposable diapers; Salvadoran coffee; on-site day care; C.C.A |
| **SOFT DRINKS** | | | | | | | | | | | |
| A & W | KO | ✓ | ✔ | ✔ | ? | ✔ | ✔ | Yes | ✓ | ✔ | |
| Barrelhead Root Beer | CADB | ✓ | ? | ? | ? | ✖ | ? | YesIN | ? | ? | ⊕; U.K. |
| Caliber[1] | GUI | | | | | | | | | | see page 330 for U.K. ratings |
| Canada Dry | CADB | ✓ | ? | ? | ✔ | ✖ | ? | YesIN | ? | ? | ⊕; U.K. |
| Coca-Cola | KO | ✓ | ✔ | ✔ | ? | ✔ | ✔ | Yes | ✓ | ? | |
| Crush | CADB | ✓ | ? | ? | ✔ | ✖ | ? | YesIN | ? | ? | ⊕; U.K. |
| Cutter | ACC | ✓ | ✓+ | ✖ | ✓ | ✓ | ✓ | No | ✓ | | Fair Share |
| Deer Park | CLX | ✓ | ✖ | ✖ | ✓ | ✓* | ✓ | No | ✔ | ✖ | |
| Evian | BSN | | | | | | | | | | see page 330 for U.K. ratings |

✔ = Top Rating   ✓ = Middle Rating   ✖ = Bottom Rating   ? = Insufficient Information

*For a more detailed explanation see key on page 14*

**SOFT DRINKS**

| Company or Product | Abbr. | $ | | | | | | | | ALERT |
|---|---|---|---|---|---|---|---|---|---|---|
| Fanta | KO | ◐ | ✓ | ✓ | ? | ✓ | Yes | ✓ | ? | |
| Fresca | KO | ◐ | ✓ | ✓ | ? | ✓ | Yes | ✓ | ? | |
| Light 'n Juicy | KO | ◐ | ✓ | ✓ | ? | ✓ | Yes | ✓ | ? | |
| Mello Yello | KO | ◐ | ✓ | ✓ | ? | ✓ | Yes | ✓ | ? | |
| Minute Maid | KO | ◐ | ✓ | ✓ | ? | ✓ | Yes | ✓ | ? | |
| Mountain Dew | PEP | ◐ | ✓ | ✓ | ✓ | ✓ | Yes | ◐ | ◐ | |
| Moussy | ACC | ✓+ | ◐ | ✓ | ✓ | ✓ | No | ◐ | ◐ | Fair Share |
| Mr. Pibb | KO | ◐ | ✓ | ✓ | ? | ✓ | Yes | ✓ | ? | |
| No-Cal | CADB | ? | ? | ? | ✗ | ? | YesIN | ? | ? | 🌐, U.K. |
| O'Doule's | BUD | ✓+ | ◐ | ✓ | ✓ | ✓ | No | ◐ | ◐ | |
| Oasis | CADB | ? | ? | ✓ | ✗ | ? | YesIN | ? | ◐ | 🌐, U.K. |
| Pepsi Cola | PEP | ◐ | ✓ | ✓ | ✓ | ✓ | Yes | ✓ | ? | |
| Perrier | SPER | ? | ? | ✓ | ✗ | ? | No | ◐ | ? | |

| Product or Company | Abbr. | | | | | | | | | ALERT |
|---|---|---|---|---|---|---|---|---|---|---|
| Ramblin' Root Beer | KO | ◡ | ✓ | ✓ | ✓ | ✓ | Yes | ✓ | ? | |
| Rocky Mountain | ACC | ✓+ | ◡ | ✓ | ✓ | ◡ | No | ◡ | ◡ | Fair Share |
| Saratoga | MO | ? | ✓ | ? | ✓ | ? | Yes | ? | ? | cigarettes; Salvadoran coffee; Work. Princ. |
| Schweppe's | CADB | ? | ? | ? | ✓ | ? | YesiN | ? | ? | ⊕, U.K. |
| Seagram's | VO | ? | ✗ | ? | ? | ✗ | No | ? | ? | ⊕ |
| Sharp's | MO | ? | ✓ | ? | ✓ | ✗ | Yes | ? | ? | cigarettes; Salvadoran coffee; Work. Princ. |
| Slice | PEP | ◡ | ✓ | ✓ | ✓ | ? | Yes | ✓ | ◡ | |
| Sprite | KO | ◡ | ✓ | ✓ | ✓ | ? | Yes | ✓ | ? | |
| Tab | KO | ◡ | ✓ | ✓ | ✓ | ? | Yes | ✓ | ? | |
| SOUP | | | | | | | | | | |
| Bovril | CPC | ✓+ | ◡ | ✓ | ✓ | ✓ | No | ✓ | ✓ | |

✓ = Top Rating   ◡ = Middle Rating   ✗ = Bottom Rating   ? = Insufficient Information

For a more detailed explanation see key on page 14

Page 299

SOFT DRINKS

| Company or Product | Abbr. | 💲 | ⚥ | 🐰 | 🐇 | 🌍 | ⚛ | 🐟 | ⬜ | ALERT |
|---|---|---|---|---|---|---|---|---|---|---|
| Campbell's | CPB | ✔ | ✔ | ✔ | ? | ✔ | No | ✔ | ✔ | on-site day care |
| Chunky Soup | CPB | ✔ | ✔ | ✔ | ? | ✔ | No | ✔ | ✔ | on-site day care |
| Continental | UN | ? | ✘ | ✔ | ✔* | ✔ | YesIN | ✔ | ? | 🌍; U.K. |
| Copperhood | ACV | ? | ✔ | ✔ | ✘ | ? | No | ✘ | ? |  |
| Cup O'Noodles | NSF |  |  |  |  |  |  |  |  | see page 344 for Japanese companies |
| Cup-A-Soup | UN | ? | ✘ | ✔ | ✔* | ✔ | YesIN | ✔ | ? | 🌍; U.K. |
| Fantastic Foods# | FFI | ✔ | ✔ | ✔ | ✔ | ✔ | No | ✔ | ✔ | some organic ingredients |
| Great American | HNZ | ✔ | ✔ | ✔ | ? | ✔ | No | ✔ | ✔ | C.C.A. |
| Habitant | CPB | ✔ | ✔ | ✔ | ✔ | ✔ | No | ✔ | ✔ | on-site day care |
| Hain | PET | ? | ? | ✔ | ? | ? | No | ✔ | ? |  |
| Harris | BN | ✔ | ✔ | ✔ | ✘ | ✔ | YesIN | ✔ | ✔ |  |
| Health Valley# | HVAL | ? | ? | ✔ | ? | ? | No | ? | ? | some organic ingredients |

| Product or Company | Abbr. | 💲 | ♀ | ✊ | 🐇 | ⚖ | ☮ | Yes/No | ⚛ | 🕊 | 🏠 | ALERT |
|---|---|---|---|---|---|---|---|---|---|---|---|---|
| Hiltons | BN | ✓ | ✓ | ✓ | ✓ | ✓ | ✓ | ✓ | YesIN | ✓ | ✓ | ✓ | |
| Home Cookin' Soup | CPB | ✓ | ✓ | ✓ | ? | ✓ | ✓ | ✓ | No | ✓ | ✓ | | on-site day care |
| Hondashi | AJI | | | | | | | | | | | | see page 344 for Japanese companies |
| Kikkoman | KIK | | | | | | | | | | | | see page 344 for Japanese companies |
| Knorr | CPC | ✓+ | ✓ | ✓ | ✓ | ✓ | ✓ | ✓ | No | ✓ | ✓ | | |
| Le Gout | K | ✓ | ✓ | ✓ | ✓* | ✓ | ✓ | ✓ | YesIN | ✓ | ✓ | ✓ | C.C.A. |
| Lipton's | UN | ? | ✓ | ✗ | ✓* | ✓ | ✓ | ✓ | YesIN | ✓ | ? | ? | 🌐, U.K. |
| Lots-A-Noodles | UN | ? | ✓ | ✗ | ✓* | ✓ | ✓ | ✓ | YesIN | ✓ | ? | ? | 🌐, U.K. |
| Mayacamas* | MAYA | ? | ? | ? | ✓ | ✗ | ? | ? | No | ? | ? | ? | |
| Oodles of Noodles | NSF | | | | | | | | | | | | see page 344 for Japanese companies |
| Progresso | PET | ? | ? | ? | ? | ✗ | ? | ? | No | ? | ? | ? | |

✓ = Top Rating   ✓ = Middle Rating   ✗ = Bottom Rating   ? = Insufficient Information

*For a more detailed explanation see key on page 14*

**SOUP**

Page 301

# SOY PRODUCTS

| Company or Product | Abbr. | 💲 | ♀ | ⚖ | 🐇 | ⚗ | 🌐 | ☢ | 🕊 | ⊞ | ALERT |
|---|---|---|---|---|---|---|---|---|---|---|---|
| Redding Ridge Farms | UN | ? | ✗ | ○ | ✓ | ✓* | ✓ | YesIN | ✓ | ? | 🌐, U.K. |
| Soup Starter | BN | ○ | ✓ | ✓ | ✓ | ✓ | ✓ | YesIN | ✓ | ✓ | |
| Souper Starters | CPB | ✓ | ✓ | ✓ | ? | ✓ | ✓ | No | ✓ | ✓ | on-site day care |
| Steero | BN | ○ | ✓ | ✓ | ✓ | ✓ | ✓ | YesIN | ✓ | ✓ | |
| Swanson | CPB | ✓ | ✓ | ✓ | ? | ✓ | ✓ | No | ✓ | ✓ | on-site day care |
| Top Ramen | NSF | | | | | | | | | | see page 344 for Japanese companies |
| Wyler's | BN | ○ | ✓ | ✓ | ✓ | ✓ | ✓ | YesIN | ✓ | ✓ | |
| **SOY PRODUCTS** | | | | | | | | | | | |
| 21st Century Foods* | TFC | ✗ | ✗ | ✓ | ✓ | ✓ | ✓ | No | ✓ | ✓ | on-site day care |
| Baker's Nutrisoy | ADM | ✓+ | ✗ | ? | ? | ✓ | ? | No | ? | ? | |
| Edensoy# | EDEN | ✓ | ✓ | ✓ | ✓ | ✓ | ✓ | No | ✓ | ✓ | some organic ingredients |
| Kikkoman | KIK | | | | | | | | | | see page 344 for Japanese companies |
| Say Moo# | HVAL | ? | ? | ? | ? | ✗ | ✓ | No | ? | ? | some organic ingredients |

| Product or Company | Abbr. | $ | ⚥ | | | | | | No/Yes | | | ALERT |
|---|---|---|---|---|---|---|---|---|---|---|---|---|
| Soylami# | TFC | ✖ | ✔ | ✔ | ✔ | ✔ | ✔ | | No | ✔ | ✔ | on-site day care |
| Tillamook Cheese | TILA | ✔+ | ✔ | ✖ | ✔ | ✔ | ✔ | | No | ✔ | ✔ | co-op |
| Tofu Cream Chie# | TFC | ✖ | ✔ | ✔ | ✔ | ✔ | ✔ | | No | ✔ | ✔ | on-site day care |
| **SUPPLIES: MISCELLANEOUS** | | | | | | | | | | | | |
| 3-in-One | RCP | ? | ? | ? | ? | ✔ | ? | | YesIN | ? | ✔ | 🌐, U.K. |
| Antrol | RCP | ? | ? | ? | ? | ✔ | ? | | YesIN | ? | ✔ | 🌐, U.K. |
| BBQ Bag | CLX | ✔ | ✖ | ✔* | ✔ | ✔ | ✔ | | No | ✔ | ✔ | |
| Black Flag | RCP | ? | ? | ? | ? | ✔ | ? | | YesIN | ✖ | ✔ | 🌐, U.K. |
| Blue Dot | GTE | ✔ | ✔ | ✔ | ✔ | ✔ | ✔ | | No | ✔ | ✔ | nuclear weapons; ✈ |
| Brita# | SLGR | ? | ? | ? | ? | ✔ | ✔ | | No | ✔ø | ? | |
| Combat | CLX | ✔ | ✖ | ✔* | ✔ | ✔ | ✔ | | No | ✔ | ✖ | |

✔ = Top Rating  ✔ = Middle Rating  ✖ = Bottom Rating  ? = Insufficient Information

*For a more detailed explanation see key on page 14*

**SUPPLIES: MISCELLANEOUS**

| Company or Product | Abbr. | $ | ♀ | | | | | | | | | | ALERT |
|---|---|---|---|---|---|---|---|---|---|---|---|---|---|
| Cutter | BAG | ? | ? | ? | ✔ | ✘○ | ✘ | ? | YesIN | ✘ | ? | ? | makes pesticides |
| D-Con | EK | ✔ | ✔ | ✔ | ✔ | ✔✱ | ✔ | ✔ | No | ✔ | ✔ | ✔ | 🐾, C.C.A. |
| Elmer's | BN | ✔ | ✔ | ✔ | ✔ | ✔ | ✔ | ✔ | YesIN | ✔ | ✔ | ✔ | |
| Energizer | RAL | ✔ | ✔ | ✔ | ✔ | ✔ | ✔ | ✔ | No | ✔ | ✔ | ✔ | |
| Eveready | RAL | ✔ | ✔ | ✔ | ✔ | ✔ | ✔ | ✔ | No | ✔ | ✔ | ✔ | |
| Flair | GS | ✔ | ✔ | ✔ | ✔ | ✔⊕ | ✔ | ✔ | YesIN | ✔ | ✔ | ✔ | |
| Fuji | FUJI | | | | | | | | | | | | see page 344 for Japanese companies |
| GE | GE | ✘ | ✔ | ? | ✔ | ✘○ | ✘ | ✘ | No | ? | ✘ | ✘ | nuclear weapons/power; 🐾: INFACT boycott |
| GTE | GTE | ✔ | ✔ | ✔ | ✔ | ✔ | ✔ | ✔ | No | ✔ | ✔ | ✔ | nuclear weapons |
| Gulf Lite | RCP | ? | ? | ? | ? | ? | ✔ | ? | YesIN | ? | ? | ✔ | 🌐, U.K. |
| Gulfwax | RCP | ? | ? | ? | ? | ? | ✔ | ? | YesIN | ? | ? | ✔ | 🌐, U.K. |
| Holiday | RCP | ? | ? | ? | ? | ? | ✔ | ? | YesIN | ? | ? | ✔ | 🌐, U.K. |
| Kingsford | CLX | ✔ | ✔ | ✔ | ✔ | ✔✱ | ✔ | ✔ | No | ✔ | ✘ | ✔ | 🌐, U.K. |

| Product or Company | Abbr. | 💲 | ♀ | | | | | | | | ⬡ ▦ | ALERT |
|---|---|---|---|---|---|---|---|---|---|---|---|---|
| Kiwi | SLE | ✓ | ✓ | ✓ | ✓ | ✓ | ✓ | Yes | ✓⊘ | ✓ | ✓ | on-site day care; C.C.A. |
| Kodak | EK | ◐ | ✓ | ✗ | ✓ | ✓⊛ | ✓ | No | ◐ | ✓ | ✓ | 🐰, C.C.A. |
| Liquid Paper | GS | ◐ | ◐ | ✓ | ✓ | ✓⊛ | ✓ | YesIN | ◐ | ◐ | ✓ | |
| Magicube | GE | ✗ | ✓ | ? | ✗○ | ✗ | ✓ | No | ✗ | ? | ✗ | nuclear weapons/power; 🐰 INFACT boycott |
| Match Light | CLX | ◐ | ✗ | ✓ | ✓* | ✓ | ✓ | No | ✓ | ✗ | ✓ | |
| Miser | GE | ✗ | ✓ | ? | ✗○ | ✗ | ✓ | No | ✗ | ? | ✗ | nuclear weapons/power; 🐰 INFACT boycott |
| Off! | SCJ | ✓+ | ✓ | ✓ | ✓* | ✓ | ✓ | YesIN | ✓ | ✓ | ✓ | 1st to ban CFCs; on-site day care |
| One Film | PRD | ✓ | ✓ | ◐ | ✓ | ✓ | ✓ | No | ◐ | ◐ | ✓ | Workplace Principles; C.C.A. |
| PAAS | SGP | ◐ | ✓ | ✓ | ✓⊛ | ✓ | ✓ | YesIN | ◐ | ✓ | ◐ | on-site day care; Workplace Principles |
| Panasonic | MTS | | | | | | | | | | | see page 344 for Japanese companies |
| Paper Mate | GS | ◐ | ◐ | ✓ | ✓⊛ | ✓ | ✓ | YesIN | ◐ | ✓ | ✓ | |

✓ = Top Rating ◐ = Middle Rating ✗ = Bottom Rating ? = Insufficient Information

*For a more detailed explanation see key on page 14*

Page 305

## SUPPLIES: MISCELLANEOUS

| Company or Product | Abbr. | $ | | | | | | | | | | | ALERT |
|---|---|---|---|---|---|---|---|---|---|---|---|---|---|
| Pencil Mate | GS | ✔ | ✔ | ✔ | ✔ | ✔⊛ | ✔ | YesIN | ✔ | ✔ | ✔ | ✔ | |
| Polaroid | PRD | ✔+ | ✔ | ✔ | ✔ | ✔ | ✔ | No | ✔ | ✔ | ✔ | ✔ | Workplace Principles; C.C.A. |
| Rit | CPC | ✔ | ✔ | ✔ | ✔ | ✔ | ✔ | No | ✔ | ✔ | ✔ | ✔ | |
| Raid | SCJ | ✔+ | ✔ | ? | ✔ | ✔* | ✔ | YesIN | ✔ | ✔ | ✔ | ✔ | 1st to ban CFCs; on-site day care |
| Raid-Max | SCJ | ✔+ | ✔ | ? | ✔ | ✔* | ✔ | YesIN | ✔ | ✔ | ✔ | ✔ | 1st to ban CFCs; on-site day care |
| Scotch | MMM | ✔ | ✔ | ✔ | ✔ | ✔* | ✔ | YesIN | ✔ | ✔ | ✔ | ✔ | ✳ |
| Snarol | RCP | ? | ? | ? | ✔ | ? | ✔ | YesIN | ✔ | ✖ | ? | ✔ | ⊕ U.K. |
| Sony | SNE | | | | | | | | | | | | see page 344 for Japanese companies |
| Spectra | PRD | ✔ | ✔ | ✔ | ✔ | ✔ | ✔ | No | ✔ | ✔ | ✔ | ✔ | Workplace Principles; C.C.A. |
| Spring Rain | RCP | ✔+ | ? | ? | ✔ | ? | ✔ | YesIN | ✔ | ✖ | ? | ✔ | ⊕ U.K. |
| Sterno | CL | ✔ | ✔ | ✔ | ✔ | ✔⊛ | ✔ | YesIN | ✔ | ✔ | ✔ | ✔ | |
| Sylvania | GTE | ✔ | ✔ | ✔ | ✔ | ✔ | ✔ | No | ✔ | ✔ | ✔ | ✔ | nuclear weapons; ☢ |
| Thompson | EK | ✔ | ✔ | ✔ | ✔ | ✔⊛ | ✔ | No | ✔ | ✔ | ✔ | ✔ | ☢; C.C.A. |

| Product or Company | Abbr. | 💲 | ⚥ | 🐰 | 🐟 | ☢ | 🐾 | | ☮ | | 🏭 | ALERT |
|---|---|---|---|---|---|---|---|---|---|---|---|---|
| **Waterman** | GS | ✓ | ✓ | ✓ | ✓ | ✓⊛ | ✓ | YesIN | ✓ | ✓ | ✓ | |
| **Wizard** | RCP | ? | ? | ? | ? | ✓ | ? | YesIN | ? | ✗ | ✓ | 🌐, U.K. |
| **SYRUPS & MOLASSES** | | | | | | | | | | | | |
| **Aunt Jemima** | OAT | ✓+ | ✓ | ✓ | ✓ | ✓ | ✓ | No | ✓ | ✓ | ✓ | Fair Share |
| **Cary's** | BN | ✓ | ✓ | ✓ | ✓ | ✓ | ✓ | YesIN | ✓ | ✓ | ✓ | |
| **Country Kitchen** | MO | ? | ✓ | ? | ✓ | ✓ | ? | Yes | ? | ? | ? | cigarettes; Salvadoran coffee; Work. Princ. |
| **Dickinson's** | SJM | ✓ | ✗ | ✓ | ✓ | ✗ | ✓ | No | ✓ | ✓ | ✓ | some organic ingredients |
| **Evans** | PET | ? | ? | ? | ? | ? | ? | No | ? | ✓ | ? | |
| **Golden Griddle** | CPC | ✓+ | ✓ | ✓ | ✓ | ✓ | ✓ | No | ✓ | ✓ | ✓ | |
| **Grandma's Molasses** | CADB | ? | ? | ? | ✗ | ✗ | ? | YesIN | ? | ? | ? | 🌐, U.K. |
| **Karo** | CPC | ✓+ | ✓ | ✓ | ✓ | ✓ | ✓ | No | ✓ | ✓ | ✓ | |

✔ = Top Rating    ✓ = Middle Rating    ✗ = Bottom Rating    ? = Insufficient Information

*For a more detailed explanation see key on page 14*

**SYRUPS & MOLASSES**

| Company or Product | Abbr. | 💲 | ⚥ | 👥 | 〰 | 🐇 | (disclosure) | 👪 | ▦ | ALERT |
|---|---|---|---|---|---|---|---|---|---|---|
| Log Cabin | MO | ? | ✓ | ✓ | ✗ | ? | Yes | ? | ? | cigarettes; Salvadoran coffee; Work. Princ. |
| MacDonald's | BN | ½ | ✓ | ✓ | ½ | ✓ | YesIN | ½ | ✓ | |
| Mrs. Butterworth's | UN | ? | ✗ | ½ | ✓ | ✓* | YesIN | ½ | ? | ⊕; U.K. |
| Old Vermont | CAG | ? | ✗ | ? | ✗ | ✗ | No | ? | ✗ | safe meat controversy; D.C.C.A.; factory farming |
| Smucker's | SJM | ✓ | ✓ | ½ | ✓ | ✓ | No | ✓ | ½ | some organic ingredients |
| Sunrise | G | ? | ? | ? | ? | ? | No | ? | ? | |
| Vermont Maid | RJR | ? | ½ | ? | ? | ✗ | Yes | ? | ? | cigarettes; D.C.C.A. |
| Vermont Maple Or. | BN | ½ | ✓ | ✓ | ✓ | ✓ | YesIN | ½ | ✓ | |
| **TEA** | | | | | | | | | | |
| Banquet | MCRK | ✓ | ✗ | ? | ✓ | ✗ | No | ? | ? | |
| Celestial Seasonings | CS | ? | ½ | ✓ | ✓ | ✓ | No | ✓ | ½ | some organic ingredients |
| Diner's Choice | K | ✓ | ✓ | ✓ | ✓* | ✓ | YesIN | ✓ | ✓ | C.C.A. |
| Eden# | EDEN | ✓+ | ½ | ✓ | ✓ | ✓ | No | ✓ | ✓ | some organic ingredients |

| Product or Company | Abbr. | 💲 | ♀ | ⚥ | ✎ | 🐾 | 🌐 | ⚖ | 🏠 | 🍼 | ⚙ | ALERT |
|---|---|---|---|---|---|---|---|---|---|---|---|---|
| Fruit Tea | MO | ? | ✔ | ✔ | ? | ✖ | ? | Yes | ? | ? | ? | cigarettes; Salvadoran coffee; Work. Princ. |
| Lipton | UN | ? | ✖ | ✔ | ✔* | ✔ | ✔ | YesIN | ✔ | ? | ? | 🌐; U.K. |
| Lyons | ALP | ✖ | ✔ | ✔ | ✔ | ✔ | ✔ | Yes | ✔ | ✔ | ✔ | 🌐; U.K. |
| Nestea | NEST | ? | ✔ | ? | ✔* | ✔ | ✔ | YesIN | ✔ | ? | ? | infant formula; Salv. coffee; 🌐; D.C.C.A.; U.K. |
| T-Time | CADB | ? | ✔ | ? | ✔ | ✔ | ✖ | YesIN | ? | ? | ? | 🌐; U.K. |
| Tea House | MCRK | ? | ✖ | ✔ | ✔ | ✔ | ✖ | No | ? | ? | ? | |
| Tender Leaf | PG | ✔ | ✔ | ✔ | ✔(*) | ✔ | ✔ | Yes | ✔ | ✔ | ✔ | disposable diapers; Salvadoran coffee; on-site day care; C.C.A. |
| Tetley | ALP | ✖ | ✔ | ✔ | ✔ | ✔ | ✔ | Yes | ✔ | ✔ | ✔ | 🌐; U.K. |
| Twining Tea | WTG | | | | | | | | | | | see page 330 for U.K. ratings |
| **TOOTHPASTE & TOOTHBRUSHES** | | | | | | | | | | | | |
| Aim | UN | ? | ✖ | ✔ | ✔* | ✔ | ✔ | YesIN | ✔ | ✔ | ? | 🌐; U.K. |

✔ = Top Rating   ✓ = Middle Rating   ✖ = Bottom Rating   ? = Insufficient Information

For a more detailed explanation see key on page 14

TEA

| Company or Product | Abbr. | $ | | | | | | Animal Testing | | | ALERT |
|---|---|---|---|---|---|---|---|---|---|---|---|
| Aqua-fresh | BECH | ✖ | ✔ | | ✔ | ✖○ | ✔ | YesIN | ✔∅ | ✔ | 🌐; Work. Princ.; on-site day care; U.K. |
| Arm & Hammer | CRCH | ✔+ | ✔ | ✔ | ✔ | ✔* | ✔ | No | ✔ | ✔ | |
| Aubrey Organics# | AUB | ? | ✔ | ✔ | | | ✔ | No | ? | ✔ | some organic ingredients |
| Check-Up | LION | | | | | | | | | | see page 344 for Japanese companies |
| Close-Up | UN | ? | ✔ | ✔ | ✔ | ✔* | ✔ | YesIN | ✔ | ✔ | 🌐; U.K. |
| Colgate | CL | ✔+ | ✔ | ✖ | ✔ | ✔❋ | ✔ | YesIN | ✔ | ✔ | |
| Crest | PG | ✔ | ✔ | ✔ | ✔ | ✔❋ | ✔ | Yes | ✔ | ✔ | disposable diapers; Salvadoran coffee; on-site day care; C.C.A. |
| Denquel | PG | ✔ | ✔ | ✔ | ✔ | ✔❋ | ✔ | Yes | ✔ | ✔ | disposable diapers; Salvadoran coffee; on-site day care; C.C.A. |
| Dentagard | CL | ✔+ | ✔ | ✔ | ✔ | ✔❋ | ✔ | YesIN | ✔ | ✔ | |
| Gleem | PG | ✔ | ✔ | ✔ | ✔ | ✔❋ | ✔ | Yes | ✔ | ✔ | disposable diapers; Salvadoran coffee; on-site day care; C.C.A. |
| Kangaroo* | DES | ? | ? | ? | ✖ | ✔❋ | ✖ | No | ? | ? | 1% For Peace |
| Oral-B | GS | ✔ | ✔ | ✔ | ✔ | ✔❋ | ✔ | YesIN | ✔ | ✔ | |
| Pearl Drops | CAR | ? | ✖ | ✔ | ✔ | ✖○ | ✔ | No | ? | ✖ | |

| Product or Company | Abbr. | $ | ♀ | | | | | | | | | | ALERT |
|---|---|---|---|---|---|---|---|---|---|---|---|---|---|
| Pepsodent | UN | ? | ✗ | ✓ | ✓ | ✓ | ✔* | ✓ | YesIN | ✓ | ✓ | ? | 🌐, U.K. |
| Prevent | JNJ | ✔ | ✓ | ✔ | ✔ | ✔⊛ | ✔ | YesIN | ✔ | ✔ | ✔ | ✔ | on-site day care; Workplace Principles |
| Reach | JNJ | ✔ | ✔ | ✔ | ✔ | ✔⊛ | ✔ | YesIN | ✔ | ✔ | ✔ | ✔ | on-site day care; Workplace Principles |
| Tom's of Maine# | TOM | ✔+ | ✗ | ✓ | ✔ | ✔ | ✔ | No | ? | ✔ | ✔ | | |
| Topol | DEPC | ? | ✓ | ✓ | ✓ | ✓ | ✓ | No | ? | ✓ | ✓ | | |
| Ultra Brite | CL | ✔+ | ✔ | ✔ | ✔ | ✔⊛ | ✔ | YesIN | ✔ | ✔ | ✔ | ✔ | |
| Ultra Character | GS | ✓ | ✔ | ✓ | ✓ | ✔⊛ | ✔ | YesIN | ✔ | ✓ | ✔ | ✔ | |
| Viadent | CL | ✔+ | ✔ | ✔ | ✔ | ✔⊛ | ✔ | YesIN | ✔ | ✔ | ✔ | ✔ | |

### VEGETABLES: CANNED, FRESH & FROZEN

| Product or Company | Abbr. | $ | ♀ | | | | | | | | | | ALERT |
|---|---|---|---|---|---|---|---|---|---|---|---|---|---|
| 21st Century Foods* | TFC | ✗ | ✔ | ✔ | ✔ | ✔ | ✔ | No | ✔ | ✔ | ✓ | ✓ | on-site day care |
| Americana Recipe | MO | ? | ✔ | ✔ | ✗ | ? | ? | Yes | ? | ? | ? | ? | cigarettes; Salvadoran coffee; Work. Princ. |

✔ = Top Rating  ✓ = Middle Rating  ✗ = Bottom Rating  ? = Insufficient Information

For a more detailed explanation see key on page 14

VEGETABLES: CANNED, FRESH & FROZEN

# VEGETABLES: CANNED, FRESH & FROZEN

| Company or Product | Abbr. | $ | ♀ | ⚥ | 🖐 | ☢ | (Yes/No) | 🐾 | ⊞ | ALERT |
|---|---|---|---|---|---|---|---|---|---|---|
| B in B | GMP | ✓ | ✓ | ✓ | ✓ | ✓ | YesIN | ✓ | ✓ | 🌐, U.K. |
| Bird's Eye | MO | ? | ✓ | ✓ | ✗ | ? | Yes | ? | ? | cigarettes; Salvadoran coffee; Work. Princ. |
| Blue Boy | CBI | ✓+ | ✓ | ✗ | ? | ✓ | No | ✓ | ✓ | |
| Blue Ribbon | MO | ? | ✓ | ✓ | ✗ | ? | Yes | ? | ? | cigarettes; Salvadoran coffee; Work. Princ. |
| Contadina | NEST | ? | ✓ | ? | ✓* | ✓ | YesIN | ✓ | ? | infant formula; Salv. coffee; 🌐; D.C.C.A.; U.K. |
| Cortland Valley | CBI | ✓+ | ✓ | ✗ | ? | ✓ | No | ✓ | ✓ | |
| Countryside | HRL | ? | ✗ | ? | ✓ | ✗ | No | ? | ? | |
| Curtice | CBI | ✓+ | ✓ | ✗ | ? | ✓ | No | ✓ | ✓ | |
| Dole | DOL | ✓ | ✓ | ? | ✓ | ✓ | No | ✗ | ✗ | pesticide sterilization suit |
| Eden# | EDEN | ✓+ | ✓ | ✓ | ✓ | ✓ | No | ✓ | ✓ | some organic ingredients |
| Farm Fresh | MO | ? | ✓ | ✓ | ✗ | ? | Yes | ? | ? | cigarettes; Salvadoran coffee; Work. Princ. |
| Farm Kitchen | CAG | ? | ✗ | ? | ? | ✗ | No | ? | ✗ | safe meat controversy; D.C.C.A.; factory farming |
| Goya | GOYA | ? | ? | ? | ? | ✗ | No | ? | ? | |

VEGETABLES: CANNED, FRESH & FROZEN

| Product or Company | Abbr. | 💲 | ♀ | ⚖ | 🐇 | (Yes/No) | ☮ | ⬚ | ALERT |
|---|---|---|---|---|---|---|---|---|---|
| Green Giant | GMP | ✓ | ✔ | ✔ | ✔ | YesIN | ✓ | ✓ | 🌐, U.K. |
| Health Valley# | HVAL | ? | ? | ✗ | ? | No | ? | ? | some organic ingredients |
| Joan of Arc | GMP | ✓ | ✔ | ✔ | ✔ | YesIN | ✓ | ✓ | 🌐, U.K. |
| Kountry Kist | GMP | ✓ | ✔ | ✔ | ✔ | YesIN | ✓ | ✓ | 🌐, U.K. |
| Le Sueur | GMP | ✓ | ✔ | ✔ | ✔ | YesIN | ✓ | ✓ | 🌐, U.K. |
| Lean Living# | HVAL | ? | ? | ✗ | ✓ | No | ? | ? | some organic ingredients |
| Libby's | NEST | ? | ✔ | ✔* | ✓ | YesIN | ✔ | ?, ? | infant formula; Salv. coffee; 🌐 D.C.C.A.; U.K. |
| Luck's | AHP | ✗ | ✔ | ✔® | ✔ | Yes | ✓ | ✓ | infant formula |
| Mariner's Cove | CBI | ✔+ | ✗ | ? | ✓ | No | ✔ | ✓ | |
| Mc Kenzie's | CBI | ✔+ | ✗ | ? | ✓ | No | ✔ | ✓ | |
| Montini | PET | ? | ? | ? | ✗ | No | ? | ? | |

| ✔ = Top Rating | ✓ = Middle Rating | ✗ = Bottom Rating | ? = Insufficient Information | |
|---|---|---|---|---|
| | For a more detailed explanation see key on page 14 | | | Page 313 |

| Company or Product | Abbr. | $ | ♀ | 👤 | ✊ | 🐾 | 🕊 |  | ⚛ | 🏭 | ALERT |
|---|---|---|---|---|---|---|---|---|---|---|---|
| Ross | UBH | ✓ | ✗ | ✗ | ✓ | ✓ | ✗ | No | ? | ? | ✗ | 🌐 U.K. |
| Salad Fixin's | DOL | ✓ | ✓ | ? | ✓ | ✓ | ✗ | No | ✗ | ✓ | ✗ | pesticide sterilization suit |
| Southland | CBI | ✓+ | ✓ | ✗ | ? | ✓ | ✓ | No | ?‑ | ? | ✓ | |
| Vegetable Classics | RJR | ? | ✓ | ? | ? | ✗ | ✓ | Yes | ✗ | ? | ? | cigarettes; D.C.C.A. |
| Victor | CBI | ✓+ | ✗ | ✗ | ? | ✓ | ✓ | No | ? | ✓ | ✓ | |
| **YOGURT** | | | | | | | | | | | | |
| Dannon | BSN | | | | | | | | | | | see page 330 for U.K. ratings |
| Light n' Lively | MO | ? | ✓ | ✓ | ? | ✗ | ? | Yes | ✗ | ? | ? | cigarettes; Salvadoran coffee; Work. Princ. |
| Lite-line | BN | ✓ | ✓ | ✓ | ✓ | ✓ | ✓ | YesIN | ✓ | ✓ | ✓ | |
| Stay 'N Shape | MO | ? | ✓ | ✓ | ? | ✗ | ? | Yes | ✓ | ? | ? | cigarettes; Salvadoran coffee; Work. Princ. |
| Stonyfield Farm# | STON | ? | ✓+ | ? | ✓ | ✓ | ✓ | No | ✓ | ✓ | ✓ | Valdez Principles; ACT‑NOW |
| Sunrise Peach | GIS | ✓+ | ✓ | ✓ | ✓ | ✓ | ✓ | No | ✓ | ✓ | ✓ | C.C.A. |
| Whitney's | K | ✓ | ✓ | ✓* | ✓ | ✓ | ✓ | YesIN | ✓ | ✓ | ✓ | C.C.A. |

| Product or Company | Abbr. | 💲 | ⚥ | ♀ | 🐾 | 🕊 | 🌍 | | | ⚖ | ALERT |
|---|---|---|---|---|---|---|---|---|---|---|---|
| Yoplait | GIS | ✔+ | ✔ | ✔ | ✔ | ✔ | ✔ | No | ✔ | ✔ | |
| Velveeta | MO | ? | ✔ | ✔ | ✖ | ? | ✔ | Yes | ? | ? | cigarettes; Salvadoran coffee; Work. Princ. |

| | | | | | | | | | | | C.C.A. |
|---|---|---|---|---|---|---|---|---|---|---|---|

✔ = Top Rating    ⍑ = Middle Rating    ✖ = Bottom Rating    ? = Insufficient Information

*For a more detailed explanation see key on page 14*

Page 315

**YOGURT**

| Company Name | Abbr. | $ ♀ ☝ ♞ ♘ ⚒ ☠ ♠ ⚡ ⊞ | ALERT |
| --- | --- | --- | --- |

## YOUR OWN WORKSHEET

Rate your own employer (any changes from year to year?):

| | | | | | | |
| --- | --- | --- | --- | --- | --- | --- |
| 1991 | | | | | | |
| 1992 | | | | | | |
| 1993 | | | | | | |

How does your employer compare to other companies in the same industry?

| | | | | | | | |
| --- | --- | --- | --- | --- | --- | --- | --- |
| Competitor 1: | | | | | | | |
| Competitor 2: | | | | | | | |
| Competitor 3: | | | | | | | |

Where should your company focus its social concerns?

# BUYING FROM
# BRITAIN

# BUYING FROM BRITAIN

New Consumer (NC), a non-profit affiliate of CEP located in Newcastle upon Tyne, England, in 1991 published its first edition of **SHOPPING FOR A BETTER WORLD**. The New Consumer guide rates 125 companies (2,500 major consumer brand names) in nine categories, seven of which are similar to CEP's. The additional two categories evaluate companies on their involvement/policies in the Third World, and political donations. The Alert column focuses specifically on four areas: alcohol, tobacco, gambling and military sales.

Since corporate practices and policies in the U.K. differ from those in the U.S., New Consumer criteria and ratings differ in some respects from those of CEP. In the Women's Advancement category, for example, the same company may receive an ✖ from CEP and a ✔ from NC. There are two reasons for this: 1) CEP looks only at advancement issues for this category and examines family benefits in a different category, while NC combines advancement and the provision of benefits; and 2) at top corporate levels women are found more commonly in the U.S. than in Britain. Having one woman on the Board or among top officers, therefore, is considered poor performance (✖) for a large American company. That rating could be boosted upward by female representation among Officials and Managers of more than 20% or a significant amount spent on doing business with women-owned firms. The New Consumer ✔ rating, on the other hand, might mean there is just one woman on the British Board; or that 10-19% of managers and 20-39% of graduates recruited are women, and there are some family benefits in place to encourage advancement.

In the Animal Testing category, there are instances where CEP has assigned a ✔* rating to a company that NC rates an ✖. On looking closely at the two rating keys, you will discover that the explanations for the differing symbols are very similar: 1) The British symbol ✖ denotes a company that tests non-medical products on animals and is funding/researching alternative testing; 2) CEP's ✔* rating is given to a company that is taking specific quantifiable and substantial steps toward elimination of animal testing. The company tests non-medical products on animals, but has reduced animal use by at least 40% over the last five years and/or has given $250,000 or more annually for alternative research.

New Consumer's Community Involvement category combines the data that CEP evaluates separately in CEP's Charitable Giving and Community Outreach categories.

The chart at the end of this section, excerpted from New Consumer's **SHOPPING FOR A BETTER WORLD**, rates British companies that make products sold in U.S. supermarkets. A + next to a company name indicates that CEP has also rated that company, so you can compare the ratings yourself. Here is the key to the NC chart.

## RATING KEY

In general a ✔✔ rating indicates a high performance in the issue as defined by the rating key. A ✔ rating means that the company has an above average record. One ✖ indicates a below-average performance, while ✖✖ indicates that the company showed little evidence of action or policies for that issue. For all categories, a rating of "?" means that there was insufficient information on which to base a rating. Each rating is made by assessing and scoring several different factors.

 **Disclosure of Information**

✔✔ The company provided substantial and substantive materials on its social and ethical policies, including completing New Consumer's questionnaire, providing publicly and non publicly available literature, and through direct dialogue.

✔ The company provided some specific information, either by partially completing New Consumer's questionnaire or by providing printed information, or through direct dialogue. Certain key questions were left unanswered.

✖ The company provided a little information or made some reference to social issues in its publicly available literature. Most key questions were not answered.

✖✖ The company provided no information or simply sent its annual report which contained no reference to social or ethical policies or practices.

 **Women's Advancement**

✔✔ Evidence that women are fairly represented in the company and that there are adequate benefits to encourage their advancement. One or more women on the U.K. Board of Directors, 20% or more managers women, 40% or more graduate recruits women, evidence of monitoring managers' hiring records and a high level of benefit provision.

✔ Evidence that steps are being taken to improve the opportunities for women. Either women are represented on the Board or women make up 10-19% of managers and 20-39% of graduate recruits. Evidence of monitoring or provisions of benefits.

✖ Some representation of women at managerial levels and above, and some provision of benefits. No women on the Board or evidence of monitoring.

✖✖ Scant evidence of women's representation or of benefits to encourage their advancement. No women on the Board, no monitoring, fewer than 10% of managerial posts filled by women and fewer than 20% of graduate recruits women. Provision of minimal benefits.

 **Ethnic Minorities Advancement**

✔✔ Evidence of ethnic minority advancement within the company including three of the following: at least one ethnic minority executive director on the U.K. Board; more than 5% of managers or graduate recruits are members of ethnic minorities; there is some form of monitoring managers' hiring records; there is support of Fullemploy (explained in section following Rating Key, under Equal Opportunities, see page 326).

✔ Evidence that steps are being taken to improve opportunities for ethnic minorities within the company, including a combination of the following: an ethnic minority non-executive director; 1 to 5% of management or graduate recruits from ethnic minorities; monitoring; and support for Fullemploy.

✖ The company may be aware that ethnic minorities are poorly represented and is taking some steps to improve opportunities, though the numbers in managerial positions are still low: fewer than 1% of managers or graduate recruits are from ethnic mi-

norities. The company has a monitoring scheme
and supports Fullemploy.

✖✖ Little evidence of steps to improve opportunities or
actual numbers of ethnic minority members in the
company.

 **Community Involvement**

✔✔ Either 0.8% or more of pre-tax profit used for charitable purposes in the U.K. or donations were continued inspite of losses; and evidence of action
including secondment of staff (volunteerism), gifts
in kind, give-as-you-earn schemes and membership
in the Per Cent Club or Business in the Community
(explained in section following Rating Key under
Charitable Giving and Community Support, see
page 327).

✔ 0.4-0.7% of pre-tax profit donated to charity in the U.K.
and evidence of non-cash donations and membership in the Per Cent Club and/or Business in the
Community.

✖ 0.2-0.3% of pre-tax profit donated to charity in the U.K.
and/or some evidence of other, non-cash, charitable
initiatives.

✖✖ Less than 0.2% of pre-tax profit donated to charity in
the U.K. and little evidence of other, non-cash, charitable initiatives.

 **Environment**

✔✔ Moderate, light or minimal impact. Evidence of an
environmental policy specific to a process, and man-

agement specifically responsible for environmental issues. Evidence of action across the majority of possible initiatives.

✔ Either very heavy or heavy impact with evidence of a process specific policy, management specifically responsible for the environment; and action across the majority of possible initiatives. Or moderate, light or minimal impact with evidence of a written environmental policy, management responsible for the environment and some positive initiatives.

✖ Either very heavy or heavy impact and either evidence of a written environment policy, management specifically responsible for the environment and a few positive actions or no policy but evidence of a number of positive actions. Or moderate or less impact with a policy and specific management responsibility and a few positive actions.

✖✖ Either moderate or less impact and no evidence of any policies, managerial responsibility or positive action. Or heavy or above impact with no policy or specific managerial responsibility and few positive actions.

## Animal Testing

✔✔ The company is not involved in any animal testing, either in-house or through outside contractors.

✔ The company tests only medical or pharmaceutical products on animals, either in-house or through outside contractors, and is funding or carrying out research into alternative tests.

✖   The company is involved in animal testing of non-medical or non-prescription products, either in-house or through outside contractors, and is funding or carrying out research into alternative tests.

✖✖   The company is involved in animal testing of non-medical and/or non-prescription products, either in-house or through outside contractors and is not funding or carrying out research into alternative tests.

 **Third World**

✔✔   A company with heavy involvement that has specific and significant positive policies for its activities in the Third World.

✔   A company with light involvement that has specific and significant policies for its activities in the Third World.

n   A company with insignificant involvement in the Third World.

✖   A company with light involvement and no significant policies for its activities in the Third World.

✖✖   A company with heavy involvement and no significant policies for its activities in the Third World.

 **South Africa**

n   No significant involvement with South Africa.

y   Either owns subsidiaries in South Africa employing fewer than 100 staff, or has licensing or franchising agreements in South Africa.

Y    Owns subsidiaries employing more than 100 staff in South Africa.

 **Political Donations**

C    Donations to the Conservative Party or free enterprise group.

L    Donations to the Labour Party or other associated group.

n    Makes no political donations.

## Alerts!

### Alcohol

A    Manufactures alcoholic drinks.

a    Retailed more than £1 million of alcoholic drinks in the last financial year.

### Tobacco

T    Manufactures tobacco products.

t    Retailed more than £1 million of tobacco products in the last financial year.

### Gambling

G    Heavily involved in the gambling industry: owns betting shops, football pools companies, bingo halls, etc.

g    Owns, leases or manufactures gaming machines.

### Military Sales

M    In the last financial year sales of military products and services amounted to more than £25 million.

m    In the last financial year sales of military products and services were more than £5 million but less than £25 million.

## Disclosure of Information

In addition to scouring all available public information, New Consumer sends each company a comprehensive four-part questionnaire. Although often disclosure is kept to a minimum, NC notes that "the way a company deals with social issues in its literature is one of the best guides" as to whether or not corporate social responsibility issues are seriously considered at that company.

## Women's Advancement

Women in the U.K. have an even more difficult road to top corporate echelons than do their American counterparts, often due to the lack of support mechanisms along the way such as Upward Mobility Committees, mentoring, and monitoring of managers' hiring records. These are now fixtures in many U.S. companies. NC takes note of progress in providing family benefits as another indication of commitment to the advancement of women. Though paid maternity leave for at least the "disability period" is "virtually universal" in Britain (certainly not the case in the U.S.!), policies such as job-sharing and flextime are fairly new and generally for salaried employees only.

## Equal Opportunities and Ethnic Minority Advancement

U.K. law requires from companies an equal opportunities statement only for people with disabilities. To ascertain the level of awareness and activity to counter other kinds of discrimination, NC asked the companies it surveyed if they had a specific individual or department to address equal opportunity hiring. It analyzed how many minorities were in top level management, what initiatives were in place to help them, and whether the company supported Fullemploy, a training and development organization committed to expanding the economic base of minority communities. Partly in response to similar U.S. groups, like the National Association for the Advancement of Colored People (Fair Share program) and Operation PUSH, many U.S. companies now have fairly aggressive recruitment programs for minorities and do business with minority-owned companies and banks. But only a tiny number of minorities have scaled the top rungs of the U.S. corporate ladder. (CEP's ratings in Minority Advancement are for U.S. only.)

## Charitable Giving and Community Support

New Consumer points out that corporate charitable giving is very different from country to country, largely depending on how the government responds financially to social welfare concerns. In the U.S., corporations have responded with an average of 1.9% of domestic pretax earnings (1990) to help offset huge cutbacks in spending by the Federal government over the last decade. The average U.K. company gives less than 0.5% of pretax earnings. NC counted both cash and in-kind company giving, and notes whether a corporation is a member of Business In the Community (a U.K. public/private partnership for community development) and The Percent Club, which asks that a company contribute no less than 0.5% of pretax U.K. profits as a condition of membership.

## Environment

Dividing companies into heavy, moderate, and light potential environmental impact categories helped New Consumer to better assess them in this area. The "heavy impact" area would include oil or chemical companies, for example. Cosmetics, electronics and pharmaceuticals would fall into the "moderate impact" group; food, furniture, and soft drinks into the "light impact" group. Companies were queried on a wide variety of actions/initiatives including: production of organic products, use of alternative energy sources, recycling, pollution control, and reduced use of packaging materials.

## Animal Testing

In both the U.S. and the U.K., companies are not required by law to perform animal tests for new non-medical or pharmaceutical products, but they are concerned that new formulations will be safe for public use. Until recently, the only accepted way to ensure safety was by the use of animal tests. Many British companies would like to move away from this stance and are now performing in-house research into viable alternatives or providing research funds to organizations such as the Fund for the Replacement of Animals in Medical Experiments (FRAME).

## The Third World

New Consumer assembled a list of developing countries with the help of the World Bank, the Brandt Report, the United Nations, and the European Community. They then focused on the level of a company's involvement in the Third World (subsidiaries, extraction of raw materials, marketing of products) and on company practices that affect communities in these countries. A U.K. company might introduce new farming technology, for example, but if only larger farmers have access to it, marginalization of smaller farmers will occur and most arable land will be controlled by agribusiness. The ratings for this complex issue concentrated on two factors: the extent of involvement of a company in the Third World; and the existence, or not, of comprehensive and applicable policies relating to the developmental impact of that involvement. NC obtained information to compile these ratings from the answers to a questionnaire and the detailed information obtained for another New Consumer publication, The Global Consumer (Gollancz, October 1991).

## South Africa

Although more than 200 U.S. firms have either completely or partially withdrawn from South Africa since 1984, many U.K. companies have chosen to stay. They assert absolute opposition to apartheid, but argue that their presence can help rather than hurt black South African workers. Of particular concern, according to New Consumer's criteria, are companies with subsidiaries remaining in South Africa that employ more than 100 people; of less concern are licensing, franchises and distributorships.

## Political Donations

There are no laws in Britain limiting the amount of donations that candidates and political parties may accept from private sources, nor are public funds provided for political activity. Though U.K. companies must publish in their annual reports any donation exceeding £200, as in the U.S., they do not have to obtain shareholders' permission to make political contributions. In 1989 Common Cause, a U.S. group critical of corporate political action committees (PACs), presented a shareholder resolution to ten major companies asking for disclosure of their PAC giving. Among the companies in this guide, the highest percentage of votes supporting the resolution was 7.6% at General Electric.

## Alerts

Though in every country there may be questionable products and services on the market that arouse public debate, New Consumer has chosen four specific areas upon which to focus attention: alcohol, tobacco, gambling, and military sales. They argue that the first three may be harmfully addictive and that the continued production and marketing of military weapons is counter-productive in a world brimming with weaponry.

| Company | Abbr. | 🔒SECRET | ♀ | ✊ | 🏭 | 🌳 | 🐋 | 🐰 | ⚙ | ALERT |
|---|---|---|---|---|---|---|---|---|---|---|
| Allied-Lyons plc+ | ALP | ✓ | ? | ✗✗ | ✗ | ✓ | ✓✓ | ✗✗ | n | C | Atg |
| Associated British Foods plc | ABF | ✗✗ | ? | ? | ✗✗ | ? | ? | ✗✗ | Y | n | a |
| The Body Shop International plc+ | BS | ✓✓ | ✗ | ✗✗ | ✓✓ | ✓ | ✓✓ | ✓✓ | n | n | |
| The British Petroleum Company plc+ | BP | ✓ | ✓ | ✓✓ | ✓ | ✗ | ✗ | ✗✗ | Y | n | tM |
| Cadbury Schweppes plc+ | CADB | ✓✓ | ✓ | ✓ | ✗ | ✓ | ✓✓ | ✗✗ | Y | n | |
| Grand Metropolitan plc+ | GMP | ✓✓ | ✓ | ✓ | ✓ | ✓ | ✓✓ | ✗✗ | Y | n | Atg |
| Guinness plc | GUI | ✓ | ✗✗ | ✗✗ | ✓✓ | ? | ? | ✗✗ | y | n | A |
| The Jacob's Bakery Limited | BSN | ✗ | ? | ? | ✓ | ? | ? | ✗✗ | n | n | A |
| Nestlé Holdings (U.K.) plc+ | NEST | ✓ | ✓ | ✗ | ✓✓ | ? | ✗ | ✗✗ | Y | n | a |
| Reckitt and Colman plc+ | RCP | ✗ | ? | ✗ | ✗✗ | ? | ? | ? | Y | C | |
| SmithKline Beecham plc+ | BECH | ✗ | ? | ✗ | ✓ | ? | ? | ✗✗ | Y | C | |
| Tate & Lyle plc | TLP | ✓✓ | ✗ | ✗✗ | ✗ | ✓ | ✓✓ | ✓ | y | C | |
| | UNG | ✓ | ? | ✗ | ✗✗ | ? | ✓✓ | ? | n | C | |

| Company | Abbr. | | | | | | | | | ALERT |
|---|---|---|---|---|---|---|---|---|---|---|
| Unilever plc+ | UN | ✓✓ | ✓✓ | ✓✓ | ✓ | ✓ | ✗ | ✓✓ | Y | n | AT |
| United Biscuits (Holdings) plc+ | UBH | ✓✓ | ✗✗ | ✗✗ | ✓ | ✓ | ✗✗ | ✓ | n | C |
| Weetabix Limited | WBX | ✗✗ | ? | ? | ✗✗ | ? | ? | ? | n | n |

✓✓ = Top Rating   ✓ = Above Average Rating   ✗ = Below Average Rating
✗✗ = Bottom Rating   ? = Insufficient Information

BRITISH COMPANIES

# BUYING FROM
# JAPAN

# BUYING FROM JAPAN

**A special 1991 issue of *Asahi Journal* surveyed 70 Japanese corporations in 11 areas of social responsibility.**

Their goal was to apply CEP's concepts in Japan, in order to raise corporate and public awareness about good corporate citizenship. For this first in their new annual issue on "The Corporation and Society," the researchers used only information provided by the companies; next year they hope to refine the questions and double the number of companies. For 1993, *Asahi Journal* plans to gather and integrate information from government and independent sources.

By special arrangement with *Asahi Journal's* editor-in-chief, Mitsuko Shimomura, we are pleased to present their analysis of Japanese consumer product companies. We include those companies with products which are sold in U.S. supermarkets and health food stores.


## RATING KEY

In *Asahi Journal*, the following icons symbolize three levels of corporate social responsibility. In the rating key these are explained using a, b, and c respectively.

 a) The bird in flight symbolizes a healthy awareness of social concerns.

b) The sitting bird indicates a more limited response.

c) The cracked egg subtly conveys the message that company social responsibility in this area is not yet born.

The chart for Japanese companies appears on page 344. Products made by the Japanese companies included in this chart may be found in their relevant product categories in the RATINGS BY PRODUCT section of the guide, beginning on page 123. Here is the key for the chart:

**Contributions:** The figures are the amount of contributions divided by the profits taken during the period under consideration.

a. 1% or more

b. 0.5%-1%

c. less than 0.5%

**Measures to Facilitate Working:** Based on the following points: (1) flex-time system; (2) 70% or more of employee's vacation time is used; (3) employee share-ownership program; (4) employee home-ownership program; (5) "stress-relief" (recreation) program; (6) educational programs.

a. 5 or more of the above standards

b. 3-4 standards

c. 2 or fewer standards

**Workplace Equality:** Based on these standards: (1) benefits provided to full-time employees also available to part-timers; (2) policy of re-hiring former employees; (3) employees with disabilities constitute 1.5% or more of workforce; (4) company facilities can accommodate wheelchairs.

a. 3 or 4 of above standards

b. 2 standards

c. 1 or no standards

**Opportunities for Women:** How many women hold management positions (section chiefs or above)?

a. 1% or more

b. less than 1%

c. no women as section chiefs or higher

**Family Benefits:** Japanese law sets a minimum of 98 days for maternity leave. Both male and female employees are considered. In this area, Japan does much better than the U.S. where most companies are just beginning to recognize the importance of assisting employees with family responsibilities.

a. Company provides (1) more than the legal minimum maternity leave, and (2) provides child care leave

b. Company provides one of the above

c. Company provides only legal minimum maternity leave

**Employment of Foreigners:** Considers these standards: (1) 0.3% or more of regular employees are foreigners; (2) 25% or more of the management staff of overseas companies (owned by or affiliated with the company surveyed) are citizens of that country; (3) 25% of all presidents of overseas companies are citizens of that country.

a. All 3 standards apply

b. 1 or 2 standards apply

c. None of the standards apply

**Environmental Awareness:** Considers these standards: (1) company applies stricter environmental standards than those required by law; (2) company has recycling program.

a. Both standards apply

b. One standard applies

c. Neither standard applies

**Community Support:** Based on these standards: (1) supports community participation of employees; (2) promotes community use of company gymnastic or educational facilities; (3) has established social services organization within the company; (4) conducts public educational programs or other public events.

a. All 4 standards apply

b. 2-3 standards apply

c. 1 or none of the standards apply

**Military involvement:** Company has or has not contracted with the Japanese Defense Agency to supply weapons.

Yes  No

**Disclosure of information:** Company does or does not make available pamphlets that provide consumers with basic necessary information about the company.

a. Pamphlets are available.

b. Pamphlets are not available.

**Survey Cooperation:** Some companies answered all or most question in the survey.  Others answered only part of the questionnaire.

a. All or most questions answered.

b. Part of the questions answered

# HIGHLIGHTS OF SURVEY

Matsushita led all 70 firms surveyed, with eight birds in flight and no cracked egg symbols. Of the 14 Japanese consumer products companies listed in SHOPPING FOR A BETTER WORLD, Sony came next after Matsushita in social responsibility. Sony received seven flying birds and no cracked eggs. Kikkoman Corp. also excelled: five flying birds and no cracked eggs. At the other end of the spectrum, Snow Brand and Lion Corporation received the most cracked egg symbols: three. Snow Brand had only three flying birds and Lion Corporation had four.

As you scan the chart on page 344, please keep in mind that the symbols assigned to companies do not incorporate independent information from government and citizen groups, but reflect exclusively information provided by the corporations themselves.

## Contributions

Eight of the 14 companies said they gave 1% or more of profits to charity; six made no response. Japanese corporations operate on a narrower profit margin than their counterparts in the U.S., focusing instead on maximization of market share and reinvestment in the business. The profit margin averages about 2.8 percent (roughly a third of the U.S. average). Tax status in Japan historically has been extremely narrowly defined, thus offering little incentive to the charitably inclined.

## Measures to Facilitate Working

Seven of the 14 companies including Sony, Matsushita, and Fuji Photo said they adhered to five or more standards that enhance the lives of workers, including: flex-time, help with home ownership, aid for outside education, profit-sharing and stress-relief (recreation) programs. The others offered three or four of these benefits. Of the 70 companies surveyed, a cracked egg "needs improvement" symbol appeared by only three. An impressive 58 companies reported that their programs for giving monetary assistance for home ownership had been in place since 1968. About 3 to 4% of American companies offer some kind of housing assistance, according to the American Affordable Housing Institute at Rutgers University.

## Equality in the Workplace

This was a difficult area for the majority of the 14 respondents, with 8 companies receiving the cracked egg symbol. At the top of the scale, only Matsushita met three or more of this category's standards. They include: 1) providing similar benefits for full and part-time workers, 2) rehiring former employees, 3) ensuring that at least 1.5% of jobs go to employees with disabilities, and 4) providing adequate facilities/access for these employees.

## Women

This is an area where Japan has historically lagged behind the U.S. and most of Europe. Companies were asked what percent of management jobs (section chiefs and above) were held by women. Among the 54 companies responding for 1989, women held an average of less than 1% of such jobs. Of our three **SHOPPING FOR A BETTER WORLD** companies, only Shiseido Co. and Kikkoman Corp. had women in more than 1% of management jobs. Asahi Breweries, Fuji Photo Film Co., Nissan Food Products Co., and Nippon Suisan Kaisha received the cracked egg symbol.

## Family Benefits

Japanese law sets an enlightened minimum of 98 days for maternity leave. The survey shows that of the 14 **SHOPPING FOR A BETTER WORLD** companies, Sony, Fuji Photo Film Co. and Matsushita allow more than that and provide child care leave as well. Among the 70 companies, the average amount of leave for child care in 1989 was 23 weeks. In this area, Japan does much better than the U.S., where most companies are just beginning to recognize the importance of assisting employees with family responsibilities. Four companies got cracked eggs: Ajinomoto Co., Lion Corporation, Shiseido Co. and Suntory.

## Internationalization of the Workplace

Only Sony and four more in the total survey earned the ✈. Standards for this category are: 3% or more of regular employees are foreigners; 25% or more of overseas staff are citizens of the country where facilities are located; and 25% of overseas operations are headed by citizens of that country. This is an important criterion for Japanese firms, as the country has traditionally preferred to have its own people in charge of overseas operations, often resulting in discrimination against non-Japanese.

## Environmental Awareness

All 70 companies responded to this subject, which is at the top of the international agenda. Six of our 14 said they went beyond environmental standards required by law and also had recycling programs. Lion Corporation, Snow Brand, and Nippon Suisan Kaisha got cracked eggs. The environmental area suffers especially from an absence of independent information from government, non-profit or other sources.

## Community Support

This category focuses on whether 1) employees are encouraged to participate in community activities, 2) company gymnastic/educational facilities are shared with the public, 3) social services are provided within the company, and 4) company conducts educational and other events for the public. Three of the 14 SHOPPING FOR A BETTER WORLD companies, Ajinomoto, Shiseido Co., and Matsushita, said they met all four standards. Only four other companies in the survey did. In SHOPPING FOR A BETTER WORLD, only Snow Brand received a cracked egg for meeting one or less.

## Military Involvement

Six companies of the 70 surveyed have military contracts to supply weapons/delivery vehicles/ammunition: Toshiba, Komatsu, Nissan, Nippon Express Company, Mitsubishi Trading Company, and Mitsui Trading Company. None in SHOPPING FOR A BETTER WORLD do.

## Survey Cooperation Disclosure

All Japanese companies included in SHOPPING FOR A BETTER WORLD said they provided consumers with basic information about the company through printed material and did respond with fairly complete questionnaire information.

# Japanese Company Addresses and Abbreviations

The addresses and phone numbers of the Japanese companies and their abbreviations, used throughout SHOPPING FOR A BETTER WORLD, are listed in the guide appearing in alphabetical order in the COMPANY ADDRESSES section and the COMPANY ABBREVIATIONS section, respectively.

| Company | Abbr. | | | | | | | | | | | |
|---|---|---|---|---|---|---|---|---|---|---|---|---|
| Ajinomoto Co., Inc. | AJI | | | | | | | | NO | | | |
| Asahi Breweries, Ltd. | ASA | | | | | | | | NO | | | |
| Fuji Photo Film Co., Ltd. | FUJI | | | | | | | | NO | | | |
| Kao Corp. | KAO | | | | | | | | NO | | | |
| Kikkoman Corp. | KIK | | | | | | | | NO | | | |
| Lion Corporation | LION | | | | | | | | NO | | | |
| Matsushita Electric Industrial Co. | MTS | | | | | | | | NO | | | |
| Nippon Meat Packers, Inc. | NPM | | | | | | | | NO | | | |
| Nissin Food Products Co., Ltd. | NSF | | | | | | | | NO | | | |
| Nippon Suisan Kaisha, Ltd. | NSK | | | | | | | | NO | | | |
| Shiseido Co., Ltd. | SHI | | | | | | | | NO | | | |

| Company | Abbr. | | | | | | | | | | | | |
|---|---|---|---|---|---|---|---|---|---|---|---|---|---|
| Snow Brand Milk Products Co., Ltd. | SNB | | | | | | | | | | NO | | |
| Sony Corp. | SNE | | | | | | | | | | NO | | |
| Suntory | SNT | | | | | | | | | | NO | | |

a = Bird in flight;   b = Sitting bird;   c = Cracked egg
*For a more detailed explanation see key on page 335*

Page 345

JAPANESE COMPANIES

# America's Corporate Conscience Awards

Each year, the Council on Economic Priorities presents our America's Corporate Conscience Awards, honoring companies for outstanding achievements or initiatives in such areas as: environmental stewardship, charitable contributions, equal opportunity, community action, and employer responsiveness to employees. CEP also bestows Dishonorable Mentions on companies whose behavior reflects blatant disregard for the environment, employee safety, or the community.

Companies may be nominated by CEP staff or advisers, outside experts familiar with corporate issues, by the companies themselves – **and by you**. Simply write us a note or call for a nomination form.

CEP's research staff then carefully examines the nominated programs, drawing on material provided by the companies themselves and on news clippings, Federal agency files, experts, legal records and other established sources of information. To qualify as a finalist, a company must not only be outstanding in the area for which it was nominated, it must also earn top ratings in at least six of CEP's **SHOPPING FOR A BETTER WORLD** categories. Furthermore, the company must agree to complete CEP's corporate questionnaire.

An independent panel of judges chooses the winners and they are announced at a gala dinner in New York City. The 1991 chairman was George Harvey, CEO of Pitney Bowes, winner of the 1990 award for Employer Responsiveness. Previous awards dinners were chaired by Colby Chandler, CEO of 1989 winner Eastman Kodak, and by James Preston, CEO of 1987 winner Avon Products.

Celebrities present the awards. Our 1991 celebration was emceed by author, editor, and sportsman George Plimpton. Susan St. James Ebersol and Ronnie Eldridge were among the presenters. In 1990, Bill Moyers served as emcee and Coretta Scott King, Ed Begley, Jr., and others presented the awards.

If you wish to nominate a company for an America's Corporate Conscience Award or want information about attending the award ceremony, please contact CEP directly at 1-212-420-1133.

## Award Winners

**1991**

Charitable Contributions ................ *Large Companies*
H.B. Fuller Company
Honorable Mention – The Stride Rite Corp.
*Small Companies*
Foldcraft Co.
Employer Responsiveness .............. .Kellogg Company
Equal Opportunity ................... Hallmark Cards, Inc.
Environment ........................... *Large Companies*
Herman Miller, Inc.
Honorable Mention – The H.J. Heinz Co.
*Small Companies*
Smith & Hawken
Community Action ..................... .Time Warner Inc.

**1990**

Charitable Contributions ........ Cummins Engine Co., Inc.
Honorable Mention – Patagonia, Inc.
Employer Responsiveness .............. Pitney Bowes, Inc.
Honorable Mention – Fel-Pro, Inc.
Equal Opportunity ............................... US West
Environment ....................................... .AT&T
Community Action .......................... .Xerox Corp.

## 1989

Charitable Contributions .................. Dayton Hudson
Honorable Mention − Newman's Own
Employer Responsiveness ................ Federal Express
Equal Opportunity .................... Eastman Kodak Co.
Environment ..................... Applied Energy Services
Honorable Mention − H.B. Fuller Co.
Community Action ................ Digital Equipment Corp.

## 1988

Charitable Contributions .... Ben & Jerry's Homemade, Inc.
Equal Opportunity ........................... Gannett Co.
Xerox Corp.
Environment ...... Minnesota Mining & Manufacturing (3M)
Community Action ......... Best Western International, Inc.
South Shore Bank
Employer Responsiveness, Family Concern ........... IBM
Opportunities for Disabled People ....... General Mills, Inc.
Animal Welfare ............ The Procter & Gamble Company
Education ................................... Gannett Co.
Improvement in Corporate Disclosure ......... Kellogg Co.

## 1987

Charitable Contributions ............... General Mills, Inc.
Polaroid Corporation
Sara Lee Corp.
Employer Responsiveness .. The Procter & Gamble Company
Equal Opportunity, .................... Avon Products, Inc.
Community Action ............................ IBM Corp.
Amoco Corp.

Honorable Mentions
South Africa ....................... Polaroid Corporation
Corporate Disclosure .................... Ford Motor Co.
Johnson & Johnson

# Dishonorable Mentions

**1991**
American Cyanamid Company
ConAgra, Inc.
Bristol-Myers Squibb Company, Gerber Products Co. and
Nestle/Carnation Food Co.

**1990**
Exxon Corp.
Perdue Farms Inc.
USX Corporation

**1989**
E.I. du Pont de Nemours & Co.
John Morrell & Co. (subsidiary of Chiquita Brands International)

**1988**
Morton Thiokol Inc.
RJR Nabisco Inc.

**1987**
A.H. Robins Co. (subsidiary of American Home Products Corporation)
American Cyanamid Company
Litton Industries
Mobil Corp.

# DISCLAIMER

The ratings in this guide are based on information current as of August 1991 and in some instances earlier. The data was gathered from:

1) extensive data from the companies themselves;

2) existing public information available in government agencies, libraries and specialized centers, or from citizens groups; and

3) advisers who are experts in our chosen categories. CEP claims no predictive value for its ratings; a company may change its behavior tomorrow.

CEP claims no knowledge of programs or problems not in the public domain or voluntarily submitted by the companies themselves or other sources.

CEP is a non-partisan organization that does not endorse any product or company.

Our ratings apply to the company as a whole and not to individual subsidiaries and divisions. Additionally, we do not purport to rate individual products. For such evaluations, we refer you to such sources as Consumer's Union and The Center for Science in the Public Interest. Our ratings are based entirely on factual information, so it is up to each consumer to decide which companies he or she wants to support.

Any questions concerning research performed by CEP affiliate New Consumer (U.K.) or the Asahi Journal (Japan) should be referred to them.

## ABOUT THE RESEARCH

In preparing this guide, the Council on Economic Priorities used information gathered in several ways:

1) questionnaires filled out by the companies themselves;

2) printed material from, or phone interviews with, company officials;

3) specialized institutions such as the AFL-CIO and trade unions, American Committee on Africa (NY), American Solar Energy Society (CO), Asahi Journal (Japan), Atlantic States Legal Foundation (NY), Black Enterprise (NY), Catalyst (VT), Center for Science in the Public Interest (DC), Citizens Clearinghouse for Hazardous Waste (VA), Citizens for a Better Environment (CA), Coalition of Labor Union Women (NY), Conservation and Renewable Energy Inquiry/Referral Service (MD), Consumers United for Food Safety (WA), Corporate Crime Reporter (DC), the Data Center (CA), Earth Island Institute (CA), Environmental Action Coalition (NY), Environmental Action Foundation (DC), Environmental Defense Fund (NY), Environmental Law Institute (DC), Families and Work Institute (NY), Food and Water, Inc. (MD), Foundation Center (NY), Friends of the Earth (DC), Government Accountability Project (DC), Greenpeace (DC), The Humane Society of the United States (DC), Independent Sector (DC), Interfaith Center on Corporate Responsibility (NY), Investor Responsibility Research Center (DC), Johns Hopkins Center for Alternatives to Animal Testing (MD), Labor Research Association (NY), National Anti-Vivisection Society (IL), National Association for the Advancement of Colored People (NJ), National Boycott News (WA), National Leadership Coalition on AIDS (DC), National Safe Workplace Institute (IL), National Toxics Campaign (MA), National Women's Economic Alliance Foundation (DC), the Natural Resources Defense Council (NY), New Consumer (U.K.), Nuclear Free

America (MD), Nuclear Information and Resource Service (DC), Organic Foods Production Association of North America (MA), People for the Ethical Treatment of Animals (MD), Renew America (DC), Rainforest Action Network (CA), Sierra Club Legal Defense Fund (CA), United Nations Environment Program (NY), University Center for Cooperatives (WI), Work/Family Directions (MA), Working Committee on Community Right to Know (DC), Worldwatch Institute (DC);

4) business and public libraries, especially for such resources as *Taft Corporate Giving Directory*, *National Data Book*, *Monthly Labor Review*, Bureau of National Affairs publications, Nexis, and Lexis;

5) government agencies such as the Bureau of Labor Statistics (DC), the Environmental Protection Agency (DC), Occupational Safety and Health Administration (DC), U.S. Department of Agriculture (DC), U.S. Small Business Administration (DC), the National Labor Relations Board (DC), and state and regional regulatory agencies;

6) advisers who are experts in our various categories. (Please see the next section for a complete list of advisers.)

After months of research, we sent each company our ratings with a request for corrections and updates.

The Council looks for comprehensive, comparable data, a task that is far more difficult in some areas than in others. For example, definitive data is publicly available on South African involvement and charitable contributions, making these issues easier to compare. Categories such as Environment, Workplace Issues, and Community Outreach are extremely complex, so that even with substantial information, data were not always comparable company-to-company. Foreign companies also do not always present comparable data. Our ability to obtain and verify data is much stronger for the domestic operations of U.S. companies.

Where firms cooperated with CEP's efforts by answering all or most of our survey, a more complete picture emerges. CEP thanks the cooperating companies for providing us with comprehensive information while some of their peers did not.

Information used for Japanese and British evaluations of companies comes entirely from Japan and Britain, respectively.

# ADVISORS

Mr. Howard G. Adams
Executive Director
National Consortium for Graduate Degrees for
Minorities in Engineering and Science, Inc. (GEM)

Mr. Richard Adams
Director
New Consumer

Mr. Randy Barber
Director
Center for Economic Organizing

Mr. David R. Brower
Chairman
Earth Island Institute

Mr. James S. Cannon
President
Energy Futures Inc.

Mr. Louis A. Clark
Executive Director
Government Accountability Project

Mr. Archie Colander
President
Amalgamated Publishers, Inc.

Reverend Maurice Culver
Executive Director
Project Equality, Inc.

Ms. Jennifer Davis
Executive Director
American Committee on Africa

Mr. Michael Jacobson, Ph.D
Executive Director
Center for Science in the Public Interest

Mr. Joseph A. Kinney
Executive Director
The National Safe Workplace Institute

Ms. Kate Rand Lloyd
Working Woman Magazine

Mr. Steven D. Lydenberg
Research Director
Kinder, Lydenberg, Domini and Co.

Mr. Joel Makower
Editor-in-Chief
Tilden Press, Inc.

Mr. Michael Mariotte
Executive Director
Nuclear Information & Resource Service

Mr. Anthony Mazzochi
Secretary-Treasurer
Oil, Chemical and Atomic Workers Union

Mr. Michael McCloskey
Chairman
Sierra Club

Ms. Susan Meeker-Lowry
Director
Catalyst

Mr. Keith Mestrich
Director of Special Services
Food and Allied Services Trades Dept., AFL-CIO

Ms. Gwen Morgan
Policy Consultant
Work Family Directions

Ms. Krishna Ahooja-Patel
Chair, Women's Studies Department
Mount St. Vincent University

Ms. Sandy Pope
Executive Director
Coalition of Labor Union Women

Mr. Steven Ross
Assistant Professor, Graduate School of Journalism
Columbia University

Ms. Ruth Ruttenberg
Ruttenberg & Associates

Mr. Ray Scannell
Director of Special Services
Bakery, Confectionery and Tobacco Workers International
Union

Robert J. Schwartz, Ph.D
Treasurer
Economists Against the Arms Race

Ms. Joan Shapiro
Senior Vice President
The South Shore Bank of Chicago

Mr. Timothy Smith
Executive Director
Interfaith Center on Corporate Responsibility

Mr. Henry Spira
Director
Animal Rights International

Mr. David Thompson
Vice President, Western States
National Cooperative Business Association

Mr. Joe Uehlein
Director, Special Projects
Industrial Union Dept., AFL-CIO

Mr. Eric Utne
Publisher/Editor
Utne Reader

# CEP Board of Directors and Staff

# The Next Step

Congratulations! By using **SHOPPING FOR A BETTER WORLD** to guide your shopping decisions, you (and over 900,000 others) have taken the first step toward casting your economic vote. There are many other ways you as a consumer can make your voice heard. Here are some suggestions:

## Letters to the Companies

Our research has shown that the Chief Executive Officer plays a major role in determining a company's commitment to social issues. Why not write to one directly? Explain what you like – or don't like – about their policies, practices or products. And if you've changed brands, tell both companies why. This is a message they'll hear loud and clear.

To help you do this, we've included the names and addresses of all the companies listed in **SHOPPING FOR A BETTER WORLD** on page 364. Here are two sample letters actually written by a consumer:

(Letter to Kellogg Co.)

I recently purchased the booklet "SHOPPING FOR A BETTER WORLD", and was happy to learn of Kellogg's support of a wide range of socially responsible issues. Your company's policies in the areas of charitable contributions, advancement of women and minorities, the environment, and family benefits are highly commendable.

Because of your practices, I not only will continue to purchase Kellogg products, but will switch to Kellogg products from those made by Philip Morris, a company seemingly lacking in social responsibility. I will urge my family and friends to do the same.

(Letter to Philip Morris Co.)

I recently purchased the booklet "SHOPPING FOR A BET-
TER WORLD", and was unhappy to learn how poorly Philip
Morris rated on a number of important social issues.

Besides its manufacture of cigarettes, which I oppose due to
their harmful effects on everyone's health, I was distressed
to see Philip Morris donated 0.6% or less of its pre-tax earnings to charitable causes, that it invests in South Africa, and
that it has a poor record of significant environmental violations, major accidents, and/or a history of lobbying against
sound environmental policies.

In light of these factors, I have made significant changes in
my shopping habits. Instead of purchasing Kraft salad dressings and cheeses and Knudson yogurt, I have switched to
Newman's Own dressing, local dairy's cheeses, and Yoplait
yogurt....

While not all of these purchasing changes are easy ones, I
feel it is important enough to the future of our world that I
take a stand through my pocketbook and urge my family and
friends to do the same. Until Philip Morris improves its position... I will continue to avoid its products.

(Please send CEP copies of the letters you write.)

## Letters to the Editors

How often have you wondered "What can one individual do?"
Well, now that you know how each of us can make a differ-
ence every time we go to the supermarket, help spread the
word! Let your friends and neighbors know about **SHOP-
PING FOR A BETTER WORLD** by writing a Letter-to-the-
Editor (LTE) to your local paper.

Tell how you've changed your buying decisions, and how it
has empowered you. And if you read an article about one of
the companies we rate – even if it's just a routine financial
story or a new product announcement – write an LTE about

its social performance. You'll help spark a broader debate on issues that concern us all.

In addition to writing about corporate social responsibility, you can also use CEP's research to address such public policy issues as economic adjustment to military cutbacks and banning chemical and biological warfare. Most small and medium-sized newspapers seldom discuss these issues. When you write a Letter-to-the-Editor you directly help stimulate and widen the debate on these vitally important matters. You'll assist us and your community by bringing CEP's informative research to many more people and making your own opinions known.

## Investing With A Conscience

As an investor, whether you have $100 or $1,000,000 to invest, you can put your principal where your principles are. Currently over $600 billion is being invested using social criteria like those in **SHOPPING FOR A BETTER WORLD**. To help you integrate your values and your investment decisions, CEP has researched and written a new book: *The Better World Investment Guide* (Prentice Hall, 1991).

But don't be fooled by the title. *The Better World Investment Guide* is not just for investors. It's for anyone who wants to learn – in detail – the behavior behind our ratings. It has in-depth profiles of 50 of America's largest publicly held companies and 50 companies most favored by ethical funds and investment advisers.

For a free CEP Research Report on socially responsible investing, please send in the coupon at the back of this guide. Or join CEP and receive a copy of *The Better World Investment Guide* free.

# Shopping Without "Paper" or "Plastic"

At one time or another we've all faced the ultimate supermarket checkout question: whether to use paper or plastic grocery bags. Many would assume that paper is better because it is a biodegradable, renewable resource. Paper bags, however, are often made from 100% virgin paper, and cause substantial environmental problems in timber extraction and manufacture. They also occupy a lot of landfill space.

A simple solution is to bring a **SHOPPING FOR A BETTER WORLD** string or canvas bag to the store and avoid the dilemma altogether. Cotton string bags fold up easily to fit into your pocket or purse and expand to carry about as much as a regular grocery bag. CEP's durable, lightweight canvas bag has an even larger carrying capacity, reinforced canvas handles and the blue and yellow **SHOPPING FOR A BETTER WORLD** logo on it. And the canvas bags are manufactured by a non-profit organization that employs disabled adults to do the sewing. To order, see the coupon at the back of this book.

# COMPANY ADDRESSES

Many consumers who purchased the 1990 edition of **SHOPPING FOR A BETTER WORLD** told us they would like the addresses, phone numbers, and names of chief officers of the companies included in the guide. Here they are. Those companies with 15 or fewer employees are noted with an asterisk (*) and those small companies with between 16 and 100 employees appear with a number sign (#) after their names. Write to the companies and tell them why you have changed your buying habits. Some companies have toll-free consumer hotlines.

21st Century Foods, Inc. *
30-A Germania Street
Jamaica Plain, MA 02130
(617) 522-7595
Rudy Canale, Owner

A&P (Great Atlantic & Pacific Tea Company)
2 Paragon Drive
Montvale, NJ 07645
(201) 573-9700
James Wood, Chairman & CEO

Abbott Laboratories
One Abbott Park Road
Abbott Park, IL 60064-3500
(708) 937-6100
Duane Burnham, Chairman & CEO

Ajinomoto U.S.A., Inc.
Glenpointe Center West 500
Frank W. Burr Blvd.
Teaneck, NJ 07666
(201) 488-1212
K. Yoshikawa, President

Alberto-Culver Company
2525 Armitage Avenue
Melrose Park, IL 60160
(708) 450-3000
Leonard H. Lavin, Chairman & CEO

Albertson's Inc.
250 Parkcenter Boulevard, Box 20
Boise, Idaho 83726
(208) 385-6200
Gary G. Michael, Chairman & CEO

Alexandra Avery Purely Natural Body Care *
68183 Northrup Creek Road
Birkenseld, OR 97016-0000
(503) 755-2446
Alexandra Avery, President

Allens Naturally *
P.O. Box 339
Farmington, MI 48332-0339
(313) 453-5410
Allen Conlon, President

Allied-Lyons PLC
c/o Hiram Walker/Allied Vintners
Riverside Drive
Windsor, Ontario N8Y 4S5 CANADA
Michael Jackaman, Chairman & CEO

American Cyanamid Company
One Cyanamid Plaza
Wayne, NJ 07470
(201) 831-2000 or 1-800-826-2544
George J. Sella, Chairman & CEO

American Home Products Corporation
685 Third Avenue
New York, NY 10017-4085
(212) 878-6138
John R. Stafford, Chairman & CEO

American Stores Company
P.O. Box 27447
709 East South Temple
Salt Lake City, UT 84102
(801) 539-0112 or 1-800-41-2863
Jonathan L. Scott, President & CEO

Amoco Corp.
200 East Randolph Drive
Chicago, IL 60601
(312) 856-6111 or 1-800-621-8889
Richard M. Morrow, Chairman & CEO

Anheuser-Busch Companies, Inc.
One Busch Place
St. Louis, MO 63118-1852
(314) 577-2000
August A. Busch III, Chairman & President

Apple & Eve, Inc. *
49 Bryant Avenue
Roslyn, NY 11576
(516) 621-1122
Gordon Crane, President

Archer Daniels Midland Co.
P.O. Box 1470, 4666 Fairies Parkway
Decatur, IL 62525
1-800-447-2301
Dwayne O. Andreas, Chairman & CEO

Aroma Vera #
3384 S. Robertson Place
Los Angeles, CA 90034
(213) 280-0407
Marcel Lavabre, President

Asahi Breweries U.S.A., Inc.
200 Park Avenue
Suite 4114-1
New York, NY 10166
(212) 878-6775

Associated Cooperatives *
322 Harbour Way, Suite 12
Richmond, CA 94801
(415) 232-1111
Terry Baird, General Manager

Atlantic Richfield (ARCO)
P.O. Box 2679
515 South Flower Street
Los Angeles, CA 90071
(213) 486-3511 or 1-800-354-1500
Lodwrick M. Cook, Chairman & CEO

Aubrey Organics #
4419 N. Manhattan Avenue
Tampa, FL 33614
(813) 877-4186
Aubrey Hampton, CEO

Aura Cacia *
1302 Nugget Lane
P.O. Box 399
Weaverville, CA 96093
(916) 623-3301
Doug Nowacki, President

Autumn-Harp, Inc. *
28 Rockydale Road
Bristol, VT 05443
(802) 453-4807
Paul Ralston, President

Aveda Corp. #
400 Central Ave. SE
Minneapolis, MN 55414
(612) 378-7400

Avon Products, Inc.
9 West 57th Street
New York, NY 10019
(212) 546-6015
James E. Preston, Chairman & CEO

Barbara's Bakery #
3900 Cypress Drive
Petaluma, CA 94954
(707) 765-2273
Gil Pritchard, President & CEO

Bayer AG
c/o Bayer USA Inc.
One Mellon Center
500 Grant Street
Pittsburgh, PA 15219
(412) 394-5500
Helge H. Wehmeier, President & CEO

Ben & Jerry's Homemade, Inc.
Route 100
P.O. Box 240
Waterbury, VT 05676
(802) 244-5641
Fred Lager, President & CEO

Body Love Natural Cosmetics *
PO Box 7542, 3303 Potrero Street #4
Santa Cruz, CA 95061
Elizabeth Jones, President

The Body Shop
45 Horshill Road
Hanover Technical Center
Cedar Knolls, NJ 07927-2003
(201) 984-9200
David Edward, CEO & President

Borden, Inc.
277 Park Avenue
New York, NY 10172
(212) 573-4000
R.J. Ventres, Chairman & CEO

Bristol-Myers Squibb Co.
345 Park Avenue
New York, NY 10154-0037
(212) 546-4000 or 1-800-457-3575
Richard M. Gelb, Chairman & CEO

British Petroleum Company p.l.c.
c/o BP America Inc.
200 Public Square
Cleveland, OH 44114-2375
(216) 586-4141
J.H. Ross, CEO

Bruno's Inc.
300 Research Parkway
P.O. Box 2486
Birmingham, AL 35201-2486
(205) 940-9400
Angelo J. Bruno, Chairman

BSN Groupe S.A.
c/o General Bisuits U.S.
891 Newark Ave.
Elizabeth, NJ 07207
(201) 527-7000

Bumpkins International #
1945 East Wilkins
Phoenix, AZ 85304
(800) 553-9302
David Lieberman, President

Cadbury Schweppes p.l.c.
c/o Cadbury Schweppes Inc.
6 High Ridge Park
P.O. Box 3800
Stamford, CT 06905
(203) 329-0911

Campbell Soup Company
Campbell Place
Camden, NJ 08103-1799
(609) 342-4800
David W. Johnson, Chairman & CEO
Consumer Hotline: 1-800-257-8443

Carter-Wallace Inc.
1345 Avenue of the Americas
New York, NY 10105
(212)339-5000
Henry H. Hoyt, Jr., CEO

Celestial Seasonings, Inc.
4600 Sleepytime Drive
Boulder, CO 80301-3292
(303) 550-5300
Barney Feinblum, President

Chevron Corporation
225 Bush Street
San Francisco, CA 94104
(415) 894-7700 or 1-800-243-8766
Kenneth T. Derr, CEO

Chiquita Brands International
Chiquita Ctr., 250 E. 5th Street
Cincinnati, OH 45202
(513) 784-8000
Carl Lindner, CEO

Church & Dwight Co., Inc.
469 North Harrison Street
Princeton, NJ 08543-5297
(609) 683-5900 or 1-800-631-5591
Dwight C. Minton, Chairman & CEO

Clientele, Inc. #
5205 N.W. 163rd Street
Miami, FL 33014
(800) 327-4660
Pat Riley, President

The Clorox Co.
PO Box 24305
Oakland, CA 94623-1305
(415) 271-7000
C.R. Weaver, Chairman & CEO

The Coca-Cola Co.
P.O. Drawer 1734
Atlanta, GA 30301
(404) 676-2121 or 1-800-638-3286
Roberto C. Goizueta, Chairman & CEO

Colgate-Palmolive Co.
300 Park Avenue
New York, NY 10022-7499
(212) 310-2000
Reuben Mark, Chairman & CEO
Consumer Hotline: 1-800-338-8388

ConAgra, Inc.
ConAgra Center
One Central Park Plaza
Omaha, NE 68102
(402) 978-4000 or 1-800-842-7518
Charles M. Harper, Chairman & CEO

Coors Co., Adolph
Mail #NH320
Golden, CO 80401
(303) 279-6565 or 1-800-642-6116
William K. Coors, Chairman & President

CPC International Inc.
P.O. Box 8000, International Plaza
Englewood Cliffs, NJ 07632-9476
(201) 894-2555
Charles R. Shoemate, Chairman & CEO

Curtice-Burns Foods, Inc.
90 Linden Place, P.O. Box 681
Rochester, NY 14603-0681
(716) 383-1850
David J. McDonald, CEO

Dannon Company
1111 Westchester Ave.
White Plains, NY 10604
(914) 697-9700

Dep Corp.
2101 E. Via Arado
Rancho Dominguez, CA 90220
(213) 604-0777
Robert Berglass, Chairman & President

Desert Essence *
P.O. Box 588
Topanga, CA 90290-0000
(213) 455-1046
Steven Silberfein, President

The Dial Corporation
1618 Greyhound Tower
Phoenix, Arizona 85077
(602) 248-4000
John W. Teets, Chairman, President & CEO

Dole Food Company, Inc.
10900 Wilshire Boulevard
Los Angeles, CA 90024
(213) 824-1500
David H. Murdock, Chairman & CEO

Dominick's Finer Foods
505 Railroad Avenue
Northlake, IL 60164
(708) 562-1000
Dan Josephs, President

Dow Chemical Co.
P.O. Box 1206
Midland, MI 48641-1206
(517) 636-8914 or 1-800-258-2436
Frank P. Popoff, President & CEO

Earth Care Paper Inc. #
4601 Hammersley Road
P.O. Box 14140
Madison, WI 53711-0140
(608) 277-2920
John Magee, President

Earth's Best, Inc. #
P.O. Box 887, Pond Lane
Middlebury, VT 05753
(802) 388-7974
Paul Luchsinger, President

Earthrise Company *
P.O. Box 1196
San Raphael, CA 94915
(415) 485-0521
Robert Henrikson, President

Eastman Kodak Co.
343 State Street
Rochester, NY 14650
(716) 724-4000
Consumer Hotline: 1-800-242-2424
Kay R. Whitmore, Chairman & CEO

Ecco Bella *
6 Provost Sq., Suite 602
Caldwell, NJ 07006
(201) 226-5799
Sally Malanga, President

Eden Foods, Inc. #
701 Tecumseh Road
Clinton, MI 49236
(517) 456-7424
Ron Roller, President

Exxon Corp.
225 East John W. Carpenter Freeway
Irving, TX 75062-2298
(214) 444-1000 or 1-800-628-3334
L.G. Rawl, Chairman

Falcon Trading Company Inc. #
1055 17th Avenue
Santa Cruz, CA 95062
(408) 462-1280
Morty Cohen, President

Fantastic Foods, Inc. #
1257 N. McDowell Blvd.
Petaluma, CA 94954
(707) 778-7801
James Rosen, President

First Brands
83 Wooster Heights Road Building 301
P.O. Box 1911
Danbury, CT 06813-1911
(203) 731-2300
Alfred E. Dudley, President & CEO

Flowers Industries, Inc.
U.S. Highway 19 South
P.O. Box 1338
Thomasville, GA 31799
(912) 226-9110
Amos R. McMullian, Chairman & CEO

Food Lion, Inc.
P.O. Box 1330
2110 Executive Dr.
Salisbury, NC 28145-1330
(704)633-8250
Tom E. Smith, Chairman & CEO

Fred Meyer, Inc.
3800 SE 22nd Avenue, P.O. Box 42121
Portland, OR 97202
(503) 232-8844
Roger G. Miller, Chairman & CEO

Fuji Photo Film U.S.A. Inc.
555 Taxter Rd.
Elmsford, NY 10523
(914) 789-8100
Osamu Inoue, President

General Electric Company
3135 Eastern Turnpike
Fairfield, CT 06431
1-800-528-7711
John F. Welch, Jr., Chairman & CEO

General Mills, Inc.
Number One General Mills Blvd
P.O. Box 1113
Minneapolis, MN 55440
(612)540-2311
H.B. Atwater, Jr., Chairman & CEO

Georgia-Pacific Corporation
133 Peachtree Street, N.E.
P.O. Box 105605
Atlanta, GA 30348-5605
(404) 521-4000 or 1-800-552-1285
T. Marshall Hahn, Jr., Chairman & CEO

Gerber Products Company
445 State Street
Fremont, MI 49413
(616) 928-2000
Alfred E. Piergallini, Chairman & CEO

Giant Eagle, Inc.
101 Kappa Drive
Pittsburgh, PA 15238
(412) 963-6200
David Shapira, CEO

Giant Food Inc.
Dept. 599, Box 1804
Washington, DC 20013
(301) 341-4100
Israel Cohen, CEO

The Gillette Company
Prudential Tower Building
Boston, MA 02199
(617) 421-7000
Alfred M. Zeien, Chairman & CEO

Goya Foods, Inc.
100 Seaview Drive
Secaucus, NJ 07096
(201) 348-4900
Joe Unanue, Jr., CEO

Grand Metropolitan PLC
c/o Grand Met Food Division
200 South Sixth Street
Minneapolis, MN 55402
(612) 330-4966
Ian A. Martin, Chairman & CEO

Grand Union Company
201 Willowbrook Boulevard
Wayne, NJ 07470
(201) 890-6000
Floyd Hall, CEO

GTE Corporation
One Stamford Forum
Stamford, CT 06904
(203) 965-2000 or 1-800-225-5483
James L. Johnson, Chairman & CEO

Guinness
6 Landmark Square
Stamford, CT 06901
(203) 323-3311

H.E. Butt
646 South Main
Box 8399
San Antonio, TX 78204
(512) 246-8000
Charles C. Butt, President & CEO

H.J. Heinz Company
P.O. Box 57
Pittsburgh, PA 15230-0057
(412) 456-5700
Anthony O'Reilly, Chairman, President & CEO

Health Valley Natural Foods #
16100 Foothill Boulevard
Irwindale, CA 91706-7811
(800) 423-4846
George Mateljan, Jr., President

Hershey Foods Corporation
P.O. Box 814
100 Mansion Road East
Hershey, PA 17033-0814
(717) 534-4000
Richard Zimmerman, Chairman & CEO

Hormel, George A. & Company
501 Sixteenth Avenue, NE
Austin, MN 55912
(507) 437-5611 or 1-800-451-7875
R.L. Knowlton, Chairman, President & CEO

Ida Grae Nature's Colors Cosmetics *
424 La Verne Avenue
Mill Valley, CA 94941
(415) 388-6101
Ida Grae, President

Int'l Research & Development Corp.
500 North Main Street
Mattawan, MI 49071
(616) 668-3336
Dr. Francis X. Wazeter, Pres. & CEO

James River Corporation
P.O. Box 2218
Richmond, VA 23217
(804) 644-5411 or 1-800-227-4177
Robert C. Williams, CEO

Jason Natural Cosmetics #
8468 Warner Drive
Culver City, CA 90291
(213) 838-7543
Jeffrey Light, President

John B. Sanfilippo & Son #
2299 Busse Road
Elk Grove Village, IL 60007
(708) 593-2300
Jasper Sanfilippo, President

Johnson & Johnson
One Johnson & Johnson Plaza
New Brunswick, NJ 08933
(908) 524-3535
Ralph S. Larsen, Chairman & CEO

Johnson & Son, Inc., S.C.
1525 Howe Street
Racine, WI 54303-5011
(414) 631-2000
Samuel C. Johnson, Chairman & CEO

Johnson Products Co., Inc.
8522 South Lafayette Avenue
Chicago, IL 60620
(312) 483-4100
Eric G. Johnson, President & CEO

Kao Corp. of America
39th Floor
437 Madison Avenue
New York, NY 10022
(212) 781-3030
K. E. Wattman, President

Kellogg Company
One Kellogg Square, P.O. Box 3599
Battle Creek, MI 49016-3599
(616) 961-2000
William E. LaMothe, Chairman & CEO

Kikkoman International Inc.
Box 784
San Francisco, CA 94101
(415) 956-7750
Yuzaburo Mogi, President

Kimberly-Clark Corporation
P.O. Box 619100, DFW Airport Station
Dallas, TX 75261-9100
(214) 830-1200 or 1-800-821-5699
Darwin E. Smith, Chairman & CEO

Kiss My Face #
P.O. Box 224
Gardiner, NY 12525-0000
(914) 255-0884
Robert MacLeod, President

The Kroger Company
PO Box 1199
Cincinatti, OH 45201-1199
(513) 762-4000 or 1-800-445-1892
Lyle Everingham, Chairman & CEO

L'Oreal S.A.
c/o Cosmair Inc.
575 Fifth Avenue
New York, NY 10017
(212) 818-1500
Guy Peyrelongue, President & CEO

Land O' Lakes, Inc.
P.O. Box 116
Minneapolis, MN 55490
(612) 481-2222
Jack Gherty, Chairman & CEO

Lion Corporation
6750 Poplar Avenue
Suite 208
Memphis, TN 38138
(901) 754-2224
Tim Ballage, General Manager of Consumer Division

Loriva Supreme Foods *
40-10 Oser Avenue
Hauppauge, NY 11788
(516) 231-7940
William S. Robertson, President

Marcal Paper Mills Inc.
Market Street
Elmwood Park, NJ 07407
(513) 762-4000 or 1-800-445-1892
Nick Marcalus, President

Mars, Inc.
6885 Elm Street
Mc Lean, VA 22101
(703) 821-4900
Forrest E. Mars, Co-President

Matsushita Electric Corporation of America
One Panasonic Way
Seacaucus, NJ 07094
(201) 348-7320
Akiya Imura, President & CEO

Mayacamas Fine Foods *
1206 East MacArthur
Sonoma, CA 95476
(707) 996-0955
Lou Williams, President

McCormick & Company, Inc.
11350 McCormick Road
Hunt Valley, MD 21031-1066
(301) 771-7301
Charles P. McCormick, Jr., Chairman & CEO

The Mead Corporation
World Headquarters
Court House Plaza NE
Dayton, OH 45463
(513) 495-3428
Burnell R. Roberts, Chairman & CEO

Melitta Bentz KG
c/o Melitta North America, Inc.
1401 Berlin Road
P.O. Box 900
Cherry Hill, NJ 08003
(609) 428-7202
Barbara Hausner, P.R. Coordinator

Minnesota Mining & Manufacturing Company (3M)
225-5N-04, 3M Center
St. Paul, MN 55144-1000
(612) 733-1110
Allen F. Jacobson, Chairman & CEO

Mobil Corporation
3225 Fallows Road
Fairfax, VA 22037-0001
(703) 846-3000 or 1-800-333-0124
Allen E. Murray, Chairman & CEO
Consumer Hotline: 1-800-333-0124

Mountain Ocean *
Box 951
Boulder, CO 80306
(303) 444-2781
Tom Benjamin, President

National Grape Co-op Association
2 South Portage St.
Westfield, NY 14787
(716) 326-3131
Everett W. Baldwin, Chairman & CEO

Nestle S.A.
c/o Nestle USA, Inc.
1133 Connecticut Avenue, NW
Suite 310
Washington, DC 20030
(202) 296-4100
Timm F. Crull, CEO

Neutrogena Corporation
5760 W 96th Street
P.O. Box 45036
Los Angeles, CA 90045
Lloyd E. Corsen, President & CEO

Newman's Own, Inc. *
246 Post Road East
Westport, CT 06880
(203) 222-0136
Paul Newman, President

Nippon Meat Packers, Inc.
c/o Day-Lee Foods, Inc.
13055 E. Molette Street
Santa Fe Springs, CA 90670
(213) 802-6800

Nippon Suisan Kaisha, Ltd.
927 North Northlake Way
Suite 210
Seattle, WA 98103
(206) 545-7271

Nissin Foods U.S.A. Co. Inc.
2001 W. Rosecrans Avenue
Cardena, CA 90249
(213) 321-6453

Ocean Spray Cranberries, Inc.
1 Ocean Spray Drive
Lakeville/ Middleboro, MA 02346
(508) 946-1000
John S. Llewellyn, Jr., President & CEO

Orjene Natural Cosmetics #
5-43 48th Avenue
Long Island City, NY 11101
(718) 937-2666
Dennis Machicao, President

Paul Penders Company, Inc. *
1340 Commerce Street
Petaluma, CA 94952
(707) 763-5828
Paul Penders, President

PepsiCo, Inc.
Anderson Hill Road
Purchase, NY 10577
(914) 253-2000
D. Wayne Calloway, Chairman & CEO

Perdue Farms Inc.
P.O. Box 1537
Salisbury, MD 21801
(301) 543-3000
Don Mabe, President & CEO

Pet Incorporated
400 South Fourth St.
St. Louis. MO 63102
(314) 621-5400
Miles Marsh, CEO

Pfizer Inc.
235 East 42nd Street, 25th Floor
New York, NY 10017
(212) 573-2323
Edmund T. Pratt, Chairman & CEO

Phillip Morris Companies, Inc.
120 Park Avenue
New York, NY 10017
(212) 880-5000
Michael A. Miles, Chairman & CEO

Phillips Petroleum Company
Phillips Building
Bartlesville, Oklahoma 74004
(918) 661-6600
C.J. Silas, President & CEO

Polaroid Corporation
549 Technology Square
Cambridge, MA 02139
(617) 577-2000 or 1-800-343-5000
I. MacAllister Booth, CEO

The Procter & Gamble Company
PO Box 599
One P&G Plaza
Cincinnati, OH 45202
(513) 983-2342
Edwin Artzt, Chairman & CEO
Consumer Hotline: 1-800-543-7310

Publix Super Markets
1936 G. Jenkins Boulevard, P.O. Box 407
Lakeland, FL 33801-0407
(813) 688-1188
George W. Jenkins, Chairman

The Quaker Oats Company
Quaker Tower
Box 9001
Chicago, IL 60604-9001
(312) 222-7111
William D. Smithburg, Chairman & CEO
Consumer Hotline: 1-800-635-3335

Rachel Perry, Inc. #
9111 Mason Avenue
Chatsworth, CA 91311
(818) 888-5881
Rachel Perry, President

Ralphs Grocery Company
1100 West Artesia Boulevard
Compton, CA 90220
(213) 637-1101
Byron Allumbaugh, Chairman & CEO

Ralston Purina Company
Checkerboard Square
St. Louis, MO 63164
(314) 982-1000
William P. Stiritz, Chairman & CEO

Reckitt & Colman plc
c/o Reckitt & Colman, Inc.
P.O. Box 941
Wayne, NJ 07474-0941
(201) 633-3600

Red Apple Companies
823 11th Ave.
New York, NY 10019
(212) 580-6800
Anthony J. Najiar, President

Revlon, Inc.
625 Madison Avenue, 7th Floor
New York, NY 10022
(212) 527-4000
Ronald Perelman, Chairman & CEO

Reynolds Metals Co.
PO Box 27003
Richmond, VA 23261
(804) 281-2000
William O. Bourke, Chairman & CEO

Rhone-Poulenc Rorer
500 Virginia Dr.
Fort Washington, PA 19034
1-800-334-9745
Robert E. Cawthorn, CEO

RJR Nabisco Inc.
401 N. Main Street
Winston Salem, NC 27102
James W. Johnston, President & CEO
Consumer Hotline: 1-800-543-3090

Royal Dutch/Shell Group of Companies
c/o Shell Oil Company, USA
One Shell Plaza
P.O. Box 2463
Houston, TX 77252
(713) 241-6161
Frank H. Richardson, CEO

Safeway Inc.
201 Fourth Street
Oakland, CA 94660
(415) 891-3000
Peter A. Magowan, CEO

San-J International #
431 Vicksburg St.
San Francisco, CA 94114
(415) 821-4041
John Perelman, V.P., Consumer Sales

Sandoz Ltd.
59 Route 10
East Hanover, NJ 07936
(201) 503-7500
Daniel C. Wagniere, CEO

Sara Lee Corp.
Three First National Plaza
Chicago, IL 60602-4260
(312) 558-8426
John H. Bryan, Jr., Chairman & CEO
Consumer Hotline: 1-800-423-4714

Schering-Plough Corp.
One Giralda Farms, Box 100
Madison, NJ 07940-1000
(201) 822-7000
Robert P. Luciano, Chairman & CEO

Scott Paper Co.
Scott Plaza I
Philadelphia, PA 19113
(215) 522-5000 or 1-800-835-7268
Philip E. Lippincott, Chairman & CEO

Seagram Company LTD.
1430 Peel Street
Montreal, PQ
Canada H3A 1S9
(514) 848-5271
Edgar M. Bronfman, CEO

Shiseido Co.
c/o Shiseido Cosmetics Ltd.
15th Floor
900 Third Avenue
New York, NY 10022
(212) 752-2644
Namio Wanikawa, President & CEO

Smith's Food & Drug Centers, Inc.
P.O. Box 30550
1550 South Redwood Road
Salt Lake City, UT 84104
(801)974-1400
Jeffrey P. Smith, CEO

SmithKline Beecham plc
1500 Spring Garden Street
Box 7929
Philadelphia, PA 19101
(215) 751-4000
Robert P. Bauman, CEO

Smucker Co., The J.M.
Strawberry Lane
PO Box 280
Orrville, OH 44667-0280
(216) 682-3000
Paul Smucker, Chairman & CEO

Snow Brand Milk Products Co., Ltd.
Fort Lee Executive Park
One Executive Drive
Fort Lee, NJ 07024
(201) 592-7359

Solgar Co. #
410 Ocean Avenue
Lynbrook, NY 11563
(516) 599-2442
Rand Skolnick, CEO

Sony Corp. of America
Sony Drive
Park Ridge, NJ 07656
(201) 930-1000
Masaaki Morita, Chairman & CEO

Source Perrier
c/o Perrier Group of America
777 Putnam Ave.
Greenwich, CT 06830
(203) 531-4100
Ronald V. Davis, CEO

Stonyfield Farms Inc. #
10 Burton Dr.
Londonderry, NH 03053
(603) 437-4040
Gary Hirshberg, President

The Stop & Shop Companies, Inc.
P.O. Box 369
Boston, MA 02101
(617) 770-8000
Lewis G. Schaeneman, CEO

Sun Company, Inc.
100 Matsonford Road
Radnor, PA 19087-4597
(215) 293-6000
Robert McClements, Jr., CEO

Suntory International Inc.
1211 Avenue of the Americas
New York, NY 10036
(212) 921-9595
Shiro Yasuno, President

Supermarkets General Corporation
301 Blair Road
Woodbridge, NJ 07095
(201) 499-3000
Jack Futterman, CEO

Tasty Baking Co.
2801 Hunting Park Avenue
Philadelphia, PA 19129
(215) 221-8500
Nelson G. Harris, CEO

Tate & Lyle PLC
c/o Domino Sugar Corporation
1251 Avenue of the Americas
New York, NY 10020
(212) 489-9000

Texaco Inc.
2000 Westchester Avenue
White Plains, NY 10650
(914) 253-4000
James W. Kinnean, President & CEO

Tillamook County Creamery Association
Box 313
4175 Highway 101 North
Tillamook, OR 97141
(503) 842-4481
D.R. Sutton, Manager

Tom's of Maine #
Railroad Avenue, P.O. Box 710
Kennebunk, ME 04043
(207) 985-2944
Tom Chappell, President

Twin Laboratories #
2120 Smithtown Avenue
Ronkonkoma, NY 11779
(516) 467-3140
David Blechman, President

Tyson Foods, Inc.
2210 West Oaklawn Drive
Springdale, AR 72764
(501) 756-4000
Don Tyson, Chairman & CEO

Unigate PLC
c/o Gardenia Foods Co. Inc.
5611 E. Imperial Hwy.
South Gate, CA 90280
(213) 862-7686

Unilever PLC
c/o Unilever United States, Inc.
390 Park Avenue
New York, NY 10022
(212) 888-1260

United Biscuits (Holdings) plc
c/o Keebler USA
One Hollow Tree Lane
Elmhurst, IL 60126
(708) 833-2900

Universal Foods Corp.
433 East Michigan Street
Milwaukee, WI 53202
(414) 271-6755 or 1-800-558-9892
Guy A. Osborn, Chairman & CEO

The Upjohn Company
7000 Portage Road
Kalamazoo, MI 49001
(616) 323-4000 or 1-800-253-8600
Theodore Cooper, Chairman & CEO

USX Corporation
600 Grant Street
Pittsburgh, PA 15219-4776
(412) 433-1121
Charles A Curry, Chairman & CEO

The Vons Companies, Inc.
618 Michillinda Avenue
Arcadia, CA 91007
(818) 821-7000
Roger E. Stangeland, Chairman & CEO

Warner-Lambert Co.
201 Tabor Road
Morris Plains, NJ 07950
(201) 540-2000
Melvin R. Goodes, Chairman & CEO

Weetabix Ltd.
c/o The Weetabix Company Inc.
20 Cameron St.
Clinton, MA 01510
(508) 368-0991

Whole Earth Foods Ltd. #
269 Portobello Road
London W11 1LR England
071-229-7545
Craig Sams, Chairman

Winn-Dixie Stores, Inc.
P.O. Box B
5050 Edgewood Court
Jacksonville, FL 32203-0297
(904) 783-5000
A. Dano Davis, Chairman

Wittington Investments Ltd.
c/o Grosvenor Marketing Ltd.
E 210 State Hwy. 4
Paramus, NJ 07652
(201) 843-1022

Wrigley, Wm. Jr. Co.
410 North Michigan Avenue
Chicago, IL 60611
(312) 644-2121
William Wrigley, President & CEO

# COMPANY ABBREVIATIONS

*Index to Company Abbreviations
arranged by abbreviation*

| | |
|---|---|
| BSN | BSN Groupe S.A. |
| BUD | Anheuser-Busch |
| BUMK | Bumpkins International # |
| CADB | Cadbury Schweppes p.l.c. |
| CAG | ConAgra |
| CAR | Carter-Wallace |
| CBI | Curtice-Burns |
| CHV | Chevron Corporation |
| CL | Colgate-Palmolive |
| CLX | Clorox Co. |
| CPB | Campbell Soup |
| CPC | CPC International |
| CQB | Chiquita Brands International |
| CRCH | Church & Dwight |
| CS | Celestial Seasonings |
| CTL | Clientele, Inc. # |
| DEPC | Dep Corp. |
| DES | Desert Essence * |
| DOL | Dole Food Company |
| DOM | Dominick's Finer Foods |
| DOW | Dow Chemical Company |
| EBI | Earth's Best, Inc. # |
| ECC | Ecco Bella # |
| ECP | Earth Care Paper Inc. # |
| EDEN | Eden Foods, Inc. # |
| EK | Eastman Kodak |
| FALC | Falcon Trading Co. # |
| FB | First Brands |
| FFI | Fantastic Foods Inc. # |
| FL | Food Lion, Inc. |
| FLO | Flowers Industries, Inc. |
| FUJI | Fuji Photo Film |
| G | Dial Corp |
| GAP | A&P(Great Atlantic & Pacific Tea Company) |
| GE | General Electric Company |
| GEB | Gerber Products |
| GF | Giant Food Inc. |
| GIA | Giant Eagle |

| | |
|---|---|
| GIS | General Mills |
| GMP | Grand Metropolitan PLC |
| GOYA | Goya Foods Inc. |
| GP | Georgia-Pacific |
| GRAP | National Grape Co-Op Association |
| GS | Gillette |
| GTE | GTE Corporation |
| GUC | Grand Union Company |
| GUI | Guinness PLC |
| HEBG | H.E. Butt Grocery |
| HNZ | Heinz Company, H.J. |
| HRL | Hormel & Co., George A. |
| HSY | Hershey Foods Corporation |
| HVAL | Health Valley Natural Foods # |
| IDA | Ida Grae Cosmetics * |
| IRDV | Int'l Research & Devl'p Corp. |
| JNJ | Johnson & Johnson |
| JNP | Jason Natural Cosmetics # |
| JPC | Johnson Products Co. |
| JR | James River Corporation |
| JSAN | John B. Sanfilippo, Inc. |
| K | Kellogg Company |
| KAO | Kao Corp. |
| KIK | Kikkoman Corp. |
| KMB | Kimberly-Clark Corporation |
| KMF | Kiss My Face # |
| KO | Coca-Cola Company |
| KR | Kroger Company |
| LAND | Land O' Lakes, Inc. |
| LION | Lion Corp. |
| LOR | Loriva Supreme Foods * |
| LORA | L'Oreal S.A. |
| MARC | Marcal Paper Mills Inc |
| MARS | Mars, Inc |
| MAYA | Mayacamas Fine Foods * |
| MCRK | McCormick & Company, Inc |
| MEA | Mead Corporation |
| MEYR | Fred Meyer, Inc |

```
MMM ...........Minnesota Mining & Manufacturing (3M)
MO ......................................... Philip Morris
MOB ............................... Mobil Corporation
MOUN .........................Mountain Ocean, Ltd. *
MTA ................................. Melitta Bentz KG
MTS ................... Matsushita Electrical Corp.
NEST ...............................................Nestle S.A.
NEWO ............................... Newman's Own*
NGNA ............................... Neutrogena Corp.
NPM .......................... Nippon Meat Packers
NSF .............................................Nissin Foods
NSK ................... Nippon Suisan Kaisha
OAT ............................. Quaker Oats Company
ORJ ..................... Orjene Natural Cosmetics #
OSC ....................Ocean Spray Cranberries, Inc.
P ...................................Philips Petroleum Company
PEP ...............................................PepsiCo, Inc.
PET ....................................................Pet Inc.
PFE ................................................ Pfizer Inc.
PG ......................... Procter & Gamble Company
PP............................... Paul Penders Company *
PRD...............................................Polaroid
PRDU ............................... Perdue Farms Inc.
PUB .....................................Publix Supermarkets
RAL .............................Ralston Purina Company
RCP .............................Reckitt & Colman plc
RED ................................. Red Apple Companies
REVL ...................................... Revlon, Inc.
RG ...........................Ralphs Grocery Company
RIS ...............................Earthrise Company *
RJR................................ RJR Nabisco Inc.
RLM ...............................Reynolds Metals Company
ROR ...............................Rhone-Poulenc Rorer Inc.
RP ................................. Rachel Perry, Inc. #
SAFE .......................................Safeway Stores, Inc.
SAND ............................................. Sandoz Ltd.
SANJ ......................San-J International Inc. #
SC ................ Royal Dutch/Shell Grp. of Companies
```

XON . . . . . . . . . . . . . . . . . . . . . . . . . . . . . . . . . . . . . . . . . Exxon Corp.

*Index to Company Abbreviations arranged by company*

# PRODUCT CATEGORY INDEX

## C

# E

# F

# H

# I

N

O

Oriental Food . . . . . . . . . . . . . . . . . . . . . . . . see Prepared Foods

# R

# S

## T

# SURVEY

Now that you have had a chance to review **SHOPPING FOR A BETTER WORLD**, we would like to know how you feel about it ... whether you've used it, whether you found it helpful, and/or have suggestions that would make in future editions better.

Please take a moment to answer these questions, tear them out along the dotted line and send them to the Council on Economic Priorities, 30 Irving Place, New York, NY 10003.

Many changes were made in this edition as a result of our readers' suggestions. We want to continue to improve the Guide and we need your help.

1. What companies, products or brands not listed in **SHOPPING FOR A BETTER WORLD** would you like to see listed in future editions? (PLEASE SPECIFY)

_____

_____

_____

2. Please rank the 12 social categories on which CEP rates companies in order of importantance?
(PLEASE SPECIFY)

_____

_____

_____

3. Would you like us to rate companies on other issues?

☐ No

☐ Yes (If Yes) Which ones? Please list

_____

_____

**4. Has SHOPPING FOR A BETTER WORLD** changed any of your shopping decisions?

☐ Yes    ☐ No

(If yes, please give a specific example, i.e., product - issue area)

_____

**5.** How often do you take a brand's ratings into account when you decide to buy a particular brand?

☐ Regularly, whenever I shop

☐ Often    ☐ Occasionally

☐ Seldom    ☐ Never

**6.** Have you written to a company as a result of their rating in the guide?

☐ Yes    ☐ No

Explain:

_____

_____

**7.** What other comments, if any, would you like to make about **SHOPPING FOR A BETTER WORLD?**

_____

_____

_____

**8.** CEP is planning to publish **TEENAGERS SHOPPING FOR A BETTER WORLD.** It would be a shorter book, and would include ratings of companies which manufacture products teenagers buy and use, such as sporting goods, fast food

restaurants, clothes and shoes, etc. How interested would
you be in this new guide?

☐ Very interested     ☐ Somewhat interested

☐ Not at all interested

8b. Why do you feel that way?

_____

_____

9. Are there any teens (age 12-21) living in your household?

☐ Yes (how many?)         ☐ No

10. If yes, did they read or use any portion of this book?

☐ Yes         ☐ No

11. If there was a **SHOPPING FOR A BETTER WORLD**
listing products teenagers use, would you buy a copy

☐ For yourself

☐ For teens you live with

☐ For teens you don't live with as a gift

☐ For other adults

12. We have been asked to publish other guides like **SHOP-
PING FOR A BETTER WORLD**. Please indicate how interested you would be in each:

|  | Very Interested | Somewhat Interested | Not at all Interested |
|---|---|---|---|
| Kids (and Parents) SBW | ☐ | ☐ | ☐ |
| Shopping for a Better Place to Work | ☐ | ☐ | ☐ |

|  | Very Interested | Somewhat Interested | Not at all Interested |
|---|---|---|---|
| Senior Citizens SBW | ☐ | ☐ | ☐ |
| Shopping for Your Home | ☐ | ☐ | ☐ |
| Shopping for Travel | ☐ | ☐ | ☐ |

## 13. Would you prefer SHOPPING FOR A BETTER WORLD to be

☐ bigger

☐ smaller

## 14. How frequently should we update SHOPPING FOR A BETTER WORLD?

☐ annually          ☐ every other year

☐ every 5 years     ☐ never

## WITH YOUR HELP, NO END IN SIGHT ...

- CEP has demonstrated that factual, careful documentation can make a difference to corporate and government priorities and performance.

- With **your** help we can increase the impact.

- Our work is supported by our nationwide membership, individual and foundation grants and sales of publications. As a member you will enjoy the convenience of having the facts at your fingertips ... facts delivered monthly in our *Research Report*, a respected and reliable source of invaluable information and updates.

- You'll also receive a free copy of **SHOPPING FOR A BETTER WORLD** and a 20% discount on all CEP books and studies.

## CEP PUBLICATIONS AND PRODUCTS

### Shopping For A Better World 1992
$7.49 or five copies for $23.95 postpaid. Special discounts are available for bulk orders. Call 212-420-1133. ITEM SBW2

### Shopping For A Better World Canvas Bag
This durable, lightweight canvas bag has the attractive blue and yellow Shopping For A Better World logo on it, reinforced handles and a larger carrying capacity than a brown paper grocery bag. $11.95/$9.95 for CEP members. ITEM CVS

### Cotton String Bag

Sturdy, comfortable handles and a large carrying capacity make this string bag perfect for carrying just about anything. It folds up easily to fit into your pocket or purse. $5.00, 2 for $8.95/$4.00 each for CEP members. ITEM STR

# FREE

Buyers of **SHOPPING FOR A BETTER WORLD** are eligible to receive **free information** from CEP.

To receive any of the free information listed below, please fill out this form and mail it to CEP, 30 Irving Place, New York, NY 10003

- ☐ Free CEP *Research Report* on:
    - ☐ Socially Responsible Investing
    - ☐ Green Consumerism
    - ☐ Actions to Save the Environment
      (folds out to a simple poster)
    - ☐ Corporate Responsibility in Japan

- ☐ A list of all the companies rated in this guide with their brand name products.

- ☐ More Information about CEP.

- ☐ More Information about CEP's Corporate Environmental Data Clearinghouse.

Name_____

Address_____

City_____

State_____ Zip_____ Phone_____

Please send information about CEP and **SHOPPING FOR A BETTER WORLD** to my friend(s):

Name(s)_____

Address(es)_____

_____

Nor:

# MEMBERSHIP FORM

☐ **YES**, enroll me as a CEP member, and send me a free copy of **SHOPPING FOR A BETTER WORLD**. I'll also receive monthly *Research Reports* and a 20% discount on all CEP publications.

☐ $25 ☐ $35* ☐ $100 ☐ $500 ☐ Other $_____

(*For a contribution of at least $35 you will receive a free copy of *The Better World Investment Guide* (Prentice Hall; 1991). See page 9 for description.

☐ Please send me ____ **SHOPPING FOR A BETTER WORLD** canvas bags @ $11.95 apiece. ($9.95 for CEP members)

☐ Please send me ____ cotton string bags @ $5.00 or two for $8.95 ($4 each for CEP members)

Name_____

Address_____

City_____ State____ Zip_____

Phone ( ) _____

Visa/MC/Amex_____

Exp._____ Signature_____

**FOREIGN ORDERS: Please add $10. Payment in US dollars only.**

Please send this form with your payment to CEP, 30 Irving Pl., New York, NY 10003-2386. Or call us (212) 420-1133. Your membership contribution (less the value of any premium you receive) is tax-deductible.

BAL2

# WHO SAYS YOU CAN'T CHANGE THE WORLD?

Every time you step up to a cash register, you vote. When you switch from one brand to another, companies hear you clearly.

You can help make America's companies more socially responsible by using this guide. Avoid products from companies whose policies you feel reflect a disregard for the public good. Buy from those that have good social records.

And stay informed by joining CEP. All members receive monthly fact-filled *Research Reports* on the issues covered in this guide. And members also receive a free copy of **SHOPPING FOR A BETTER WORLD** every year!

So join today! Simply fill out the reverse side of this page and mail it to CEP with your tax-deductible contribution.

$25/year: Regular Member ($15 Limited Income)

$35/year: Special Member – Receive a free copy of *The Better World Investment Guide* (Prentice Hall, 1991)

$100/year: Donor – Receive the above plus all CEP books and studies released in that year.

$250/year: Sponsor – All the above plus a free in-depth report on any company we are currently tracking.

$500/year: Patron – All the above plus first class mailing of monthly Research Report, annual listing in Research Report and an invitation to Executive Director's Reception at our America's Corporate Conscience Awards (ACCA).

$1,000/year: Director's Circle – All the above plus reserved seating with CEP's Director at ACCA and a listing in our annual report.

---

**MEMBERSHIP/ORDER FORM ON REVERSE SIDE**